Divyakant Agrawal   K. Selçuk Candan
Wen-Syan Li (Eds.)

New Frontiers in Information and Software as Services

Service and Application Design Challenges
in the Cloud

Springer

Volume Editors

Divyakant Agrawal
University of California at Santa Barbara
Department of Computer Science, Santa Barbara, CA 93106, USA
E-mail: agrawal@cs.ucsb.edu

K. Selçuk Candan
Arizona State University
School of Computing, Informatics
and Decision Systems Engineering
Tempe, AZ 85287-8809, USA
E-mail: candan@asu.edu

Wen-Syan Li
SAP China
Shanghai, 201203, China
E-mail: wen-syan.li@sap.com

ISSN 1865-1348   e-ISSN 1865-1356
ISBN 978-3-642-19293-7   e-ISBN 978-3-642-19294-4
DOI 10.1007/978-3-642-19294-4
Springer Heidelberg Dordrecht London New York

Library of Congress Control Number: 2011920956

ACM Computing Classification (1998): H.3.5, J.1, H.4.1, K.4.4, C.4

Typesetting: Camera-ready by author, data conversion by Scientific Publishing Services, Chennai, India

Printed on acid-free paper

Springer is part of Springer Science+Business Media (www.springer.com)

Preface

The need for a book focusing on the challenges associated with the design, deployment, and management of information and software as services materialized in our minds after the success of the two consecutive workshops (WISS 2009 and WISS 2010) we organized on this topic in conjunction with the IEEE International Conference on Data Engineering (ICDE).

Over the recent years, the increasing costs of creating and maintaining infrastructures for delivering services to consumers have led to the emergence of cloud-based third-party service providers that rent out network presence, computation power, storage, as well as entire software suites, including database and application server capabilities. These service providers reduce the overall infrastructure burden of small and medium (and increasingly even large) businesses by enabling rapid Web-native deployment, lower hardware/software management costs, virtualization and automation, and instant scalability. The emergence in the last decade of various enabling technologies, such as J2EE, .Net, XML, virtual machines, Web services, new data management techniques (including column databases and MapReduce), and large data centers contributed to this trend. Today grid computing, on-line e-commerce and business (including CRM, accounting, collaboration, and workforce management) services, large-scale data integration and analytics, IT virtualization, and private and public data and application clouds are typical examples exploiting this database and software as service paradigm.

While the financial incentives for the database and software as service deployments are obvious, convincing potential customers that outsourcing their data is a viable alternative is still challenging. Today, major customer demands from these third-party services include competitive pricing (including pay-per-use), performance-level and service-level assurances, and the flexibility to move services across third-party infrastructures or maybe to in-house private clouds maintained on-premise. Behind these demands lie serious concerns, including the security, availability, and (semantic and performance) isolation provided by the third-party infrastructures, whether these will work in accordance with in-house components, whether they will provide sufficiently complete solutions that eliminate the need of having to create complex hybrids, whether they will work with other clouds if needed, and whether they will be sufficiently configurable but still cost less.

Note that, while tackling these demands and concerns, the service provider also needs to find ways to optimize the utilization of its internal resources so as to ensure the viability of its own operations. Therefore, the immediate technical challenges faced by providers of information and software as service infrastructures are manifold and include, among others, security and information assurance, service level agreements and service class guarantees, workflow modeling, design patterns, and dynamic service composition, resource optimization and multi-tenancy, and compressed domain processing, replication, and high-degree parallelization.

The chapters in this book, contributed by leaders in academia and industry, and reviewed and supervised by an expert editorial board, describe approaches for tackling these cutting-edge challenges. We hope that you will find the chapters included here as indicative and informative about the nature of the coming age of information and software as services as we do.

November 2010

Divyakant Agrawal
K. Selçuk Candan
Wen-Syan Li

Editorial Advisory Board

Table of Contents

Service Design

Study of Software as a Service Support Platform for Small and Medium
Businesses 1
    Chang-Jie Guo, Wei Sun, Zhong-Bo Jiang, Ying Huang,
    Bo Gao, and Zhi-Hu Wang

Design Patterns for Cloud Services 31
    Jinquan Dai and Bo Huang

Service Security

Secure Data Management Service on Cloud Computing
Infrastructures.. 57
    Divyakant Agrawal, Amr El Abbadi, Fatih Emekci,
    Ahmed Metwally, and Shiyuan Wang

Security Plans for SaaS 81
    Marco D. Aime, Antonio Lioy, Paolo C. Pomi, and Marco Vallini

Service Optimization

Runtime Web-Service Workflow Optimization 112
    Radu Sion and Junichi Tatemura

Adaptive Parallelization of Queries Calling Dependent Data Providing
Web Services 132
    Manivasakan Sabesan and Tore Risch

Data-Utility Sensitive Query Processing on Server Clusters to Support
Scalable Data Analysis Services 155
    Renwei Yu, Mithila Nagendra, Parth Nagarkar,
    K. Selçuk Candan, and Jong Wook Kim

Multi-query Evaluation over Compressed XML Data in DaaS 185
    Xiaoling Wang, Aoying Zhou, Juzhen He, Wilfred Ng, and
    Patrick Hung

The HiBench Benchmark Suite: Characterization of the MapReduce-
Based Data Analysis 209
    Shengsheng Huang, Jie Huang, Jinquan Dai, Tao Xie, and Bo Huang

Multi-tenancy and Service Migration

Enabling Migration of Enterprise Applications in SaaS via Progressive
Schema Evolution 229
    Jianfeng Yan and Bo Zhang

Towards Analytics-as-a-Service Using an In-Memory Column
Database 257
    *Jan Schaffner, Benjamin Eckart, Christian Schwarz, Jan Brunnert,
    Dean Jacobs, and Alexander Zeier*

What Next?

At the Frontiers of Information and Software as Services 283
    K. Selçuk Candan, Wen-Syan Li, Thomas Phan, and Minqi Zhou

Author Index 301

Study of Software as a Service Support Platform for Small and Medium Businesses

Chang-Jie Guo, Wei Sun, Zhong-Bo Jiang, Ying Huang,
Bo Gao, and Zhi-Hu Wang

IBM China Research Lab, ZGC Software Park No. 19, Beijing, China
{guocj,weisun,jiangzb,yinghy,bocrlgao,zhwang}@cn.ibm.com

Abstract. Software as a Serivce (SaaS) provides software application vendors a Web based delivery model to serve big amount of clients with multi-tenancy based infrastructure and application sharing architecture so as to get great benefit from the economy of scale. In this paper, we describe the evolution of the small and medium businesses (SMB) oriented SaaS ecosystem and its key challenges. On particular problem we focus on is how to leverage massive multi-tenancy to balance the cost-effectiveness achieved via high shared efficiency, and the consequent security, performance and availability isolation issues among tenants. Base on this foundation, we further study the concepts, competency model and enablement framework of customization and configuration in SaaS context to satisfy as may tenants' requirements as possible. We also explore the topics on service lifecycle and the subscription management design of SaaS.

Keywords: Software as a Service, Multi-tenancy, Customization, Service Lifecycle Management, Subscription, Small and Medium Businesses (SMB).

1 Introduction

Software as a Service (SaaS) is gaining momentum with the significant increased number of vendors moving into this space and the recent success of a bunch of leading players on the market [1]. Designed to leverage the benefits brought by economy of scale, SaaS is about delivering software functionalities to a big group of clients over Web with one single instance of software application running on top of a multi-tenancy platform [2]. Clients usually don't need to purchase the software license and install the software package in their local computing environment. They use the credentials issued by the SaaS vendor to log onto and consume the SaaS service over Web through an Internet browser at any time and from any where with Internet connections.

Today's economic crisis makes it imperative that organizations of all sizes find new ways to perform their operations in a more cost-effective fashion. This is particularly true for small and medium size businesses (SMBs) which often operate with thinner margins than their larger enterprise counterparts [3]. From this point of view, SaaS is a delivery model that has everything to lure SMBs -- easy installation, low cost. As a consequence, SMBs can afford those more powerful enterprise applications, such as Customer Relationship Management (CRM), Enterprise Resource Planning (ERP) and

D. Agrawal et al. (Eds.): Information and Software as Services, LNBIP 74, pp. 1–30, 2011.
© Springer-Verlag Berlin Heidelberg 2011

Supply Chain Management (SCM), via SaaS alternatives to the traditional, on-premise software packages of the past. It thus has achieved a prosperous development and covered most of the well-known application areas during the past several years. According to a recent survey [4], 86% of the 600+ SMBs that participated in the survey said they expected to deploy SaaS in their organization over the next year. Further, 55% of the survey participants indicated that they were planning to spend the same or even more on IT over the next year.

As more people are diving deep into the market, the SMBs oriented SaaS evolves gradually into a complex ecosystem. In the ecosystem, the service provider hosts many applications recruiting from different software vendors in the centrally-managed data centers, and operates them as the web delivered services for a huge number of SMBs simultaneously. Furthermore, some value-added service resellers (VARs), also appeared to help distribute, customize and compose the services to end customers more efficiently. All of these roles collaborate together to create a healthy and scalable SaaS value chain for the SMB market. The SMBs greatly reduce their operating costs and improve the effectiveness of their operations. Other stakeholders of the ecosystem share the revenues by providing support in the different stages of the service lifecycle, such as service creation, delivery, operation, composition and distribution. To enable the ecosystem and value chain, several technical challenges are inevitable introduced, especially compared with the traditional license software based business model.

- *Massive multi-tenancy* [2] refers to the principle of cost saving by effectively sharing infrastructure and application resources among tenants and offerings to achieve economy of scale. However, the tenant would naturally desire to access the service as if there is a dedicated one, which inevitably results to the security, performance and availability isolation issues among tenants with diverse SLA (service level agreement) and customization requirements.
- *Self-serve customization* [14] Many clients, although sharing the highly standardized software functionalities, still ask for function variants according to their unique business needs. Due to the subscription based model, SaaS vendors need take a well designed strategy to enable the self-serve and configuration based customization by their customers without changing the SaaS application source code for any individual customer.
- *Low-cost application migration* may help service providers recruit more offerings in a short time, since the service vendors needn't pay too much efforts in transformation. However, one issue is most of existing applications are on-premise or with very initial multi-tenancy features enabled. Another challenge is the extremely heterogenous programming models.
- *Streamlined service lifecycle* [15] refers to the management processes of services and tenants in many aspects like promotion, subscription, on-boarding, billing and operation etc. It focuses on optimizing the delivery efficiency and improving the process flexibility to satisfy the dynamically changing requirements.
- *On-demand scalability* refers to effectively deliver the application and computational resources to exactly match the real demands of clients. Today, this study is mostly located in cloud computing [5]. One key challenge is the on-demand allocation/de-allocation of resources in a dynamic, optimized and transparent way.

The existing IT infrastructure, middleware and programming models are difficult to satisfy the requirements and challenges described above, which show in many aspects. For example, software vendors should pay significant development efforts to enable their applications with the capabilities to be run as SaaS services. Meanwhile, the service providers are assailed by seeking a secure, flexible and cost-effective infrastructure and platform to effectively deliver and operate the SaaS services in the massive multi-tenancy scenarios. Furthermore, they also need well-designed management processes and programming toolkits to attract more software vendors, value added service builders and resellers to join the ecosystem, and recruit, promote and refine the services in a more efficient way.

This paper will introduce our experiences and insights accumulated in the real industry practices, to set up an effective and profitable SaaS ecosystem for the large-scale service provider to deliver internet-based services to a huge amount of SMB clients by working with plenty of service vendors. This paper focuses on exploring the key customer requirements and challenges of the ecosystem from three important aspects, e.g. massive multi-tenancy, flexibility and service lifecycle management, and the corresponding technologies having the potential to resolve them in practice.

The rest of this paper is organized as follows: Section 2 illustrates the evolution of SaaS ecosystem for SMB market. The next three sections are the main body of this paper. Section 3 focuses on massive multi-tenancy, which is the most important characteristic of SaaS. It explores how to achieve the cost effectiveness via effective resource sharing mechanisms, and the consequent security, performance and availability isolation issues among tenants. Section 4 will explore the configuration and customization issues and challenges to SaaS vendors, clarify the difference between configuration and customization. A competency model and a methodology framework have been developed to help SaaS vendors to plan and evaluate their capabilities and strategies for service configuration and customization. Section 5 targets to the service lifecycle and the subscription management design of SaaS. A subscription model is introduced first to capture the different entities and their relationships involved in SaaS subscription. Then a method supported with service structure patterns and business interaction patterns analysis is presented to empower a SaaS provider to design an appropriate subscription model for its service offering. A case study is also made to demonstrate the effectiveness of the method at the end of this paper. Section 6 introduces related works, and finally Section 7 concludes this paper and discusses future works.

2   SMBs Oriented SaaS Ecosystem

In the primary SaaS model, service (software) vendors are responsible for all stages of the complete service lifecycle. As illustrated in Fig. 1, they have to develop and host the SaaS applications by themselves. To promote the businesses, they should define a suitable go-to-market strategy to connect the potential SMB customers to persuade them to subscribe the services. Furthermore, service vendors need also pay significant efforts in the daily operations of the services, like charging the monthly "hosting" or "subscription" fees from customers directly.

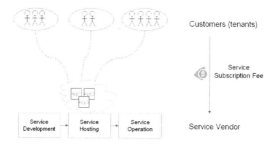

Fig. 1. The Primary SaaS Eco-system

SaaS customers, e.g. tenants, wish to get cost-effective services that address their critical business needs via a continuous expense rather than a single expense at time of purchase to reduce the Total Cost of Ownership (TCO). Meanwhile, the quality of the services, such as the security, performance, availability and flexibility, should be ensured at an acceptable level, considering the web based multi-tenant environments. Furthermore, the capability of highly on-demand scalability is also strongly required to adapt the dynamic and diverse requirements of their rapid business developments.

In this case, service vendors should accumulate enough knowledge in SaaS domain and have an insight into the architecture design of the SaaS applications. They need pay great efforts to enable those SaaS specific features, such as multi-tenant resources sharing patterns, isolation mechanisms, SLA management, service subscription and billing etc. This demands that developers own more strong technical skills, and inevitably increases the development cost and cycle.

Things could be a lot worse if the service vendors want to build more than one SaaS applications. They have to repeat the effort one by one since the implementation of the SaaS specific features have already been closely tangled with the business logics of each application. It may produce multiple independent and silo SaaS applications, which is not scalable to both development and management.

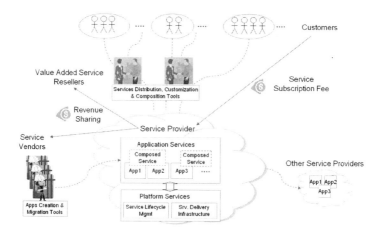

Fig. 2. The Advanced SaaS Ecosystem

Fig. 2 shows a more complex ecosystem, in which a new role, e.g. the service provider instead of the service vendor, will take full responsibility for hosting and operating the SaaS applications, and focus on providing better service quality to customers. In general, service providers may not develop applications by themselves, but tend to recruit from the service vendors and share the revenue with them in a certain way. In this case, service vendor becomes the pure SaaS content provider, while the value propositions of service provider in the ecosystem are as follows.

First, service provider sets up a cost-effective, secure and scalable runtime environment to deliver the applications of service vendors as services. It includes the hosted infrastructure, middleware and common services for SaaS enablement as well as the management and operation support, such as subscription, metering, billing, monitoring etc. To be noted, all of these features are provided in a standard "platform as service" way, independent of the applications running above. It's somehow similar to the BSS/OSS (Business/Operation Support System) platform of a telecom carrier, but targets to the SaaS domain.

Secondly, service provider also provides a suite of programming packages, sandbox, migration and offering lifecycle management tools for service vendors to quickly develop, test, transform and on-board their SaaS applications. In this case, service vendors need only focus on the user interfaces, business logics and data access models of their applications, without concerning with the detailed implementation of the SaaS enablement features. Those applications following the given programming specifications can easily run as services inside the hosted environment of service provider. Obviously, it can greatly reduce the development or migration costs of SaaS applications, and has potential to attracting more service vendors for a short time.

According to the definition of Wikipedia [6], a value-added reseller (VAR) is a company that adds some feature(s) to an existing product(s), and then resells it (usually to end-users) as an integrated product or complete "turn-key" solution. In the SaaS ecosystem, the value proposition of VAR mainly comes from two aspects:

- *Service Distribution*: The economics of scales demands the service provider to recruit a large volume of subscribed customers. In general, the VARs are geographically closer to end customers, and more familiar with the businesses and requirements of SMBs. By building a well-designed distribution network with resellers, service provider may recruit more SMB customers with least costs of go-to-market. In practice, service resellers may have pre-negotiated pricing that enables them to discount more than a customer would see going direct, or share the revenue with service provider.
- *Service Engagement*: The value propositions of VARs can also be added by providing some specific features for the customer's needs which don't exist in the standard service offerings, such as services customization, composition and integration with the on-premise applications or processes. Customers would purchase these value added services from the resellers if they lack the time or experiences to satisfy these requierments by themselves.

3 Massive Multi-tenancy

3.1 Overview of Multi-tenancy Patterns

Multi-tenancy is one of the key characteristics of SaaS. As illustrated in Fig. 3, in a multi-tenant enabled service environment, the user requests from different organizations and companies (referred as tenants) are served concurrently by one or more hosted application instances and databases based on a scalable, shared hardware and software infrastructure. The multi-tenancy approach can bring in a number of benefits including the improved profit margin for service providers through reduced delivery costs and decreased service subscription costs for clients. It makes the service offerings attractive to their potential clients, especially the SMB clients within very limited IT investment budget.

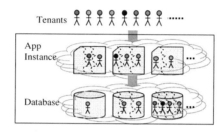

Fig. 3. A Multi-Tenant Enabled Service Environment

To achieve the economies of scale, the multi-tenant approach wishes to increase revenues by recruiting large number of clients and reduce the average service delivery costs per client by serving these clients with highly sharing infrastructure and application resources. Although higher resources sharing level can effectively drive down the total costs for both service consumers and providers, there are essential conflicts between cost-effectiveness and isolation among tenants. From the user experience, QoS (Quality of Service) and administration perspectives, the tenants would naturally desire to access and use the services as if there were dedicated ones. Therefore, isolation should be carefully considered in almost all parts of architecture design, from both non-functional and functional level, such as security, performance, availability, administration etc.

Generally, there are two kinds of multi-tenancy patterns: multiple instances and native (or massive) multi-tenancy, as illustrated in Fig. 4. The former supports each tenant with its dedicated application instance over a shared hardware, Operating System (OS) or a middleware server in a hosting environment whereas the latter can support all tenants by a single shared application instance over various hosting resources.

The two kinds of multi-tenancy patterns scale quite differently in terms of the number of tenants that they can support. The multi-instances pattern is adopted to support several up to dozens of tenants. While the native multi-tenancy pattern is used to support a much larger number of tenants, usually in the hundreds or even thousands. It is interesting to note that the isolation level among tenants decreases as the

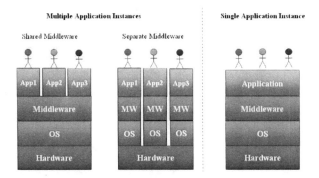

Fig. 4. Multi-tenancy Patterns: Multiple Instances Vs. Native (Massive) Multi-tenancy

scalability level increases. By using native multi-tenancy to support more tenants, we should put more efforts to prevent the QoS of one tenant from being affected by other tenants in the same sharing multi-tenancy environment.

The selection of multi-tenancy technology depends on the specific application scenarios and the target clients' requirements. For example, a large enterprise may prefer to pay a premium for multiple instances to prevent the potential risks associated with resource sharing. While most SMB companies would prefer services with a reasonable quality at lower costs, and care less about particular kinds of multi-tenancy patterns that the service providers use. Therefore, in this paper, we will focus on the native multi-tenancy pattern to explore how to achieve cost-effectiveness with acceptable isolation level for the SMB oriented SaaS ecosystem.

3.2 Cost-Effectiveness

Typically, most SaaS offerings target to SMB clients with very limited IT budgets. It's well known that low price is one of the most important reasons that SaaS can attract the attention of SMB customers. Therefore, the success of SMB oriented SaaS extremely depends on cost effectiveness and scalability, e.g. economics of scale. This trend is quite obvious, especially in the emerging markets.

For example, in China, one SMB with 3 concurrent users need only pay about $300 per year to subscribe the online accounting and SCM applications [7]. Meanwhile, the service provider, which is the biggest ERP software vendor of China SMB market, wishes to recruit several hundred thousands or even one million subscribed SMB customers in future several years. The scale of tenant number is predictable since China owns over 40 million SMBs in 2009. The key challenge is that how to make it profitable within such low pricing model.

First, from the view of service provider, it should extremely reduce the expense of service delivery infrastructure including the hardware, software and utility of hosting center, e.g. bandwidth, power, space etc., and save the costs of human resources to maintain the service operation lifecycle.

In this case, the multiple instances pattern in Fig. 4 is not practical as the small revenue generated from each tenant won't justify the allocation of dedicated hardware/software resources for the tenant. Actually, many resource types can be shared among tenants in a more fine-granular and cost effective way if we take some kind of suitable resource management mechanism. These resources are located in different tiers and artifacts of SaaS applications, like user interface, business logic and data model. Table 1 gives some of these resources in a J2EE based SaaS application.

Table 1. Sharable multi-tenant resources in the J2EE based SaaS application

Layer	Components	Sharable Resources
Persistent Data Model	Database Access (JDBC, SDO, Hibernate, JPA etc.)	✧ Data Source & Connection Pool
		✧ DB Account
		✧ Database/Schema/Table/Buffer Pool etc.
	File / IO	✧ Directory
		✧ File
	Directory Server (LDAP)	✧ Directory Tree
		✧ Schema
Business Logic	Authentication & Authorization	✧ Organization Structure / Privileges Repository
		✧ Login / authorization modules
	Global Java Object	✧ Static variable
		✧ Variable of Singleton Class
	Remote Access (Socket/Http, RMI, CORABA, JNDI, Web Service etc.)	✧ Remote Services
		✧ Connection Parameters like URI, port, username, password etc.
	EJB	✧ Stateful EJB instance
		✧ Data source connection, table of Entity Bean
		✧ Queue, sender's identity of MDB
	Logs	✧ Log file location, content, format and configuration
	Cache	✧ Cache Container
Process/Workflow	BPEL Process Template	✧ Template Level Attribute, Activity, Link Condition etc.
	Human Task	✧ Verb, Task UI etc
	Business Rule	✧ Rules
User Interface	JSP	✧ Application Scope Variable (tag, usebean, applicationContext etc.)
		✧ Declaration variable
		✧ Logo,Style,Layout etc.
	Servlet	✧ Single-thread servlet
		✧ servletContext

For each kind of sharable resource type, we start from identifying all the potential sharing and isolation mechanisms, and evaluate them according to the estimation of the degree of cost saving. The additional management costs introduced by different level of resources sharing should be considered carefully. Since current administration tools for application, middleware and database are totally unaware of the concept of tenants, service providers have to pay more efforts and human resources to execute those multi-tenancy related operations manually because of lacking tenant-aware toolkits and automation processes.

For people to understand better, we take the database access as an example [8], and identified at least three kinds of resources sharing patterns in Fig. 5.

- ♦ *E1: Totally isolated*: each tenant owns a separate database
- ♦ *E2: Partially shared*: multiple tenants share a database, but each tenant owns a separate set of tables and schema

- *E3: Totally shared*: multiple tenants share the same database, tables and schema. In this pattern, records of all tenants are stored in a single shared table sets mixed in any order, in which a tenant ID column is inserted in each table to associate the data records with the corresponding tenants

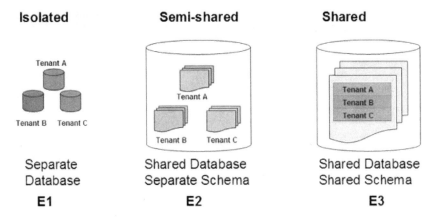

Fig. 5. Data tier resource sharing patterns in the multi-tenant context

Obviously, *E3* is more cost effective than another two patterns in the infrastructure level resources consumption. However beside the isolation issues that we will further discuss later, it also introduces additional costs in data management and maintenance.

For example, per-tenant data backup and restore is a very typical feature that should be provided in a multi-tenant environment. Existing DBMS only supports database and table-space level backup and restore mechanism, which can work well in pattern *E1* since the smallest operation unit of a tenant is also the database.

While in *E3*, the records of all tenants are stored inside a same set of tables, which makes the existing backup and restore mechanism hardly identify and separate data from the dimension of tenant. In this case, the administrator has to execute the work manually and results to significant effort. Therefore, to automate the operation process and cut the maintenance cost, current DBMS management toolkits should be enhanced and transformed as tenant awareness.

Secondly, as for service vendors, the development and upgrading costs of SaaS applications should be as small as possible. There are also many software vendors who have already accumulated a lot of on-premise applications in different industries. Most of these applications are very mature and verified in the markets. If they can be quickly transformed into multi-tenant applications with least effort, the SaaS ecosystem will become more attractable to both end customers and service vendors.

One practical approach is to provide a multi-tenancy enablement layer to hide the complexities of enabling the multi-tenancy capability by encapsulating the detailed implementation of multi-tenant resources sharing and isolation mechanisms. By leveraging the (nearly) transparent programming interfaces, build-time libraries and runtime components (or plug-ins of middleware), the enablement layer relieves most of developers from those complicated multi-tenant issues by simulating a virtualized single-tenant application development environment.

To keep consistency, we still take the database as the example. It's well known in a standard J2EE application, people generally access database via the standard JDBC interface or some frameworks above it, such as the iBatis, Hibernate and JPA. To support pattern *E3* in Fig. 5, the layer provides a specific multi-tenant JDBC wrapper (or driver), which can intercept the database access requests of the application and retrieve the data of the tenant of the current logon user in an implicit way. Since the multi-tenant wrapper takes the same programming interfaces of standard JDBC, the developers are almost multi-tenancy non-awareness and like writing a single tenant application. Similarly, to transform those existing on-premise applications, the developers can simply re-compile the application by replacing the JDBC libraries, without needing change any source codes.

3.3 Security Isolation

In the multi-tenant scenarios, besides those traditional security mechanisms (i.e., authentication, authorization, audit etc.), one also needs to consider additional potential security risk introduced by other tenants who share the same application instance and resources. This section focus on the security technologies in the massive multi-tenant system to safeguard the security of each tenant at similar security levels as those of the traditional single-tenant applications.

Access Control Isolation. It refers to the mechanism to prevent a user from getting the privileges to access resources belonging to other tenants. There are generally two kinds of access control isolation patterns: implicit filter and explicit permission. Paper [9] introduced how to apply these two patterns into a multi-tenant data model. Actually, we can further generalize the two patterns to realize the access control isolation of other resources through proper designs of the filter and permission mechanisms.

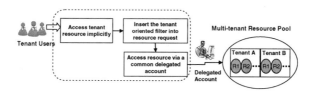

Fig. 6. Process of Implicit Filter Based Access Control Isolation Pattern

- *Implicit Filter Based Access Control Isolation:* In this pattern as illustrated in Fig. 6, when one tenant requests to access shared resources, a common platform level account is delegated to handle this request. The delegated account is shared by all tenants and has the privileges to access resources of all tenants. However, the key of this mechanism is to implicitly compose a tenant-oriented filter that will be used to prevent one user from tapping into resources of other tenants. There are some typical and practical filters for different kinds of resources, such as the SQL sub-statement like "*Where TenantID=xxx*", tenant specific XML context/scope in the configuration file, and one additional tenant aware parameter or dimension of the *if/then ruleset* or *decision table* in business rule etc.

- ◆ *Explicit Permission Based Access Control Isolation:* In this pattern, access privileges for the resources have been explicitly pre-assigned to the corresponding tenant accounts by using the Access Control List (ACL) mechanism. Therefore, there is no need to leverage an additional common delegated account across tenants.

Let's take the database resource sharing pattern *E3* in Fig. 5 as an example too. According to the approaches described above, we may leverage either the application-level or DBMS-level database access control isolation mechanisms.

In the former, all tenants share a common database account to access their own data records. A sub-clause needs to be inserted into the SQL statement, to filter out data records not belonging to the current tenant. For example, for an application query such as *Select name, address, phone From CustomerData*, the query would need to be re-written as *Select name, address, phone From CustomerData Where TenantID='xyz'*.

Although easy to implement, application-level access control isolation has some potential security risks. For example, SQL injection [10], which is a technique that exploits a security vulnerability occurring in the database layer of an application, may occur when user input is either incorrectly filtered for string literal escape characters embedded in SQL statements or user input is not strongly typed and thereby unexpectedly executed. In the multi-tenant context, a well-designed user input may bypass the sub-clause used to filter out other tenants' data. A typical example of cross tenant SQL injection is as follows:

Suppose the original SQL statement is *Select * From Sales_Order Where TenantID = 'xyz' And SOID = '" + Order_Id + "'*. If the Order_Id variable is crafted in a specific way by a malicious user, the SQL statement may do more than the code author intended. For example, setting the Order_Id variable as: *'123' or '0'='0'*. Then, the new SQL statement becomes: *Select * From Sales_Order Where TenantID = 'xyz' And SOID = '123' or '0'='0'*. Obviously, in this case, all tenants' orders residing in the shared table will be accessed illegally.

In the DBMS-level access control isolation, each tenant is assigned a dedicated database access account and connection which only has privileges to access its own resources. It should depend on some kind of access control mechanism support by DBMS in native. For example, Label-Based Access Control (LBAC) [11] is a new security feature provided by DB2 v9, which allows you decide exactly who has read and write access to individual rows and individual columns, and thus greatly increases the control you have over who can access your data. In this way, it can completely prevent potential SQL injection attack.

Information Protection Isolation. This topic is intended to protect the integrity and confidentiality of each tenant's critical information. In other word, one should prevent the critical information of one tenant from being read or modified by other unauthorized tenants and users via hacking attempts.

Typically, the information may be accessed by unauthorized requesters when data is stored in database or in memory, exchanged among different application components, and transferred through networks. A traditional way to protect the information content is through data encryption and digital signature. However, in a multi-tenant system, the mechanism of sharing the same set of keys among all tenants is obviously meaningless since it can only prevent external attackers, but not other tenants who also have the access to the keys. Therefore, in this case, each tenant should own a unique set of keys, without disclosing to other tenants, to encrypt its critical and private information.

Theoretically, we may encrypt all the information with the strongest encryption algorithm in any situation. However, the security is about trade-offs of information security and performance. We should strive for good-enough security, not for more security than necessary. From a practical point of view, we suggest the following principles when making the tradeoffs with respect to the security in multi-tenant systems:

- *Encrypt or digitally sign the most critical information only:* Generally, the criticality of data can be measured by application specific domain knowledge (i.e. financial data may have higher priority) and the SLA requirements of the tenants.
- *Select a suitable encryption algorithm:* Generally, encryption algorithms with stronger security may result in poorer performance. In some cases, we may take mixed encryption algorithms for the tradeoffs. For example, use the public and private key cryptography algorithm to protect symmetric keys which are finally used to encrypt data [9].
- *Consider the information access frequency:* The performance will suffer more if the data with higher access frequency is encrypted.

3.4 Performance Isolation

The objective of performance isolation mainly includes two aspects. First, prevent the (potentially bad) behaviors of one tenant from adversely affecting the usage performance of other tenants in an unpredictable manner. Secondly, avoid the unfairness among tenants in terms of usage performance. One should prevent the unbalanced situations where some tenants achieve very high performance at the cost of others while all of them sign the same SLA. However, the fairness doesn't mean absolute equality: the performance of one tenant is related to its corresponding SLA. It's reasonable to provide higher performance for the tenant who pays more for a better SLA.

As we all know, the resource allocation mechanisms have major impact on the system performance. [12] In this section, we explore the merits and shortcomings of several resource management mechanisms, and provide guidelines on how to effectively leverage them in the complex multi-tenant environments.

- *By Tenant Resource Reservation:* Enforce fixed quotas per tenant for different resources. This approach can guarantee to meet the minimal SLA requirements of a tenant. However, it does not have the flexibility to share the idle resources, and may significantly reduce the throughput and scalability of the hosting service platform, especially in the high-load situations.

♦ *By Tenant Resource Admission Control*: Enforce the admission control policies or limitations per tenant for different resources to prevent potentially bad behaviors. The admission policies may be static or even dynamic ones dependent on the states of the system during the runtime. For example, "if the system load is less than a certain degree, then the maximal number of concurrent users per tenant should be fifteen, else be ten."

♦ *Tenant Oriented Resource Partition*:   It refers to the capability of distributing different kinds of available resources among a number of partitions. Each tenant will be assigned to a certain resource partition. Tenants sharing the same partition should follow the same resource management policies, and be separated from those tenants outside the partition. Obviously, this separation improves the isolation capabilities among tenants who don't belong to the same partition. The challenge is how to improve the resources efficiency among partitions. One potential approach is a well-designed placement algorithm to distribute tenants with different loads and SLAs among multiple partitions to balance the loads of all partitions.

In practice, we suggest to take a hybrid performance isolation pattern. First, the tenants are categorized into different groups according to their specific SLA requirements and behavior patterns studied by statistical data collected during the runtime. Then, the approaches mentioned above, including resources reservation, admission control and partition, etc., would be applied selectively to achieve the best balance between the resource utilization efficiency and the performance isolation.

3.5 Availability (Fault) Isolation

The service availability is one of the most important SLA metrics of a hosted application. Study [13] in this area have concerned with how to design a high availability system. However, the native multi-tenant system presents a new challenge: how to prevent the propagation of faults among tenants sharing the same application instance, or the so-called tenant oriented fault or availability isolation.

In traditional single tenant system, the availability is usually measured by following formula:

$$ST\text{-}Availability = MTTF / (MTTF + MTTR) \qquad (1)$$

Where, *MTTF* is Mean Time To Failure, *MTTR* is Mean Time To Repair. Therefore, the availability is expressed as a ratio of the average service available time to the total system cycle time.

While in a multi-tenant system, the formula should be revised by taking the tenants into consideration. Suppose the total number of tenants is N, and the average number of infected tenants is X when a fault occurs. We can define the availability of the multi-tenant system as following:

$$MT\text{-}Availability = 1 - MTTR / (MTTF + MTTR) * X / N \qquad (2)$$

Obviously, consider the *MTTF*, *MTTR* and *N* as the constants, the average infected tenant number X should be the key factor of the availability of the hosted service.

In other words, the goal of tenant oriented fault isolation is to reduce X/N, the ratio of fault propagation among tenants, as much as possible.

Based on the analysis above, we give out several principles to handle the challenge of preventing fault propagation in a multi-tenant system:

- *Fault Detection & Diagnosis*: It's the first stage to detect that something unexpected has occurred and quickly identify the currently infected tenant(s). This implies that each tenant should have the ability to monitor the states of its own running instance, and report to the service platform in a timely manner via the mechanisms like *heart-beating* and *periodical simulations*.
- *Fault Propagation Prevention*: Once having detected the faults occurred to certain tenants, we need to take immediate actions to prevent them from propagating to other tenants so as to reduce the infection ratio X/N. Although the specific approaches to reach this goal depend very much on particular kinds of the fault (category), one basic principle is to force the faster release of the critical shared resources to avoid the possible fault propagation. Furthermore, certain isolation technologies discussed in the previous sections (e.g., the partitioning) can also help prevent fault propagation among tenants.
- *On-Line Repair*: In the native multi-tenant system, the faults of those ill tenants should be repaired while the application instance is still running. Two possible approaches are: (1) *Tenant oriented service restart*: First suspend or kick out all active users and instances of the ill tenant, release resources it currently owns, and try to correct the error via modifying (potentially) wrong data or information, then "restart" the service of the tenant (activate users or instances). (2) *Tenant oriented service restore*: In this approach, we clear all data of the ill tenant, and restore to one of its previous backup versions.

Beside the fault isolation, the data redundancy is another very important approach to provide fault tolerance. While in the native multi-tenant system, one particular problem is to balance the cost and the tenants' specific requirements on SLA. Generally, the cost associated with providing this feature is a reduction of storage capacity available, since the implementations require one or more duplications of the tenant's data set. For each tenant, more copies of data mean better SLA but higher cost. Therefore, the design of data redundancy mechanism should be fine granular and tenant awared to flexibly allocate suitable copies of data for each tenant, which can save the operation cost by the greatest degree while not violating the commitment on availability.

4 Flexibility: Configuration and Customization

4.1 Configuration and Customization in Multi-tenancy Environment

The fundamental design point of SaaS is to serve hundreds and thousands of clients through one instance of software application. SaaS vendors don't develop and keep different software versions for any individual client. The most ideal case for SaaS vendors is that every client feel comfortable using a completely standardize offering. However this ideal case usually doesn't happen in enterprise software application area. As illustrated in Fig.7, In general with the functional complexity increase of the software, the more potential tailoring efforts need be involved to serve a specific client. Web e-Mail is one SaaS service with relatively simple functions, that is why clients usually just need to tailor the service with parameters based setting, e.g. e-mail box storage size; account number. Industry generic CRM is one service with medium level of function complexity that is why you see many CRM SaaS vendors offer much stronger tailoring capabilities through configuration and customization tools. As SaaS leverages economy of scale of clients' number through a long tail play, therefore the more complex of the software, it becomes more non-appropriate to explore SaaS model as client may ask very complex tailoring requirements which can not be handled effectively with Web based delivery model in multi-tenancy environment. That is why the most successful SaaS services stay at CRM, Human Resource Management (HRM), Finance & Administration (F&A) and Collaboration (email, web-conference, etc) spaces [16].

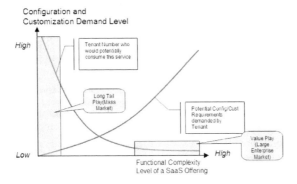

Fig. 7. Configuration and Customization Demands vs. Functional Complexity of a SaaS

Tailoring a SaaS service can leverage two major approaches: Configuration and Customization. These two terms usually get people confused about their differences. Actually different SaaS vendors use different terms in different contexts. We try to clarify the difference between them. As depicted in Fig.8, In order to make a standardized SaaS offering to serve a specific client, we need to tailor it into a tenantized offering by satisfying this client's unique requirements. Both Configuration and Customization can support this tailoring effort into certain level. The crux of the difference is complexity. Configuration does not involve source code change of the SaaS application. It usually support variance through setting pre-defined parameters, or

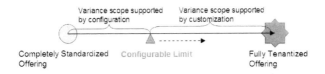

Fig. 8. Configuration and Customization

leveraging tools to change application functions within pre-defined scope, e.g. adding data fields, changing field names, modifying drop-down lists, adding buttons, and changing business rules, etc. Configuration can support tailoring requirements within pre-defined configurable limit. Customization involves SaaS application source code changes to create functionality that is beyond the configurable limit.

Comparing with Configuration, Customization is a much more costy approach for both SaaS vendors and clients. As Customization involves SaaS software source code changes, that produces many issues which involve significant cost, for example: Requiring people with higher skills with higher wage to work on Customization; Allocating resources and infrastructure to manage software code versions; involving much longer lifecycle brought by code development/debugging/testing and deployment; and losing business opportunity from those clients who can not accept the Customization complexity and cost [17]. The Customization is becoming much more complex in SaaS context, as SasS vendors need to maintain every piece of Customization code tenant by tenant. Upgrading the SaaS application should not lead into losing of any single tenant's customization code. Therefore wherever possible, SaaS should avoid Customization by using Configuration to meet clients' tailoring requirements and enlarge configurable limit as far as possible toward client's unique requirements.

4.2 Configuration and Customization Competency Model

To facilitate strategy definition and execution discussion around SaaS configuration and customization, we introduce the Configuration and Customization Competency Model described in Fig. 9. There are 5 levels of competencies have been defined from "Entry", "Aware", "Capable" levels to "Mature" and "World Class" levels. This model can be used in the assessment of SaaS application to identify improvement goals around configuration and customization through necessary benchmarking with market leader's competency level. Different level of competency can enable different level of variance requirements through different technical approaches supported by ranges of SaaS services from completely standardized offering across all the tenants to fully tenantized offering for any individual tenant. In theory, the higher of the competency level, the more customers and the more complex variance requirements the SaaS service can

Level of Competency	Description	Approach	Variance Level Supported	
Entry	Highly standardized offering without any configuration and customization support	Well design the functionalities as standardized offering to cover targeted customers	None	Completely Standardized Offering
Aware	Relatively standardized offering with pre-defined variance points	Offer parameterized configuration	Low	
Capable	Relatively standardized offering with user defined configuration	Offer self serve configuration tool to empower customers	Medium	
Mature	Base offering with programable enviroment to enable user preferred customization	Offer scripting based programming for very flexible customization	High	
World Class	Offer a platform supported by programming model and tools to enable extremely strong customization or even new application development	Offer well defined programming model and tools to enable extensive customization and new application development	Extremely High	Fully Tenantized Offering

Fig. 9. SaaS Configuration Competency Model

support. However different SaaS vendors may have different strategies in terms of targeted customer segments, supported scope of variance, etc. If the SaaS strategy is well defined, the SaaS service can succeed on the market even its configuration and customization competency only stays at "Entry" level or "Aware" level.

The configuration and customization to a SaaS application can happen in many different perspectives. Summit Strategies Inc analyzed the configuration and customization capabilities of SaaS in different implementation layers of the software, which include: Presentation Logic, Application Logic, and Database Logic [18]. Here we try to analyze this issue from clients' requirements point of view as follows.

As illustrated by the Fig. 10, SaaS tenants can potentially have configuration and customization requirements from many different perspectives. Each tenant may raise the following challenges to the SaaS vendor: "I need more fields to describe my business documents"; "Our manager wants a new report/dashboard to analyze sales data"; "Our organization has no role of procurement manager"; "The workflow of our business is different with what you can support". Any of these challenges can be divided into implications to different perspectives of the SaaS application, e.g., Data, User Interface, Organization Structure, Processing Logic, Workflow, Business Rules, For example: When tenant wants to change the default data structures provided by the SaaS vendor, the configuration and customization tools should support.

"Add Custom Field", "Change Field Name", "Change Field Type"; When tenant wants to change workflow pre-built by SaaS vendor, the configuration and customization tools should support "Switch on/off Tasks", "Add New Tasks", "Reorder the Tasks", "Change Roles for a Task". If you analyze those change impact relationship" lines on the figure, you will notice "Data Configuration and Customization" and "Organization Structure Configuration and Customization" are the two most important perspectives, any change of these two perspectives will potentially bring major impact to many other perspectives including User Interface, Workflow, Business Rules, etc.

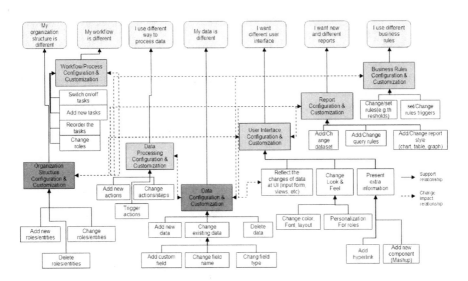

Fig. 10. Perspectives of Configuration and Customization Requirements

For example: If tenant changes a data structure, then the user interface to support the input and view of the data should be changed as well; If tenant changes the roles' definition, then the workflow need to be changed accordingly for those tasks handled by those roles. Therefore SaaS vendors should put much more effort to well design Data and Organization Structure layers to support easy configuration and customization. It is also very important to consider the impacts and establish the linkages between the other software artifacts and the changes of Data and Organization structure.

4.3 A Framework to Plan and Execute Configuration and Customization Strategy

It is very important to define the appropriate software functional scope to be offered as SaaS. It is extremely critical for SaaS vendors to have the right strategy and software architecture to support Configuration and Customization. This is the foundation to support a SaaS service to pursue economical scale.

Fig. 11. A Framework to Plan and Execute Configuration and Customization Strategy

As illustrated in the above figure, we introduce a framework to guide the plan and execution of SaaS configuration and customization strategy. This framework consists of a methodology and supporting analysis tools.

Understand Environment. The first step of the methodology is to make necessary investigation to understand the environment related with the configuration and customization of the SaaS service. There are two main areas need to be investigated: client requirements and market leader competency level. The objective of analyzing customer requirements is to identify the targeted customer segment and the required variance scope. As illustrated in Fig. 12, a customer segmentation analysis can be conducted by segmenting the whole market into 4 quadrants divided by two major dimensions: uniqueness of requirements and capability to acquire alternative solution. In general, the customers in quadrant III should be the primary targeted customer segment of SaaS service as these customers have relatively low level of variance requirements and has relatively weak capability to acquire alternative solution (e.g. invest on a custom developed application) other than the SaaS service. Quadrant I is

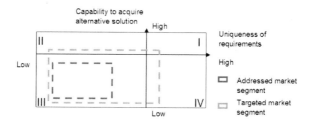

Fig. 12. Customer Segment Analysis

usually a difficult segment for SaaS service to win as each of the customers in this segment has very unique requirements and they have the capability to explore other alternatives.

Customers in quadrant II and IV are the segments where customers are usually in marginal position. If the SaaS vendors could offer strong, easy and low cost configuration and customization capabilities, they can win more customers in these two segments. The SaaS vendor can leverage survey and interview with selected potential customers to develop such a customer segment analysis. There are two important elements of this analysis. The first one is to well define the SaaS application function scope and complexity level so as to make clients fall into quadrant III as many as possible; the second one is to determine the addressed market segment and targeted segment through enhanced configuration and customization according to the investigated variance requirements.

Market leader's competency level investigation can help SaaS vendor to well position itself in the competition environment from configuration and customization perspective, which is an important exercise to support target competency level definition discussed later in this paper.

Define Strategy. SaaS vendor should determine how they plan to support the required configuration and customization requirements in the targeted customer segment. To facilitate the discussion, we abstract the potential strategies around Configuration and Customization into four Models illustrated in the table below.

Table 2. Different Configuration and Customization Approaches

	Model A: Native Design	Model B: Smooth Evolvement	Model C: Pulse Evolvement	Model D: Failure Management
Description	Thoroughly analyze the common configuration and customization requirements before building the SaaS application; Design the application for extensive configuration and customization; provide powerful web based tools for tenants to configure and customize the SaaS service by themselves or other system integrator vendor.	SaaS vendors need to spend effort to support every single tenant's configuration and customization requirements. But SaaS vendors have a way to manage the cost by leveraging tools & assets, and gradually reduce the cost spend on configuration and customization per tenant.	SaaS vendors collect configuration and customization requirements from a group of tenants. Upgrade application to satisfy the requirements demanded by a big group of tenants when the return on investment can be justified by potential benefits brought by the effort.	SaaS vendors support configuration and customization for individual tenant. They fail to manage the cost within a scope required by a profitable business.
Approach	Provide programming model, web based tools and API for tenants to conduct configuration and customization in self-service mode. SaaS vendors won't change application code for any individual tenant.	SaaS vendors change application codes according to tenants' requirements. They deploy management tool and process to manage the cost spent on each tenant.	SaaS vendors change application codes when the configuration and customization requirements are defined and justified by a big group of tenants' demand.	SaaS vendors change application codes according to each tenant's requirements. They don't have effective tools and process to manage the cost spent on each tenant.
Possible Scalability	Very High	Medium-to-Low	Medium-to-High	Very Low
Application Complexity	Medium-to-Low	Medium	Medium	High

As shown in Fig. 13, the four approaches, "Native Design" (Model A), "Smooth Evolvement" (Model B), "Pulse Evolvement" (Model C), "Failure Management" (Model D), have different level of impact on the SaaS service delivery cost spent on each tenant from configuration and customization. As shown on the following figure, Model D is obviously a bad one which every SaaS vendors should avoid to get into. The other three models can all support sustainable SaaS service business with different profit margins. They can be good choice according to specific SaaS business context in terms of: application complexity, scalability target, the vendor's understanding of the market, the budget situation, etc. In general, Model B is more appropriate for SaaS targeting very limited number of clients as supporting each individual tenant's unique requirements is a very expensive strategy. If a SaaS vendors want to explore very high scalability to leverage very big economical scale (Long tail play), then Model A would be the best approach. The easiest approach for a SaaS vendor starts from is Model C, they learn the market along the process and eventually can be evolved into Model A when they clearly define and build configuration and customization capabilities needed by the large amount of tenants they want to acquire and serve.

Model A can only be built out through deep understanding of the potential configuration and customization requirements associated with the SaaS service. It takes specially designed software architecture and provides web based tools for easy and extensive configuration and customization without changing the SaaS application source code.

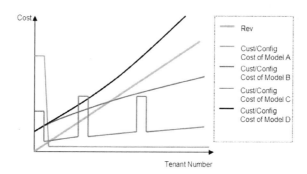

Fig. 13. The Impact on Configuration and Customization Cost of Different Approaches

Access Competency. This step is extremely important for those traditional software application vendors who plan to explore SaaS as a new delivery model. The configuration and customization might not be a big challenge for applications vendors who have been successfully addressing consumer market and SMB market. These vendors usually take volume play model and do not support individual customer's variance requirements. They can jump start to explore SaaS by transforming their applications into multi-tenancy enabled with Web interface. However the configuration and customization issue is a big challenge for those application vendors who have been addressing medium to large enterprise market. Though they have well packaged application as a base, these vendors are usually paid by their customers to take custom development approach to satisfy each individual customer's unique variance requirements.

In many cases, source code level customizations are involved if the application has no well defined configuration framework. But in the traditional application delivery model, the vendor can afford that because they are paid by the end customer to do so. This approach can not be replicated in SaaS delivery model. SaaS has subscription based usage pattern. The very small amount upfront investment made by the tenant and monthly based subscription fee can not support the total cost spent on source code level customization. Therefore these application vendors should be very careful and make necessary assessment about their competency around configuration and customization before they decide to move their application to the SaaS delivery model.

We introduced the configuration and customization competency model with several major perspectives to be studied for a SaaS application in section 4.2. These perspectives can be categorized into 6 groups: data structure and processing, organization structure, user interface, workflow, business rule and reporting. This model can be used to assess the competency of the existing software application from configuration and customization aspect. As illustrated by an example in Fig. 14, a benchmark study can also be conducted to compare with market leader's competency so as to clearly identify competency improvement goals. This study does not mean that every SaaS vendor should improve the competency to the higher level from every perspective. If a vendor's application is pretty similar with other existing SaaS services on the market from function aspect, then higher level configuration and customization competency can help the vendor to get stronger competitive advantages.

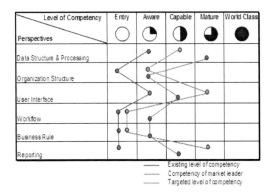

Fig. 14. Competency Assessment and Gap Analysis

Identify Gaps and Actions. Through the competency benchmark study, the competency gaps can be identified to guide the actions' definition. The example in Fig. 14 shows the gaps and improvement goals especially in user interface and reporting perspectives. With the analysis in section 3, the competency improvement goal could be further developed into specific actions. For example, to improve the configuration and customization capability for reporting function of the application, the actions need to be identified to support *"Add/Change dataset"*, *"Add/Change query rules"* and *"Add/Change report style (chart, table, graph)"*. If we go through every configuration and customization perspectives according to figure 3, we can generate a long list of actions which implies very complex design challenges for the SaaS application.

It is critical to have well designed principals and approach to tackle all the actions in a unified and consistent way.

As we discussed in table 2, there are different approaches which can enable different competency level requirements. Parameterized Configuration can enable "Aware" level variance through setting pre-defined parameters and options by end user in the runtime environment. Self Serve Configuration tool leverages an application variance metadata framework and a series of simple point-and-click wizards, users can design custom user interfaces and modify the structure of the data model and the application's business logic (workflow, business rules, etc). But the scope of configuration is constrained by the metadata framework. Scripting based programming, a version of end-user programming, allow for larger scope customization by the end user by extending the features of the tool using a constraint scripting language to guarantee security and avoid script generated damage to the core application. World Class SaaS service make their application coupled with a development environment and a formal programming model that can be used by user to build new application code or modify compiled code to match their requirements. Different SaaS vendors take different approach and develop their own implementations. [19] There is not a generic and platform independent approach for SaaS vendors to use today. There is a strong opportunity for research activities.

5   Service Lifecycle Management

5.1   SaaS Service Lifecycle Overview

Generally speaking, SaaS has a different lifecycle compared to a traditional software product. The stages like requirements analysis, development and testing are still very fundamental; however, new activities are required in addition. The following figure shows an overall SaaS lifecycle.

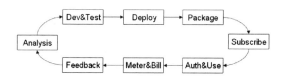

Fig. 15. An Overall SaaS Lifecycle

After a software application has been developed and deployed, it needs to be packaged by defining business terms, applying billing policies, and so on before it's ready to be subscribed to as a service offering by a customer. There are multiple ways to subscribe, including self-service or subscription via service reseller or operator. If a customer successfully subscribes to a service offering, then users can be authorized to access it. Based on metered usage information the customer will be billed periodically. Usually, feedback and analysis are essential steps to further improve a software application or customer service.

In real practice, the lifecycle may be different from the complete one showed above (e.g., there's a certain kind of SaaS, which is developed and consumed via the Web where no explicit deployment step is required). Another example is customer triggered provisioning, which occurs when one service is very popular and being subscribed to by a large number of customers. Additional deployments may be required to ensure a reasonable response time and satisfied customers.

5.2 Service Subscription Model

Subscription instantiates a service offering by providing customer-specific billing policy parameters and service level configurations. A service authorization is given based upon the subscription result and governing constraints or rules. For example, the maximum number of users is specified at subscription time and becomes a constraint for authorization.

To separate the concerns and build a flexible connection between software implementation and business operation, we refine the concept of service into a service element and a service offering in a general SaaS context. Fig. 16 shows the subscription model, and the key entities are described as follows.

- Software application is the deployment unit, and one application contains one or more service elements.
- Service element is the access and metering unit. There may be dependencies between service elements, and optionally, a service element has targeted customer types.
- Service offering is the subscription unit packaged from a service element, and business terms and billing policies are defined for a service offering.

Subscription enables a tenant to register for a service offering, while authorization gives a user to access a service instance. Here the service instance is generated from the subscription, and it is actually the instance of a service element.

The subscription model congregates different types of considerations around the entities of software application, service element and service offering, thus building a solid foundation for SaaS subscription management. But in real practice, the relationships among these entities and the ecosystem roles can be very complex, especially as the SaaS area evolves. Based on our in-market practice and study, we summarize the relationships into two groups of patterns, service structure and business interaction, which focus on connections among key entities and interactions among ecosystem roles, respectively.

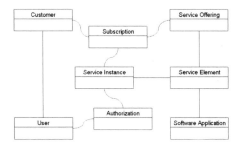

Fig. 16. SaaS Subscription Model

Subscription requirements provide input for pattern selection, as shown in Fig. 17. After both groups of patterns have been decided, they will be composed to get the final subscription design. More than one pattern can be selected for each group. If a conflict arises upon composing service structure patterns and business interaction patterns, either business- or technical-oriented requirements/pre-conditions should be adjusted. As an example, the application and service element may need to be re-engineered to support certain business interaction patterns.

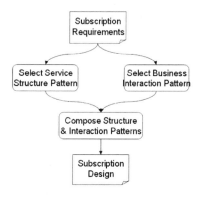

Fig. 17. Pattern-based Approach

Service Structure Patterns. Service structure patterns are described as following several categories:

- *Single Service*: Service offering contain only one service element, which must be selected when subscribing
- *Independent Multiple Services*: Service offering contains more than one service elements. One or more of them can be selected when subscribing. There's no dependency between any two of them.
- *Dependent Multiple Services*: Service offering contains more than one service elements. There are dependencies between service elements. And if one service element has been selected when subscribing, then the service elements it depends on must be selected.
- *Composed Service*: Service offering is composed of more than one service offerings. And the service elements of each offering are implemented respectively.
- *Proxy Service*: Service offering O_1 has more than one service elements. One (or more) of them is from another service offering O_2. And O_1 and O_2 are owned by different providers. This pattern becomes even more complex when there are dependencies between service elements of O_1.

For space reasons, we purposely have not included the problem and example sections for each pattern. To give one example, consider the case of the Dependent Multiple Services structure pattern. In a transaction based application like order management, reporting is a useful function built on top of the transaction history. When delivered as a SaaS, the Dependent Multiple Services pattern accurately describes this structure, and puts constraints for subscription in a systematic way.

The process of selecting a service structure pattern is shown in Fig. 18 as a non-exclusive decision tree. It can be visited more than once to decide related patterns. To illustrate, when packaging service offerings from another provider, both Proxy Service and Composed Service patterns can be selected.

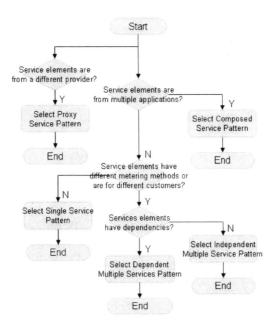

Fig. 18. Service Structure Pattern Selection

Business Interaction Patterns. Typical business interaction patterns are described as followings:

- *Self-Service*: Customers directly subscribe to service offering from service provider.
- *Hub-Spoke*: The hub customer subscribes to service offering from provider and the spoke customers subscribe to service offering from the hub customer. (Or the hub customer subscribes to service offering on behalf of spoke customers.)
- *Distribution*: The reseller subscribes to service offering from provider and the customers to service offering from the reseller. (Or the reseller subscribes to service on behalf of the customers.)
- *Delegated*: The provider subscribes to service offering from another provider on behalf on its customers. (This usually happens together with the proxy structure pattern.) After subscription, the provider is authorized to sell the corresponding service offering.

The runtime results for subscription actions are included. E.g. in the Distribution pattern, a reseller subscribes to a service offering from a provider, and in turn, customers subscribe to the service offering from the reseller. The permanent result at runtime is both the reseller and the customers will obtain related privileges of the corresponding service offering.

We also describe the selection of business interaction patterns in Fig. 19. This is a degenerate decision tree and all the patterns can be selected as long as the proposed conditions can be satisfied.

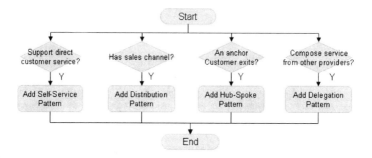

Fig. 19. Business Interaction Pattern Selection

5.3 Case Study: Service Subscription of the Retail B2B Case

We apply the pattern-based design approach for subscription management in a real case in this section. A retail Business to Business (B2B) service is an industrial application to facilitate the interaction between a retailer and its suppliers via web. There are three main functional modules: retailer's portal (RP), supplier's portal (SP) and Transaction Notification (TN). RP and SP depend on each other with two-way data exchange, and TN depends on either RP or SP as a data source. When delivered as a SaaS, SP and RP can be charged by service period while TN is more suitable to adopt quantity-based charging model. The provider in this context has a strong sales channel network and provides very limited direct customer service support.

With pre-conditions stated above, we can first decide the service structure. RP and SP serve specific customers respectively, and although user of TN is not restricted by customer type, TN fits a different metering method from RP and SP. Thus, we can get the following structure by selecting Dependent Multiple Services pattern, and the graphic representation is shown in Fig. 20.

In the retail industry, usually, one retailer has hundreds or thousands of suppliers, and it's the anchor customer for the retail B2B service. But since a provider has limited customer service capability, we can only select the Distribution pattern for business interaction, which means the provider depends on resellers to get customers. If the provider offers (or wants to build) direct customer service, then, the Hub-Spoke pattern can also be adopted, and accordingly.

Both patterns are workable, and the retailer and its suppliers finally get their required services. But the business relationship and the follow-up service operation are totally different. In the Hub-Spoke model, a total billing report will be issued from the provider to the retailer. And the retailer collects a service fee from the suppliers. While in the Distribution model, a third party customer service company (reseller) is introduced, who will deal with retailer and suppliers for billing and other customer interactions. The provider no longer directly touches either the retailer or the suppliers anymore. Based on different business considerations, dissimilar decisions will be made.

Fig. 20. Service Structure for Retail B2B Service

6 Related Work

In the hosted applications of the early 90s [20][21], companies only moved their hardware and applications from their premises to the data centers, and paid a premium to have their applications hosted. This was a typical single-tenancy scenario without any hardware or software sharing. To reduce the operation cost, some hosting service providers [22] started to run multiple application instances with the same code base on a shared hardware or software infrastructure. In fact, many such technologies [23] are applicable to support the multi-tenant pattern including partition, virtual OS, resources partitions, and virtual middleware server.

To achieve more benefits from the concept and practice of the shared efficiency, pioneers in this domain started building their solutions of hosted applications around the multi-tenancy rather than simply leveraging the on-premise application hosting model. [21] In recent years, the native multi-tenancy model, as exemplified in SaaS [24][25][26][27][28], achieves great successes. However, most of them are specific applications or application types such as CRM. [25][28]

Fred & Gianpaolo studied the similar topics [9][29]. They provided a high-level description of the architecture of a SaaS application, and discussed the challenges and benefits of developing and offering SaaS. Their work mainly focused on the multi-tenant data model from the security and scalability perspectives. There are already some studies [23] on the tradeoffs of resources utilization and isolation. The authors of [30][31] introduced the OS level performance isolation mechanisms, by leveraging the reservation or partition technologies on system resources. White and Miles [13] presented four principles on fault tolerance and availability to deal with the fault isolation issues.

As for the customization and configuration, there are many academic research and industrial best practices available already. For example: Software Configuration Management theory was developed by Roger Pressman through software engineering research[32]; SAP software applications have strong configuration and customization capabilities through Graphic User Interface(GUI) based tool and script based programming tool(ABAP)[33]. The leading SaaS vendors have developed profound configuration and customization capabilities as well, for example, Salesfoce.com provides Apex to facilitate the extensive application configuration and customization on the Web based on the multi-tenancy architecture. [34]

In the telecommunications industry, subscription information is the basis for service life cycle management. For example, to handle the relationships and interactions among a service user, subscriber and retailer, the Telecommunication Information Networking Architecture (TINA) specifies a subscription management information model [35], and also related service components [36]. Lee et al. provide a three-tier CORBA based framework to implement a service subscription information management system in a TINA environment [37]. Compared with a general publish/subscription system, research and practice in this area are more concerned with the service subscription process and data model in the telecommunication industry context. Subscription management for Web services is mainly concerned with issuing event notifications and handling the communication between two parties, the subscriber and the registry. For example, Universal Description Discovery and Integration (UDDI) introduces a type of entity called subscription in its information model for a service requestor to keep track of changes of other UDDI entities like businessEntity, businessService, and so on [38]. UDDI defines corresponding application protocol interface (API) sets to handle the interaction between a subscriber and a registry in both synchronous and asynchronous models. Liu et al. introduces a "consumer centric" service discovery and subscription approach based on the concept of Community-of-Interest (CoI) [39][40]. CoI is a collection of several services with similar functionalities and different qualities of service (QoS). In a CoI model, the subscriber does not communicate with any individual service directly, instead, it interacts with CoI which is responsible for scheduling the subscription to real target service providers dynamically to achieve the best choice for either QoS or another objective. Mietzner et al. propose multi-tenancy patterns and variability descriptors to package multi-tenancy aware configurable composite SaaS applications, based on Service Component Architecture (SCA) [41]. They study service structure from a configurability perspective, and subscription is not explicitly covered.

7   Summary

As more people are diving deep into the market, the SMBs oriented SaaS evolves gradually into a complex ecosystem. It involves many stakeholders with different requirements and value propositions, such as customer (tenant), service provider, service (software) vendor and value-added service reseller and so on. This paper targets to explore the technologies to set up a healthy and profitable SaaS ecosystem to operate many SaaS applications recruiting from service vendors for a huge number of SMB customers. According to the customer requirements and experiences we accumulated via real customer engagement, this paper focuses on exploring three most important challenges of the ecosystem, e.g. massive multi-tenancy, flexibility and service lifecycle management, and the corresponding technical solutions.

First, this paper introduces how to leverage the massive multi-tenancy technologies to achieve the cost effectiveness by effectively sharing resources of the infrastructure, middleware and application instance among tenants. Due to the essential tradeoff between the high shared efficiency and isolation among tenants, we also explore many approaches to support better security, performance and availability isolation in the multi-tenant environments.

Configuration and customization are the critical perspectives for SaaS vendors to design their offerings to satisfy as many customers' requirements as possible in the targeted customer segment and application domain In this paper, we clarified the concepts of configuration and customization in SaaS context, and introduced competency model and a framework to help SaaS vendors to plan their offerings from configuration and customization enablement point of view.

This paper also explores the topics on service lifecycle and the subscription management design of SaaS. We present a method which can guide a SaaS provider in designing subscription management according to its application's characteristics and targeted business model. Structure pattern and interaction pattern are the key components of this method which are summarized from various types of SaaS businesses. Finally, we also leverage a case study to demonstrate the effectiveness of the method.

References

1. Sun, W., Zhang, K., Chen, S.-K., Zhang, X., Liang, H.: Software as a service: An integration perspective. In: Krämer, B.J., Lin, K.-J., Narasimhan, P. (eds.) ICSOC 2007. LNCS, vol. 4749, pp. 558–569. Springer, Heidelberg (2007)
2. Guo, C.J., Sun, W., Huang, Y., Wang, Z.H., Gao, B.: A Framework for Native Multi-Tenancy Application Development and Management. In: The 9th IEEE International Conference on E-Commerce Technology and the 4th IEEE International Conference on Enterprise Computing, E-Commerce, and E-Services, pp. 551–558. IEEE Press, Tokyo (2007)
3. How SMBs Can Save Money Using SaaS, `http://itmanagement.earthweb.com/features/article.php/3803136/How-SMBs-Can-Save-Money-Using-SaaS.htm`
4. Microsoft Sees Growing SaaS Opportunity Among SMBs, `http://www.pcworld.com/businesscenter/article/161925/microsoft_sees_growing_saas_opportunity_among_smbs.html`
5. The Cloud Wars: $100 billion at stake. Technical Report, Merrill Lynch (2008)
6. WikiPedia, `http://en.wikipedia.org/wiki/Value-added_reseller`
7. Youshang.com, `http://www.youshang.com/en/compare.html`
8. Build A Multi-tenant Data Tier With Access Control and Security, `http://www.ibm.com/developerworks/db2/library/techarticle/dm-0712taylor/`
9. Multi-Tenant Data Architecture, `http://msdn.microsoft.com/en-us/library/aa479086.aspx`
10. WikiPedia, `http://en.wikipedia.org/wiki/SQL_injection`
11. DB2 Label-Based Access Control, a practical guide, Part 1: Understand the basics of LBAC in DB2, `http://www.ibm.com/developerworks/edu/dm-dw-dm-0605wong-i.html`
12. Urgaonkar, B.: Dynamic Resource Management in Internet Hosting Platforms. Doctoral Thesis, University of Massachusetts Amherst (2005)
13. White, R.V., Miles, F.M.: Principles of Fault Tolerance. In: Applied Power Electronics Conference and Exposition, pp. 18–25. IEEE Press, San Jose (1996)
14. Sun, W., Zhang, X., Guo, C.J., Sun, P., Su, H.: Software as a Service: Configuration and Customization Perspectives. In: Congress on Services Part II, 2008. SERVICES-2, pp. 18–25. IEEE Press, Beijing (2008)
15. Jiang, Z., Sun, W., Tang, K., Snowdon, J.L., Zhang, X.: A Pattern-based Design Approach for Subscription Management of Software as a Service. Technical Report, IBM China Research Lab (2009)
16. Summit Strategy Inc., Software-Powered Services Net-Native Software-as-Services Transforms the ISV Business Model. Technical Report
17. Rohleder, C., Davis, S., Günther, H.: Software Customization With XML. Issues in Information Systems VI(2) (2005)
18. Summit Strategy Inc., Software Powered Services Net Native SaS Transforms The Enterprise Application. Technical Report
19. Datamonitor ComputerWire, SaaS Customization. Technical Report

20. Gray, T.: Application Service Provider - A new way of software application delivery. Melbourne (2002)
21. Gianforte, G.: Multiple-Tenancy Hosted Applications: The Death and Rebirth of the Software Industry. RightNow Technologies Inc (2005)
22. Kobilsky, N.: SAP CRM On-demand. SAP Forum (2006)
23. BEA Weblogic Application Consolidation Strategies, http://dev2dev.bea.com/pub/a/2003/10/Heublein.html
24. Software as a Service (SaaS): An Enterprise Perspective, http://msdn.microsoft.com/en-us/library/aa905332.aspx
25. Salesforce.com Corporation, http://salesforce.com
26. Waters, B.: Software as a service: A look at the customer benefits. Journal of Digital Asset Management 1(1), 1 (2005)
27. Software as a Service (SaaS) Resource Center, http://www.deitel.com/softwareasaservice/SoftwareAsAService_ResourceCenter_Articles.html
28. Rightnow Technologies Inc., http://www.rightnow.com/products/
29. Architecture Strategies for Catching the Long Tail, http://blogs.msdn.com/gianpaolo
30. Verghese, B., Gupta, A., Rosenblum, M.: Performance isolation: sharing and isolation in shared-memory multiprocessors. In: Proceedings of the 8th Conference on Architectural Support for Programming Language and Operating Systems, San Jose, pp. 181–192 (1998)
31. Pérez, C.O., Rutten, M., Steffens, L., van Eijndhoven, J., Paul Stravers, S.: Resource Reservations in Shared-memory Multiprocessor SOCS. Philips Research Laboratories, Technical Report, Eindhoven, The Netherlands
32. Pressman, R.: Software Engineering: A Practitioner's Approach. McGraw-Hill Science, New York
33. Getting Started: ABAP, SAP Community Network, https://www.sdn.sap.com/irj/sdn/go/portal/prtroot/docs/webcontent/uuid/90e7556d-ed76-2910-1592-b6af816225cc
34. Introduction to the Apex Platform, http://salesforce.com
35. TINA 1.0 Specification, Service Component Specification Computational Model and Dynamics Version 1.0b (1998), http://www.tinac.com/specifications/documents/comp.pdf
36. TINA 1.0 Specification, Overall Concepts and Principles of TINA Version 1.0 (1995), http://www.tinac.com/specifications/documents/overall.pdf
37. Lee, J.C.-K., Mohapi, S., Hanrahan, H.E.: Service Subscription Information Management in a TINA Environment using Object-Oriented Middleware. In: Intelligent Network Workshop, pp. 121–125. IEEE Press, Los Alamitos (2001)
38. UDDI V3.0.2, http://www.oasis-open.org/committees/uddi-spec/doc/spec/v3/uddi-v3.0.2-20041019.htm
39. Liu, X.Z., Zhou, L., Huang, G., Mei, H.: Consumer-Centric Web Services Discovery and Subscription. In: IEEE International Conference on e-Business Engineering, pp. 543–550. IEEE Press, Hong Kong (2007)
40. Liu, X.Z., Huang, G., Mei, H.: Towards Service Discovery and Subscription based on Community-of-Interest. In: Proceedings of the Second IEEE International Symposium on Service-Oriented System Engineering, pp. 167–174. IEEE Press, Washington (2006)
41. Mietzner, R., Leymann, F., Papazoglou, M.: Defining Composite Configurable SaaS Application Packages Using SCA, Variability Descriptors and Multi-Tenancy Patterns. In: Third International Conference on Internet and Web Applications and Services, pp. 156–161. IEEE Press, Los Alamitos (2008)

Design Patterns for Cloud Services

Jinquan Dai and Bo Huang

Intel China Software Center
No. 880 Zi Xing Road, Shanghai, P.R. China, 200241
{jason.dai,bo.huang}@intel.com

Abstract. The transition to cloud computing is a disruptive trend that poses huge challenges to the software and service architecture. There are dramatic differences between delivering software as services in the cloud for millions to use through their occasionally disconnected clients, versus distributing software as bits for millions to run on their PCs. In particular, cloud services need new design patterns and programming models for their partitioned data set with many copies that are independently changed. This is a huge software challenge and a major barrier to the adoption of cloud computing. For instance, big websites spend 70% of their efforts on the undifferentiated heavy lifting (e.g., partitioning, replication and scaling) versus 30% on the differentiated value (feature) creation. This chapter will review the challenges for cloud services and some of the emerging solutions to address those challenges, based on our experience in building cloud service platforms as well as the industry best practices.

Keywords: cloud computing, cloud service, scalability, availability, reliability, design patterns, service architecture.

1 Introduction

The transition to cloud computing is a disruptive trend that poses huge challenges to the software and service architecture. There are dramatic differences between delivering software as services in the cloud for millions to use through their occasionally disconnected clients, versus distributing software as bits for millions to run on their PCs. First, services must be highly scalable, supporting millions of concurrent users at peak. Second, services must have low latency, minimizing the wait time of users. Third, services must be always available, even in times of server or network failures. Fourth, services can evolve much more quickly (with, say, weekly or bi-weekly releases) than packaged products, because they only run inside the cloud. Those requirements have two important implications on the underlying software as follows.

- **The data center is the computer**

In order to meet the requirements of high scalability, high availability and low latency, services are developed to run on mega data centers [1], as opposed to shrink-wrapped software running on individual PCs. The data centers have a scale-out shared-nothing architecture (made up of tens of thousands of independent, commodity servers) and are geographically distributed. And there is also a move to

D. Agrawal et al. (Eds.): Information and Software as Services, LNBIP 74, pp. 31–56, 2011.
© Springer-Verlag Berlin Heidelberg 2011

many small, cheap, independent and less reliable data centers (e.g., containerized data centers [2] [3]) that are geo-distributed, for the sake of cost and energy effectiveness [4].

In this model, cloud services can achieve high scalability only through partitioning, and achieve high availability only through redundancy. Therefore, services need to be architected to have their data and computing partitioned among independent servers, and to have their data (asynchronously) replicated across independent servers and data centers.

- **The application is always offline**

Despite the increasingly ubiquitous wireless connectivity, clients will be occasionally disconnected. In addition, due to ubiquitous service compositions (e.g., SOA and service APIs), data integrations (e.g., mashup and widget), as well as data replications across multiple servers and data centers, remote services and data will be occasionally unavailable to the applications (either in the cloud or on the clients).

If those applications have to wait for the remote services and data when disconnected, cloud services will be extremely slow and have low availability. Therefore, the application needs to work with an assumption that it is always offline, by making progress based on its local states as much as possible (e.g., using Google Gears [5] that provides an environment for web applications to run offline or Microsoft Sync framework [6] that automatically synchronizes data between clients and services), and by interacting with remote partners asynchronously to reconcile their states.

In summary, cloud service platforms are drastically different from traditional distributed systems. The classic definition of a distributed system is a *"collection of independent computers that appear to the users of the system as a single computer"* [7]. Traditionally, efforts in this area (such as distributed transactions, quorum protocols, atomic broadcast, RPC, synchronous request-response, and tightly coupled schema) all attempt to mask the existence of independence from the applications. On the other hand, cloud computing is composed of, and more importantly, acknowledges the existence of many small, independent, and unreliable components (e.g., clients, servers, data centers and services) that may be occasionally disconnected.

Consequently, cloud services need new design patterns and programming models for the partitioned data set with many copies that are changed independently [8]. This is a huge software development challenge and a major barrier to the adoption of cloud computing. For instance, developers of big websites usually spend 70% of their efforts on the undifferentiated heavy lifting (e.g., partitioning, replication and scaling) versus 30% on the differentiated value (feature) creation [9]. This chapter will review the challenges for cloud services and some of the emerging directions for solutions to address those challenges, based on our experience in building cloud service platforms as well as the industry best practices.

The rest of the chapter is organized as follows. Section 2 describes how the cloud services manage their partitioned data set using the new data model. Section 3 reviews the computing models adopted by cloud services to distribute their computations across many independent servers. Section 4 discusses the challenges for cloud service to manage distributed agreement across many independent components and how those challenges can be addressed. Section 5 describes how to cope with the inconsistency across multiple data replicas in cloud services using relaxed consistency models. Finally, section 6 concludes the chapter with possible future works for both the industry and the academic community.

2 Data Model

Traditionally, enterprise systems store their data in relational databases. However, the complex management, general querying and transaction support offered by an RDBMS is overkill for most of the service applications. This excess functionality results in high performance penalty, expensive hardware and highly skilled personnel for operations, making it a very inefficient solution. In addition, traditional distributed relational database systems focus on providing a complete relational model with transactional (ACID) consistency to the partitioned and/or replicated data, and are therefore limited in scalability and availability [10].

Although many advances have been made, it is still difficult to scale-out databases or use smart partitioning and replication schemes. Many big websites have to build their own (semi-) structured data storage systems from scratch (e.g., Google's *Bigtable* [11] system, Amzon's *Dynamo* [10] system and Yahoo's *PNUTS* [12] system); and others just use the traditional RDBMS as dumb row stores and build their own access and management logics above the databases (e.g., the eBay architecture [13], sharding in MySpace [14] and Flickr [15], and Microsoft SQL data service [16]), as illustrated in Fig. 1.

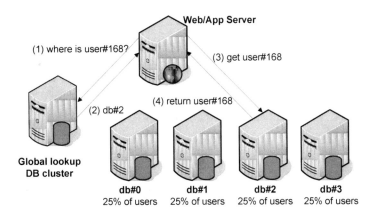

Fig. 1. In this simple example of data access layer (above traditional databases), each of the servers (*db#0* – *db#3*) contains a subset of the user profiles. When the web server needs to access the profile of *user#168*, it first looks up the profile location, which is stored at the global lookup DB cluster. After the location (server *db#2* in this example) is determined, the web server can directly go to server *db#2* for the profile.

2.1 Requirements of Cloud Services

Cloud services need a new data model to deal with their unique requirements and challenges as follows.

- **Data partitioning**

  In cloud services, data are usually horizontally partitioned along primary access paths [19] [20] (e.g., by individual users), and spread around independent servers. For instance, Fig. 2 illustrates the horizontal partitioning of databases in the eBay architecture [13]. Therefore, the new data model should allow the programmers to express the data partitioning as a program abstraction, and to design the applications around collections of partitioned data.

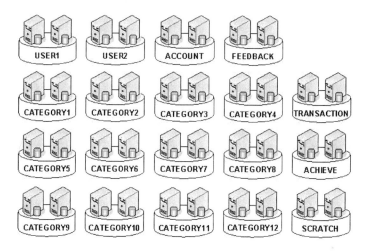

Fig. 2. eBay horizontally splits its databases (e.g., *user* and *category* tables) into individual shards, which are standalone database servers containing a slice of the main database

- **Dynamic schema**

  Cloud services need to both evolve quickly and provide high availability; consequently changes to the data schema need to be handled seamlessly in a system running 24 by 7, 365 days a year. Therefore, the new data model should allow the schema of objects to be flexibly defined and dynamically changed.

  For instance, in Amazon SimpleDB [21], data are organized into *domains* that are collection of *items* described by attribute-value pairs; conceptually, a domain is analogous to a relational table with each item corresponding to a row and each attribute corresponding to a column. However, unlike traditional databases, Amazon SimpleDB has a much more flexible data schema, as illustrated in Fig. 3.

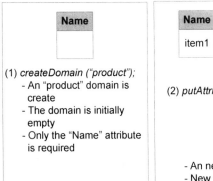

Name

(1) *createDomain ("product");*
  - An "product" domain is create
  - The domain is initially empty
  - Only the "Name" attribute is required

Name	Category	Color	Size
item1	sweater	blue, red	small

(2) *putAttribute (domain=>"product",*
              Name=>"item1",
              Category=>"sweater",
              Color=>"blue",
              Color=>"red",
              Size=>"small");
  - An new item "item1" is added
  - New attributes "Category", "Color" and "Size" are added
  - Multiple values are associated with the "Color" attribute

Name	Category	Color	Size	Material
item1	sweater	blue, red	small	
item2	shoes	black	9	leather

(3) *putAttribute (domain=>"product",*
            Name=>"item2",
            Category=>"shoes",
            Color=>"black",
            Size=>"9",
            Material=>"leather");
  - An new item "item2" is added
  - Values of different types are associated with the "Size" attribute of "item1" and "item2"
  - New attributes "Material" is added to "item2" only

Fig. 3. Amazon SimpleDB has a very flexible schema. New attributes can be dynamically added on the fly and only associated with specific items, multiple values can be associated with an attribute of an item, and two items in the same domain can have different types of values for the same attribute.

- **Local transaction (only)**

In cloud services, distributed transactions (including techniques such as two-phase commit, Paxos, and quorum protocols) are not used, due to their performance cost and fragility [20] [22]. Therefore, the new data model should enforce that only local transactions (within a node) can be used and that distributed transactions are not allowed.

For instance, in Google Megastore [23] [24] each data object is known as an *entity* and each entity have a *parent entity*. Consequently entities forms a forest of trees through their parent-relationship, and all entities in the same tree (i.e., with the same root entity) belong to the same *entity group*. All entities in a group are stored in the same Megastore node, and a single transaction can only operate entities in the same entity group.

- **Incremental scaling**

In cloud services, the size of the data manipulated by the applications grows significantly large over time. What previously fits in one machine may need to be repartitioned to multiple machines later. Therefore, the new data model should allow the applications to scale incrementally (i.e., one machine at a time), by dynamically spreading the data in a small set of machines to a larger set as the load grows and new machines become available.

2.2 New Data Model: Uniquely Keyed Elements

Typically the new data model for cloud services comprises a collection of *uniquely keyed elements* [22], as described in detail below and illustrated in Fig. 4.

1) Each element represents a disjoint set of data (which are typically described as property-value pairs and whose properties may be dynamically changed). An application comprises many elements; for instance, a web application usually supports many users, and each user can be represented as an element identified by the unique user ID.

2) All the data within a single element is guaranteed to reside on a single machine (ignoring replication); different elements may be located in different machines. That is, the data set of the application is partitioned around those uniquely keyed elements.

3) The application locates a specific element through its unique key. The physical location of the element is determined by the lower layer (e.g., the data store), and is likely to change as the requirement for scaling changes and the deployment evolves. Therefore, the application cannot make assumptions about the locations of elements, except that a single element is guaranteed to reside on a single machine.

4) The application can only perform atomic transactions within a single element. Transactions cannot span multiple elements, because there is no guarantee that they will reside on the single machine all the time

In summary, the data model for cloud services requires that the service has the notion of element as a programming abstraction, designs its business logic and data set around the collection of elements, uses the unique key to locate a specific element, and assumes lack of atomicity across different elements. This data model is implicitly adopted by many Internet-scale services in the industry today (such as Amazon SimpleDB [21], Google MegaStore [23] [24], Microsoft Windows Azure table storage [25] and Microsoft SQL data service [16]).

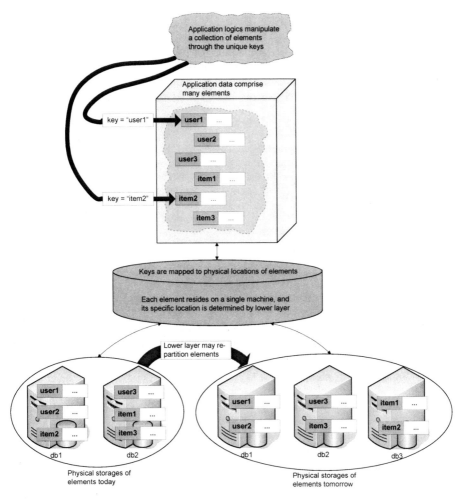

Fig. 4. The application's data are factored into elements, each of which has a unique key. The lower layer guarantees each element always resides on a single machine; however, it may re-partition the elements as requirements for scaling change.

2.3   Data Access in the New Data Model

An element is just a logical concept that represents a disjoint set of data; those data can be stored in any form that is appropriate for the service, such as SQL records (possibly across many tables). The partitioning should be as fine-grained as possible because the underlying data store will never split an element. On the other hand, data querying patterns should also be taken into considerations during the data partitioning, as some data accesses are very challenging to support in the new data model.

- **Primary-key based access**

Primary-key based access to records is not only predominant for cloud services, but also the most efficient and preferred way in the new data model, as long as the primary key includes the unique identifier of the element that contains the record (e.g., the primary key of every record that belongs to a *user* element may contain the unique user ID).

- **Simple queries**

It is also straightforward to efficiently support some simple forms of queries in the new data model, especially those against a specific element (and preferably over some indexed fields).

- **Arbitrary, ad-hoc queries**

On the other hand, it is very challenging, if not impossible, to support arbitrary, ad-hoc queries in the new data model, especially those that can potentially access an arbitrary number of elements (e.g., finding all the users whose birthdays are today where each user is an individual element).

In general, it is unclear what the most efficient way is to support this type of queries. One possible implementation of such queries is through distributed query; that is, (partial) queries are sent to all the nodes which then return partial results to a central place to assemble the final result. Unfortunately, distributed query is limited in performance and scalability as the data set grows in size.

An alternative implementation is two-level lookup through alternative indices; that is, identifiers of the elements containing the records are first determined by looking up an alternative index and only those elements are then queried. Since all elements or servers are not queried, two-level lookup usually has better performance and scalability; however, the service needs to deal with the potential inconsistency as the alternative index can get out-of-sync with the element data [22].

In practice, only a predefined, business critical subset of those ad-hoc queries will be supported for the service. For instance, social network services usually need to solve the *hairball* problem [26]. That is, those services need to organize the per-user information (e.g., groups that a user belongs to) as an individual element so that they can efficiently access such information by the user ID; on the other hand, they also need to access the per-user information by searching for the data to find the users (e.g., all the users belonging to a given group). Those predefined queries are typically supported through extensive use of prepared statements and bind variables [13], and through data *demornalization* [15] (that is, storing data redundantly along all primary access paths, usually in an asynchronous manner).

For instance, in FriendFeed [27] data are stored as JSON objects with unique IDs in the primary database tables, which are then horizontally partitioned based on the primary keys. In order to efficiently access these data by searching on a secondary property, a separate "index" database table is created and asynchronous updated to contain the mapping between the secondary property and the unique ID

[28]. Though redundant data are stored in index tables (hence the denormalization), the primary tables can be queried more efficiently through the index tables.

2.4 Existing Cloud Data Stores

The new data model of cloud services has led to the emergence of many new cloud data stores, characterized by the ability to scale to thousands of nodes and petabytes of data, fault tolerance, flexible schema and simplified query API.

For instance, Google's Bigtable [11] system provides a sparse, distributed, column-oriented table store to many of its services (e.g., Google Maps, Google Earth and Orkut [17]). In Bigtable, each value is indexed by the tuple *(row, column, timestamp)*, as illustrated in Fig. 5. The Bigtable API provides functions for looking up, writing and deleting values using the specific row key (possibly with column names), and for iterating over data in several consecutive rows using the start row key (possibly with column names). In addition, Bigtable supports single-row transaction, which can be used to perform atomic read-modify-write sequences on data stored under a single row key; however, it does not support general transactions across row keys.

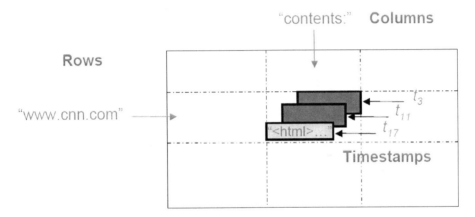

Fig. 5. The conceptual view of Bigtable is a sparse, distributed, multi-dimensional table, where each value is indexed by the tuple (row, column, timestamp) [17]

Physically, rows are ordered lexicographically and dynamically partitioned into row ranges (or *tablets*). Each tablet is assigned to a single *tablet server*, which handles the all data accesses requests to its tablet, as illustrated in Fig. 6. Mutations are first committed to the append-only log on the Google File System (GFS) [18] and then write to the in-memory *memtable* buffer; the data in the tablet are stored in *SSTable* (ordered, immutable map from keys to values [17]) files on GFS, and a read operation is executed on a merged view of the sequence of SSTables and the memtable. In addition, columns can be group to different *locality groups*, and separate SSTables are generated for different locality groups in each tablet.

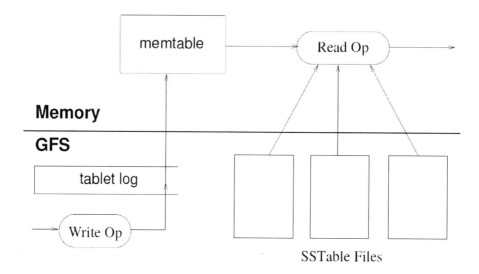

Fig. 6. The tablet server is responsible for handling the read/write requests to its tablet, using the in-memory memtable buffer, the write-ahead log in GFS, and the SSTables data files in GFS [11]

The location of each tablet is stored in the special *root* and *METADATA* tables that are themselves stored in Bigtable, and the root table is never split. The client caches (and prefetches) tablet locations by looking up the *root* and *METADATA* tables, and directly communicates with the tablet servers for data accesses. The largest Bigtable cluster in Google scales to more than 70 petabytes of data over several thousands of servers [17].

Unlike Bigtable, Amazon's Dynamo system [10] provides a distributed key-value store to many core services in Amazon's ecommerce platform (e.g., the shopping cart service). It has a primary-key only interface, exposing two operations (*get* and *put*) for reading and writing a specific object using its *key*.

Physically, objects in Dynamo are dynamically assigned to different *storage nodes* using consistent hashing [27]. That is, Dynamo hashes the key of each object and the hash output range is treated as a fixed circular space or ring (i.e., the largest hash value wraps around to the smallest hash value). Each storage node is also hashed to a value in the space, which represents its position on the ring. A specific object is assigned to a storage node by first hashing its key to yield its position on the ring, and then walking the ring clockwise to find the first node with a position larger than the object's position. Therefore a storage node is responsible for the region in the ring between it and its predecessor in the ring; consequently the departure or arrival of a node only affects its immediate neighbors and other nodes remain unaffected. To further improve load distributions, in Dynamo each physical node may contain one or more "virtual hosts", and each virtual host is assigned to a position in the ring.

In Dynamo, every storage node maintains the mapping from each node to its tokens (i.e., virtual hosts in the ring), using a peer-to-peer, gossip-based distributed failure detection and membership protocol. By adopting such a full membership model, the client can send the get/put requests to any storage node (through a generic load balancer), and the storage node can directly forward the request using the mapping; on the other hand, though this model works well for couple of hundreds of nodes, scaling such a design to run with tens of thousands of nodes is not trivial due to overheads in maintaining the full membership [10].

Similar to Bigtble, Yahoo's PNUTS [12] system is a distributed table store where data organized into tables of records with attributes. Unlike Bigtable, PNUTS supports *selection* and *projection* from a single table, in addition to the primary-key based accesses (e.g., *get*, *set* and *delete* operations). Though multi-record transactions are not supported, PNUTS provides the atomic *test-and-set-write* operation that can be used to implement single-row transactions without any locks.

Physically, tables in PNUTS are horizontally partitioned into groups of records called *tablets*. Tablets are scattered across many *storage units*, which is responsible for storing the tablets and handling the access requests. Schema flexibility is supported by storing records as parsed JSON objects.

The assignment of tablets to storage units in PNUTS are determined by a single pair of active/standby *tablet controller*, which is responsible for moving a tablet between storage units for load balancing or recovery and when a large tablet must be split. Each data access request from the clients can be received by any of the many *routers* (through a generic load balancer) in PNUTS. Each router fetches (and caches) the location information of all tablets from the tablet controller, and forwards the request to the appropriate storage unit. For a query that spans multiple tablets, the *scatter-gather engine* in the router is responsible for splitting it into multiple individual requests for single tablet accesses, and assembling the final results.

Though these cloud data stores have different design and implementation details, they do share similar design patterns to address the unique challenges of cloud services. The data in these systems are horizontally partitioned in a dynamic way to achieve incremental, almost-infinite scalability. The data access API (mostly primary-key based) exposed by these systems is much more restrictive compared to relational systems; in particular, only single-record transactions are supported. The data schemas are also very flexible in these systems. A lot of emerging open source cloud data stores, such as HBase [30], Hypertable [31], Cassandra [32] and Voldemort [33], are inspired and strongly influenced by these systems.

3 Computing Model

To support the requirements of high scalability, high availability and offline behaviors, cloud services need a new model for distributing computations across many independent components. The general computing mode for cloud services to scale is through stateless computing with scale-out, with shared durable backing store, as illustrated in Fig. 7. For different types of applications, the detailed models may be different, as described in the following sections.

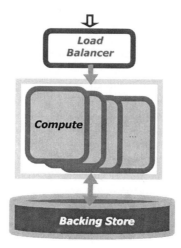

Fig. 7. The general computing model to scale is through stateless computing with scale-out, with durable backing store underneath. Many compute instances are forked on different nodes and are completely stateless; consequently, processing work are routed through load balancers and can be handled by any of the compute instances.

3.1 Large-Scale Data Processing

Internet-scale cloud services routinely generate terabytes (or even petabytes) of data and process these data for inference of patterns (using, e.g., machine learning and analytic queries). This type of large-scale data processing is usually performed in batch style, and the *MapReduce* [34] model proposed by Google provides a very attractive framework for the large-scale data processing in the cloud.

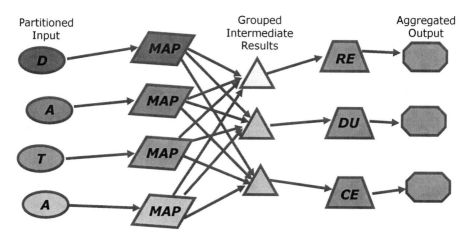

Fig. 8. The dataflow of the MapReduce model is shown. The input data are first partitioned into splits, each of which is processed by a map function in parallel. Each group of the intermediate map output are then processed by a reduce function in parallel to generate the aggregated final results.

At a high level, a MapReduce program essentially performs a group-by-aggregation in parallel over a cluster of servers, as illustrated in Fig. 8. The application has one input that can be trivially partitioned. In the first stage a *map* function, which dictates how the grouping is performed, is applied to the partitioned input by different machines in parallel. In the second stage a *reduce* function, which performs the aggregation, is applied to each group produced in the first stage, again by different machines in parallel.

The MapReduce model allows users to easily develop data processing programs that can be scaled to thousands of servers, without worrying about the details of parallelism. It is most appropriate for the batch-style, throughput-oriented, stateless (or append-only) computing, where the input has a huge amount of data and is trivially partitionable.

3.2 Interactive Cloud Services

Unlike the batch-style data processing, interactive cloud services need to process a huge number (e.g., millions) of concurrent user requests using some stateful workflow and with very low (e.g., sub-second) latency. If the processing of each individual request just requires small to moderate efforts, the service typically adopts the *Pre-Fork* model, which is geared towards this type of high-concurrency, low-latency and stateful computing, as illustrated in Fig. 9.

In the PreFork model, a pool of web or application servers runs exactly the same application, and a specific request from the client can be routed (through the load-balancers) to any server, which then starts a new process (or thread) to handle the incoming request [20]. In this model, the web or logic tier is completely stateless, as user session flow moves through different servers/processes, and the state data are stored in the data tier (which is shared by all the servers and processes).

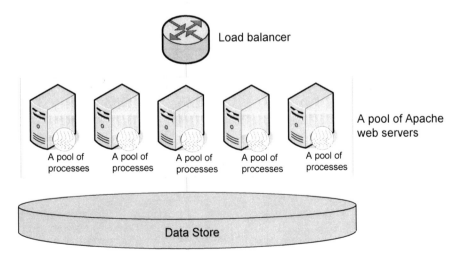

Fig. 9. The PreFork model using the Apache web servers in a typical web site is shown. Each server in the web server pool runs the Apache HTTP server, which maintains a pool of processes. Each HTTP request can be handled by any process on any server.

3.3 Complex Service Compositions

For complex cloud services, a monolithic 2- or 3-tier architecture holding all the business and display logic (e.g., the PreFork model) poses a lot of challenges to the independent scalability, availability and feature evolvement of different components in the cloud service [35]. As a result, complex cloud services are usually composed of many independent and autonomous services using the service-oriented architecture (*SOA*), where each individual service is relatively simple and usually adopts the PreFork model. For instance, the architecture of Amazon's platform is loosely coupled and built around services, comprising hundreds of services and a number of application servers that aggregate the information from the services, as illustrated in Fig. 10. The application that renders the Amazon.com gateway pages is one such application server, which calls more than 100 services to collect data and construct the page for the user [35].

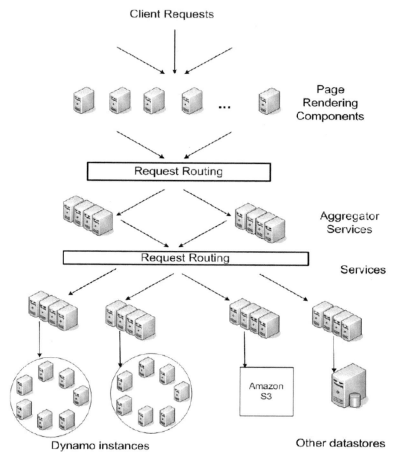

Fig. 10. Amazon's platform is a service-oriented architecture, where dynamic web content is generated by page rendering services which in turn query many other services [10]

However, adopting SOA as a design pattern and programming model presents a few important implications and challenges to cloud services as follows.

- **Independent services interconnected by messaging**

Service oriented architecture characterizes a collection of independent services, which are autonomous, opaque and probably stateful. Services communicate with each other exclusively through messages whose formats (schema) and semantics are well defined. The messages contain operators, which reflect its intended purpose (i.e., a business function of the service), as well as the operands to the operators. Each service will only do a limited set of things for its partners based on the prescribed messages. The essence of SOA lies in independent services that are interconnected by messaging [36], as illustrated in Fig. 11.

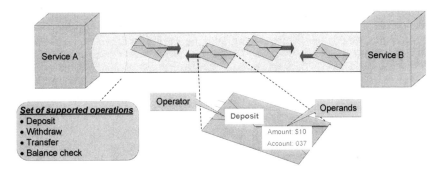

Fig. 11. Service-oriented architecture comprises independent services interconnected by messaging. The only way to interact with the service is via the prescribed messages, each of which invokes the application logic to perform some fixed operations on the private data.

This provides a very firm encapsulation of the service. That is, each service comprises a chunk of code and data that are private to that service; the only way to interact with the service is via the prescribed messages, each of which invokes the application logic to perform some fixed operations on the private data. No other knowledge of the private code or data is shared with other services.

- **At-lease-once messaging**

In the SOA model, each service may run in a pool of servers using, say, the PreFork model; in addition, different services run on different server pools and communicate through messages. However, given the unreliable servers and networks, most applications use at-lease-once message delivery (e.g., resending the message indefinitely until it is acknowledged), as illustrated in Fig. 12.

In at-least-once messaging, it is essential that retries of the messages always have the same contents that do not change as copies of the message move around. Therefore, it is critical to design for messages that are both *immutable* (that is, each message is uniquely identified and that identifier yields immutable contents for the message) and *stable* (i.e., having an unambiguous and unchanging interpretation across space and time) [36]. In addition, when a message is sent, the schema for the message must be immutable too.

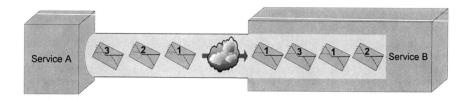

Fig. 12. At-lease-once messaging may lead to message tries and out-of-order arrivals of messages. In this example, *message1* is lost and a retry of *message1* arrives after *message2*; in addition, the acknowledgement of *message1* is also lost, and a duplicated retry of *message1* arrives after *message3*.

In practice, those requirements are usually achieved by binding time-stamps or versions to the data, and by not recycling important identifiers. Consequently, the schema and the content of the message can be associated those *version dependent identifiers* [36] (e.g., the price of product A on 2007/12/31 instead of the current price of product A).

- **Idempotent, commutative, and associative processing**

At-lease-once messaging guarantees that the message be delivered and processed at lease once (but perhaps more than once), if the system remains operational indefinitely. A consequence of this semantics is that the service must tolerate duplicated messages and the out-of-order arrival of messages.

To cope with message retries, the service has to process duplicated messages correctly. Typically, this is achieved by designing the services to be *idempotent* [22]. The processing of a message is idempotent if a subsequent execution of the processing does not change the semantics of the application state. For instance, if the operation only reads the data, it is *naturally idempotent* (even if a log record describing the read-operation is written).

On the other hand, processing messages that are not naturally idempotent requires ensuring each message is processed exactly once (i.e., the change of the semantics of the application state must happen exactly once). In practice, the service needs to maintain the log of the messages it has received and/or processed, to ensure the same message will not be processed more than once. In addition, if a response is required, the same response message must be returned.

Similarly, to cope with message reordering, it is essential to design the service to be *commutative* and *associative*; that is, it can process the out-of-order arrival of messages correctly.

- **Asynchronous integrations**

The essence of SOA lies in independent services that are interconnected by messaging. However, the services may still expect synchronous request/response interactions (i.e., service A sends a request to service B and blocks waiting for a response from B), just as in the traditional web architecture or remote procedure calls. On the other hand, it is more preferable to have different services decoupled and integrated via asynchronous interactions, e.g., using the event driven architecture.

Asynchronous integrations have several advantages [20] [37]. If services A and B integrate asynchronously, each can be scaled independently of the other; and they can have independent availability characteristics (e.g., A can continue to make progress even if B is down or distressed). In addition, asynchronous processing reduces user experience latency at the cost of data/execution latency, and allows the infrastructure to be scaled for the average load instead of the peak.

Of course, it is sometimes impractical to decompose the typical web application into components that perform all external interactions asynchronously. For instance, it would be difficult to transform user login into an asynchronous flow, otherwise the interactions with the users would become unnatural. However, it is desirable to move as much processing as possible to asynchronous flows.

4 Distributed Agreement

Cloud computing is composed of many independent and unreliable components (e.g., clients, servers, data centers and services) that may be occasionally disconnected, and one of its most critical problems is how to manage distributed agreement across those independent components without distributed transactions [22]. When the applications (either in the cloud or on the clients) attempt to make decisions across multiple elements or services, they have to accept and cope with the uncertainty (including race conditions, partial failures and other exceptional events). When distributed transactions can be used, that uncertainty is manifest in the locks held on data and is managed by the transaction manager. Without distributed transactions, the management of uncertainty is typically implemented in the business logic. For instance, eBay does not use distributed transactions in their architecture; instead, they manage the distributed agreement through careful ordering of database operations and asynchronous recovery [13] [20].

The absence of distributed transactions means that the applications must accept the uncertainty (races and failures) when making decisions across different elements, and they usually manage the uncertainty through complex, workflow-style *apology-oriented computing* [38] [39] as described below.

- **Tentative operation**
  Without atomicity across different elements, the applications must read/write different elements in different transactions to reach distributed agreement. Instead of committing changes to each element directly, the application first performs a *tentative operation* on the element, requesting a commitment but leaves open the possibility of cancellation. For instance, in the *Promise* [40] model, the client can specify some predicates over resources (e.g., account balance larger than $100) as a *promise request* to the service; once the promise is granted, the service guarantees the predicates will be maintained over a specific period of time.

  The tentative operation is similar to reservations on an element. After successfully completing the tentative operation on the element, the application is isolated from the effects of concurrent activities with respect to the element. In addition, the business logic of the applications accepts the uncertainty of partial failures because the operation is only tentative and needs to be either confirmed or cancelled later.

- **Confirming and cancelling operations**

If all the tentative operations on different elements are successful, they are then confirmed and the changes are committed. As the application is isolated from the concurrent activities, those changes are guaranteed to be valid and the *confirming operations* are guaranteed to succeed.

On the other hand, if there are any failures after the tentative operations are completed (e.g., a subsequent tentative operation fails), those completed tentative operations are then cancelled. The *cancelling operations* are not simple undo operations; instead, they are usually special logics that *programmatically apologize* and compensate for the effects of tentative operations.

Every tentative operation is eventually confirmed or cancelled, and the confirmations and cancellations are sometimes time driven. In addition, due to the concurrent nature of services, different operations and cancellations must be reorderable.

- **Asynchronous recovery**

There may be failures during the confirming and cancelling operations. Therefore, those operations are usually performed by asynchronous flows. In practice, the messages requesting the operations are transactionally enqueued, and then an asynchronous or batch process performs those operations repeatedly until they are successful. Consequently, those operations may be retried or reordered, and they must be designed to be idempotent, commutative and associative themselves.

In summary, apology-oriented computing manages distributed agreement through complex, workflow-style processing that assumes a lack of atomicity across elements and services, which is essential for highly scalable and highly available cloud services. Classic (distributed) transaction approaches emphasize read-write semantics and hence they are typically implemented with locking. On the other hand, the Escrow [41] transactional model deals with highly concurrent commutative operations (e.g., addition) against numeric data; it allows many transactions to perform their operations concurrently against a hot-spot value, by logging the operations and recording high and low limits for the possible values. At a high level, the apology-oriented computing generalizes the Escrow transactional model and applies the technique at a different granularity.

The following case study illustrates how a simple item-purchase service can be implemented using service-oriented architecture with apology-oriented computing. Unfortunately, it is unclear what the right programming abstraction is for this type of complex, workflow-style processing.

Case Study: Item Purchase

In this (overly) simplified example, a user *($user_id)* can purchase one item *($item_id)* as long as the number of the item in stock *($amount)* is larger than zero, and the balance of the user account (*$balance*) is no less than 100.

In traditional database system settings, the data set can be stored into three tables (namely, the *Items*, *Users* and *Orders* tables), as shown on the right of Fig. 13. Using an ACID-style transaction, the purchase workflow can be accomplished as illustrated on the left of Fig. 13.

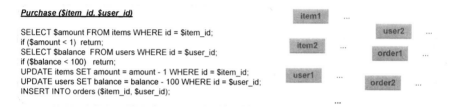

```
Purchase ($item_id, $user_id)

BEGIN;
SELECT $amount FROM items WHERE id = $item_id;
if ($amount < 1)  ABORT;
SELECT $balance  FROM users WHERE id = $user_id;
if ($balance < 100)  ABORT;
UPDATE items SET amount = amount - 1 WHERE id = $item_id;
UPDATE users SET balance = balance - 100 WHERE id = $user_id;
INSERT INTO orders ($item_id, $user_id);
COMMIT;
```

Items	Users	Orders
id	id	id
amount	balance	item_id
...	...	user_id
		price

Fig. 13. With traditional databases, the purchase workflow can be implemented using ACID transactions

```
Purchase ($item_id, $user_id)

SELECT $amount FROM items WHERE id = $item_id;
if ($amount < 1)  return;
SELECT $balance  FROM users WHERE id = $user_id;
if ($balance < 100)  return;
UPDATE items SET amount = amount - 1 WHERE id = $item_id;
UPDATE users SET balance = balance - 100 WHERE id = $user_id;
INSERT INTO orders ($item_id, $user_id);
```

Fig. 14. Without distributed transactions, a naïve implementation of the purchase workflow cannot cope with the uncertainty correctly

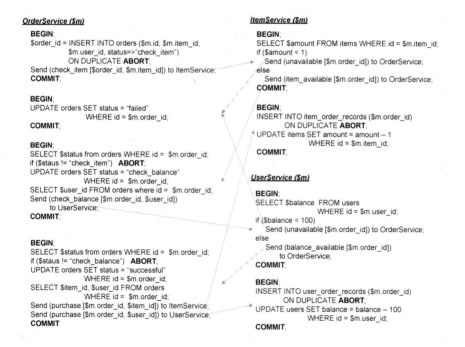

```
OrderService ($m)

BEGIN;
$order_id = INSERT INTO orders ($m.id, $m.item_id,
              $m.user_id, status=>"check_item")
           ON DUPLICATE ABORT;
Send (check_item [$order_id, $m.item_id]) to ItemService;
COMMIT;

BEGIN;
UPDATE orders SET status = "failed"
            WHERE id = $m.order_id;
COMMIT;

BEGIN;
SELECT $status from orders WHERE id =  $m.order_id;
if ($staus != "check_item")  ABORT;
UPDATE orders SET status = "check_balance"
            WHERE id =  $m.order_id;
SELECT $user_id FROM orders where id =  $m.order_id;
Send (check_balance [$m.order_id, $user_id])
         to UserService;
COMMIT;

BEGIN;
SELECT $status from orders WHERE id =  $m.order_id;
if ($staus != "check_balance")  ABORT;
UPDATE orders SET status = "successful"
            WHERE id = $m.order_id;
SELECT $item_id, $user_id FROM orders
            WHERE id =  $m.order_id;
Send (purchase [$m.order_id, $item_id]) to ItemService;
Send (purchase [$m.order_id, $user_id]) to UserService;
COMMIT
```

```
ItemService ($m)

BEGIN;
SELECT $amount FROM items WHERE id = $m.item_id;
if ($amount < 1)
    Send (unavailable [$m.order_id]) to OrderService;
else
    Send (item_available [$m.order_id]) to OrderService;
COMMIT;

BEGIN;
INSERT INTO item_order_records ($m.order_id)
         ON DUPLICATE ABORT;
UPDATE items SET amount = amount – 1
         WHERE id = $m.item_id;
COMMIT;
```

```
UserService ($m)

BEGIN;
SELECT $balance  FROM users
            WHERE id = $m.user_id;
if ($balance < 100)
    Send (unavailable [$m.order_id]) to OrderService;
else
    Send (balance_available [$m.order_id])
         to OrderService;
COMMIT;

BEGIN;
INSERT INTO user_order_records ($m.order_id)
         ON DUPLICATE ABORT;
UPDATE users SET balance = balance – 100
            WHERE id = $m.user_id;
COMMIT;
```

Fig. 15. An implementation of the purchase workflow using service-oriented architecture is shown. Though each service can properly handle duplication and out-of-order arrivals of messages, they still cannot cope with the uncertainty correctly.

Fig. 16. The purchase workflow is implemented using apology-oriented computing, which can correctly manage the uncertainty

However, cloud services need to partition the data set into elements, each of which may reside on different servers; for instance, there can be three different types of elements in the services (namely, the *item*, *user* and *order* elements), as show on the right of Fig. 14. Since distributed transactions that access multiple elements are not allowed, a naïve implementation of the purchase workflow is shown on the left of Fig. 14, which unfortunately cannot properly manage the uncertainty (i.e., races and failures).

A better implementation of the purchase workflow using service-oriented architecture is illustrated in Fig. 15. Each of those services can tolerate duplicated messages and the out-of-order arrival of messages, by building idempotence, commutativity and associativity into its processing. However, they cannot cope with the lack of atomicity and the uncertainty correctly.

Finally, Fig. 16 illustrates an implementation of the purchase workflow using service-oriented architecture with apology-oriented computing, which can correctly deal with the lack of atomicity and the uncertainty (i.e., races and failures).

5 Consistency Model

In cloud services, the partitioned data set (i.e., elements) is replicated (across clients, servers and data centers) to support high availability and offline behaviors. Consequently, cloud services need a new consistency model for the partitioned data set with many independently changed copies.

Traditional distributed database systems provide transactional (AICD) consistency for the replicated data using techniques such as two-phase commit and quorum protocols. However, as determined by the *CAP theorem* (first conjectured by Eric Brewer [42] and later confirmed by Gilbert and Lynch [43]), out of three properties of a shared-data system (namely, *data consistency*, *system availability* and *tolerance to network partition*), one can only achieve two at any given time. An important observation is that in large-scale distributed systems, network partitions are inevitable and consequently consistency and availability cannot be achieved at the same time. Traditional database systems emphasize on consistency over availability, and take the approaches that tradeoff the availability of the data under certain failure scenarios.

On the other hand, cloud services usually focus more on availability and usually work with the *BASE* [44] model – *basically available*, *soft state* and *eventually consistent*. That is, in practice cloud services manage their replicated data using the relaxed or weak consistency model (e.g., eventual consistency [45]) instead of the transactional consistency model (i.e., serializability).

5.1 Weak Consistency due to Asynchronous Replications

In the data storage system of cloud services, each element may be N-way replicated; a write-operation must successfully update W replicas before it completes, and a read-operation must access R replicas for the value. If $W+R > N$, the system has what are called quorum update and read architectures, and can guarantee strong consistency because the write set and the read set always overlap. For instance, in the synchronous RDBMS replication scenario, the system has $N=2$, $W=2$ and $R=1$ and always guarantees strong consistency.

On the other hand, in practice data are usually asynchronously replicated in cloud services, and consequently weak consistency will arise because the system has $W+R \leq N$. For instance, in the asynchronous RDBMS replication scenario, the system has $N=2$, $W=1$ and $R=1$ and cannot guarantee strong consistency.

Therefore, cloud services must be able to tolerate possible inconsistency (or weak consistency) brought by asynchronous replications [46]. The simplest form of asynchronous replications is master-slave replications (e.g., MySQL replication [47] and replications between the Facebook data centers [48]), where write-operations can only update the master the slaves are read-only (as illustrated in Fig. 17). For this type of replications, the service needs to properly handle the potential *replication lag* (i.e., the time window when the slave is behind and hence inconsistent with the master), and the possible nontransparent master failover (i.e., a slave may take over without latest changes on the master) [46].

In addition, the high availability, disconnection support and offline behaviors required by cloud services mandate we sometimes design away from master or authoritative copies. Consequently, asynchronous multi-master replications (e.g., Flickr shards [15]) are sometimes preferred, in which write-operations can update any one of the replicas (as illustrated in Fig. 18). For this type of replications, the service also needs to properly handle the potential transactional conflicts.

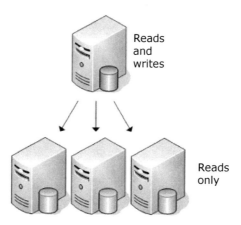

Fig. 17. In master-slave replications, the service can only write the master while it can read any one of the master/slave servers

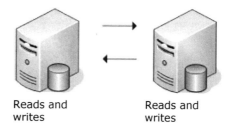

Fig. 18. In multi-master replications, the service can write and read any of the replicas

5.2 Possible Weak Consistency Models

A consequence of the weakly consistent data storage system is that after a write-operation completes, subsequent read-operations may not return the updated value. Consequently, it may lead to conflicting changes that must be detected and resolved. For instance, in Amazon SimpleDB [21], after the data are successfully written, it takes some time for the update to propagate to all the copies of the data; the data will eventually be consistent, but an immediate read might not show the change.

Due to those challenges, the general weak consistency model can be very confusing to both the service users (e.g., Facebook users will be confused when they do not see a post on someone's "wall" that they have just made) and the service developers [49]. It is therefore very important to precisely specify the weak/eventual consistency models used in the service (with possible constraints for performance, availability and user-friendliness tradeoffs), so that it can be easily understood and reasoned about. Unfortunately, it is unclear what the right system abstraction of relaxed consistency model is to the users and developers, though several application-specific solutions do exist.

- **User perception**

In practice, relaxed consistency models are usually defined in easy-to-understand terms (e.g., wall-clock time) for service users. One option is for cloud services to guarantee that stale data will go away within certain wall-clock time (e.g., a new listing in Craigslist may not appear in a search for five minutes), which is usually well understood and accepted by the users. To support this model, the data storage system can choose to synchronize data or expire the cache periodically, instead of updating all data replicas immediately.

In addition, it is also common for cloud services to provide *session consistency* (a practical variant of *read-your-writes* consistency [7]) by sticking a user session to a particular server. For instance, both Flickr [15] and Facebook [48] attempt to assign an (active) user to the same server to get around of the potential replication lag.

- **Application (developer) model**

Session consistency can be used for the service applications; in addition, for services developers, relaxed consistency models can be also defined using more complex semantics. Some data storage systems provide mechanisms for conflict detection and resolutions, which are typically based on versioning and require application-specific knowledge.

For instance, in Dynamo a specific object is assigned to a host using consistent hashing, and that host also replicates its object at the N-1 clockwise successor nodes in the ring [10]. That is, Dynamo replicates each of its objects on N hosts (the *preference list* of the object). It treats the result of each change as a new and immutable version of the data (using the *vector clock* [7]), and allows for multiple versions of an object to be present in the system at the same time. When a client wishes to update an object, it must specify which version to update by passing a *context* obtained from an earlier read operation.

When a storage node receives a *put* request, it generates the vector clock for the new version and writes the new version locally; it then sends the new version to nodes in the preference list and waits for at least W-1 nodes to respond. When a node receives a *get* request, it requests all existing versions of the object from nodes in the preference list and waits for R responses before returning the result to the client. If multiple conflicting versions of the object are received, it returns all the versions that are causally unrelated (encoded in the *context*). Typically, Dynamo is configured to have N larger than $R+W$ for better latency and availability, which only guarantees the eventual data consistency.

In addition, in PNUTS data are replicated across multiple (typically geographically distributed) *regions*, where each region contains a full complement of system components and a complete copy of each table [12]. It supports *record-level mastering* among the replicas; that is, one of the replicas is designated as the master, independently for each record, and all updates to that record are forwarded to the master. Updates of a given record are propagated to non-master replicas asynchronously (using a publish/subscribe message system), and are applied to all the replicas in the same order.

Based on the record-level mastering, PNUTS provides *per-record timeline consistency* by associating each record with a *version* number that is incremented on every write, and providing a whole range of API calls with varying level of consistency guarantees.

- *Read-any*: the record returned may be a stale version.
- *Read-critical(required_version)*: the record returned is newer than or the same as the *required_version* (obtained from previous *write* requests).
- *Read-latest*: the record returned is the latest version.

6 Conclusions and Future Works

Cloud service platforms are drastically different from traditional distributed systems, in that, instead of masking the existence of independent components from the applications, they need to acknowledge the existence of many small, independent, and unreliable components (clients, servers, data centers and services) that may be occasionally disconnected. Consequently, they need new design patterns to manage the partitioned data set with many copies that are changed independently.

In practice, the service usually partitions its data set into collections of uniquely keyed elements, designs its business logic using service-orient architecture with apology-oriented computing, and manages its data replicas using relaxed consistency models.

In addition, there are still a lot of problems that are both difficult and interesting in the new model of cloud services. In particular, it is unclear what the most efficient way is to support queries beyond primary-key based accesses for the partitioned data set, what the right programming abstraction is for the complex workflow-style processing, and what the right system abstraction of the relaxed consistency model is to the service users and developers. Therefore, cloud computing and services present wonderful challenges and opportunities to both the industry and the academic community.

References

1. Hamilton, J.: An Architecture for Modular Data Centers. In: Third Conference on Innovative Data Systems Research (CIDR 2007) (January 2007)
2. Patterson, D.A.: Technical perspective: the data center is the computer. Communications of the ACM 51(1) (January 2008)
3. Sun Modular Datacenter, http://www.sun.com/service/sunmd/

4. Church, K., Greenberg, A., Hamilton, J.: On Delivering Embarrassingly Distributed Cloud Services. In: Seventh ACM Workshop on Hot Topics in Networks (HotNets-VII) (October 2008)
5. Google Gears, http://gears.google.com/
6. Microsoft Sync framework, http://msdn.microsoft.com/sync/
7. Tanenbaum, A.S., van Steen, M.: Distributed Systems: Principles and Paradigms. Prentice Hall, Englewood Cliffs (January 2002) ISBN: 978-0130888938
8. Dai, J.: Design Patterns for Internet-Scale Services. In: Proceedings of the 25th International Conference on Data Engineering (ICDE 2009) (March 2009)
9. Vogels, W.: Ahead in the Cloud - The power of Infrastructure as a Service. In: 2008 MySQL Conference & Expo (April 2008)
10. DeCandia, G., Hastorun, D., Jampani, M., Kakulapati, G., Lakshman, A., Pilchin, A., Sivasubramanian, S., Vosshall, P., Vogels, W.: Dynamo: Amazon's Highly Available Key-value Store. In: ACM Symposium on Operating Systems Principles (SOSP 2007) (October 2007)
11. Chang, F., Dean, J., Ghemawat, S., Hsieh, W.C., Wallach, D.A., Burrows, M., Chandra, T., Fikes, A., Gruber, R.E.: Bigtable: A Distributed Storage System for Structured Data. Seventh Symposium on Operating Systems Design and Implementation (OSDI 2006) (November 2006)
12. Cooper, B.F., Ramakrishnan, R., Srivastava, U., Silberstein, A., Bohannon, P., Jacobsen, H., Puz, N., Weaver, D., Yerneni, R.: PNUTS: Yahoo!'s hosted data serving platform. In: Proceedings of the VLDB Endowment, vol. 1(2) (August 2008)
13. Shoup, R., Pritchett, D.: The eBay Architecture. In: SD Forum 2006 (November 2006)
14. Whitcomb, A., Benedetto, J.: Running a Megasite on Microsoft Technologies. In: Microsoft Mix 2006 Conference (March 2006)
15. Pattishall, D.: Federation at Flickr: Doing Billions of Queries per Day. In: 2007 MySQL Conference & Expo (April 2007)
16. Kakivaya, G.: SQL Data Services Under the Hood. In: PDC 2008 (October 2008)
17. Dean, J.: Large-Scale Distributed Systems at Google: Current Systems and Future Directions. In: The 3rd ACM SIGOPS International Workshop on Large Scale Distributed Systems and Middleware (LADIS 2008) (October 2009)
18. Ghemawat, S., Gobioff, H., Leung, S.-T.: The Google File System. In: 19th ACM Symposium on Operating Systems Principles (October 2003)
19. Hamilton, J.: On Designing and Deploying Internet-Scale Services. In: 21st Large Installation System Administration Conference (LISA 2007) (November 2007)
20. Shoup, R.: eBay Marketplace Architecture: Architectural Strategies, Patterns, and Forces. In: QCon 2007, San Francisco (September 2007)
21. Amazon SimpleDB, http://aws.amazon.com/sdb/
22. Helland, P.: Life beyond Distributed Transactions: an Apostate's Opinion. In: Third Conference on Innovative Data Systems Research (CIDR 2007) (January 2007)
23. Barrett, R.: Under the Covers of Google App Engine Datastore. In: Google I/O Conference 2008 (May 2008)
24. Furman, J.J., Karlsson, J.S., Leon, J.-M., Lloyd, A., Newman, S., Zeyliger, P.: Megastore: A Scalable Data System for User Facing Applications. In: SIGMOD 2008 (June 2008)
25. Nilakantan, N., Castro, P.: Windows Azure Table - Programming Cloud Table Storage. In: PDC 2008 (October 2008)
26. Hamilton, J.: Scaling LinkedIn, http://perspectives.mvdirona.com/2008/06/08/ScalingLinkedIn.aspx
27. FriendFeed, http://www.friendfeed.com/

28. Taylor, B.: How FriendFeed uses MySQL to store schema-lessdata, http://bret.appspot.com/entry/how-friendfeed-uses-mysql
29. Karger, D., Lehman, E., Leighton, T., Panigrahy, R., Levine, M., Lewin, D.: Consistent hashing and random trees: distributed caching protocols for relieving hot spots on the World Wide Web. In: Proceedings of the Twenty-Ninth Annual ACM Symposium on Theory of Computing (May 1997)
30. HBase project, http://hadoop.apache.org/hbase/
31. Hyptertable project, http://www.hypertable.org/
32. Cassandra project, http://incubator.apache.org/cassandra/
33. Voldemort project, http://project-voldemort.com/
34. Dean, J., Ghemawat, S.: MapReduce: Simplified Data Processing on Large Clusters. In: Sixth Symposium on Operating Systems Design and Implementation (OSDI 2004) (December 2004)
35. O'Hanlon, C.: A Conversation with Werner Vogels. ACM Queue 4(4) (May 2006)
36. Helland, P.: Data on the Outside versus Data on the Inside. In: Second Conference on Innovative Data Systems Research (CIDR 2005) (January 2005)
37. Pritchett, D.: Architecting for Latency. In: QCon 2007, San Francisco (September 2007)
38. Helland, P.: The Irresistible Forces Meet the Moveable Objects. TechEd EMEA (2007)
39. Finkelstein, S., Brendle, R., Jacobs, D.: Principles for Inconsistency. In: Fourth Conference on Innovative Data Systems Research (CIDR 2009) (January 2009)
40. Greenfield, P., Fekete, A., Jang, J.: Isolation Support for Service-based Applications: A Position Paper. In: Third Conference on Innovative Data Systems Research (CIDR 2007) (January 2007)
41. O'Neil, P.E.: The Escrow transactional method. ACM Transactions on Database Systems (TODS) 11(4) (December 1986)
42. Brewer, E.: Towards robust distributed systems. In: Principles of Distributed Computing (PODC 2000) (July 2000)
43. Gilbert, S., Lynch, N.: Brewer's conjecture and the feasibility of consistent, available, partition-tolerant web services. ACM SIGACT News 33(2) (June 2002)
44. Pritchett, D.: BASE: An ACID Alternative. ACM Queue 6(3) (May/June 2008)
45. Vogels, W.: Eventually Consistent. ACM Queue 6(6) (October 2008)
46. Helland, P., Campbell, D.: Building on Quicksand. In: Fourth Conference on Innovative Data Systems Research (CIDR 2009) (January 2009)
47. MySQL Replication, http://dev.mysql.com/doc/refman/5.1/en/replication.html
48. Engineering @ Facebook's Notes, Scaling Out, http://www.facebook.com/note.php?note_id=23844338919
49. Armbrust, M., Fox, A., Patterson, D.A., Lanham, N., Trushkowsky, B., Trutna, J., Oh, H.: SCADS: Scale-Independent Storage for Social Computing Applications. In: Fourth Conference on Innovative Data Systems Research (CIDR 2009) (January 2009)

Secure Data Management Service on Cloud Computing Infrastructures*

Divyakant Agrawal[1], Amr El Abbadi[1], Fatih Emekci[2],
Ahmed Metwally[3], and Shiyuan Wang[1]

[1] Department of Computer Science
University of California at Santa Barbara
Santa Barbara, CA 93106, USA
{agrawal,amr,sywang}@cs.ucsb.edu
[2] LinkedIn Corporation
2029 Stierlin Court, Mountain View, CA 94043, USA
femekci@linkedin.com
[3] Google Inc.
1600 Amphitheatre Parkway, Mountain View, CA 94043, USA
ametwally@gmail.com

Abstract. Data outsourcing or database as a service is a new paradigm for data management in which a third party service provider hosts a database as a service. The service provides data management for its customers and thus obviates the need for the service user to purchase expensive hardware and software, deal with software upgrades and hire professionals for administrative and maintenance tasks. Since using an external database service promises reliable data storage at a low cost it is very attractive for companies. Such a service would also provide universal access, through the Internet to private data stored at reliable and secure sites in cloud computing infrastructures. However, recent governmental legislations, competition among companies, and data thefts mandate companies to use secure and privacy preserving data management techniques. The data provider, therefore, needs to guarantee that the data is secure, be able to execute queries on the data, and the results of the queries must also be secure and not visible to the data provider. Current research has been focused only on how to index and query encrypted data. However, querying encrypted data is computationally very expensive. Providing an efficient trust mechanism to push both database service providers and clients to behave honestly has emerged as one of the most important problem before data outsourcing to become a viable paradigm. In this paper, we describe scalable privacy preserving algorithms for data outsourcing in cloud computing infrastructures. Instead of encryption, which is computationally expensive, we use distribution on multiple sites that are available in the cloud and information theoretically proven secret sharing algorithms as the basis for privacy preserving outsourcing. The technical contributions of this paper is the establishment and development of a framework for efficient fault-tolerant scalable and theoretically secure privacy preserving data outsourcing that supports a diversity of database operations executed on different types of data.

* This research was partially supported by the NSF under grant IIS-0847925.

D. Agrawal et al. (Eds.): Information and Software as Services, LNBIP 74, pp. 57–80, 2011.

Keywords: Distributed Computing, Data Outsourcing, Cloud Computing, Data Security, Data Privacy.

1   Introduction

Internet-scale computing has resulted in dramatic changes in the design and deployment of information technology infrastructure components. Cloud computing has been gaining in popularity in the commercial world, where various computing based capabilities are provided as a service to clients, thus relieving those clients from the need to develop expertise in these capabilities, as well as the need to manage and maintain the software providing these services. Amazon, for example, has created the service EC2, which provides clients with scalable servers; as well as another service S3, which provides scalable storage to clients. Recently, NSF partnered with Google and IBM to offer academic institutions access to large scale distributed infrastructure under the NSF CLuE program. There has clearly been a radical paradigm shift due to the wide acceptance of and reliance on Internet and Web-based technologies.

One of the reasons for the success of Internet-scale computing is the role it has played in eliminating the size of an enterprise as a critical factor in its economic success. An excellent example of this change is the notion of *data centers* which provide clients with the physical infrastructure needed to host their computer systems, including redundant power supplies, high bandwidth communication capabilities, environment monitoring, and security services. Data centers eliminate the need for small companies to make a large capital expenditure in building an infrastructure to create a global customer base. The data center model has been effective since it allows an enterprise of any size to manage growth with the popularity of its product or service while at the same time also allows the enterprise to cut its losses if the launched product or service does not succeed. During the past few years we have seen a rapid acceleration of innovation in new business paradigms and data centers have played a very important role in this process.

In addition to the physical infrastructure needed to support Internet and web-based applications, such applications have data management needs as well. To enable more sophisticated business analysis and user customization, e-commerce applications maintain data or log information for every user interaction rather than only storing transaction data (e.g. sales transactions in the retail industry). This trend has resulted in an explosive growth in the amount of data associated with these applications. Storage and retrieval of such data poses monumental challenges especially for relatively small-sized companies since the cost of data management is estimated to be five-to-ten times higher than the data acquisition cost [1]. More importantly, in-house data management requires a much higher level skill-set to deal with the issues of storage technologies, capacity planning, fault-tolerance and reliability, disaster recovery, and DBMS and Operating Systems software upgrades. Most commercial entities would rather direct their valuable technical resources and engineering talent to focus on their business applications instead of becoming full-time data management companies.

Due to the above concerns, *data outsourcing* or *database as a service* has emerged as a new paradigm for data management in which a third party service provider hosts a database and provides the associated software and hardware support. The Database Service Provider (DBSP) provides data management for its customers, and thus obviates the need for the customer to purchase expensive hardware and software, to deal with software upgrades, and to hire professionals for administrative and maintenance tasks. Since using a DBSP promises reliable data storage at a low cost, it is very attractive for large enterprises such as commercial entities, intelligence agencies, and other public and private organizations. Such a service would also provide universal access through the Internet to private data stored at reliable and secure sites. A client company can outsource their data, and its employees then have access to the company data irrespective of their current locations. Rather than carrying data with them as they travel or logging remotely into their home machines, employees can store and access company data with the DBSP, thus eliminating the risk of data lost or theft. Additionally, employees do not have to deal with the hurdle of accessing the company's VPN to sign on to specific database machines, nor do they have to face issues of machine crashes and data unavailability.

Although the data outsourcing paradigm has compelling economic and technical advantages, its adaptation has not mirrored the success of data centers. The main reason for this failure is the concern of data security and privacy. Recent governmental legislations, competition among companies, and data thefts mandate that enterprises use secure and privacy preserving data management techniques. It is usually not preferred in data outsourcing to use a trusted external database service where service providers and clients are honest and clients do not hesitate to share their data with database service providers. Thus the research challenge is to build a robust and efficient service to manage data in a secure and privacy-preserving manner. The DBSP, therefore, needs to guarantee that data is secure, that the results of the queries must also be secure, and that the queries can be executed efficiently and correctly,

Previous research in the context of secure data outsourcing has focused on these areas independently. In the case of ensuring *security* or equivalently *confidentiality* of outsourced data, most of the research is concerned with ensuring that even though the data is outsourced to a third party, the individual data values should not be discernible to the service provider [1,2,3,4,5,6,7,8,9]. In the case of ensuring the security of query results, *private information retrieval* is used. This problem has been studied as the theoretical formulation where the client must be able to retrieve the ith element from N data elements without the service provider discovering that the client is interested in the ith element [10,11,12,13,14,15,16]. Finally, in the last case we are concerned with malicious service providers, and therefore need to ensure completeness and correctness of user queries in that the results returned by the service provider are indeed the exact answers to the user queries [17,18,19,20,21]. Although one of challenges of secure data outsourcing is providing query efficiency, it is not the only problem. Since thousands of clients per database service provider are expected, the scalability of the proposed techniques and the availability of the services are also very important concerns. However, current proposals do not consider these issues and assume a simple scenario consisting of an always available DBSP and a simple service user. If, for example, the service provider corrupted the data, it would be impossible to recover it for the service user. To be able to use external DBSPs in real-world settings, there must be a mechanism to verify that data has been corrupted and to recover the data. *Providing a trust mechanism* to ensure both DBSPs and clients behave honestly has emerged as one of the most important problem that must be overcome before data outsourcing becomes a viable paradigm. Clearly, a wide adaptation of data outsourcing will only be possible if all these issues are adequately addressed in the same framework.

In this paper, we propose a scalable secure and privacy-preserving framework for data outsourcing. Instead of computationally expensive encryption mechanism, which is used in most proposed approaches [22] and in the commercial arena [23], we use distribution on multiple service provider sites and information theoretically proven secret-sharing algorithms as the basis for privacy preserving outsourcing. Our approach trades the expensive computation in encryption mechanism with relatively modest communication overhead. We formulate our framework and present the essential idea in Section 3. We then develop practical solutions for efficient data retrieval in Section 4 and for processing different queries in Section 5. We outline possible extensions for making our framework a mature data management service in Section 6.

2   Background

2.1   Encryption-Based Data Security

Current research on data security use encryption to hide the content of the data from service providers [1,3,5,7,8,9]. Agrawal et al. [24] use a commutative encryption to answer intersection and join queries over two private databases in an *honest-but-curious* environment. Both operations require a privacy-preserving intersection primitive. The privacy-preserving property would allow that each of the parties only learn about the entities in the data sources that are common to both parties. No other information is revealed other than the total size of the list. The join operation is built upon the privacy-preserving primitive.

The concept of *database as service* has been of interest to the research community under various guises. NetDB2 [1] was developed and deployed as a database service on the Internet. NetDB2 directly addresses two of the main challenges in developing databases as a service, namely data privacy and performance. NetDB2 uses encryption to ensure privacy and is the first work that directly addresses and evaluates the issue of performance, which is critical for success in databases. Recently [25] proposed using homomorphic encryption to support secure aggregate outsourcing. In [19] Sion introduced the notion of query execution assurance in outsourced databases, namely, assurances are provided by the database server that the served client queries were in fact correctly executed on the entire outsourced database. In [26], the problem of using a single key for data encryption is raised. In such a context, third parties with authorization to access this data either have a complete view of the outsourced data, or, if different users have varying authorizations, the data owner needs to participate in the query execution to filter results. The communication overhead makes these solutions unsatisfactory, and in [26] a hierarchical key assignment scheme is proposed and efficiently supported. Anciaux et al. [27] address the interesting problem of executing privacy preserving operations on both public as well as private data, when the latter are stored on smart USB keys.

The computational complexity of encrypting and decrypting data to execute a query increases the query response time. Therefore, this complexity is one of the bottlenecks in current solutions [24]. In fact, Agrawal et al. [24] show that computing a privacy preserving intersection problem using encryption results in a very high time complexity. The cost estimation of encryption based approach on a synthetic data consisting of 10 documents at one site and 100 documents at another site (each with 1000 words) could take as much as 2 hours of computation and approximately 3 Gigabits of data transmission. Similarly, for a real dataset consisting of approximately 1 million medical records, the encryption based approach takes approximately 4 hours of computation time and and 8 Gbits of data transmission. Scannapieco et al. [28] propose using an embedding of the data in a Euclidean space to avoid complex cryptographic computations. This approach has the added benefit of performing privacy preserving approximate data matching, as well as preserving the privacy of the database schema. Another problem with the data encryption approach is that finding the required tuples to execute the query over encrypted data is a significant challenge. In order to solve this problem, current proposals reveal some information about the content of the data to be used in filtering the required tuples [1,2]. With a good filtration mechanism, the communication cost of retrieving data from service providers would be less and thus the query response time would be much better. However, the quality of the filtration process strictly depends on the amount of information revealed to the service provider. Therefore, there is a privacy performance tradeoff in these solutions. Finally, in order to execute range queries efficiently order preserving data encryption mechanisms have been proposed [3]. However, it has also been argued that order preservation may weaken data security [5].

2.2 Private Information Retrieval

Interestingly, the problem of private information retrieval has been a research topic for more than a decade. The problem was first proposed in the context of a user accessing third-party data without revealing to the third-party his/her exact interests [11]. An example scenario is an analyst who wants to retrieve information from an investor database made available by a certain company, but who would not like his/her future intentions be exposed to that company. Although the original formulation of this problem was with respect to third-party data it is very much applicable in the context of outsourced data. In particular, users may not want to reveal their queries to the service provider since this information can compromise the privacy of their behavior patterns.

Formally, private information retrieval is stated as follows: the database is modeled as a string x of length N held at a remote server, and the user wants to retrieve the bit x_i for some i, without disclosing any information about i to the server [11]. A trivial solution would be for the user to retrieve the entire database. A simple proof establishes that if we only have one server, the trivial solution is the best we can hope for [11]. A way to obtain sub-linear communication complexity is to replicate the database at several servers. It has been shown that with k servers the communication complexity can be reduced to $O(N^{\frac{1}{2k-1}})$. There is a long history of theoretical research in this area and most solutions rely on the availability of multiple servers or multiple service providers [11,12]. If a database server is restricted to perform only polynomial-time computations, single server solutions are also available to achieve sub-linear communication complexity [10,13,14,15].

The notion of private information retrieval which ensures privacy of user queries has also been extended to the case where the privacy of data is a concern. This is referred to as *symmetric private information retrieval* [29,30,31]. A necessary ingredient in all these proposals is the requirement that the database privacy can only be maintained through data replication, i.e., multiple *non-cooperating* database servers are needed. The drawback of these formulations is that their focus is primarily on the cryptographic frameworks to ensure user query and database privacy. Furthermore, the only types of database queries that are supported are address queries in which the specific key for the data-item must be specified a priori. It is not clear if these techniques can easily be generalized to a full range of database operations involving selection queries, join queries, and aggregation and group-by operators. In fact, in a recent work by Sion and Carburnar [16], the authors have challenged the computational practicality of both private information retrieval and symmetric private information retrieval. In that, the authors through extensive experimentation and evaluation have established that the private information retrieval protocols are several orders of magnitude slower than the trivial protocol of transferring entire database to the client to ensure user privacy. Also, they predict this trend to hold even after accounting for hardware advances as far ahead as 2035. The only way these protocols can be leveraged is by deploying 100s to 1000s of CPUs to perform the underlying arithmetic to realize the cryptographic operators. Thus, in essence the authors doubt the viability of private information protocols in practice and state that alternative approaches are wanted to address the very *real* and *practical* problem of data outsourcing. As will be outlined later in the paper, our approach to database outsourcing is also relied on data distribution on multiple servers. However, in contrast to private information retrieval, our approach does not incur expensive computation cost, and it can withstand attacks from collusion of multiple servers.

2.3   Information Distribution

In the area of computer and data security, there is an orthogonal approach which is based on information dispersal or distribution instead of encryption. Most of this work on security arose in the context of communicating a secret value from one party to another. Many approaches rely on encrypting the secret value using encryption keys and ensure that the information can only be revealed to a party that has the key. Shamir [32] proposed an orthogonal scheme that does not rely on the notion of keys. Instead, he proposed splitting the secret into n pieces such that the secret value can only be revealed if one has access to any k of these n pieces, $k < n$. This scheme is shown to be information-theoretically secure as long as there is some guarantee that the adversary cannot access k pieces. Unlike encryption methods, Shamir's secret sharing algorithm is computationally efficient. Our intent is to take a distributed approach towards secure data outsourcing in that we want to explore using secret-sharing approach and multiple service providers. The advantage of this approach is that it addresses both data security as well as privacy-preserving querying of outsourced data.

Although robust, secret sharing does not defend against mobile adversaries [33] which attack several of the secret shares, thus potentially revealing the secret. Proactive secret sharing [34,35] has been proposed where the shares are updated periodically, thus preventing the adversary from retrieving the secret. Earlier work assumed synchronous systems, while more recently Zhou et al. proposed proactive secret sharing in an asynchronous system [36]. Aggarwal et al. [4] use a partitioning approach for data outsourcing in that multiple service providers are used and data is vertically partitioned among these service providers so that no service provider has complete understanding of the data.

In [37,38], we proposed using Shamir's secret sharing algorithm to execute privacy preserving operations among a set of distributed data warehouses. In [37], a middleware, Abacus, was developed to support selection, intersection and join operations. This approach was designed for data warehouses and took advantage of the dimension table in the star scheme to hide information using inexpensive one-way hash functions. In [38], this work was generalized to any type of database, and used distributed third parties and Shamir's secret sharing algorithm to secure information and support privacy preserving selection, intersection, join and aggregation operations (such as SUM and MIN/MAX operations) on a set of distributed databases. Similar to [24,38], Aggarwal et al. [39] propose a method for finding the kth ranked element approximately in the union of more than two databases using secure multi-party computation.

3   Overview of the Proposed Framework

In this section, we formulate the secure data outsourcing problem and then briefly discuss our proposed approach towards an effective solution. As discussed in the introduction, our goal in making data outsourcing a reality is to ensure we overcome some of the challenges that arise in the adoption of data outsourcing in the computing industry. In particular, although encryption based solutions have existed for some time in the research arena, they have not been widely adapted due to the enormous computational and I/O overhead associated with them. Our approach instead is to use data dispersion on multiple servers instead of data encryption to achieve data security and privacy of user queries. This approach is not only efficient, but also exploits the paradigm of Internet-scale computing by taking advantage of the large number of available resources.

Assume that a client, which we refer to as the *data source* D, wants to outsource its data to eliminate its database maintenance cost by using the database service provided by database service providers $DAS_1, ..., DAS_n$. D needs to store and access its data remotely without revealing the content of the database to any of the database services. For the sake of this discussion, assume D has a single table $Employees$, with employee names and salaries, in its database and stores $Employees$ using the services provided by $DAS_1, ..., DAS_n$. After storing $Employees$, D needs to query $Employees$ without revealing any information about either the content of the table or queries. D can pose any of the following queries over time:

1. Exact match queries such as: *Retrieve all information about employees whose name is 'John'*.
2. Range queries such as: *Retrieve all information about employees whose salary is between 10K and 40K*.

3. Aggregate queries such as MIN/MAX, MEDIAN, SUM and AVERAGE. Aggregates can be over ranges for example *sum of the salaries of employees whose salary is between 10K and 40K*. In addition, they can be over exact matches such as *average of the salaries of all employees whose name is 'John'*.

There are several privacy preserving proposals addressing exact match queries and range queries [1,3,4], however, these proposals are not complete and reveal some information about the underlying data, for example the range of employee salaries, to the database service provider. We propose a complete approach to execute exact match, range, and aggregation queries in a privacy preserving manner. The goal is to build a practical scalable system and answer queries without revealing any information. Throughout the paper, we will assume that there are two kinds of attributes in tables namely *numeric attributes* such as salary and *non-numeric attributes* such as name. Furthermore, we will assume that exact match queries are over non-numeric attributes, and range queries and aggregation queries are over numeric attributes. We will contrast the work in [1,2] referred to as *data encryption*, wherever appropriate, with our proposed technique so as to highlight the differences and compare them.

In our solution, data is divided into n shares and each share is stored in a different service provider. When a query is generated at a data source, it is rewritten, the relevant shares are retrieved from the service providers, and the query answer is reconstructed at the data source. In order to answer queries, any k of the service providers must be available. The main idea here is that the service providers are not able to infer anything about the content of the data they store, and still the data source is able to query its database by incurring reasonable communication and computation costs.

In the data encryption model, data source D encrypts each tuple in the table and saves the encrypted tuples at the service provider DAS. Using one service provider is enough in this scheme. When a query comes, data source D retrieves **all** tuples from the service provider DAS and decrypts them. Then, it finds the required tuples for the query and answers the query using them. Since the encrypted form of data is stored at service provider DAS, DAS will not know anything about the content of the data it stores. However, it cannot help with query processing since the entire encrypted database has to be transferred to the data source for query processing.

We start by discussing simple techniques of outsourcing a singleton numeric attribute such as salary in an idealized environment. Then, we generalize our techniques to deal with more complex operations, and propose extensions for non-numeric data. In the proposed secret sharing model, the goal is to divide a secret value and to distribute shares to the service providers such that the providers cannot figure out the secret even if they combine their shares. The solution is based on Shamir's secret sharing method [32]. Data source D divides the numeric value v_s into n shares and stores one share at each service provider, DAS_1, DAS_2, ..., DAS_n, such that knowledge of any k ($k \leq n$) shares in addition to some secret information, X, known only to the data source is required to reconstruct the secret. Since, even complete knowledge of $k-1$ service providers cannot reveal any information about the secret even if X is known, this method is information theoretically secure [32].

In the secret sharing method, data source D chooses a random polynomial $q(x)$ of degree $k-1$ where the constant term is the secret value, v_s, and secret information X

Algorithm 1. Secret Sharing Algorithm

1: *Input:*
2: v_s: Secret value;
3: D: Data source of secret v_s;
4: DAS: Set of service providers $DAS_1, ..., DAS_n$ to distribute secret;
5: *Output:*
6: $share_1, ..., share_n$: Shares of secret, v_s, for each service provider DAS_i;
7: *Procedure:*
8: D creates a random polynomial $q(x) = a_{k-1}x^{k-1} + ... + a_1x^1 + a_0$ with degree $k-1$ and a constant term $a_0 = v_s$.
9: D chooses secret information X which is n random points, $x_1, ...x_n$, such that $x_i \neq 0$.
10: D computes share coming from v_s for each service provider DAS_i, $share(v_s, i)$, where $share(v_s, i) = q(x_i)$.

---

which is a set of n random points, each corresponding to one of the database service providers. Then, data source D computes the share of each service provider as $q(x_i)$, $x_i \in X$ and sends it to database service provider DAS_i. To reconstruct the secret value v_s, the data source retrieves shares from the service providers. The shares can be rewritten as follows:

$$shares(v_s, 1) = q(x_1) = ax_1^{k-1} + bx_1^{k-2}... + v_s$$
$$shares(v_s, 2) = q(x_2) = ax_2^{k-1} + bx_2^{k-2}... + v_s$$
$$\vdots$$
$$shares(v_s, n) = q(x_n) = ax_n^{k-1} + bx_n^{k-2}... + v_s$$

The secret value can be reconstructed using any k of the above equations since there are k unknowns including the secret value v_s. In order to reconstruct the secret value v_s, any set of k service providers will need to share the information they have received, and they need to know the set of secret points, X, used by D. Since only data source D knows X, only it can reconstruct the secret after getting at least k shares from any k of the service providers.

We illustrate the secret sharing model using a concrete example. Assume that data source D needs to outsource the salary attribute of an *Employees* table using 3 database service providers, DAS_1, DAS_2 and DAS_3. In order to do this, it chooses 5 random polynomials with degree one for each salary value in the table whose constant term is the salary ($n = 3$ and $k = 2$). In addition, secret information X, $X = \{x_1 = 2, x_2 = 4, x_3 = 1\}$, is also chosen one for each database service provider. Therefore, the polynomials would be $q_{10}(x) = 100x + 10$, $q_{20}(x) = 5x + 20$, $q_{40}(x) = x + 40$, $q_{60}(x) = 2x + 60$ and $q_{80}(x) = 4x + 80$ for salaries $\{10, 20, 40, 60, 80\}$ respectively. Then, it sends $\{q_{10}(x_i), q_{20}(x_i), q_{40}(x_i), q_{60}(x_i), q_{80}(x_i)\}$ to service provider DAS_i to store them. The data outsourcing step is illustrated in Figure 1. Note that neither the polynomials nor the salaries are stored at the service provider and Figure 1 shows the information stored at each of the service provider. When a query is initiated at the data source, it needs to retrieve the shares corresponding to all salaries from the

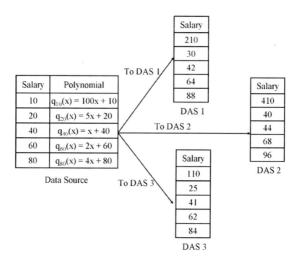

Fig. 1. Demonstration of Example 1

service providers, i.e., $\{q_{10}(x_i), q_{20}(x_i), q_{40}(x_i), q_{60}(x_i), q_{80}(x_i)\}$ from DAS_i. After this, it needs to find out the coefficient of each polynomial q and thus all secret salaries (note that receiving any k shares is enough for this since the polynomials are of degree $k-1$). In our example, data source D needs to receive shares from any 2 of the service providers and uses the set of secret values X, to compute the coefficients of polynomials $q_{10}, q_{20}, q_{40}, q_{60}$ and q_{80} and thus salaries, 10, 20, 40, 60 and 80 can be retrieved.

As seen from the above example, our approach for secure data outsourcing is based on data distribution or information dispersal. In that regard our work can be seen as the continuation of the proposal from the Stanford group that articulated a data partitioning approach for data outsourcing [4]. The Stanford approach relied on vertical partitioning of relations to prevent a single data service provider from having a complete information. Thus the level of security provided is not very high in such a scheme. We instead use the secret-sharing approach that is information-theoretically proven to be secure and therefore provides much higher levels of security guarantees.

4   Practical Solutions for Secure Data Outsourcing

In this section, we extend the simple technique described in the previous section to only retrieve the required data from service providers or a small superset and thus reduce the computation and communication cost in query processing. In the simple solution described above, the database service providers are primarily used as storage servers. They do not play any role in the query processing itself and therefore the proposed approach is not practical. This will result in a large communication cost since the entire database needs to be retrieved from the service provider for every query. Furthermore, the data source itself will become a processing bottleneck since it needs to process all user queries. in fact, this is exactly the same overhead as in the case of data encryption with a single server. In the rest of the paper we use this idealized solution as a starting point and propose refinements to make the solution more practical and scalable. For clarity and continuity of exposition, we first discuss how Hore et al. [2] overcome these problems in the data encryption approach and then show how we can expand the secret sharing approach to also avoid retrieving all the data.

4.1 Efficient Retrieval

In order to reduce the communication and computation costs incurred in the idealized approach of the data encryption based data outsourcing, database service providers need to filter some of the data and send only a superset of the required data for the query. However, the database service providers cannot know which tuples are needed to execute the query since they have the encrypted form of the tuples. For example, If a query asking for salaries more than 40 is posed, the service provider needs to send all salaries since the service provider cannot know the salaries more than 40. If there was a method to determine a superset of the salaries more than 40 over the encrypted domain, then only tuples in this subset need to be sent. In order to find such a superset, data source D puts labels on the encrypted data [2]. For the above example, these labels are basically ranges of salaries. Data source D stores the encrypted form of each salaries with the salary range. Therefore, data source D stores the encrypted value and range-label pairs, e.g., $\{(E(10), [0 - 10]), (E(20), [10 - 20]), (E(40), [40 - 50]), (E(60), [50 - 60]), (E(80), [80 - 90])\}$ where E is an encryption function. This labeling allows the service provider to filter some of the salaries. For example salaries $E(10)$ and $E(20)$ can be filtered using labels since their range labels show that they cannot be more than 40.

There is a privacy-efficiency tradeoff in this scheme. The labels reveal some information about the content of the data to the service provider. For example, the service provider can deduce the number of salaries in each range and thus get an idea about the sum of the salaries paid. In order to reduce this information leakage, the ranges should be large. However, large ranges result in poor performance in query execution since the filtering process is not efficient with large ranges. The ranges should be small to filter more data and thus reduce the costs of communication and computation. However, data source D reveals more information if the ranges are small. Thus, there is a privacy-performance tradeoff and the performance of this method strictly depends on the sizes of ranges.

In contrast, we now propose an extension to the secret sharing method, which will allow the retrieval of only the required tuples from the service providers instead of a superset. The key observation to achieve this is that the order of the values in the domain $DOM = \{v_1, v_2,...,v_N\}$ needs to remain the same in the shares of the service providers. In other words, if data source D needs to outsource secret values from domain DOM and $v_1 < v_2 < ... < v_N$, the shares of a service provider DAS_i, $share(v_1, i), share(v_2, i), .., share(v_n, i)$, derived from $v_1, v_2,.., v_N$ respectively need to preserve the order (i.e., $share(v_1, i) < share(v_2, i) < .. < share(v_N, i)$). Since the order of the shares at the service provider is not preserved in the solution in Section 3, database service providers cannot filter the data. However, If we had a mechanism to construct the polynomials calculating shares in an order preserving manner for a specific domain, then data source D could retrieve only the required tuples instead of a superset to answer a query. We now propose an order preserving polynomial building technique to achieve this goal. Without loss of generality, we will assume that polynomials are of degree 3 and in the following form $ax^3 + bx^2 + cx + d$ (i.e., $k = 4$). Given any two secret values v_1 and v_2 from a domain DOM, we need to construct two polynomials $p_{v_1}(x) = a_1x^3 + b_1x^2 + c_1x + v_1$ and $p_{v_2}(x) = a_2x^3 + b_2x^2 + c_2x + v_2$ for these values such that $p_{v_1}(x) < p_{v_2}(x)$ for all x points if $v_1 < v_2$. The key observation for our solution is that $p_{v_1}(x) < p_{v_2}(x)$ for all positive x values if $a_1 < a_2$, $b_1 < b_2$, $c_1 < c_2$ and $v_1 < v_2$. We first present a straightforward approach to construct a set of order preserving polynomials and show why it is not secure. Then, we present a secure method for constructing such order preserving polynomials.

A straightforward method to form a set of order preserving polynomials for a specific domain is to use monotonically increasing functions of the secret values to determine the coefficients of the polynomials. In this scheme, we need three monotonically increasing functions f_a, f_b and f_c to find the coefficients of the polynomial $p_{v_s} = ax^3 + bx^2 + cx + v_s$ which is used to divide the secret value v_s. The coefficients of the polynomial p_{v_s} are the values of the monotonically increasing functions of the secret value v_s where $a = f_a(v_s)$, $b = f_b(v_s)$ and $c = f_c(v_s)$. Therefore, for two secret values v_1 and v_2 ($v_1 < v_2$) and their respective polynomials $p_{v_1}(x) = f_a(v_1)x^3 + f_b(v_1)x^2 + f_c(v_1)x + v_1$ and $p_{v_2}(x) = f_a(v_2)x^3 + f_b(v_2)x^2 + f_c(v_2)x + v_2$, the value of $p_{v_1}(x)$ is always less than the value of polynomial $p_{v_2}(x)$ for all x values. Since any service provider DAS_i gets the value of the polynomials at point x_i, the share coming from secret value v_1, $share(v_1, i)$ would always be less than the share coming from the secret value v_2, $share(v_2, i)$ (i.e., $p_1(x_i) < p_2(x_i)$). However, this solution is not secure enough to hide secret values from the service providers. For example, assume the following monotonic functions are used: $f_a(v_s) = 3v_s + 10$, $f_b(v_s) = v_s + 27$ and $f_c(v_s) = 5v_s + 1$. Then, the share of data source DAS_i from secret value v_1 would be $p_1(x_i) = (3v_1 + 10)x_i^3 + (v_1 + 27)x_i^2 + (5v_1 + 1)x_i + v_1$ which is $p_1(x_i) = (3x_i^3 + x_i^2 + 5x_i + 1)v_1 + (10x_i^3 + 27x_i^2 + x_i)$. Basically, the secrets are multiplied by the same constants and then the same constant is added to compute the share of a service provider for all secret values. Therefore, if a service provider is able to break this method for one secret item can determine the complete set of the secret values. Thus this approach is not secure. One possibility is that instead of using simple monotonic functions, more complex monotonic functions can be employed. The scheme still remains vulnerable since if an adversary is able to break one secret value, it can determine the rest of the values.

Since the above approach to construct an order preserving polynomial is not secure, we propose another scheme to build order preserving polynomials for values from a specific domain. In particular, we propose a secure method using different coefficients for each secret value so that service providers cannot know the relation between secret values except the order. In polynomial construction, the coefficients a, b and c are chosen from the domains DOM_a, DOM_b and DOM_c. Since the coefficients can be real numbers, the sizes of the coefficient domains are independent from the data domain size. For finite domain $DOM = \{v_1, v_2, ...v_N\}$, the domains DOM_a, DOM_b and DOM_c are divided into N equal sections. For example DOM_a is divided into N slots : $[1, \frac{|Dom_a|}{N}]$ for v_1, $[\frac{|Dom_a|}{N} + 1, 2\frac{|Dom_a|}{N}]$ for v_2,...,$[(N-1)\frac{|Dom_a|}{N} + 1, |Dom_a|]$ for v_N. After this,

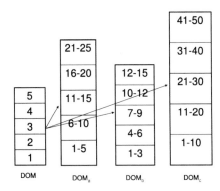

Fig. 2. Demonstration of Order Preserving Polynomial Construction

coefficient a_{v_i} for value v_i is selected from the slot $[(i-1)\frac{\lfloor Dom_a \rfloor}{N}+1, i\frac{\lfloor Dom_a \rfloor}{N}]$ with the help of hash function h_a which maps v_i to a value from $[(i-1)\frac{\lfloor Dom_a \rfloor}{N}+1, i\frac{\lfloor Dom_a \rfloor}{N}]$. The other coefficients b_{v_i} and c_{v_i} are computed similarly with the hash functions from domains Dom_b and Dom_c. Finally, the polynomial used to divide the secret value v_i into shares would be $p_{v_i}(x) = a_{v_i}x^3 + b_{v_i}x^2 + c_{v_i}x + v_i$.

Assume data domain is $DOM = \{1, 2, 3, 4, 5\}$, and we want to construct order preserving polynomials of degree 3 for this domain. In order to do this, we need to find 3 coefficients a, b and c for each value in DOM. Furthermore, assume coefficients a, b and c are chosen from the domains $Dom_a = [1, 25]$, $Dom_b = [1, 15]$, and $Dom_c = [1, 50]$ respectively. The domain of each coefficient is divided into 5 equal pieces since we have 5 elements in domain DOM. For example Dom_a is divided into 5 pieces: $[1, 5]$, $[6, 10]$, $[11, 15]$, $[16, 20]$ and $[21, 25]$. The other domains are divided into similar slots as shown in Figure 2. Coefficients a, b and c for secret item 3 are selected from the third slots in domains Dom_a, Dom_b and Dom_c respectively with the help of the hash functions h_a, h_b and h_c. Assume for the sake of this example hash function h_a maps secret value 3 to 13 which is in the third slot of Dom_a, h_b maps it to 7 in the third slot of Dom_b, and h_c maps it to 23 in the third slot of Dom_c. Then, the resulting polynomial for secret value 3 would be $p_3(x) = 13x^3 + 7x^2 + 23x + 3$. Similarly, the polynomial for secret value 5, $p_5(x) = 24x^3 + 14x^2 + 44x + 5$, can be constructed with the same method using the values from the 5th slot of each domain. The main observation here is that the value of polynomial $p_5(x)$ is always greater than the value of polynomial $p_3(x)$ for all positive x values, since the values in the 5th slot are bigger than the values in the 3rd slot. After constructing the polynomial for the secret value v_i, p_{v_i}, data source D divides the secret value v_i into n pieces to be sent to each of the service providers. In other words, D stores $p_{v_i}(x_1)$ at DAS_1, $p_{v_i}(x_2)$ at DAS_2,...,$p_{v_i}(x_n)$ at DAS_n. The secret value v_i is reconstructed as described in Figure 1 after retrieving these shares from the service providers. The service provider DAS_i storing $p_{v_i}(x_i)$ for the secret value v_i cannot know the secret value v_i. Because it does not know x_i and anything about the domains of the coefficients Dom_a, Dom_b and Dom_c.

We now consider the security of the proposed polynomial construction technique. Basically, we discuss what a service provider can infer from the stored data and then show that it cannot know the content of the data with the inferred information. From the stored data, service provider DAS_i can know an upper bound on the sum of the domain sizes (i.e., $|DOM| + |Dom_a| + |Dom_b| + |Dom_c|$). This can only happen when it stores the last secret value from DOM and the coefficients are mapped to the last slots of the domains for the last secret value v_N in the domain. Assume this worst case. Then, the polynomial for secret value v_N would be $P_{v_N}(x) = |Dom_a|x^3 + |Dom_b|x^2 + |Dom_c|x + v_N$ and the share of DAS_i would be $share(i, v_N) = P_{v_N}(x_i) = |Dom_a|x_i^3 + |Dom_b|x_i^2 + |Dom_c|x_i + v_N$. From this share, DAS_i can only know an upper bound on the sum of the sizes of the domains and that upper bound is too loose to infer something about the content of the data. Therefore, we claim that the database service providers can only know an upper bound on the sum of the domains from the stored information. Furthermore, database service provider DAS_i cannot know each domain size or the exact value of the sum of the coefficient domain sizes even if it knows the secret point x_i, in the worst case scenario described above. Because, there are 4 unknowns, Dom_a, Dom_b, Dom_c and v_N, in the share of DAS_i, $share(i, v_N) = P_{v_N}(x_i) = |Dom_a|x_i^3 + |Dom_b|x_i^2 + |Dom_c|x_i + v_N$ (assuming x_i is known). Thus, these unknowns cannot be found.

We now discuss the general case. If database service provider DAS_i knows the secret point x_i and the sum of the coefficient domain sizes $|Dom_a| + |Dom_b| + |Dom_c|$, it cannot infer anything about the secret items (even with simple hash functions mapping the secret values to the first values in the slot are used). Assume hash functions h_a, h_b and h_c map secret values to the first values in each slot. Let the coefficients of polynomial $p_{v_i}(x)$ with these simple hash functions be $a = v_i \frac{|Dom_a|}{N}$, $b = v_i \frac{|Dom_b|}{N}$ and $c = v_i \frac{|Dom_c|}{N}$. Then, the share of DAS_i would be:

$$p_{v_i}(x_i) = v_i \frac{|Dom_a|}{N} x_i^3 + v_i \frac{|Dom_b|}{N} x_i^2 + v_i \frac{|Dom_c|}{N} x_i + v_i$$

In addition to its share, if DAS_i knows the sum of the sizes of the domains which is $|Dom_a| + |Dom_b| + |Dom_c|$, there are 5 unknowns ($|Dom_a|$, $|Dom_b|$, $|Dom_c|$, $|DOM|$ and v_i) and 2 equations. Therefore, the unknowns and thus the secret value is not revealed to database service provider DAS_i even with these simple hash functions. In our scheme, a service provider can only derive an upper bound on the sum of the domains $|Dom_a| + |Dom_b| + |Dom_c| + |DOM|$ but not the secret point x_i. In addition, the hash functions map secret values to any value not only the first value in the slot. Thus, a database service provider DAS_i cannot know the secret value v_i even if it knows the secret point x_i. The service provider DAS_i storing $\{p_{v_1}(x_i), p_{v_2}(x_i),...,p_{v_N}(x_i)\}$ cannot know the secret values $\{v_1, v_2,..,v_N\}$.

In addition to the above security guarantees, for two secret values v_i and v_j from the same domain, data source DAS_i will get its shares $share(v_i, i) = p_{v_i}(x_i)$ (share of DAS_i from v_i) and $share(v_j, i) = p_{v_j}(x_j)$. If $v_i < v_j$ then $share(v_i, i) < share(v_j, i)$ due to the polynomial construction method. That is, for any two secret values v_i and v_j from the same domain, the shares of data source DAS_i, $share(v_i, i) = p_{v_i}(x_i)$ (share of DAS_i from v_i) and $share(v_j, i) = p_{v_j}(x_j)$, preserves the order (i.e., if $v_i < v_j$ then $share(v_i, i) < share(v_j, i)$).

5   Query Processing

In this section, we briefly discuss how different queries are processed in the secret sharing data outsourcing framework. We consider exact match, range, aggregation and join
queries. In each case, we will illustrate how the encryption scheme solves the problem
and contrast it with our approach.

5.1   Exact Match Queries

An example of an Exact Match Query would be "retrieve the names of all employees
whose salary is 20". In the data encryption model [2,1], all the attributes are encrypted
and the service provider only knows the encrypted values. Queries are formulated in
terms of the encrypted values, and tuples corresponding to those encrypted values are
retrieved. In order to process this query in this scheme, data source D rewrites the query
as follows: Retrieve the employees whose salary is $E(20)$, where $E()$ is the encryption
function of data source D. After retrieving these tuples, data source D decrypts them
and answers the query. For this kind of query, the communication and computation is
performed for the tuples which are needed to execute the query. Thus, encryption is a
good method for exact match queries. In the secret sharing model, data source D needs
to retrieve shares from the service providers. Therefore, it rewrites k queries one for
each service provider. For example, the rewritten query for DAS_i would be: Retrieve
the tuples of all employees whose salary is $share(20, i)$, where $share(20, i)$ is the
share of service provider DAS_i for the secret value 20. In order to find $share(20, i)$,
data source D first constructs[1] the polynomial for secret item 20, $p_{20}(x)$, and then it
computes the shares, $share(20, i) = p_{20}(x_i)$. After retrieving the corresponding tuples
from the service providers, data source D computes the secret values. The computation
and communication is only performed for those tuples which are needed to answer the
query. The communication cost is k times that of the encryption method. However,
solving a polynomial is significantly less computationally expensive than decrypting an
item.

5.2   Range Queries

In order to process range queries in the encryption model [2,1], labels are associated
with the encrypted tuples. These labels indicate the range of the particular encrypted
values. The labels are used to find a superset of the answer in the data encryption
method. For example, to execute the query asking for the employees whose salaries
are between 20 and 50, the service provider sends all the tuples which may be needed
to answer the query using the labels. The efficiency of the data encryption method depends on how much privacy is preserved with labeling. Therefore, there is a tradeoff
between privacy and performance in this method. In order to answer the same query in
the secret sharing method, data source D rewrites n queries (one for each of the service provider). For example, the query sent to service provider DAS_i is: All employees

---

[1] Note that the polynomials are not stored at the data source which would amount to storing
the entire data itself. Instead, the polynomials are generated as part of the front-end query-
processing at the data source.

whose salaries are between $share(20, i)$ and $share(50, i)$. In order to compute shares, $share(20, i)$ and $share(50, i)$, two order preserving polynomials, $p_{20}(x)$ and $p_{50}(x)$, are constructed ($share(20, i) = p_{20}(x_i)$ and $share(50, i) = p_{50}(x_i)$). Service provider DAS_i, then, sends the tuples of all employees whose salaries are between $share(20, i)$ and $share(50, i)$. Since we have an order preserving polynomial construction technique for the domain, DAS_i can send only the required tuples. After getting this information from the service providers, data source D executes the query by solving the polynomials. Therefore, the computation and communication is performed for those tuples which are required to answer the query. In addition to this, no information about the underlying data is revealed to the service providers as opposed to the data encryption method. We note that in the context of range queries the data encryption method has some amount of information leakage due to the range labels associated with the numeric attribute. Furthermore, even though the data source only communicates with only one database service provider the query result of a range query is a superset of the final answer. This results in two drawbacks. First, there is inherent communication overhead associated with this scheme. The second which is more important is that the data source also needs to have a query processor to perform range filtering at its end. In contrast, the secret sharing scheme does not require any data filtering on the data source, hence the scheme can work with thin clients. However, as was the case earlier, the secret sharing scheme does need to communicate with multiple service providers. The consequence of this overhead does result in greater fault-tolerance and data availability in the presence of failures since only k of n database service providers are needed to compute the query result.

5.3   Aggregation Queries

We consider *Sum/Average, Min/Max/Median* aggregation queries. We classify aggregation queries in two class: 1) Aggregations over Exact Matches 2) Aggregation over ranges. We illustrate aggregation query processing techniques with the following example queries:

- Q1: Sum/Average of the salaries of the employees whose name is "John" (Sum/Average over Exact Match).
- Q2: Sum/Average of the salaries of the employees whose salary is between 20 and 40 (Sum/Average over Ranges).
- Q3: Min/Max/Median of the salaries of the employees whose name is "John" (Min/Max/Median over Exact Match).
- Q4: Min/Max/Median of the all salaries of the employees whose salary is between 20 and 40 (Min/Max/Median over Ranges).

Processing aggregation queries in the data encryption method is straightforward but inefficient. There are two major problems preventing data encryption method from developing efficient techniques: 1) The order is not preserved in the encrypted domain. 2) Although homomorphic encryption makes it possible to perform arithmetic operations on encrypted data [40], the complexity of its computation grows enormously with the number of operations needed to perform on the cipher text. Labels are used to find the candidate tuples which can be Max/Median/Median and they are sent to the data source.

Then, the data source decrypts the incoming tuples and finds the answer. Therefore, the amount of computation and communication depends on the size of the superset and the size is usually much bigger than the necessary (this is needed to protect the privacy). In order to execute queries Q1 and Q2, the service provider sends all the tuples satisfying the conditions of the queries such as name is John and salary is between 20 and 40. It uses labels while finding the salaries between 20 and 40. After getting these tuples, the data source decrypts them and performs the summation after that. The query response time strictly depends on the computation and communication performed and thus the number of tuples needed to execute the query.

Processing aggregation queries in our framework consists of two steps. In the first step, service providers receive the rewritten queries from the data source and perform an intermediate computation. In the second step, the data source receives the intermediate results from all of the service providers and computes the final answer. The above queries are rewritten as follows and sent to the service provider DAS_i :

- Q1: Sum/Average of the salaries of the employees whose name is $share('John', i)$.
- Q2: Sum/Average of the salaries of the employees whose salary is between $share(20, i)$ and $share(40, i)$.
- Q3: Min/Max/Median of the salaries of the employees whose name is $share('John', i)$.
- Q4: Min/Max/Median of the all salaries of the employees whose salary is between $share(20, i)$ and $share(40, i)$.

Then, DAS_i finds the tuples needed to answer these queries and performs an intermediate computation over them. We will extend our approach used in [37,38]. These intermediate results are then sent to the data source D. After getting all of these intermediate results, data source D computes the final answer. In this scheme, only the intermediate results need to be sent by service providers while a superset of the required tuples needs to be sent in data encryption method. Therefore, the communication cost is negligible e.g., sending a single value referring to the shared sum. Thus the query response time is much faster in this scheme.

5.4 Join Operations

So far in our development, we assumed data sources have only one table for the sake of the presentation and thus did not consider join operations involving multiple tables. We now demonstrate that our technique can be applied if these tables are related to each other through referential keys and join is based on these keys. Consider a simple schema consisting of two tables Employees (EID, Name, Lastname, Department, Salary) and Managers (EID, ManegerID, ManagerUserName, Password). A possible query may ask for the salaries of all managers. To execute this query, these two tables should be joined using the attribute EID. Our scheme can be directly applied to execute this query since join is based on two attributes which are from the same domain and our polynomials are constructed for each domain not for each attribute. Therefore, this join can be done by the service provider at the service provider site. However, if a join is based on two attributes from different domains such as Name and ManagerUserName, then the proposed approach cannot be used for this kind of joins. Thus, the query asking for the salaries of the managers whose name is the same as the ManagerUserName cannot be answered with the proposed scheme. Such extensions and generalizations will be the focus of our proposed research.

In the same vein, if we need to compare two attributes from different domains to execute a query, the proposed technique cannot be applied. For example, a query asking for employees whose salary is 10 times their ages cannot be answered efficiently with our technique. On the other hand, a query asking for the employees whose salary is more than the salary of their managers can be executed efficiently. Furthermore, a query asking for the employees whose salary is 2 times the salary of their managers can be executed efficiently too. The execution of these queries are straightforward with the basic methods. In order to answer all kinds of queries efficiently with the proposed technique, we need to represent all attributes with a *universal domain*. If we had such a domain, we can compare all attributes with each other and join tables based on any subset of the attributes. Exploring the possibility of defining a universal domain will be also be a subject of our research investigation.

6   Extensions

6.1   Different Types of Data

We have considered only numeric attributes so far and the proposed technique is for numeric attributes. Of particular interest is the question of representing non-numeric data, and potentially compressed data. We will now illustrate a simple approach for demonstrating how to apply our scheme for non-numeric attributes. In particular, we need to convert them to numeric attributes. For example, the attribute name length of 5 characters(i.e., VARCHAR(5)), can be represented as a numeric attribute although it is in fact a non-numeric attribute. For the sake of this discussion, assume the characters in names can be one of the letters in the English alphabet and they can be shorter than 5 characters. Thus, the regular expression for this attribute is $(A|B|....|Z|*)^5$ where $*$ represents blank. For instance, name "ABC" is rewritten as "ABC**" while name "FATIH" is rewritten as "FATIH" (because it already has 5 characters). The name attribute consists of a combination of 27 possible characters which are enumerated $(* = 0, A = 1, B = 2, C = 3..., Z = 26)$. and thus, each name can represent a number in a number system of base 27. For example, name "ABC**" can be rewritten as $(12300)_{27}$ which corresponds to 21998878 in decimals. With this simple enumeration technique, non-numeric attributes can be converted into numeric attributes and then the proposed outsourcing technique can directly be applied. With the proposed enumeration technique execution of widely used queries over non-numeric attributes can be handled easily. For example, a query asking for employees whose name starts with "AB" or a query asking employees whose name is between "Albert" and "Jack" can be converted into range queries and executed with the range query processing technique discussed earlier.

6.2   Database Updates

Although our discussion so far has focused on database queries, we would like to note that the proposed techniques are also applicable for database updates. An update would involve retrieving the shares corresponding to the tuples that need to be updated by using the querying approaches discussed above. The actual values for the tuples are reconstructed at the client, and the relevant updates are performed. A new polynomial is constructed and the new shares are distributed to all the service providers. Alternatively, lazy updates as well as incremental updating of values could be incorporated to reduce the communication overhead.

6.3   Fault-Tolerance

As we alluded earlier, the secret sharing method does provide some level of fault-tolerance and data availability in the presence of failures. There are two issues related to fault tolerance: 1) Service availability and 2) Malicious service providers. Both of these issues are very important in using database services. In our scheme, a polynomial of degree $k - 1$ is used to divide the secret and thus k shares and parties are needed to compute the secret. Therefore, in the secret sharing scheme if k of the n service providers are available, the queries can be answered using the shares coming from these service providers. Another important problem is dealing with malicious service providers. These malicious service providers may corrupt the shares they store (intentionally or unintentionally). Therefore, there must be a mechanism to detect the malicious behaviors and to execute queries correctly in spite of their existence.

Malicious behavior is closely related to the issue of query correctness as discussed in the introduction. We argue that indeed the secret sharing method can be made robust in the presence of malicious database service providers. Consider the case when in response to a query, each of the n service providers send their shares or intermediate results to the data source. Then the data source solves the linear system and computes the secret values which are the answer of the queries. The main challenges in a malicious environment is that a service provider may lie while processing queries (perhaps because it has been compromised). In that case, the result of the query will not be correct. We consider n service providers where t of them can be malicious. In this case, receiving k shares is not sufficient, since t of the malicious service providers could have sent shares. Therefore, $k + t$ shares are needed for retrieve the data. However, if the number of trustworthy service providers is less than $k + t$, the data cannot be retrieved. Therefore, the number of trustworthy service providers, $n - t$, should be more than $k + t$. Then, the following relation between k, t and n has to be satisfied to ensure correct decisions: $k + t \leq n - t$, i.e., $k \leq n - 2t$.

In the case of aggregation queries, each of the n service providers aggregate their shares and send the result to the query poser. Then the query poser solves the linear system and computes the aggregated value. Since the results coming from service providers are k consistent (i.e, any k of n equations give the same value for the aggregate), solving the linear system for any k of them is sufficient if all service providers are honest. However, in a hostile environment some of the service providers could be malicious and could send incorrect values, thus solving one linear system of k equations is not sufficient. There are $\binom{n}{k}$ different possible groups of linear systems that could be used to find the aggregate. If there are $n - t$ honest service providers, then the solutions of $\binom{n-t}{k}$ linear systems would give the same value, which is the answer of the query. However, any other linear system with at least one malicious service provider would give a different value. Two different linear systems $Ax_1 = a$ and $Bx_2 = b$, produce the same solution, i.e., $x_1 = x_2$, and $x_1 = x_2$ if $b = BA^{-1}a$. The probability of the solution of two linear systems to be the same is equal to the probability of getting this b with randomly chosen numbers, which is $1/|Dom|^k$. This is because service providers do not know the matrices A and B. The probability of two sets of results coming from service providers giving the same incorrect value is infinitely small for large domains. We plan to use this property to deal with malicious behaviors and query correctness in the context of secure data outsourcing framework. In particular, we will explore methods for (1) increasing fault-tolerance, (2) identifying malicious behavior and (3) verifying the correctness of query responses.

6.4 Management of Private and Public Data

Once data has been stored at a database service provider, a user may not only want to query his/her own private data, but possibly some public data provided by the database service provider. In fact, the database service provider can thus provide a value added incentive: not only storing the client's private data, but also providing seamless access and integration with a large repository of public data. For example, a client's data may contain her private collection of friends, including information such as phone numbers, addresses, etc. The server may have a database of restaurants and their addresses. The client can exploit the public data to request restaurants that are close to a friend's house, without revealing any private information about the friend, i.e., their name, address, phone number, etc. The combining or *mash-up* of public and private data is especially pertinent in the context of applications arising from national security. Consider the case of an agency such as the FBI that tracks suspicious individuals. Now consider many other public/private agencies such as the TSA that need to correlate the travelers at San Francisco International Airport with the FBI List. This example illustrates the need for *secure mash-up* of public and private data. This problem has recently been addressed in the more limited context of private data stored in a smart USB key [27]. The problem of executing database queries on both private and public data in the context of data outsourcing at database service providers is left as future work.

6.5 Efficiency, Usability and Security Tradeoffs

The proposed privacy preserving data outsourcing methodology is based on Shamir's secret sharing algorithm. Started by Shamir [32] and Blakley [41] independently, the research on secret sharing schemes is quite rich. According to Stinson [42], there were about 68 papers on secret sharing schemes in 1992, and more than 200 papers in 1998. Under Shamir's model, a group of entities with conflicting interests cooperate. More advanced secret sharing algorithms address a variety of issues such as access structures which are methodologies determining which subsets of players should be used to compute the secret and which subsets should not. Furthermore, issues regarding the verifiability properties of the secrets by the players or whether the players or even the dealer is malicious or just curious but honest are also addressed. In a way, any of the newer schemes are "better" than Shamir's scheme according to some criterion. For our purposes, we believe such schemes are not needed. We believe Shamir's secret sharing scheme is sufficient to solve most of the privacy issues in data outsourcing. What we care deeply about is that there is perfect secrecy (in the information theoretic sense), i.e., the participants receive and provide the shares but learn absolutely nothing about the secret; Shamir's scheme provides that for us. That does not mean, however, it is the most usable and efficient scheme even for our purposes. The first observation we make is the secret sharing polynomial in Shamirs scheme is defined over a finite field $GF(p)$, and thus, all arithmetic computations (additions, subtractions, multiplications, and inversions) are performed *modulo p* where p is a prime number. Shamir suggests a 16-bit prime number, which provides 64,000 shares, which is plenty for many applications. The arithmetic *modulo p* however is not efficient arithmetic; particularly multiplications and inversions are expensive. Each time a secret is distributed or collected (by computation) such computations need to be performed which will be costly. It would much more efficient if instead of *mod p* arithmetic, we perform *mod 2* or *mod* 2^{32} arithmetic which are more efficiently performed in general-purpose computers. It was shown by McEliece and Sarwate [43] that in fact a secret sharing scheme with parameters $[k - 1, n]$ is equivalent to a $[n + 1, k]$ Reed-Solomon code. This has provided a new avenue for creating secret sharing schemes in which one relies on maximum distance separable codes. Furthermore, arithmetic over $GF(2)$ and elliptic curves over $GF(q)$ are also possibilities. For example, secret sharing schemes over arbitrary Abelian groups employ polynomials degree $log(n)$ where every participant gets approximately $log(n)$ shares [44]. In some cases, the information rate is suboptimal. We would like to investigate the efficiency properties of secret sharing schemes in order to find the optimal one for a given architecture, whose basic parameters are the number of data outsourcing centers and the communication latency and throughput of the network connecting them. We believe engineering aspects of secret sharing is an important component in our research. In this paper, we have proposed the secret sharing schemes as a privacy-preserving tool for data outsourcing because we think encryption is an inefficient mechanism for achieving privacy in large distributed (and outsourced) data bases. While implementing secret sharing schemes, we need to determine a family of secret sharing methods, which are engineered for the particular scenarios they are being used for and thus would be the most efficient.

7   Concluding Remarks

Secure data outsourcing or data management service is complimentary to the notion of data centers in that it will enable enterprises to outsource both application processing as well as data management to external entities and thus leveraging from economies of scale resulting in significant efficiencies in the Information Technology infrastructures. In this paper, we have presented a scalable secure and privacy-preserving framework for data outsourcing in the cloud. Instead of encryption, which is computationally expensive, we used distribution on multiple data provider sites and information theoretically proven secret-sharing algorithms as the basis for privacy preserving outsourcing. Our approach is also very practical in that it only retrieves the required tuples for answering a query. We plan to extend our framework to support all kinds of data operations, be fault tolerant and be able to query on both private and public data.

References

1. Hacigumus, H., Iyer, B.R., Li, C., Mehrotra, S.: Executing SQL over encrypted data in the database service provider model. In: SIGMOD Conference (2002), http://citeseer.ist.psu.edu/hacigumus02executing.html
2. Hore, B., Mehrotra, S., Tsudik, G.: A privacy-preserving index for range queries. In: Proc. of the 30th Int'l. Conference on Very Large Databases VLDB, pp. 720–731 (2004)
3. Agrawal, R., Kiernan, J., Srikant, R., Xu, Y.: Order preserving encryption for numeric data. In: SIGMOD 2004: Proceedings of the, ACM SIGMOD International Conference on Management of Data, pp. 563–574. ACM Press, New York (2004)
4. Aggarwal, G., Bawa, M., Ganesan, P., Garcia-Molina, H., Kenthapadi, K., Motwani, R., Srivastava, U., Thomas, D., Xu, Y.: Two can keep a secret: A distributed architecture for secure database services. In: CIDR, pp. 186–199 (2005)
5. Kantarcıoğlu, M., Clifton, C.: Security issues in querying encrypted data. In: Jajodia, S., Wijesekera, D. (eds.) Data and Applications Security 2005. LNCS, vol. 3654, pp. 325–337. Springer, Heidelberg (2005)
6. Hore, B., Mehrotra, S., Tsudik, G.: A privacy-preserving index for range queries. In: Proceedings of the International Conference on Very Large Data Bases (2004)
7. Li, J., Omiecinski, E.R.: Efficiency and security trade-off in supporting range queries on encrypted databases. In: Jajodia, S., Wijesekera, D. (eds.) Data and Applications Security 2005. LNCS, vol. 3654, pp. 69–83. Springer, Heidelberg (2005)
8. Shmueli, E., Waisenberg, R., Elovici, Y., Gudes, E.: Designing secure indexes for encrypted databases. In: Jajodia, S., Wijesekera, D. (eds.) Data and Applications Security 2005. LNCS, vol. 3654, pp. 54–68. Springer, Heidelberg (2005)
9. Yang, Z., Zhong, S., Wright, R.: Privacy-preserving queries on encrypted data. In: Gollmann, D., Meier, J., Sabelfeld, A. (eds.) ESORICS 2006. LNCS, vol. 4189, pp. 479–495. Springer, Heidelberg (2006)
10. Kushilevitz, E., Ostrovsky, R.: Replication is not needed: Single database, computationally-private information retrieval. In: Proceedings of the FOCS (1997)
11. Chor, B., Goldreich, O., Kushilevitz, E., Sudan, M.: Private infomation retrieval. Journal of the ACM 45(6), 965–982 (1998)
12. Stern, J.: A new and efficient all-or-nothing disclosure of secrets protocol. In: Ohta, K., Pei, D. (eds.) ASIACRYPT 1998. LNCS, vol. 1514, pp. 357–371. Springer, Heidelberg (1998)
13. Kushilevitz, E., Ostrovsky, R.: One-way trapdoor permutations are sufficient for non-trivial single-server private information retrieval. In: Preneel, B. (ed.) EUROCRYPT 2000. LNCS, vol. 1807, p. 104. Springer, Heidelberg (2000)
14. Cachin, C., Micali, S., Stadler, M.: Computationally private information retrieval with polylogarithmic communication. In: Stern, J. (ed.) EUROCRYPT 1999. LNCS, vol. 1592, p. 402. Springer, Heidelberg (1999)
15. Chang, Y.: Single database private information retrieval with logarithmic communication (2004)
16. Sion, R., Carbunar, B.: On the computational practicality of private information retrieval. In: Proceedings of the Networks and Distributed Systems Security (2007)
17. Devambu, P., Gertz, M., Martel, C., Stubblebine, S.: Authentic third-party data publication. In: Proceedings of the IFIP Workshop on Database Security (2000)
18. Mykletun, E., Narasimha, M., Tsudik, G.: Authentiction and integrity in outsourced databases. In: Proceedings of the ISOC Symposium on Network and Distributed Systems Security (2004)
19. Sion, R.: Query execution assurance for outsourced database. In: Proceedings of the Interntional Conference on Very Large Data Bases (VLDB 2005) (2005)

20. Pang, H., Jain, A., Ramamritham, K., Tan, K.: Verifying completeness of relational query resultts in data publishing. In: Proceedings of the ACM International Conference on Management of Data (SIGMOD 2005) (2005)
21. Narasimha, M., Tsudik, G.: Authentication of outsourced databases using signature aggregation and chaining. In: Li Lee, M., Tan, K.-L., Wuwongse, V. (eds.) DASFAA 2006. LNCS, vol. 3882, pp. 420–436. Springer, Heidelberg (2006)
22. Sion, R.: Secure data outsourcing. In: Proceedings of the 33rd International Conference on Very Large Data Bases, pp. 1431–1432 (2007)
23. Agrawal, R., Asonov, D., Srikant, R.: Enabling sovereign information sharing using web services. In: SIGMOD Conference, pp. 873–877 (2004)
24. Agrawal, R., Evfimievski, A., Srikant, R.: Information sharing across private databases. In: Proc. of the 2003 ACM SIGMOD International Conference on on Management of Data, pp. 86–97 (2003)
25. Ge, T., Zdonik, S.B.: Answering aggregation queries in a secure system model. In: Proceedings of the 33rd International Conference on Very Large Data Bases, pp. 519–530 (2007)
26. di Vimercati, S.D.C., Foresti, S., Jajodia, S., Paraboschi, S., Samarati, P.: Over-encryption: Management of access control evolution on outsourced data. In: Proceedings of the 33rd International Conference on Very Large Data Bases, pp. 123–134 (2007)
27. Anciaux, N., Benzine, M., Bouganim, L., Pucheral, P., Shasha, D.: Ghostdb: querying visible and hidden data without leaks. In: Proceedings of the ACM SIGMOD International Conference on Management of Data, pp. 677–688 (2007)
28. Scannapieco, M., Figotin, I., Bertino, E., Elmagarmid, A.K.: Privacy preserving schema and data matching. In: Proceedings of the ACM SIGMOD International Conference on Management of Data, pp. 653–664 (2007)
29. Ostrovsky, R., Shoup, V.: Private Information Storage. In: Proceedings of the STOC (1997)
30. Gertner, Y., Ishai, Y., Kushilevitz, E., Malkin, T.: Protecting data privacy in private information retrieval schemes. In: Proc. of the Thirtieth Annual ACM Symposium on Theory of Computing, pp. 151–160. ACM Press, New York (1998)
31. Naor, M., Pinkas, B.: Oblivious transfer and polynomial evaluation. In: Proc. of the Thirty-First Annual ACM Symposium on Theory of Computing, pp. 245–254. ACM Press, New York (1999)
32. Shamir, A.: How to share a secret. Commun. ACM 22(11), 612–613 (1979)
33. Ostrovsky, R., Yung, M.: How to withstand mobile virus attacks (extended abstract). In: PODC 1991: Proceedings of the Tenth Annual ACM Symposium on Principles of Distributed Computing, pp. 51–59 (1991)
34. Herzberg, A., Jarecki, S., Krawczyk, H., Yung, M.: Proactive secret sharing or: How to cope with perpetual leakage. In: Coppersmith, D. (ed.) CRYPTO 1995. LNCS, vol. 963, pp. 339–352. Springer, Heidelberg (1995)
35. Jarecki, S.: Proactive secret sharing and public key cryptosystems. Master's thesis, MIT (1995), http://citeseer.ist.psu.edu/jarecki95proactive.html
36. Zhou, L., Schneider, F.B., Renesse, R.V.: APSS: Proactive secret sharing in asynchronous systems. ACM Transactions on Information System Security 8(3), 259–286 (2005)
37. Emekci, F., Agrawal, D.P., El Abbadi, A.: ABACUS: A distributed middleware for privacy preserving data sharing across private data warehouses. In: Alonso, G. (ed.) Middleware 2005. LNCS, vol. 3790, pp. 21–41. Springer, Heidelberg (2005)
38. Emekçi, F., Agrawal, D., El Abbadi, A., Gulbeden, A.: Privacy preserving query processing using third parties. In: ICDE, p. 27 (2006)
39. Aggarwal, G., Mishra, N., Pinkas, B.: Privacy-preserving computation of the k'th-ranked element. In: Cachin, C., Camenisch, J.L. (eds.) EUROCRYPT 2004. LNCS, vol. 3027, pp. 40–55. Springer, Heidelberg (2004)

40. Gentry, C.: Fully homomorphic encryption using ideal lattices. In: STOC 2009: Proceedings of the 41st Annual ACM Symposium on Theory of Computing, pp. 169–178 (2009)
41. Blakley, G.R.: Safeguarding cryptographic keys. In: Proceedings of the National Computer Conference, American Federation of Information Processing Societies, vol. 48, pp. 313–317 (1979)
42. Stinson, D., Wei, R.: Bibliography on secret sharing schemes, http://www.cacr.math.uwaterloo.ca/dstinson/ssbib.html
43. McEliece, R.J., Sarwate, D.V.: On sharing secrets and reed-solomon codes. Communications of ACM 24(9), 583–584 (1981)
44. Cramer, R., Fehr, S.: Optimal black-box secret sharing over arbitrary abelian groups. In: Yung, M. (ed.) CRYPTO 2002. LNCS, vol. 2442, pp. 272–287. Springer, Heidelberg (2002)

Security Plans for SaaS

Marco D. Aime, Antonio Lioy, Paolo C. Pomi, and Marco Vallini

Politecnico di Torino
Dip. Automatica e Informatica
Torino, Italy
security@polito.it
http://security.polito.it

Abstract. The SaaS paradigm offers several advantages, mostly in terms of direct and indirect cost reduction, but its deployment must be carefully planned to avoid several security pitfalls. In this chapter we analyse the security of various SaaS architectures, from pure multi-tenant SaaS to advanced outsourcing services and virtualisation as a service.

We first analyse the SaaS-specific threats, then we discuss a portfolio of best practices for mitigating these threats, and finally we introduce a conceptual framework to formalise security-related requirements associated to the SaaS context.

Our work is mainly intended to help SaaS customers in understanding security issues of SaaS and planning adequate countermeasures for risk reduction.

1 Introduction

The main advantage of SaaS consists in outsourcing to a service provider the management of hardware devices, software licenses and configuration tasks. Obviously, these costs need to be shared among different customers, to be profitable. SaaS introduces some changes in classical security management and raises some additional security issues. On one hand, small entities can adopt strong security and dependability solutions that would otherwise be too expensive for a single small entity. On the other hand, customers loose the direct control over some parts of their information system and are scared by the consequent menaces caused by the outsourcing. Furthermore, sharing the same resources among different tenants creates serious concerns. Consequently, a SaaS provider must offer and demonstrate convincing security solutions for strong protection of its services and access links against external attackers, for effective independence and isolation among the customers instances of the service, and to allow customers to verify the effective application of contractual conditions.

In this chapter, we first analyse the security threats affecting the SaaS paradigm and then we suggest appropriate security controls to increase the security and reliability of SaaS. Finally, we present an approach to asses SaaS security, and define the responsibilities of the customer and the provider in case of failure despite the adoption of security solution for risk mitigation.

D. Agrawal et al. (Eds.): Information and Software as Services, LNBIP 74, pp. 81–111, 2011.

2   SaaS Threat Model

SaaS involves different actors, namely customers and providers: the first use the (application) service provided by the latter.

A SaaS customer generally uses a multi-level / multi-lateral security model to remotely access the service. For example, a company will have different users accessing the software with different privileges.

A SaaS service can be offered to a single customer, but often is designed with a multi-tenant architecture, where the same service is offered to multiple customers.

Although a SaaS application appears as a monolithic piece of software to the customer, it can actually be implemented with a multi-provider architecture. The provider could fully host applications with its own data centre, or in turn could exploit resources from other parties. For example, a provider could use hardware resources (computational power or data storage) from a third-party data centre. Therefore, when studying the security of a SaaS service, we must consider four threat sources: the customer-provider interaction, the cross interactions between different customers of the same provider, the interactions between the SaaS provider and sub-providers, and finally external attackers targeting any part of the SaaS service. In the following sections we discuss these threats grouping them into two categories: threats originated by the provider and threats born from the SaaS architecture.

Note that we do not analyse general threats that could affect any software independently of its SaaS nature (as a malicious user exploiting an application vulnerability for privilege escalation) but we consider those cases where the SaaS paradigm influences the exploitability or impact of these threats.

2.1   Provider-Originated Threats

There are intentional and unintentional threats that can originate by the SaaS provider, as it can behave dishonestly or just make operational errors.

Customer data violation. As long as application data are stored at (or at least accessed by) the provider, it is able to perform arbitrary actions on them. Possible threats are unauthorised read, unauthorised modification, forging and deletion. Therefore, as in any other outsourcing technique, SaaS requires a reasonably trusted provider as well as strategies for data protection to mitigate the exposure and impact of this threat.

Unreliable computation. A provider can alter computations and give unreliable service to the customer. Moreover, a provider can perform unauthorised/unsolicited actions impersonating the customer. For example, think of a service that supplies marketing information: the provider could collude with another customer (a competitor) and modify the service to return forged results, or just a subset of the correct results to benefit the competitor. A similar scenario could involve a service that performs elaborations useful for prototype analysis:

the provider could modify the service to randomly return wrong results to slow down the development process of one customer.

Given these threats, SaaS should be equipped with integrity verification functions. However, this is not sufficient and redundancy strategies (e.g. performing duplicate computations and comparing results between different providers) should be considered as well.

Misbehaviour hiding. A provider may tamper with data, actions, or events related to SaaS execution to hide its – intentional or unintentional – violation of contractual conditions. For example, a provider may forge log files or tamper with audit systems to hide violations of SLA, QoS, or agreed isolation mechanisms. On another hand, a provider can perform unauthorised actions in place of the customer, tampering the auditing systems to attribute these actions to the customer.

It is therefore clear that correct log and monitoring data must be available and usable as a proof in case of dispute about satisfaction of the contractual conditions or liability of performed actions. Consequently, SaaS should always be implemented with proper auditing functions (e.g. log files, monitoring systems) capable to provide trustworthy and non-repudiable information about SaaS execution. Additionally, the "separation of duties" principle should be followed, with the auditor being a different entity from the provider.

2.2   Architectural Threats

Even assuming reliable provider behaviour, the migration from a self-managed infrastructure to SaaS creates risks affecting customers data, provider-side computations, and provider-customer communications.

Manipulation of shared resources. The SaaS model implies that some resources are shared among several customers. They could be just hardware resources (in implementations based on virtualisation) as well as distributed storage services, multi-user software, and even application processes (when following a pure multi-tenant paradigm).

Customer data stealing or tampering is a more severe problem in SaaS than in a traditional environment because the provider typically hosts and manages data of different tenants. Furthermore, to minimise hardware and energy costs, the provider likely stores different customers' data on the same shared servers. Thus, if the provider is unable to guarantee complete data isolation and protection, a customer could steal data belonging to other tenants (such as an innovative project) or modify data to compromise their integrity. Having a shared platform and shared data highly increases the effectiveness of common traditional attacks, such as session hijacking, cross-site scripting, and SQL or command injection Less sophisticated attacks may aim to cause just an application or system crash to affect data availability or randomly damaging data.

Network access threats. Adopting SaaS typically implies migrating from an Intranet-based environment to an Internet-based one. Since Internet is outside the control domain of both the provider and the customer, this raises specific security issues.

Common network threats (e.g. sniffing, tampering) affect communication confidentiality and integrity. Furthermore, also communication availability is negatively influenced by the use of Internet, as it is basically a best-effort network and - additionally - faults or attacks might decrease or block the availability of the service and thus impact on customer activities. Therefore, mechanisms to protect SaaS access should be considered as well as topologies that minimise the impact of network unavailability.

Authentication. Since a SaaS application is accessed via network, access control is mandatory and cannot be based on network addresses (as sometimes happens in a Intranet) due to address spoofing.

Not all possible authentication architectures are suitable for access control in SaaS. For instance, sharing the same authentication mechanism between SaaS and non-Saas applications should be absolutely avoided as there is the risk that a provider gets hold of a general-purpose authentication credential, valid not only for the SaaS application but also for other customer applications not hosted on this provider.

In fact authentication and authorisation are functions that should be separated from the application logic when moving to the SaaS paradigm. They must become self-contained and managed sub-services, acting as external components of the SaaS application. This means that they may be provisioned independently of the main application software, for example hosted at a different provider or - even better - directly managed by the customer with a single-sign-on (SSO) schema.

Bad subcontractors. Since a SaaS provider may actually use sub-providers to offer its own service, there are hidden dependencies that are not evident to the customer. The simplest example is a customer that has contracted two different providers for the same service to increase its availability, but actually the availability is not increased if both providers use the same sub-contractor for the hardware platform. Also the interactions between the sub-providers are a risk factor if not adequately protected. Therefore the internal architecture of the provider should be not only well designed and protected, but also exposed to the customer for his own risk analysis.

3   SaaS Security Mechanisms and Best Practices

Security is of utmost importance for widespread SaaS adoption, given the threats listed in the previous section. On one hand, potential customers are interested to adopt SaaS solutions to reduce their costs, but before doing so they need strong warranties on the reliability and trustworthiness of this architectural change. On the other hand, high security can create a competitive advantage for providers to attract more customers. In this section we analyse the available security controls and best practices that can be adopted to mitigate the SaaS risks, considering both these perspectives.

3.1   Service Redundancy

In order to protect the system against availability threats, redundant architectures are commonly implemented to guarantee service also in case of an
infrastructural failure. SaaS easily permits implementing different redundancy
schemas.

When application management is fully delegated to the service provider, the
implementation details of service redundancy are not decided by the customer,
but disclosing them helps in raising trust in the provider. In fact, detailing the
internal architecture of a provider is a good step to persuade customers in trust-
ing and adopting the provider's services, may be after an evaluation by a security
expert under non-disclosure agreement.

In other cases, like in Infrastructure As A Service (IAAS), the provider manages only the basic platform and customers directly select which (virtual) machines they need and configure their interconnection topology. Therefore in this
case the customers directly manage dependability techniques, including redundant (virtual) machines and redundant links.

Finally, SaaS permits implementing a novel way to replication: *provider replication*, where there are more providers of the same solution and they are used
simultaneously to enhance application dependability.

Service redundancy is typically implemented with physical or logical replication, depending by the type of attack/failure to prevent.

Physical replication implies the replication of critical hardware elements. In
some cases, it requires just server replication, whereas in more critical situation it
involves whole network trunks or entire data centres. Obviously, these solutions
are used to mitigate risks related of hardware faults and typically only providers
can adopt them, to improve the offered dependability level. Customers can adopt
physical replication only by the provider replication technique, but also in this
case, the problem of *bad subcontractors* (Sec.2.2) may decrease the effectiveness
of this approach.

On another hand, *logical replication* implies the allocation of more instances
or virtual machines for the same process, without requiring different hardware
devices, thus reducing also costs and energy consumption. This approach is used
to protect the system from logical attacks, like DoS (Denial-of-Service), and to
reduce timeouts when process switching is needed due to a hardware failure. This
solutions knows a wide application in SaaS infrastructures. The replication may
be implemented at virtual machine (VM) level, both by the customers (that
benefit from reduced costs of a VM with respect to a physical machine) and
by the service providers, that can replicate machines hosting the service. The
replication of VM for providers can be performed in two different ways: balancing
the requests among all the customers or, as we discuss later, assigning a VM per
customer (thus offering a better warranty on the SLA, Sec.3.3)

One common problem in service replication regards correctly routing the requests for a single service to the different parallel servants [7]. The simpler solution
consists in performing address translation, by translating the same service URL
to different servants URLs, in order to assign the clients to different servants, for

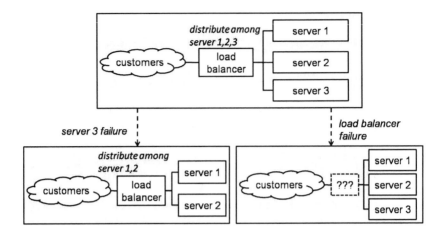

Fig. 1. Replication with central equipment

example with round-robin DNS or NAT. Otherwise ad-hoc devices (load balancers) can redirect in a transparent manner each request to the servants and possibly redirect back the servants' answers. Note that in all these cases the component responsible for this translation becomes a critical part of the solution, as shown in Fig. 1. Finally, DNS-based address translation allows clients caching translated addresses and continuing to work without continuously accessing the translator, whereas the other approaches cannot do this. On another hand, in case of failure of a servant, the DNS-based solution is slower in propagating the change than the others.

Another approach consists in statically configuring different servants to answer only to the request of a portion of the possible clients. For example (Fig. 2), configuring the N servants to answer only those requests whose client address is IP mod $N = x$, where $0 < x < (N - 1)$ and x is different for every servant. Of course, in case of faults, the value of N must be properly updated. In this solution, the distribution of the work is done in a statical manner and cannot take into account the changes in the workload.

Also the task of distributing requests can be managed either by the provider or by the customer, depending upon who manages the replication. Customers must be aware that if they manage the replication by themselves then they must consider the balancing component as the weakest link of the chain. When balancing via the DNS, it is also feasible delegating this task to a different provider, whereas in other cases the balancing task is typically under the customer or provider control.

3.2   Diversity Implementation

While service replication prevents damages caused by "instance faults" (i.e. faults of a specific software instance), diversity implementation [2] is the answer to issues originating from "class faults", defects that are present in all the instances of an object. The main class faults in information systems are *software vulnerabilities*

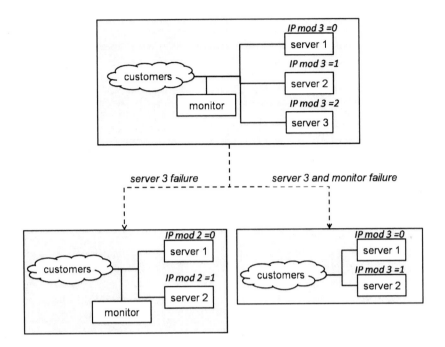

Fig. 2. Replication without central equipment

[31] and programming bugs. Furthermore, common software problems are exacerbated by SaaS, since it often uses Virtual Machine Monitors (VMM) that exhibit several security issues [9].

Diversity implementation may occur at different levels of the system, from hardware architecture, to operating system, and up to application software. It consists in using two or more different implementations of the same requirements, to mitigate risks related to implementation defects, that could be used, for example, in vulnerability exploitation.

SaaS technologies allow diversity implementation at different levels, more widely than in traditional architectures. On one hand, the service provider can internally apply this technique for its own infrastructure and hosting services, like in non-SaaS situations. On the other hand, customers could exploit these techniques when there are available compatible service components from the same or different service providers. The provider could offer alternative implementations of the same functionalities. Indeed, this approach is quite feasible for IAAS, offering different OSes and VMMs. On the contrary, using this approach at higher levels is more difficult because would require creating different applications implementing the same business-level functionality. However, also in this case, the provider could follow this path and invest in this solution - for example, for infrastructural components - to attract more customers.

If there is the chance to have an application service offered by different providers, customer can exploit this technique too, to prevent the unreliable computation issues. For example, we can imagine to have different SaaS providers offering a search engine. Using only one provider implies a strong trust on its results. In fact, if the information returned is wrong, the customer cannot verify it. Conversely, it is possible to use more than one engine at the same time, combining their results in different ways based on the customer's requirements. It is possible accepting only the information that all the providers confirm, for a maximum correctness/integrity of the data, or on the contrary merging all the data to maximise the results breadth. The Byzantine General problem [19] supposes to have N different sources and f of them are wrong: to have the warranty that a data is correct, it is necessary that $N \leq 3f$. Therefore, under the hypothesis of single fault, three providers are needed to thwart this attack.

Depending on the nature of the attack that we want to prevent, we use in different manner this technique.

When using several implementations in parallel, the application data are more vulnerable since it is sufficient a single vulnerability among the different implementations to attack the system. However, as a payback, to cause a complete denial of service, it is necessary finding an exploitable vulnerability in each implementation: consequently, it is more resistant from the availability point of view. Fig. 3 illustrates this diversity solution.

Conversely, it is common using replicated security devices in series to enable the "defence in depth" strategy. For example, this is widely applied for perimeter defence where a network is protected by two firewalls in a sequence: to penetrate such

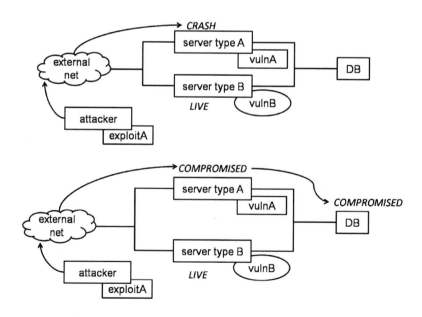

Fig. 3. Diversity implementation of application equipment

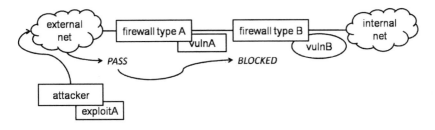

Fig. 4. Diversity implementation of security equipment

a network, the attacker must find and exploit a vulnerability for each device. In practice, since it is difficult having more implementations of the same application, this approach is limited to security devices put in series. This case is exemplified in Fig. 4.

3.3   Isolation

Isolation is the typical countermeasure against fault and attack propagation [8]. Since SaaS architectures imply the sharing of resources among different tenant, inter-tenant attacks and attacks propagation are one of the main obstacle to SaaS wide application. Consequently, the SaaS platform must guarantee a reasonable level of isolation, that can be implemented at logical or physical level, with different costs and different strengths.

Logical isolation is performed with configuration strategies, without any modification to the underlying hardware platform. It encompasses several techniques to separate the tasks of different customers of the same provider: spawning a dedicated instance of the SaaS module, exploiting virtualisation by allocating a dedicated virtual machines, or using VPN (Virtual Private Network) and VLAN (Virtual LAN) technologies to separate network trunks. On the other hand, *physical isolation* requires reserving actual dedicated physical machines or network trunks, isolated via firewalls. It is evident that logical solutions are weaker but cheaper, whereas physical ones are stronger but more expensive. Furthermore, logical isolation can be configured and exploited at run-time, while physical isolation must be planned at design time, requiring proper hardware devices and longer times for implementation and modifications (in the case of new customers).

Isolation can be applied into two orthogonal directions: *vertically*, among the different parts of the SaaS application, and *horizontally*, among the different tenants of the same SaaS application, as shown in Fig. 5.

Vertical isolation can be considered as an implementation of *multilevel security*, and it is a protection for the SaaS service against external attackers. In other words, it means isolating service components from each other. Virtualisation is a cheap technique to provide vertical isolation: we spawn virtual machines, providing isolation among them by means of virtualisation platforms like Xen, VMware, or VirtualPC, without using hardware elements. Physical approaches

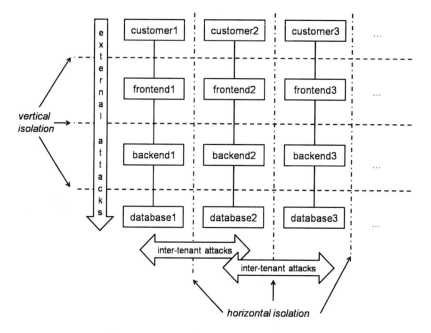

Fig. 5. Vertical and horizontal isolation

are more consolidated [13] and largely adopted in general. In fact, separating application components onto different machines mitigates fault propagation from one component to another via the execution environment or the shared resources. Moreover, we can also achieve isolation by means of firewalls between different network trunks, so mitigating the risk of network fault propagation. Physical solutions are very suitable for implementing vertical isolation, since the service architecture is known at design time.

On another hand, horizontal division is strictly related to the classical *multilateral security* concept [1]. In fact, since one of the most relevant menace is the multi-tenancy nature of SaaS architectures, a strong isolation among tenants is an attractive solution to create trust in the provider environment. Physical solutions are not suitable for horizontal isolation, since the number of tenants is typically dynamic. Furthermore, SaaS economic return is based on resource sharing, that conflicts with the physical isolation approaches. On the countrary, logical approaches can be applied at run-time and dynamically changed. A first mechanism consists in having different service instances for different customers. In case of a multi-tier service, to be more effective, every service component must adopt the same solution. A dedicated virtual machine can be assigned to each tenant, in order to exploit the virtualisation platform for isolation. Then, a dedicated virtual network can be created for every customer, to prevent shared connections menaces. This solution is a particularly good match with the SaaS security requirements; in fact, virtualisation is one of the enabling technologies to protect SaaS environments.

The possible coarseness of isolation in SaaS is strongly related to the type of service under discussion. IAAS allows a VM-level isolation, while PaaS and SaaS, that expose entire applications can offer a dedicate VM for tenant, a dedicated instance per tenant, or assuring that the isolation performed by the application is enough. Even if such isolation is expensive from the SaaS provider perspective, in many cases it is necessary to be attractive for customers worried about such security issues. Furthermore, a stronger isolation can assure higher level of SaaS compliance, since the performance level offered to every tenant are less interconnected.

3.4   Channel Protection

Channel protection is mainly used to protect critical data in transit between parties over untrusted networks (e.g. the Internet) or inside a virtualised environment. We distinguish three different scenarios: site-to-site, nomadic user, and end-to-end. In the *site-to-site* scenario, two or more companies establish a virtual private network (VPN) between their gateways to link their sites. The channel is protected only among VPN gateways. In SaaS this technique finds application to protect the interactions among different (sub-)providers or between a customer and its provider. This is the case when the application is displaced at the provider while the critical data remain by the customer. In the *nomadic users* scenario, the users access remotely (via an untrusted network) the service of a provider. In this case the users protect their the access by using a VPN client to connect to the VPN gateway placed at the provider's site. Therefore the channel is protected from the user's client to the VPN gateway, independent of the network hosting the client. In a SaaS environment, the *nomadic user* VPN technique allows the users of a customer to securely access the SaaS service but, in this case, the provider is directly involved in remote access with its VPN gateway and consequently it directly manages Authentication, Authorisation and Accounting (AAA) for the customer's users. Finally in the *end-to-end* scenario the interaction between two entities is fully protected from source to destination. In SaaS this permits to displace services at different providers, with fully protected interactions irrelevant of the communication links. However the massive use of end-to-end protection channels increases the number of network connections and the overhead introduced by security protocols.

The approach selected for channel protection impacts not only security but also performance of the SaaS application. When using individual channels (as in the end-to-end or nomadic user cases) there is more flexibility and higher isolation between the tenants, but at the price of an increased number of network channels, which is usually bad in term of performance (due to the set-up/teardown time and the TCP slow start algorithm). Conversely, a site-to-site VPN approach performs better in terms of network throughput, but offers lower security due to limited coverage (only the "external" part of the channel) and no separation among the individual channels carried inside the same VPN.

Channel protection technologies. Two main technologies - IPsec and SSL/TLS - can be used to create the protected channels described in the scenarios of the previous section.

A site-to-site secure channel can be built using IPsec in tunnel mode at gateways, to establish a VPN between customer and provider, or among different (sub-)providers. An alternative approach is to create a SSL/TLS VPN (working at layer 4 of the ISO/OSI stack), more flexible and easy to configure than IPsec (e.g. OpenVPN). This is because IPsec needs to configure key exchange services that may conflict with firewall and be incompatible with address translation policies.

SSL/TLS and IPsec VPN can also be adopted in the nomadic user mode. However it is necessary to configure a VPN remote access gateway at the provider's side and each user must install and configure an individual VPN client to perform remote access and join the VPN.

More choices are available to protect interactions in the end-to-end scenario. The first class of solutions is based on a VPN-like approach, establishing a secure virtual channel end-to-end between two different parties without gateways, for example by adopting IPsec in transport mode at the end nodes. The second approach uses application protocols layered on top of a secure transport protocol, as in the case of HTTP, POP or SMTP over SSL. This has the benefit of easy configuration, as it is performed only server-side and at application level, compared to an IPsec transport channel that must be configured at OS level and at both ends (client and server).

Obviously, for best-of-breed channel security, it is also possible to carry a SSL-based application inside a site-to-site VPN channel, that provides a double line of defense and has the additional benefit of protecting the external routing too.

3.5   Access Control

Access control is very important for SaaS as its applications may be used simultaneously by several users of the same tenant and several tenants. This section discusses the approaches and the architectures to provide access control in SaaS environment.

First of all, we distinguish between access control at network and application level. When a service is outsourced, we should guarantee the same security level of the traditional environment. The adoption of network-level access controls permits to authenticate and authorise users regulating the access to the provider through an untrusted network (such as Internet). However, considering the multi-level and multi-tenancy nature of SaaS, this approach may be insufficient and not enough fine-grained to secure a SaaS application. For example let us consider an application available for two or more customers, divided into several components (services). The adoption of a separate VPN between each customer and the service provider guarantees that the services are reachable at network-level only from authorised users. However, to guarantee that only authorised users can perform tasks using the services, application-level access control mechanisms are needed.

The choice of application-level access controls should take into account scalability (as often users and services increase more rapidly than expected) and interoperability properties (because SaaS often needs interaction with different providers). A typical access control approach requires user identification (authentication) and the evaluation of the user access rights to the resources (authorisation). The application-level access controls available in traditional environments are often based on user's roles, as in RBAC (Role-Based Access Control). Typically in a single-domain system roles are assigned based on user identity. However, in a multi-level provider scenario, the adoption of RBAC is not easy because a user could need access to services of different providers and, for each of them, we should define and evaluate its identity and roles. To overcome these issues, access control mechanisms based on attributes have been developed. This approach allows to authorise a user performing an authentication based on a set of attributes (that are exchanged between the providers) rather than on user identity. In addition, it allows to define policies at a higher level by using attributes both for user identification and to regulate access to the resources.

Monolithic and distributed implementations. Traditional environments usually implement access control with a monolithic approach. Often authentication and authorisation are performed as a centralised task on a single system or, as an independent task for each system offering a service (e.g. each system has a different ACL to control access to its own resources). The key point of these approaches is that the access control is anyway performed always within the organisation borders. However, in a multi-level provider environment these approaches are not feasible because the users need access, in a transparent way (without performing a new authentication for each system), to resources which are scattered onto several providers. To satisfy this requirement, typical for grid computing, several approaches and architectures have been developed. An interesting proposal is [30] that discusses a set of architectures for accessing the grid resources without the user's identity. To satisfy SaaS access control requirements we start considering these architectures and adopting an attribute-based approach. This work considers the Service Provider (SP) as the element that offers SaaS to companies and that directly interacts with the users (tenants). The Resource Provider (RP) interacts with the SP to offers a specific service that composes the SaaS application. In addition, a SP could interact with different RPs. An Attribute Server (AS) contains information useful for authentication and authorisation and can be part of the SP. By using these basic building blocks, different architectures can be created. In the "Complete Trust" architecture, the RP relies both for authentication and authorisation on the SP, and the users are anonymous at the RP side. The SP interacts with the AS providing authorisations and negotiates resource or service with the RP masquerading this to the users. In the "Medium Trust" model, the SP only performs authentication while the RP authorises resource utilisation or service consumption. The RP relies on the SP or another third party to obtain the user's attributes. Practically, these attributes are stored into the AS and retrieved by the RP. This solution clearly separates the user's identity (evaluated at the SP) from the authorisation policies defined for consuming a service. In addition, the use of an attribute-based authorisation at the RP permits to define more fine-grained policies. For example, it is possible to differentiate service properties (as QoS or performance) for different user classes or service providers.

Displacing the access control components. The authentication and authorisation tasks may be split into three different components: Policy Enforcement Point (PEP), Policy Decision Point (PDP) and Policy Repository (PR). We consider the PEP as the point where the policy is applied, the PDP as the point where user's credentials are evaluated and the PR as the point where the policy is stored. While in traditional environments PEP, PDP and PR are deployed internally at the company, the SaaS approach introduces novel solutions to distribute these components.

First we can separate the PEP from the PDP and PR, displacing the enforcement point at the provider and the PDP/PR at the customer. As a result, the SaaS applications rely on the customer directly managing the access control policies, credentials and the related tasks. To provide network-level access control in this scenario, a VPN gateway can be used as a PEP. To provide application-level access control, the provider should host the portion of the application able to perform authentication while the customer directly manages the access control policies and users' credentials. Finally the PEP and PDP/PR interactions require protection and are therefore carried out using SSL/TLS or IPsec.

As an alternative, in a multi-provider architecture we can displace the PEP to a provider and the PDP and PR to another one. In this case, the company entirely relies on external providers and does not directly manage access control policies or credentials. The network-level access control is not affected by this change. However, adding a second provider requires to move the PDP/PR from the customer to the new provider and to secure the PEP-PDP interactions between the two providers.

Authentication and authorisation techniques. In traditional web applications, TLS secure channels are often used to protect the application-level user authentication exchange. Normally TLS is configured to only authenticate the server using its X.509 certificate and then the user credentials (as username/password) are exchanged at application level inside the secure channel. However this requires each application server to perform user authentication and would be rather difficult to apply in a SaaS environment composed by several services relying on different providers. This scenario suggests that a SaaS application needs adopting the browser-based Federated Identity Management (FIM) protocols. This introduces a third party entity, the Identity Authority (IA), that is responsible to identify the user and generate a token for consuming service at the SP. The TLS protocol is typically used to protect the data exchange among browser, IA and SP but not to identify the user. User identification is often provided by a token created via a Single Sign-On (SSO) architecture that identifies the users using a centralised authentication server (CAS) and then providing them with a token that the user can consume at the application servers to prove his identity. Several approaches have been developed to implement the FIM using the Security Assertion Markup Language (SAML); for example, the Liberty Alliance project and WS-* specifications both describe a set of protocols and profiles to implement FIM. [12] and [16] analyse the issues and propose a set of solutions to provide secure SAML Single Sign-on Browser/Artifact, one of the most important three-party authentication protocol. The major issues are (1) the browser and issuing server have no cryptographic trust relationship, and (2) weak security for the Same Origin Policy (SOP). In a few words, the first issue allows attacks to web browser to steal the authentication token and reuse it spoofing the user's identity because the token is not bound to the user's web browser. The SOP allows access from a web object (e.g. HTTP cookie) to another one that respects the same policy, or in simple words, that is part of the same application. In the web context, the same application is identified by domain name, protocol and port. However an attack to the DNS can circumvent the SOP, allowing to manipulate or steal a web object like cookies (e.g. using an XSS attack).

In particular [16] suggests to adopt the following approaches to protect the SAML single sign-on. SAML 2.0 Holder-of-Key Assertion Profile [25] describes the issuing and processing of a holder-of-key SAML assertion. This adopts a TLS client and server authentication and the SAML token is bound to the public key of the client's certificate. More in detail, the SAML token contains a Holder-of-Key assertion that includes the client's public key. As a result, the token is valid only for the user that can prove to be the owner of the associated identity, by using his private key. The Locked Same Origin Policy approach [17] suggests to take reliable security decisions on client's browser using the server's public key. The mechanism works as follows: (1) when the browser receives a cookie, it memorizes the related server's public key, and then (2) the browser sends the cookie only to the server that is able to prove its identity (presenting the same public key). The third approach is to bind the SAML token to the TLS session. In this mechanism, the server deduces that the data sent, in response to the token, is directed to the client that shares the same TLS session.

Another approach different from single sign-on and described in [5] is the TLS-Federation that adopts the TLS protocol and a client certificate authentication in federated scenario. The TLS-Federation IA exploits X.509 certificates to express the statements about user identities and supports different authentication methods (e.g. X.509 credentials, username/password, one time passwords). This approach works as follows: every time the user navigates from a service provider to another, its identity is re-established (in a transparent way for the user) performing the TLS-handshake (using a different challenge). In addition, [16] suggests that the TLS-Federation can be integrated with SAML in order to carry the token inside the X.509 client certificate.

3.6 Service Integrity

Attesting the service integrity is very important for SaaS as it allows customers to verify that the service is un-tampered when it is using their data.

The most promising solution to perform this task is the one developed by the Trusted Computing Group [33]. Trusted Computing (TC) is an emerging technology aimed to enforce a specific behaviour of computer systems and to protect the cryptographic keys used by the systems [23]. In the SaaS scenario, the most interesting TC idea consists in its ability to trustworthy measure the software components as they are executed and to report these measures to external entities. The components are identified using their digest and the report is protected by using a digital signature. Special hardware elements – called Roots of Trust (RoT) because their behaviour is trusted "a priori" – guarantee the reliability of the measurements collected and reported.

To trustworthy report the integrity measurements to an external entity, one of these roots of trust vouches for the accuracy of information in order to persuade an external verifier that the system is in the reported configuration. This is named "remote attestation".

In a SaaS scenario the provider could offer to its customers an interface to request a remote attestation of the service, whenever they want to verify its integrity. In this way, the customer can compare the integrity measurement received with the "good" one stored in advance (may be at contract time) and verify that nothing is changed and the system is untampered.

This solution is very promising and fits well with the SaaS needs, but, since it is based on specific hardware capabilities (the TPM, Trusted Platform Module) subject to some hardware attacks, a dishonest provider could physically manipulate the TPM to override the controls. Therefore a TC-based integrity solution for SaaS should always be accompanied by some reliable audit track to at least identify the hardware attacks that occurred.

3.7 Accounting and Auditing

Accounting and auditing are common tasks to track resource consumption and to identify which user performed a certain operation. However in SaaS we should consider different views of accounting and auditing for the customer and the provider, accordingly to the separation of duties (SoD) paradigm. For example, the auditor of the provider should verify that only authorised users can access the SaaS application but should not trace which operations are performed on the SaaS components. Instead this task is reserved to the auditor of the customer, that should check the operations performed by the customer's users. Thus these data should be available only for the customer as reports to verify user operations, behaviour of the outsourced application, and to take evidence of the effective quality of service (QoS). At the provider side, accountability can also be used for billing purposes, taking into account which service features are requested (e.g. at run-time) or subscribed by the customer. Log generation is a common solution to produce evidences about user operations. We can distinguish two different log types: system and network log. A base system log contains AAA information, run-time processes with state and resource consumption. Using TC-based features it is possible to extend the base system log adding integrity measures of the process images and configuration files for tracing modifications (e.g. when a process is tampered). The network log instead is useful to trace interactions among services and to detect SaaS application behaviour against defined policies. Accordingly to the separation of duties paradigm, system and network logs are split for customer and provider accountability and auditing related tasks.

Log separation. Two different solutions can be used to isolate the provider and customer logs. The simplest solution for customer logs is to share a symmetric key among the customer and the SaaS components involved in the logging tasks. These perform log operations, cipher data with the shared key and save information at the provider. The customer, using his copy of the shared key, is able to decrypt the log data and analyse them. This solution is simple but requires sharing a symmetric key and logs are recorded at the provider that generated them. To improve security while still using a single provider, we can use public and private keys. The application components cipher data using the public key of the customer, that may decrypt them using its private key. To decrease the computational tasks related to the use of asymmetric keys, application components and customer can share a symmetric key for encryption and decryption, protected using the asymmetric key approach. For example, the customer chooses a symmetric key that is ciphered with the public key of the application and sent to it for use in log encryption. A second solution improves log isolation by storing logs at another provider. As a result the application components log and send ciphered data to another provider (using one of the previous approaches). In this case the application provider only stores its own (system) logs while the application logs are stored remotely at the second provider.

3.8 Anomaly Detection

The anomaly detection task allows to monitor network traffic (e.g. bandwidth utilisation) and process behaviour to identify attacks and service availability. Monitoring and Intrusion Detection Systems (IDS), in traditional environments, are typically displaced at the internal network and related data is collected and analysed.

Anomaly detection is important in SaaS because availability and reliability are crucial properties, as the application is outsourced and the provider should prove that its service is working as defined in the SLA. However, when a company decides to migrate its application from a traditional model to the SaaS approach, the anomaly detection task should be modified accordingly. First of all it is necessary to correctly place the sensors and define the aggregation point for collected data. Second the customer's data, derived from network monitoring, should be classified and isolated from the others. Finally, the collected data should be available for customers to perform analysis.

Virtualisation technologies can be exploited to achieve anomaly detection is SaaS. We suggest to install an agent on every VM hosting customer's components, in order to collect information like network reachability, service status, and others. A set of VM able to collect and analyse reported data, can be located at different provider or at the customer. In this case, data integrity and confidentiality can be protected using symmetric/asymmetric keys or a combination of these, similarly to the log approach.

3.9   Data Protection

Data security is a crucial point in SaaS, because the provider processes customers' data. Consequently, ensuring and disclosing an adequate protection is essential.

Basic data protection is obtained by defining proper access control policies, which define the entities entitled to access and manipulate the data. These policies are enforced through authorisation and isolation techniques. However, following a defense-in-depth strategy, additional protection techniques should be used to strengthen the access control mechanisms and/or reduce the potential damage in case the intended policy is violated.

Among these additional techniques, cryptography (in the form of information encryption and/or authentication codes) should be exploited whenever data have confidentiality and integrity requirements. Furthermore, the provider must also implement techniques (e.g. data backup services) to prevent and eventually react to loss of data availability, while paying attention to not conflict with confidentiality and integrity requirements.

Encryption solutions can be roughly distinguished in data and storage encryption, depending to which coarseness data are cyphered. Data encryption, means that a selected set of data is cyphered, while storage is intended as cyphering disks images or blocks, independently by their type and peculiarity. Even if encryption is intended for protecting data confidentiality, it can be easily exploited to offer also data integrity.

Data encryption can be efficiently applied only by those applications that permit providers to manage customers' data at a sufficiently coarse level to encrypt just them, like application-level SaaS and Database As A Service. In such applications, data are stored in a Data Base Management Systems (DBMS). *Data encryption* is supported by many widely used systems, like Oracle DB, Microsoft SQL Server, PostgreSQL, and DB2. Since data encryption is especially useful as an additional measure against unforeseen policy violation, its usage in place of authorisation mechanisms is strongly discouraged [26] due to problems in key revocation and difficulties in managing such mechanisms as authorisation. Furthermore, this solution must be used carefully, since it affects performance-critical component: it must be limited to data really critical, considering that such protection prevents the creation of indexes on the cyphered columns and affects the database performance.

To work with encrypted data there are two possible approaches: decrypting them before use or performing privacy homomorphic operation on encrypted data.

Some specialists suggest to perform the decryption with scripts directly at the database, in order to impact the performance as little as possible. According to this approach, encryption keys can be stored inside the database (in a different table or embedded in the scripts), externally in a file on the same machine, or given to the client applications that has to include them in the query.

Privacy homomorphism [3] allows executing some types of query directly on encrypted data. Consequently, the decryption of data is not required to perform some operations (like `exact select, equijoin, projections`) and allows not sharing the secret key with the DBMS. This approach can be feasible to store critical data at the provider, allowing the customer to maintain his data secret towards the provider. Unfortunately, this approach is quite preliminary, and limited to a subset of operations, consequently its application is currently uncommon.

Storage encryption exploits hardware and/or operating system capabilities to encrypt large amount of data without any distinction for their nature, except for their location. The application of these solutions in a SaaS environment is mainly in IaaS when the customer data are not managed at all. Of course, customers can apply internally standard data protection, but this is not related to SaaS technology. This solution can be applied at different levels, depending on the type of storage. Storage can be directly encrypted with the adoption of cryptographic file systems, as supported by many modern operating systems [4], or exploiting hardware-capable encrypting disks [28]. This solution is very effective in case a disk is stolen, as the data are typically encrypted with symmetric algorithms and the keys are stored elsewhere in a secure environment (for example, at the customer premise). In general, this solution is effective against third party unauthorised subjects, while is ineffective in a multi-tenant environment where they typically share the same physical resources. Storage encryption can also be used to protect customers from each other, but only if different partitions or disks are reserved for each of them. In Storage Area Network (SAN) there are different approaches to perform data protection. Some approaches assume that the underlying storage server is trusted and prevents attacks from outsiders [11,20]. On the contrary other approaches [10,22] do not trust storage servers and propose to protect also data in transit over the SAN. These solutions typically propose a centralised approach, that can be avoided by performing encryption of disk block with symmetric keys, that in turn are encrypted with every public key of the SAN entities allowed to access the blocks [18].

Backup is an important process for data protection in any kind of environment. Backup, be it in the form of *Cold standby* or *Hot standby* implies having more copies of the same data. While problems related to their correlation are widely discussed and are not interesting here, backup protection must be specifically addressed for SaaS. In fact, data backup is often delegated to the provider, which must then guarantee the same level of data protection for the copies as for the live data. In other words, backups must be encrypted as live data are. It could be a reasonable request that only the data owners can decipher their backups, for example, by using symmetric backup encryption keys that are in turn encrypted with the data owner's public key. Conversely, this solution is not practical if the customer completely delegates the management of the system to the provider and simply requires that the system is properly running. In both these cases, particular importance must be given to loss of encryption credential loss, that could completely prevent the data recovery process. In case of cold standby, performed with the adoption of a virtual machine, it is reasonable cyphering the VM image when it is not running. Even if less expensive than whole disk encryption, this approach implies encrypting a lot of not critical data and requiring an unjustified amount of resources.

4   Assessing SaaS Security

In the previous sections, we have shown how SaaS introduces new threats, and how various security technologies can mitigate their effects. Security evaluation and awareness becomes essential to draw the proper bar when designing or acquiring a specific SaaS solution, and reasoning on security implications should be an integral and relevant part of SaaS planning and contracting.

Information risk analysis [15] (only "risk analysis" hereinafter) provides standard methods to reason on security threats, consequences, and countermeasures. We argue that SaaS planning must always include risk analysis tasks to build an explicit map of the risks shared between the customer and the provider. Moreover, SaaS raises some peculiar requirements to risk analysis practice. We discuss here how to use risk analysis tools to satisfy these requirements, and thus improve security awareness and confidence in SaaS.

4.1   Risk Analysis When Planning SaaS

Most risk analysis methodologies explicitly model the following root concepts:

- assets: parts of the information system relevant for risk analysis;
- dependencies: relationships among assets;
- threats: potential incident scenarios;
- vulnerabilities: characteristics of the information system that influence the materialisation or consequences of the threats;
- controls: characteristics and parts of the information system that mitigate the vulnerabilities.

Assets are assigned a value, generally articulated along multiple security dimensions. Popular dimensions include the classic confidentiality, integrity, and availability, and may include others like authenticity and accountability. Note that the same security dimension may have different semantics depending on the asset type: for example integrity has a completely different meaning when applied to a message rather than a platform.

Threats' manifestations cause impacts that degrade the value of vulnerable assets, while controls may prevent/reduce this degradation. The risk analysis process systematically studies the relationship between system assets, selected controls, and threats to characterise the chance that a certain threat manifests itself and causes certain impacts.

A tenet in risk analysis is that the real value resides in higher level assets (business processes and critical information), while concrete threats are associated to lower-level assets. Risk analysis correlates this information by modelling dependencies between assets. Dependencies describe how assets values propagate from high-level assets to lower level ones (e.g. a business process depending from some software and hardware equipment), and how threats propagate from lower level assets to influence higher level ones (e.g. an integrity loss at a process exposing confidential data).

Applying risk analysis concepts to SaaS planning and contracting has some peculiar advantages beyond standard security practice:

- help customers to identify formally to what extent their system is going to depend on the SaaS provider;
- help customer and provider to agree formally on the partition of security responsibilities;
- help customers in comparing alternative SaaS offers that are different in terms of security features.

On the other side, SaaS puts some constraints on the risk analysis (RA) process, briefly discussed here as C1 ... C4:

(C1 - multi-party risk allocation). RA should distinguish to which party (customer or provider) every risk is allocated. Risk transfer is often included among risk treatment options, but standard methodologies do not model where the risk is actually reallocated.

(C2 - explicit risk dependencies). RA should explicitly represent all the events and relationships that have relevance to the manifestation of a threat and to the assessment of its impact. All methodologies model assets-to-threats associations and compute evaluations of impacts, but several ones fail to provide an explicit and formal representation of the information that has determined the computed values.

(C3 - proper asset abstraction). In a SaaS context, several details on the underlying system infrastructure could not be shared between customer and provider. Standard RA methodologies devote great effort to infrastructure modelling, while only few and recent approaches support rich modelling of the application logic that is often the most relevant part of a SaaS service architecture.

(C4 - SaaS specific threats). Obviously, RA for SaaS requires a model of its specific threats, as described in Sec. 2, and a model of the SaaS security building blocks, as discussed in Sec. 3. Note that no SaaS specific or proprietary control has been discussed, but rather we considered SaaS-oriented deployment of standard security controls. Therefore, as nearly all RA methodologies support customisation and extension of asset and threat libraries, they should be in principle able to satisfy this constraint.

We can design/describe a SaaS oriented risk analysis process by selecting components from a variety of standard methodologies. In particular, we can borrow from OCTAVE [6] the use of threat trees to explicitly model risk dependencies, from SDL [14] and TAM [21] the rich application functional description, and from ISO-27005 [15] the standard risk concept framework. Note that the threat trees are strongly related to attack trees, first proposed by Schneier [29]. The core task becomes building a set of attack trees/graphs that formally (1) identify the possible incidents that may affect the SaaS environment, and (2) identify responsibilities in preventing each incident. We will call these objects "risk dependency graphs", or briefly "risk graphs".

4.2   Formal Model of SaaS Risks

A risk graph for SaaS includes – as graph nodes (N) or edges (E) – SaaS components, their interactions, security dimensions and dependencies, threats and vulnerabilities.

Components and interactions model the assets and include at least:

- organisations (N), such as customers and providers;
- roles (N), representing different kinds of actors interacting with the application (e.g. users and administrators);
- components (N), that is data, software, and platform elements composing the SaaS environment;
- interactions (N) between roles and components, and among components.

A suitable concrete example is the application modelling of TAM [21] extended to multi-organisation representation.

The selected asset model it must be enriched with proper security dimensions to model assets' value and security dependencies. In particular, we consider two other graph element types:

- assets' security dimensions (N), representing assets' values;
- security dependencies (E), identifying relationships between security dimensions, both inter- and intra-assets.

Threats are introduced in the graph by using the following elements:

- threats (N), that is potential incidents (including faults and attacks) that may affect the SaaS service;
- vulnerabilities (E), representing the threats' impacts in terms of degraded assets' security dimensions.

Logical connectors distinguish between correlated (AND) and uncorrelated (OR) edges in the graph.

As an example, Fig. 6 shows a simple risk graph. It represents attacker A compromising the integrity of component C1. Then, having acquired the C1 identity, A invokes operation O2 on component C2 and thus compromises the confidentiality of data D (owned by the customer). The invocation of operation O2 also causes the generation of (authentic) audit data L2.

It is worth discussing the importance of *application interactions* within the model. At high level, they model SaaS security policies in terms of virtual operations allowed for each role over the SaaS components, including CRUD[1] operations over data. At low level, they model functional relationship between

---

[1] Create, Read, Update, Delete.

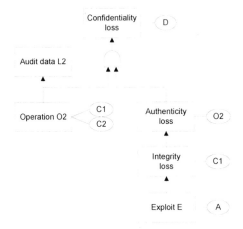

Fig. 6. Basic risk graph

components, including data communication and service invocation. A sequence of component interactions has a global effect that can be expressed in terms of high-level virtual operations. In other words, virtual operations depend upon one or more component interactions. Within this model, threat actions can be represented as unauthorised interactions, and their impact assessed in terms of security dimensions at the involved components. For example, the unauthorised invocation of operation O on DBMS component C results in the unauthorised reading of the stored data D, and degrades its confidentiality.

A second observation is relative to *asset abstraction* suitable for SaaS modelling. Risk analysis methodologies recognise that business level information and service depend upon software processes and hardware components. Software and hardware are modelled themselves as hierarchy of sub-components. With SaaS, several details of the server platform and network infrastructure are not interesting to the customer, or the provider prefers to avoid their full disclosure. We assume platform and infrastructure nodes in the risk graph to have a high level of granularity, even if this is not strictly a requirement of our approach. For instance, in case of virtualisation technologies, a group of virtual machines could be dynamically hosted on a set of physical machines. The hosting machines, or even the whole set, could be represented as a black box. The virtual machines will depend on the integrity of the platform box represented as an atomic property.

A third aspect deserving attention is about *security controls*. The relationship between threats, controls, and security dimensions is recursive [32]. Some threat may degrade some security dimension at some asset and a control is introduced to remove this vulnerability. Now, however, the new control may be subject to some threat compromising its integrity and effectiveness. Risk graphs can be built recursively by identifying assets, threats relevant to assets, controls relevant to threats, threats relevant to controls, and so on. The process can stop when the generated set of risk graphs allows defining a risk allocation that satisfies the customer.

Once built, each risk graph explicitly represents the risk dependencies within a specific threat scenario. A classic risk analysis process would associate each risk graph with a risk level, classify all the generated graphs based on their risk level, and select appropriate risk treatment actions. On the countrary, our approach focuses on formally sharing responsibilities between customer and provider to prevent the manifestation of the threat scenario. We call this task "risk allocation". Technically, every threat node is associated to an organisation node to represent that the organisation has accepted responsibility for the selected event. The mix of resulting responsibilities is then summarised in a per graph responsibility. In this way, risk graphs are customised as part of the SaaS contracting phase to agree formally on security responsibility sharing.

Fig. 7 extends the graph in Fig. 6 with a sub-graph that models a new risk scenario in which the attacker A can steal the user's smart-card SC and invoke operation O1 on component C1 to obtain the same overall effect (data D disclosure) as in the basic risk scenario. Additionally, the figure also shows a possible risk allocation: the integrity violation at C1 is allocated to provider P as it is responsible for platform integrity, while the case of unauthentic invocation of operation O1 is allocated to customer C because physical protection of user tokens is responsibility of the customer.

To build effective risk graphs and risk allocations, the following set of basic validation rules (R1 ... R5) should be applied:

(R1) every risk graph must include one or more nodes corresponding to the integrity failure of some SaaS component, otherwise the risk is either globally accepted (and its allocation become irrelevant), or should be avoided by changing the SaaS design (e.g. adding a proper countermeasure to prevent it).

(R2) every attack graph must include one or more nodes corresponding to the generation of some audit data, otherwise the risk manifestation could not be effectively detected, the risk should be accepted, and its allocation is useless. If the impact is unacceptable, a change in the SaaS design should be considered (e.g. introducing additional logging and/or auditing features).

(R3) every pair of risk graphs differing in the allocation of some threat action must also differ in the generation of some unaffected (authentic) audit data. If this is not the case, it would be impossible to distinguish between the manifestations of the two risk scenarios, and the allocation could not be enforced.

(R4) every attack graph must be assigned to one organisation as the global risk taker. No rule exists to select the global risk allocation from the allocation of the specific threats actions within the graph. The global allocation of every risk graph is a contractual decision. In case agreement is difficult, the parties should consider splitting the graph into sub-graphs whose allocation appear less controversial.

(R5) every risk graph must be rooted in one or more nodes that represent impacts relevant to the customer (e.g. a virtual unauthorised operation along

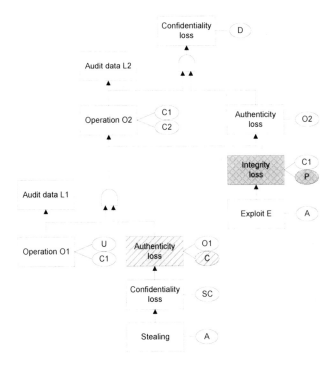

Fig. 7. Augmented risk graph with risk allocation

with its effects in terms of damaged security dimensions), otherwise there
is a partial risk scenario whose allocation could be misleading. In fact, we
may not be considering some relevant countermeasures that, if effective,
should fully mask the effects of the partial risk scenario at global level.
Expanding/merging should be considered for this kind of risk graphs.

As an example, the two risk scenarios in Fig. 7 can be differentiated based on
their audit data sets: in the smart-card stealing scenario, the system logs that
smart-card SC requested operation O1. Therefore, customer and provider could
agree to split the risk graph in two independent risk graphs. The first graph,
including the C2 integrity violation scenario, is globally allocated to provider P.
The second, including the smart-card stealing scenario, is globally allocated to
customer C. The two new graphs are distinguished by the different sets of audit
data: L2 for what concerns the first graph, L2 plus L1 in the second graph. This
agreement is illustrated in Fig. 8.

Now suppose that, after further analysis, the first graph is expanded to model
that the provider could forge audit data L1 making the two graphs indistinguish-
able. Then two options become available: either the SaaS design is changed to
accommodate some countermeasure against L1 forging, or the two risk graphs
are merged and the resulting graph is globally allocated to either the provider
or the customer. Choosing the first option, the interface of C1 is modified to let

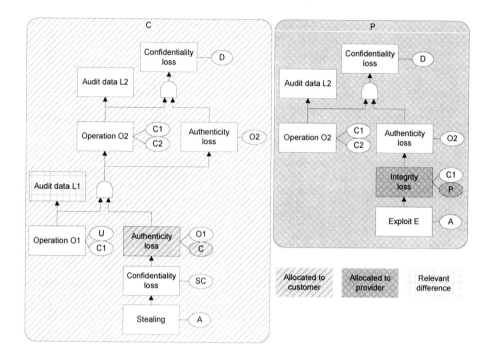

Fig. 8. Global risk allocation

every O1 invocation to be unpredictably identified and signed with the user's smart-card. In the second case, the customer may substantially opt for accepting the risk of provider misbehaviour, or the provider may take all the risks caused by design limits in its SaaS implementation.

Note that we have not presented any rule to validate the completeness of the generated risk graphs set. Lack of formal completeness is a limit of all risk analysis methodologies. Practically, they heavily rely on analyst's security expertise to achieve a satisfying level of confidence in the analysis, including its completeness. A more detailed discussion of this point is out of focus here but we can state that having a good functional model of the SaaS application greatly helps in ensuring that all the risk belonging to the following classes have been taken into account:

- every high-level operation involving SaaS data/components, even those not explicitly modelled, could take place as consequence of some threat scenario;
- every SaaS component, including security controls, could loose integrity due to some successful attack, if proper controls have not been placed to prevent it;
- every SaaS data, including security data, could loose confidentiality and integrity due to some successful attack, if some controls have not been placed to prevent it.

4.3   Examples of Risk Graphs Usage

This section presents some simple examples of risk graphs and risk allocations, related to some of the aspects discussed in Sec. 3, namely data protection, service isolation, and authentication/authorisation.

In the first example (Fig. 9), the risk graph shows how deploying a per-customer web front-end reduces the risk associated to XSS attacks [27]. Without isolation, a user from customer Ca that is able to store some XSS code (e.g. by using SQL injection techniques [27]) would also affect the confidentiality of data belonging to other customers, e.g. customer Cb. The risk of user misbehaviour could be allocated to customer Ca (left side of the graph), but obviously not for what concerns the impacts on other customers (right side of the graph).

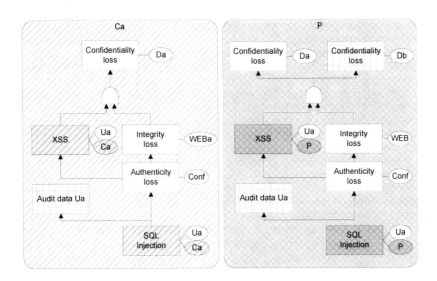

Fig. 9. Example 1

The second example (Fig. 10) illustrates how proper authentication and authorisation design can help managing risks of unauthorised operations. If authentication and authorisation decisions are delegated to the customer, e.g. with an identity management system like SAML [24], it is possible to discriminate an insider attack at the provider. In fact, an unauthorised operation could not be matched with an authorisation assertion signed by the customer. Referring to the top part of the graph, availability of the SAML assertion S demonstrates that either the user Ua requested (maybe erroneously) the operation Del, or that the authentication and authorisation service Auth operated by the customer was tampered with. Both risk scenarios can be allocated to customer Ca. Conversely, in the bottom graph, unavailability of any authorisation assertion for operation Del suggests that an insider attack at the provider is the most likely origin. This risk graph is thus allocated to provider P.

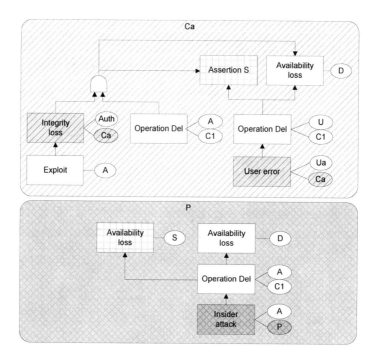

Fig. 10. Example 2

The last example (Fig. 11) deals with data encryption. Without data encryption, it is not possible to discriminate, and thus allocate, the risk of disclosure by a misbehaving authorised user, against the risk of provider equipment being compromised. For instance, in the top graph, it is not possible to discriminate disclosure by user Ua, and integrity loss at database DBS. Data encryption allows allocating the risk of unauthorised disclosure to the customer, and the risk of a vulnerable encryption mechanism to the provider. For example, storage encryption performed by the operating system without trusted computing base does not protect data against software bugs (e.g. introduced by third party contractors at the provider). On the other side, even trusted computing techniques are vulnerable to attacks exploiting physical access. The critical factor is that the access to unencrypted data is difficult to track, while the fallacy of an encryption method and platform integrity is likely to become a public fact and/or it can be practically demonstrated. Within Fig. 11, the bottom graph states that violation of data D confidentiality is allocated to provider P if it is possible to demonstrate a manifest platform vulnerability at database DBS. Audit information about the database platform's characteristics can be practically implemented through different mechanisms, including trusted computing techniques.

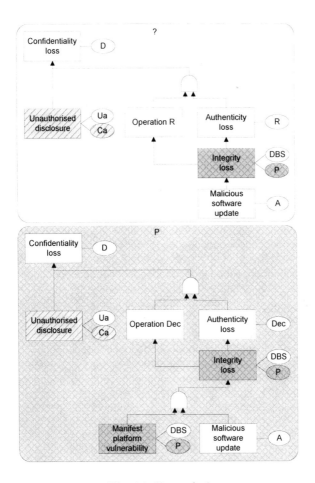

Fig. 11. Example 3

5   Conclusions

From the analysis in this chapter, it is clear that the SaaS environments are potentially affected by several security problems, that might impact their adoption. This is partly due to their nature of distributed networked system and partly to their specific characteristics of multi-tenant multi-provider software environment.

However well-known protection techniques can be adopted to mitigate and in some cases completely counter these security problems. This target can be reached by carefully considering all the risks. Since SaaS is a complex environment, a formal risk analysis approach should be taken, coupled with best practices to cover the unacceptable risks.

Following this approach, we are confident that SaaS will achieve a security level at least comparable to that of the applications being replaced by it, and therefore will become an asset in the design and operation of future software architectures and services.

References

1. Anderson, R.J.: Security Engineering: A Guide to Building Dependable Distributed Systems, pp. 161–184. Wiley, Chichester (2001)
2. Avizienis, A., Kelly, J.P.J.: Fault tolerance by design diversity: Concepts and experiments. Computer 17(8), 67–80 (1984)
3. Bertino, E., Sandhu, R.: Database security - concepts, approaches, and challenges. IEEE Transactions on Dependable and Secure Computing 2(1), 2–19 (2005)
4. Blaze, M.: A cryptographic file system for unix. In: Proceedings of the First ACM Conference on Computing and Communication, pp. 2097–2102 (June 1993)
5. Bruegger, B.P., Hühnlein, D., Schwenk, J.: TLS-Federation - a secure and relying-party-friendly approach for federated identity management. In: BIOSIG, pp. 93–106 (2008)
6. Caralli, R.A., Stevens, J.F., Young, L.R., Wilson, W.R.: Introducing OCTAVE allegro: Improving the information security risk assessment process. CMU TR (May 2007), http://www.cert.org/archive/pdf/07tr012.pdf
7. Cardellini, V., Casalicchio, E., Colajanni, M., Yu, P.S.: The state of the art in locally distributed web-server systems. ACM Comput. Surv. 34(2), 263–311 (2002)
8. Clark, D.D.: RFC 816: Fault isolation and recovery (July 1982)
9. Ferrie, P.: Attacks on more virtual machine emulators. Symantec Advanced Threat Research (2008)
10. Fu, K.: Group sharing and random access in cryptographic storage file systems. Master's thesis, Massachusetts Institute of Technology (1999)
11. Gobioff, H.: Security for a High Performance Commodity Storage Subsystem. PhD thesis, School of Computer Science, Computer Science Department, Carnegie Mellon University (1999)
12. Gross, T.: Security analysis of the SAML single sign-on browser/artifact profile. In: Omondi, A.R., Sedukhin, S.G. (eds.) ACSAC 2003. LNCS, vol. 2823, p. 298. Springer, Heidelberg (2003)
13. Harris, S.: CISSP Exam Guide, 3rd edn., pp. 337–413. McGraw-Hill/Osborne
14. Howard, M., Lipner, S.: The Security Development Lifecycle. Microsoft Press, Redmond (2006)
15. ISO. ISO 27005 - Security techniques - Information security risk management. ISO Standard (2005)
16. Jensen, M., Schwenk, J., Gruschka, N., Iacono, L.L.: On technical security issues in cloud computing. In: IEEE International Conference on Cloud Computing, pp. 109–116 (2009)
17. Karlof, C., Shankar, U., Tygar, J.D., Wagner, D.: Dynamic pharming attacks and locked same-origin policies for web browsers. In: CCS 2007: Proceedings of the 14th ACM Conference on Computer and Communications Security, pp. 58–71. ACM Press, New York (2007)
18. Kim, Y., Narasimha, M., Maino, F., Tsudik, G.: Secure group services for storage area networks. IEEE Communications Magazine 41, 92–99 (2003)
19. Lamport, L., Shostak, R., Pease, M.: The byzantine generals problem. ACM Transactions on Programming Languages and Systems 4, 382–401 (1982)
20. Mazieres, D., Kaminsky, M., Kaashoek, M.F., Witchel, E.: Separating key management from file system security. In: Proceedings of the 17th ACM Symposium on Operating Systems Principles, pp. 124–139 (1999)
21. Microsoft Corporation. Microsoft Threat Analysis & Modeling v2.1 (March 2007), http://blogs.msdn.com/threatmodeling/

22. Miller, E.L., Freeman, W.E., Long, D.D.E., Reed, B.C.: Strong security for network-attached storage. In: USENIX Conference on File and Storage Technologies (FAST), pp. 1–14 (January 2002)
23. Mitchell, C.: Trusted Computing. IEEE Press, Los Alamitos (2005)
24. OASIS. Assertions and protocols for the OASIS security markup language (SAML) v2.0. OASIS Standard (March 2005), http://saml.xml.org
25. OASIS. SAML V2.0 holder-of-key assertion profile, version 1.0. OASIS Standard (July 2009), http://docs.oasis-open.org/security/saml/Post2.0/sstc-saml2-holder-of-key.pdf
26. Oracle Corporation. Database encryption in oracle9i. Oracle Technical Whitepaper (Febraury 2001), http://www.oracle.com/technology/deploy/security/oracle9i/pdf/f5crypt.pdf
27. OWASP Foundation. Owasp top 10 - the ten most critical web application security vulnerabilities (2007), http://www.owasp.org/index.php/Top_10_2007
28. Schmid, P.: Momentus 5400 FDE.2: Data Encryption On-a-Drive. Tom's hardware review, http://www.tomshardware.com/reviews/momentus-5400-fde,1742.html
29. Schneier, B.: Attack trees. Dr. Dobb's Journal (December 1999)
30. Squicciarini, A.C., Bertino, E., Goasguen, S.: Access control strategies for virtualized environments in grid computing systems. In: IEEE International Workshop on Future Trends of Distributed Computing Systems, pp. 48–54 (2007)
31. Stallings, W.: Cryptography and Network Security, 4th edn. Prentice Hall, Englewood Cliffs (2005)
32. Stoneburner, G., Goguen, A., Feringa, A.: Risk management guide for information technology systems. NIST Special Publication 800-30 (July 2002), http://csrc.nist.gov/publications/nistpubs/800-30/sp800-30.pdf
33. Trusted Computing Group (2009), https://www.trustedcomputinggroup.org

Runtime Web-Service Workflow Optimization[*]

Radu Sion[1] and Junichi Tatemura[2]

[1] Computer Sciences, Stony Brook University
Stony Brook, NY 11794
sion@cs.stonybrook.edu
[2] NEC Research Labs, 10080 N. Wolfe Rd.
Cupertino, CA 95014
tatemura@sv.nec-labs.com

Abstract. Increasingly, business models build on mechanisms for online interaction. Web Services, business workflows and service orchestrations provide essential tools for staging successful networked business to business (B2B) or business to customer (B2C) transactions.

One of the important online interaction quality metrics is perceived response time. The ability to sustain a high throughput and provide fast service effectively means more business and associated revenue. Downtimes and slow transactions can be a strong deterrent for potential customers. The ability to automatically monitor and optimize response performance becomes more important than ever.

In this paper we propose a solution for optimizing web service business workflow response times through dynamic resource allocation. On-the-fly monitoring is combined with a novel workflow modeling algorithm that discovers critical execution paths and builds "dynamic" stochastic models in the associated "critical graph". One novel contribution of this work is the ability to naturally handle parallel workflow execution paths. This is essential in applications where workflows include multiple concurrent service calls/paths that need to be "joined" at a later point in time. We discuss the automatic deployment of on-the-fly monitoring mechanisms within the resource management mechanisms. We implement, deploy and experiment with a proof of concept within a generalized web services business process (BPEL4WS/SOAP) framework. In the experiments we show the natural adaptation to changing workflow conditions and appropriate automatic re-allocation of resources to reduce execution times.

Keywords: Web Services, Workflows, Response Time Optimization.

1 Introduction

To achieve maximum performance with a finite set of resources, these need to be (re)allocated preferably for each new instance of a workflow execution. Because it is often hard for human system operators to perform such allocations

---

[*] An extended abstract [1] of this paper appeared in ICWS 2005.

D. Agrawal et al. (Eds.): Information and Software as Services, LNBIP 74, pp. 112–131, 2011.

appropriately, to achieve maximum utilization and response times, an ability to automatically do so becomes more important than ever. In [2] Gillmann, Weikum and Wonner propose an adaptive workflow management solution integrating service quality awareness with stochastic modeling of workflows, an approach well suited in the case of single-threaded workflows with non-concurrent paths.

There exist scenarios however, where such static stochastic models cannot be applied. These include workflows with parallel threads of (potentially) mutually interacting services. A classical example is the case of a manufacturing company workflow, issuing a request to a supplier A for various parts and, *occasionally* also to a supplier B (simultaneously). A static stochastic model of the workflow could not possibly accommodate this conditional scenario. Moreover if the two parallel workflow paths A and B interact (e.g. by messaging), things complicate further.

Here we propose to build upon the stochastic modeling approach introduced in [2] and provide a solution able to handle such dynamic and parallel workflows. Our solution is based on the on-the-fly discovery of workflow critical paths [3] and their analysis within an adaptive resource reallocation framework.

While there exist likely scenarios for single-webservice invocation workflows, here we analyze mainly workflows invoking an average of more than one web - service in their lifetime. This is of interest as we are not as much concerned with individual web services but rather the the ability to perform global workflow optimization through web service resource (re)allocation. We also note that, while we scope our solution for web service business workflows, it arguably extends to arbitrary frameworks.

We also implemented and experimented with a proof of concept within a web services based business workflows (i.e. BPEL [4]) framework. The design is multi - layered: the first layer enables the ability to transparently monitor execution times for the component workflow states (web service calls) and collect associated execution times. The second layer reasons about these collected statistics dynamically, with the aim to optimize global responsiveness (workflow execution times). This layer then originates resource (re)allocation recommendations to the third layer handling resource allocation.

The main contributions of our work include: (i) a solution for on-the-fly optimization of average workflow response time, adaptive to a dynamic environment (e.g., workload patterns, available server resources, network congestion), (ii) a proof-of-concept implementation of monitoring architecture components, enabling run-time profiling and data collection on open-standard Web Service platforms, (iii) a "dynamic" stochastic workflow modeling approach for workflows with concurrent paths, and (iv) the experimental analysis thereof. Moreover, we note that our model is based on a critical path as a construction as opposed to existing models which only consider simple execution paths.

The paper is structured as follows. Section 2 introduces the web service execution monitoring framework. Section 3 defines the modeling framework and establishes an execution-aware weighting scheme for workflow tasks. Section 4 discusses the resource allocation algorithm. In Section 5 we explore limits and improvements to our solution. Section 6 presents experimental results and Section 7 explores related work. Section 8 concludes.

2   Web Service Wrapping

Statistics and local information about individual web service performance are essential in building any solution for evaluating and optimizing of overall orchestration/workflow behavior. The process of collecting these statistics has to be non-intrusive and transparent from both a programming and deployment point of view. More specifically, we are concerned here with the ability to assess local and remote web service response times within an existing, deployed BPEL [4] workflow which invokes a set of external services. One of the main difficulties in designing an automated solution for this derives from the requirement to be able to associate each response time sample with both the corresponding web service and a specific workflow instance.

For the purpose of optimizing overall workflow behavior, we need the ability to monitor composing individual web service behavior directly for each execution instance, with a minimal overhead. In our solution, we propose to enable this through a novel call-tracing mechanism, namely *invocation wrappers*. An invocation wrapper is a software component (e.g. Java class) associated with a specific web service that acts as a proxy for it (within a workflow execution engine, e.g. invoked from the associated BPEL file) while also collecting execution time statistics into a common repository. In Figure 1 (a) a traditional BPEL web service invocation/call is depicted. Figure 1 (b) illustrates the same call, wrapped within an associated invocation wrapper (ws_wrapper). In summary, invocation wrappers are used for dynamic and transparent response time profiling.

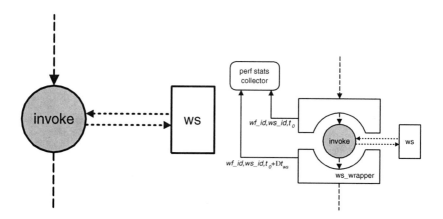

Fig. 1. (a) A remote web service is accessed in a traditional BPEL invocation. (b) Transparent monitoring entails automatically modifying the BPEL flow description with calls to invocation wrappers instead of direct web service invocations.

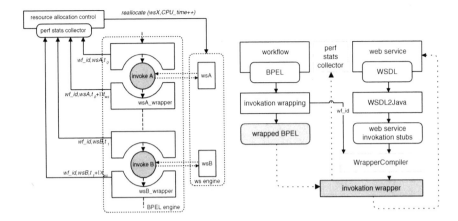

Fig. 2. (a) When multiple web services compete, the resource allocation is greatly improved if on-the-fly workflow performance awareness is built in. (b) The invocation wrapper is automatically produced by the wrapper compiler from the java invocation stubs generated by a WSDL to java converter and a unique identifier for the current workflow.

Naturally, most workflows invoke multiple web services throughout their lifetime. When multiple web services are coming into play, an optimization of the global workflow execution/response time can be achieved by an adaptive resource allocation scheme, considering each invoked component, see Figure 2 (a).

For (mainly) economic reasons, invocation wrappers need to be non-intrusive from both a programmer's and runtime deployment point of view. Legacy applications are to be handled and assuming a runtime profiling aware programming model is not always natural. Thus, the monitoring framework has to provide for automatic transparent invocation wrapping for targeted web services within a BPEL process.

Achieving this goal entails two dimensions. First, the workflow specification file (BPEL, omitted due to space constraints) needs to be augmented with invocation wrapper calls instead of direct web service invocations. A traditional call to a web service method $getValue(String name)$ is wrapped by invoking the wrapper instead. An additional ("wf_id") parameter is added to its signature, initialized with a per-workflow unique identifier. This parameter is used to associate the collected web service execution statistics with their corresponding workflow. Additionally, the wrapper partner will have an associated WSDL [5] file derived from the original web service description file augmented with the new method signature(s), passing workflow identification information to the wrapper. The second stage in automatically wrapping a web service invocation provides for each wrapped web service an invocation wrapper. The invocation wrapper is to be automatically generated (see Figure 2 (b)) by a specialized wrapper compiler (an extension of WSDL2Java) that takes as input a unique current workflow identifier and a web service invocation stub and generates the invocation wrapper. The wrapper is in effect a modified version of the web service invocation stub, augmented with code that profiles the current execution and stores the associated data in a specialized (system-wide) statistics collector bean.

3   Workflow Modeling

Once the monitoring framework is in place, our solution deploys a novel inference mechanism able to model and predict workflow behavior and associated optimizing resource (re)allocations for the composing tasks. Here we outline this model.

3.1   Stochastic Workflow Modeling

In [6] and [2] Gillman et al. motivate and discuss the issue of service quality guarantees in the framework of workflow management for e-services. A solution based on static stochastic modeling of workflow behavior is provided.

The core algorithm starts by defining the concept of a "flow process", a "stochastic process with a finite set of states". Certain conditions and assumptions are then associated with the transitions between these states, including: (i) "the time until the flow process performs the next transition is randomly distributed", (ii) there is a given (static) probability of the flow process entering a certain state, and (iii) this probability is independent of the time the process spent in the current state and also (iv) "independent of the process's earlier history".

A stochastic model is built for a given workflow using the assumptions above. It is then coupled with a "performance model" in which each service call (server) is modeled by "considering only its mean service time per request and the second moment of this metric". By estimating these values (through "collecting and evaluating online statistics") and feeding them into the stochastic model, resource allocation requirements are inferred for optimizing execution times.

Limitations. The static stochastic approach is certainly suited for a number of workflow scenarios under given assumptions. One of the most restrictive assumption is the requirement that the Markov model transition probabilities are history independent (point (iii) above, "independent of the time period that the flow process spent in ... [a previous state]").

There are scenarios however (see Figure 3), where such static stochastic models cannot be applied. These include workflows with parallel threads of (potentially) mutually interacting services. A classical example could be the case of a manufacturing company workflow, issuing a request to a supplier A for various parts and, *occasionally* also to a supplier B (simultaneously). A static stochastic model of the workflow could not possibly accommodate this conditional scenario. Moreover, input data-dependency in workflow transitions is often occurring and this dependency is mostly related to the past history of the flow, thus directly conflicting with point (iv) in Section 3.1 above.

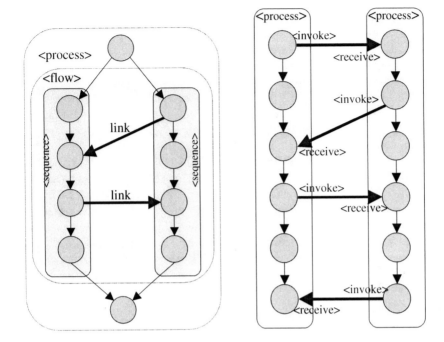

Fig. 3. Scenarios where a direct stochastic approach cannot model workflow behavior. (a) Concurrent sequences within a process (b) Concurrent processes

Yet another important aspect that cannot be handled by a purely stochastic approach is the scenario of parallelism, e.g. inter-thread or inter-process asynchronous communication within the same workflow. (in the previous example, if the two parallel workflow paths A and B interact, e.g. by messaging) For this aspect, an apparent solution would be to augment the semantics of transitions with synchronization primitives, however this is highly likely leading to an unintuitive, complex model. In the following we show how "dynamic" stochastic modeling over the space of graphs defined by workflow-instance critical paths can be used to naturally handle these issues.

3.2   Instance Critical Paths

Starting from the need to address the limitations outlined above, we propose an alternative to simple stochastic modeling, more suited to handling these and other specific workflow-modeling challenges. Our solution relies on the concept of workflow *critical paths*. Critical paths aim to capture the most time-consuming activities within a workflow. In other words, the question that is answered is: which of the composing workflow tasks have the most impact on the overall workflow execution time ? Traditionally [7] [8], a workflow critical path is defined as the *longest execution path* from the initial task to the final task of the workflow. Here we use a by-construction runtime definition, designed specifically to leverage data available from the monitoring framework. Our definition computes critical paths for workflow instances on the fly by processing runtime execution statistics. In the following we are using the term *critical path* or *instance critical path* to denote a path within a workflow *instance* (not schema).

Let there be a workflow composed of a set of states/tasks $\mathbb{S} = \{S_0, S_1, S_2, ..., S_n\}$ and transitions $\mathbb{T} \subset \mathbb{S} \times \mathbb{S}$ (i.e. $(S_i, S_j) \in \mathbb{T}$ iff. there exists a workflow transition from task S_i to task S_j). Let $O(S_i) = \{X | \forall (S_i, X) \in \mathbb{T}\}$, the set of all potential "target" (child) transitions of S_i and $I(S_i) = \{X | \forall (X, S_i) \in \mathbb{T}\}$ the set of all "incoming" transitions of S_i (see Figure 4 (a)).

Let there be a set of predicates $\mathbb{P}$ defining the semantics of workflow execution, in particular its transition schedule. Each task S_i with a single incoming transition $(|I(S_i)| = 1)$ is considered to immediately start executing. For each task , the execution behavior is defined by a conditional "incoming transition evaluation" expression, $SYNC_{S_i} : I(S_i) \rightarrow \{true, false\}$ that govern the transition execution. S_i only starts executing if $SYNC_{S_i}()$ becomes true. $SYNC_{S_i}$ can evaluate an arbitrary boolean formula on the state of the incoming transitions. We assume that $SYNC_{S_i}$ is expressed in a normal conjunctive form.

Considering a certain workflow instance, for each task S_i, let τ_i be the time when S_i starts executing and $\tau_i + \delta_i$ the time when S_i finishes (i.e. is removed from $A()$, the set of active tasks, see definition below). If for example $SYNC_C(AC, BC) = (AC$ and $BC)$, then task C is not executing until both transitions AC and BC are done by the workflow, i.e. when both tasks, A and B finish executing. To be noted that in this particular case, C starts executing at time $\tau_C = max(\tau_A + \delta_A, \tau_B + \delta_B)$. For each task S_i, the outgoing transitional behavior is modeled by a specific function, $TRANS(S_i)$ which determines which of the transitions in $O(S_i)$ are to be pursued upon completion. These semantics of business workflows allow for multiple parallel "threads". If for example $TRANS(C) = \{D, E\}$ then, after completing C, the workflow is "split" into two parallel execution threads starting in D and E. Because of this, at each point in time, several tasks in (S) can be "active". Let $A(t) \subset \mathbb{S}$ (or shorter $A()$, for current time) be the set of active tasks of the given workflow at time t.

Let S_0 and S_n (by convention) be the initial, respectively final task of the workflow. In the following we are only concerned with workflow instances that are terminating. In other words, the flow execution starts in state/task S_0 ($A(0) = \{S_0\}$) at time τ_0 and ends when task S_n is reached ($S_n \in A()$) at a time τ_n[1]. A business workflow is then completely described by $\mathbb{S}$, $\mathbb{T}$ and $TRANS_{S_i}() (\forall) S_i \in \mathbb{S}$. For the purpose of evaluating and, more importantly, optimizing runtime behavior, this defining description needs to be augmented with the ability to model workflow performance by handling more "measurable" quantities. For a workflow instance, the monitoring framework provides execution and transition statistics. For each task $S_i \in \mathbb{S}$, let $TS(S_i)$ be the set of all pairs of corresponding (τ_i, δ_i) times. Let $TS = \cup_{i \in (0,n)}(TS(S_i))$. Also, let $TR(S_i, t) \subset O(S_i)$ be the

---

[1] Naturally, one main goal for workflow optimization is minimizing the execution time, $(\tau_n - \tau_0)$.

set of transitions "fired" after task S_i completes at time t. These statistics are collected by the monitoring framework. $TR()$ effectively models $TRANS(S_i)$. Let $TR = \cup_{i \in (0,n)}(TR(S_i))$.

Sequential Workflow. If, for any two task executions i, j with (τ_i, δ_i), $(\tau_j, \delta_j) \in TS$ we have $(\tau_i + \delta_i) \leq \tau_j$ or $(\tau_j + \delta_j) \leq \tau_i$, (i.e. $(\tau_i, \tau_i + \delta_i) \cap (\tau_j, \tau_j + \delta_j) = \emptyset$) then the workflow effectively behaves sequentially[2]. In this case we define the workflow critical path c as an ordered (by start times τ_i) sequence of (S_i, τ_i) pairs such that: for any two pairs $(S_i, \tau_i), (S_j, \tau_j) \in c$ there exists a transition $(S_i, S_j) \in TR(S_i, \tau_j)$ and $(S_0, \tau_0), (S_n, \tau_n) \in c$.

Parallel Workflow. For each execution instance of a parallel workflow (i.e. where there exist $i, j \in (0, n)$ such that $(\tau_i, \tau_i + \delta_i) \cap (\tau_j, \tau_j + \delta_j) \neq \emptyset$) we define the critical path cp as an ordered sequence of (S_i, τ_i) pairs, by construction as described in Figure 4 (b). $conj\_trans(SYNC_A)$ is defined as follows. If $SYNC_A = (XA \vee YA) \wedge (ZA \vee WA) \wedge ...$ (normal conjunctive form on truth-values of incoming transitions), then for each pair of expressions $(XA \vee YA)$, $conj\_trans(SYNC_A)$ contains the one expression corresponding to the "faster" firing transition (the expression becomes true faster). For example if $(\tau_X + \delta_Y) < (\tau_Y + \delta_Y)$, then XA fires first (if $XA \in TR(X, (\tau_X + \delta_Y)))$ and XA is included in $conj\_trans(SYNC_A)$.

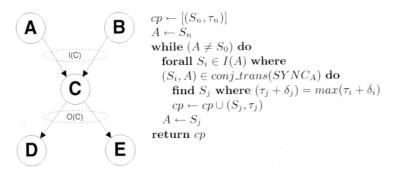

Fig. 4. (a) Incoming and outgoing task transitions (for task C) (b) Critical path construction algorithm

Thus, by construction, a critical path (see Figures 5 (a), 5 (b)) aims to capture the true workflow service bottlenecks from a parallel execution perspective. At each step we select the transition corresponding to the task that is the "latest" to finish among the transitions *required* for the continuation of the execution. As will be seen in Section 5.2 inter-thread asynchronous messaging can also be naturally expressed by critical path semantics.

---

[2] Its (potentially) parallel behavior is "masked" by the non-"overlapping" nature (in terms of execution) of all participating tasks.

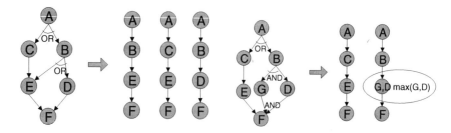

Fig. 5. (a) Potential critical paths for a workflow behaving sequentially. (b) Potential critical paths for a parallel workflow.

3.3 Critical Graph

Minimizing a given workflow instance response time is naturally equivalent to minimizing the execution time of its corresponding critical path. Optimizing workflow execution over multiple instances however, is a more challenging task, especially considering history and input data-dependent transitions. In the following we devise a method that aims to accurately and adaptively model average future workflow response time behavior using previously seen multiple execution instances. This model is then to be used in recommending tasks for resource re-allocations with the final goal to optimize global response time.

Let there be a set of m observed past workflow execution instances and their corresponding critical paths $C = \{c_1, ..., c_m\}$. For each critical path $c_i \in C$, let t_i be the starting time of its initial task (S_0). Because all the critical paths are ultimately composed of subsets of the original workflow graph (and contain by nature at least the initial (S_0) and final (S_n) tasks), intuitively we "group" them into a *critical graph* $g(t)$[3] by colluding all common tasks of each critical path into a graph "node" as shown in Figure 6 (b). Each such node S_i corresponds to an observed critical path task. Because of the collusion effect, each S_i is naturally augmented with a set of timestamps ($TS(S_i)$) corresponding to the τ-value on each critical path where the associated task appeared. Some nodes in the critical graph are going to be more "hot/active" than others. For example in Figures 6 (a) and (b) task B is occurring more frequent compared to D for example. Thus, intuitively, in order to optimize overall performance it could be helpful to rank the tasks accordingly and then use this ranking to recommend appropriate allocation of resources.

The first idea that comes to mind is the use of a stochastic Markov model to augment the critical graph and build a probabilistic weight of each occurring graph state (task) according to its occurrence frequency. Thus, for each task $S_i \in g$, we count its number of observed executions $|TS(S_i)|$, normalize over all tasks in g and use this as a frequency weight:

---

[3] Because of its dynamic nature, the critical graph will "look different" at different points in time, hence the $g(t)$ notation. For simplicity reasons in the following we are using g instead to mean the graph at the current time.

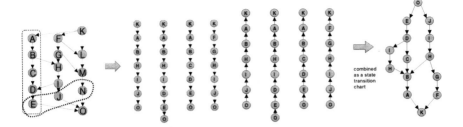

Fig. 6. (a) Four sample observed critical paths in different execution instances of the given workflow. (b) Composing multiple observed critical paths into a critical graph.

$$w(S_i) = \frac{|TS(S_i)|}{\sum_{S_j \in g} |TS(S_j)|} \tag{1}$$

There are several drawbacks to this formula. Because of its static nature, it does not adapt to workflow behavior changes easily. Hot current tasks are being potentially out-weighted by hot tasks in the far past. To fix this we propose an idea similar to the memory-aware Markov model described in [9], namely the use of time-locality in the weight computation. For each task S_i, we can determine its occurrence time from the collected statistics available in $TS(S_i)$. Let $times(S_i) = \{\tau | \forall \delta, (\tau, \delta) \in TS(S_i)\}$. Thus, if t is the current time, (1) becomes[4] (see also [9]):

$$w(S_i) = \frac{1}{\sum_{S_j \in g} |TS(S_j)|} \times \sum_{\tau \in times(S_i)} e^{-(t-\tau)} \tag{2}$$

Equation (2) does a far better job in adapting to workflow changes by its inherent time-locality awareness. Nevertheless, because of the data-dependent nature of workflow tasks, there arises another problem, namely the ability to handle different execution times for different observed instances of a given task. That is, task S_i can have a varying impact on the resulting workflow performance if each of its execution instances behave differently. For example, instances of a task that were quite frequent but fast executing in the far past might be less important overall than more recent instances of the same task that are not as frequent but much slower executing. We propose to somehow consider also observed execution times in the computation of the task's weight. Thus (2) becomes:

$$w(S_i) = \frac{1}{\sum_{S_j \in g} |TS(S_j)|} \times \sum_{(\tau, \delta) \in TS(S_i)} \delta e^{-\alpha(t-\tau)} \tag{3}$$

Equation (3) associates a weight to a task, by considering both its time locality as well as its execution duration. A recent task is weighted more than an older

---

[4] For illustrative purposes, this is not normalized to 1.0 but can be easily brought to a normalized form if required.

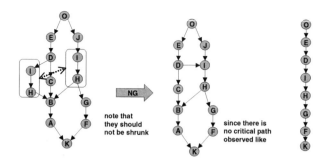

Fig. 7. Pruning the critical graph for efficiency is not trivial. Care should be taken to not introduce additional incorrect critical paths in the result (e.g., $O - E - D - I - H - J - F - K$).

one. A hot task is also weighted more than one less frequently occurring. A slow executing task is also assigned a higher weight than a fast executing one. The global parameters $\alpha \in (0, 1]$ is defining the importance of the start-time and execution duration respectively in one task's weight. There is a trade-off to be observed between a prevalent time-locality aware behavior and a more execution time dependent weighting. See also Section 6.

It is worth noting that, apparently, for efficient parsing and storage reasons, the critical graph seems to allow an additional pruning/canonical reduction step meant to reduce its size while maintaining its entire transition structure. For example, in the graph in Figure 7, apparently the transition from I to H, occurring multiple times, can be "collapsed" into one single instance. If such optimization techniques are to be deployed however, care should be taken to not introduce additional incorrect critical paths in the resulting "optimized graph". In this particular case, the proposed optimization is not sound, in that it introduces a critical path $(O - E - D - I - H - J - F - K)$ that was never observed in the initial construction process.

4   Resource Allocation

The weights defined by equation (3) define an ordering on a set of tasks, with the recent, hot, slow executing tasks being weighted higher. This ordering features a certain degree of adaptability, also tunable from the α parameter. As tasks become slower and/or less frequent the weights naturally adjust. Intuitively, these weights provide an "importance" metric for executing tasks, that could be used in the resource (re)allocation process to speed up the global workflow execution. Thus, the next step in the optimization process sorts the tasks appearing in the critical graph according to their weight and proposes a weight-proportional (re)allocation of additional resources to the higher-weighted ones. This aims to reduce the task execution time and thus the global workflow execution time (as the weight models the importance of this task in the global workflow).

4.1   Resource Model

Let us model the resource allocation process in more detail. Let there be the notion of a resource (e.g. CPU time) that can be quantified and allocated to each workflow composing task. Let r_i be the allocated amount for considered task S_i. Intuitively, in many scenarios there (arguably) exists a direct dependency between r_i and the task execution time δ_i. The more resources a task receives, the less time it should take executing. For illustrative purposes let this dependency be (see Figure 8 (b)) increasing and such that there exists a certain point, $min(\delta_i)$, below which the execution time of S_i does not improve, even if more resources (i.e. than $max(r_i)$) are allocated. Also, let $min(r_i)$ be the minimal amount of resources that S_i can function with. Thus, for any task S_i we have $r_i \in (min(r_i), max(r_i))$.

Given this model, let us construct a resource allocation algorithm that would optimally handle a fixed amount of total resources r to a given set of tasks. For simplicity purposes, let us make yet another assumption. Once a workflow starts executing, each task has continuously allocated an amount of resources of at least $min(r_i)$ (we do not model out-swapping). Thus $r > \sum_i min(r_i)$.

If $r > \sum_i max(r_i)$ each task could be allocated a maximum required amount of resources, thus functioning at its best potential. In this over-provisioning scenario, resource allocation can not improve workflow execution time. Thus, we are mainly concerned with the case when

$$r \in (\sum_i min(r_i), \sum_i max(r_i))$$

This is the case where all tasks are functioning (with minimal resources $min(r_i)$), but resource allocation can improve execution times for the highest weighted tasks.

4.2   Algorithm

We propose a resource allocation algorithm (see Figure 8 (a)) as a continuously running separate thread with control ability over resources and the execution environment of the composing workflow tasks (i.e. webservices).

The algorithm starts by assessing the "distance" between the current and the previously (at the time of the last allocation) computed task weights. If this difference exceeds a certain threshold $((\Delta_W(W_A, W_B) > \theta))$, resource reallocation is initiated. Tasks are allocated the remaining resources, according to their respective weights. $\Delta r_i(x) = \frac{w_i}{sumw_j} \times x$, represents the chunk to be allocated to task S_i out of the total remaining resource amount x. The thread then sleeps for a certain amount of time before resuming execution[5].

Increased Adaptivity. What if $\Delta_W(W_A, W_B) > \theta$ is too restrictive for the given workflow and will never be satisfied ? In other words, what if the task

---

[5] Alternately, this delay between allocation evaluations could be replaced by, or combined with an active notification mechanism activated by changes in the workflow response time for example

$W_A \leftarrow$ **null**
while (**true**) **do**
  $W_B \leftarrow$ **compute** weights according to (3)
  sort W_B
  if $(\Delta_W(W_A, W_B) > \theta)$ **then**
    $res \leftarrow (r - \sum_j min(r_j))$
    forall $w_i \in W_B$ (in sorted order) **do**
      $r_i \leftarrow min((min(r_i) + \Delta r_i(res)), max(r_i))$
      $res \leftarrow res - (r_i - min(r_i))$
    $W_A \leftarrow W_B$
  sleep *delay*

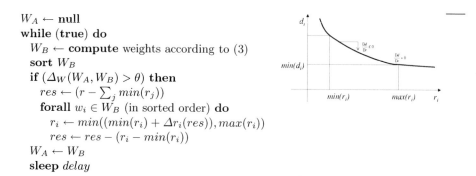

Fig. 8. (a) Resource allocation algorithm (running thread). (b) Proposed task execution time – resource dependency.

weights vary but to a degree that is insufficient to exceed the threshold. While the threshold value was introduced to fight the scenario of continuous re-allocations without much benefit, workflow behavior is hardly possible to bound ahead of time. It might be useful to "force" a re-allocation to be performed if too much time has elapsed since the last one. This idea can be coupled with the threshold mechanism in a natural way by changing the re(allocation) triggering condition into:

$$\Delta_W(W_A, W_B) + \varphi \Delta t > \theta$$

where Δt is the time elapsed since the last re(allocation) operation and *varphi* $\in$ $(0, 1)$.

5   Discussion

5.1   Allocation Stability

The resource allocation algorithm (Figure 8) suffers from a potential instability problem. If some resources get reallocated from a task A to a task B because currently, $w(A) < w(B)$, it is likely that in the next execution instance, δ_A is going to increase (as less resources are available to A). This in turn will yield an increase in $w(A)$. This might result in $w(A) > w(B)$, thus prompting resource allocations in the opposite direction, from B to A.

The effect of this instability is controllable however. Reallocation only happens when the distance between the weight vectors exceeds θ. Thus, small changes within individual weights might not be of impact right-away. Also, further fine-tuning can be achieved by choosing an appropriate β (lowering the impact of execution time in the weight computation).

The algorithm can be modified to provide a complete solution to this issue as follows. Keep a history for each task S_i, remembering its two past differing associated weights (for past reallocation cycles) $w^1(S_i)$, $w^2(S_i)$. $w^2(S_i)$ is the current weight of the task. Lets assume that $w^1(S_i) > w^2(S_i)$ (the task was allocated more resources as a result of $w^1(S_i)$ and then its weight dropped, possibly because of an associated speedup). Let $w^3(S_i)$ be the future weight that would be associated with this task if resources would be (de)allocated according to the current weight $w^2(S_i)$. The future weight can be estimated by approximating δ_i from the past execution times in $TS(S_i)$ and by assuming no new task execution happens before the next reallocation. If $w^2(S_i) < w^3(S_i) \approx w^1(S_i)$ (close to the original weight) the de-allocation would obviously result in oscillation; the algorithm should NOT de-allocate any resources that were allocated to S_i but rather ignore it and proceed to the next task, by reallocating the remaining resources.

In other words, we check if the weight of a task went down because of its increased speed (after allocation). If the future weight of the task is going to be back up (similar to the old weight) this might result in instability, thus needs to be avoided. We argue that this (or a similar) heuristic can significantly reduce or even completely eliminate oscillations and instability. Additionally, a variation of the algorithm could be to only de-allocate an upper-bounded fraction (η) of the resources of a given task. Considering an assumed relationship between task execution time and allocated resources, this ensures that the task slowdown can be upper bounded, thus the weight variation due to reallocation, limited.

5.2   Asynchronous Messaging

Asynchronous communication between parallel tasks (see Figure 9 (a)) needs to be considered when optimizing overall workflow execution times because the messaging constructs and semantics have a direct impact on these times. Fortunately, it turns out that asynchronous messaging can be naturally handled within the critical paths framework with a minimal set of associated algorithm extensions.

For each asynchronous communication instance between two parallel processes (sequences of tasks) P_1 and P_2, there exists a *invoke* ($P_1 \rightarrow P_2$) and a *receive* ($P_1 \leftarrow P_2$) semantic link. Because of the nature of asynchronous messaging and the BPEL business flows, from the execution flow and times point of view, these links behave effectively like transitions between tasks in P_1 and P_2. Thus, our main extension to the algorithm involves the critical path construction mechanism in Section 3.2. Instead of considering only the explicit transitions in $\mathbb{T}$ we augment this set with these links and treat them as transitions in the rest of the algorithm. The message initiation via *invoke* is virtually instantaneous (message goes in P_2's incoming mailbox), it can be ignored for simplicity. Thus let $\mathbb{T}^* = \mathbb{T} \cup receive\_links$, where $receive\_links$ is the set of all pairs of tasks (X, Y) like in Figure 9 (a), where Y is a receive activity and X initiates a reply message for Y.

In the following let us analyze the extended critical path construction in the case of two parallel processes. There are two possible asynchronous messaging scenarios. In the first case (Figure 9 (b)), process P_1 initiates an asynchronous message exchange with P_2, continues executing and eventually blocks waiting for a reply. In other words, the reply arrives *after* (at time $t_x > t_2$) it is expected. In

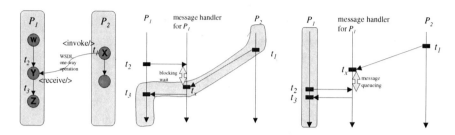

Fig. 9. (a) Asynchronous messaging scenario between two workflow processes/threads. (b) Reply arrives *after* it is looked for. Process 1 blocks waiting. The current workflow instance critical path naturally includes the *invoke* activity in process 2 and the blocking *receive* in process 1. (c) Reply arrives *before* it is looked for and becomes queued. Process 1 continues virtually un-interrupted ($(t_3 - t_2) \approx 0$) upon executing *receive*. The critical path includes just tasks within process 1 (as process 2 is faster and "keeps up", thus not impacting overall execution time).

this case, intuitively, the workflow execution is impacted by t_x, thus by the reply activity/task X. The critical path should thus contain $\{(W, \tau_W), (X, t_1), (Z, t_3)\}$.

In the second scenario, the reply arrives *before* (at time $t_x < t_2$) it is expected in P_1 and is queued in P_1's message handler. Thus, in this case, the workflow execution is not impacted at all by the reply and process P_1 continues un-interrupted with activity Z. The critical path construction mechanism should result in a path containing $\{(W, \tau_W), (Z, t_3)\}$ (τ_W not figured).

5.3   Limited Storage

In Section 3.3 a certain assumption was underlying the definition of task weights. A virtually infinite amount of memory was required to keep one task's execution history in $TS(S_i)$. This is sometimes not desirable.

This can be solved by observing that equation (3) is suitable for a natural incremental computation. If we change the notation such that $w(t)$ denotes the weight of task S_i as computed at current time t, then we have a dependency between $w(t)$ and $w(t + \Delta t)$ for any $\Delta t > 0$ as follows:

$$w(t + \Delta t) = \frac{1}{s_{t+\Delta t}} \times [e^{-\alpha \Delta t} s_t w(t) + \sum_{(\tau, \delta) \in TS(S_i) \wedge \tau > t + \Delta t} \delta e^{-\alpha(t - \tau + \Delta t)}]$$

where $s_t = \sum_{S_j \in g} |TS(S_j)|$ such that $\forall (\tau, \delta) \in TS(S_i)$, $\tau < t$. In effect, this reformulation shows the natural ability to compute the task weight dynamically out of a previous task weight incrementally, thus requiring virtually no additional storage.

In practice, when given a limited storage window for each task, another solution is easier to implement and identical from a theoretical point of view. Instead of the exponential weight in (3), which often presents representation accuracy issues, use the following linear version of the weight definition:

$$w(S_i) = \sum_{(\tau,\delta) \in TS(S_i)} \frac{\delta}{t - \tau} \tag{4}$$

Then, compute a task weight after seeing a certain fraction of m (e.g. $\frac{m}{2}$) worth of task instances and store that weight $w^1(S_i)$ instead of the seen instance stats. Repeat. This process will result in a set of task weights (e.g. one for each $\frac{m}{2}$ instances seen) that represent a summarized view of the execution history of S_i. There is only a fixed number of these weights that we remember, and the "older" ones are gradually discarded.

When computing the current task weight, we then consider all the actual time stamps in the remaining window and compute a weight $w^2(S_i)$. Then the current weight is going to be defined by

$$w(S_i) = \chi w^1(S_i) + (1 - \chi)w^2(S_i)$$

, where $\chi \in (0, 1)$. $w^1(S_i)$ is then replaced by $w^2(S_i)$ and the process continues. Depending on how much memory is available, for more accuracy, this mechanism can be extended by storing multiple weights and having multiple χ values in computing the final weight.

Yet another optimization that can be deployed derives from the fact that it is likely that some tasks are going to be more active than others. If stats keeping memory is shared, storage can be distributed according to the estimated/previous frequency of each task, such that statistics about very active tasks are going to be more accurate than for less active ones.

6   Experiments

We implemented a proof-of-concept package (wfx.*) of the workflow modeling and resource allocation algorithms presented. Our implementation allows the definition, virtual execution, monitoring and resource allocation for arbitrary workflows and associated tasks. We also implemented experimental versions of our wrapper technology and tested it with the IBM BPWS4J Engine.

We performed experiments and analyzed the behavior of various classes of workflows. For illustration purposes here we discuss a simple minimal

Here we are discussing a simple, yet illustrative workflow depicted in Figure 10 (a). This workflow is simple enough to be easy to comprehend and is composed of an initial traditional stochastic flow (that can be handled by simple stochastic modeling [2]) followed by concurrent execution of tasks 6 and 7 (they start simultaneously, upon completion of 5) and a conjunctive join condition[6] for task 8.

---

[6] Handling conjunctive joins is one of the important novel use scenarios that our solution handles.

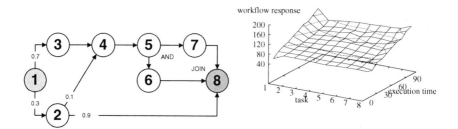

Fig. 10. (a) Simple parallel workflow. Transitions 5-7 and 5-6 are triggered simultaneously. (b) Average workflow response time as a function of individual service times for the workflow in (a). It can be seen (as intuitively expected) that tasks 1 and 8 have a higher impact on the workflow execution (they are executed every time).

To assess, the initial impact of each task in the global execution times, in Figure 10 (b) the overall workflow response time is depicted as a function of the individual task execution times. It can be seen that (as can be inferred from the workflow schema), task 1 seems to correlate stronger (steeper incline) with the global workflow times, than task 2 for example. Task 2 is only triggered 30% of the time which would explain its lower observed weight in the overall times.

Validating the critical weights is of significant importance if the allocation mechanism is to function properly and recommend appropriate resource allocations. In the experiment depicted in Figure 11 (a) gradually increasing task execution times naturally result in higher weights, prompting the allocation of additional resources.

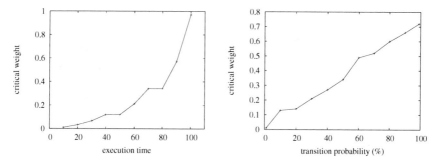

Fig. 11. (a) The critical weights accurately follow increases in task execution times, prompting additional resource allocation. Pictured is task 4 in the workflow in Figure 10 (a). (b) As the transition probability increases (for task 2 in Figure 10 (a)), the associated critical weight follows almost linearly.

In Figure 11 (b) we can see how higher transition probabilities (e.g. for task 2) yield almost linearly following values in the resulting weights. This shows that there exists a natural direct relationship between the weighting process (and additional resource allocation) and the task execution frequency. This in effect ties our work with the work in [2] and shows that it also correctly handles stochastic aspects.

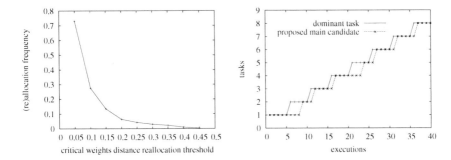

Fig. 12. (a) The stability and frequency of the resource (re)allocation process can be controlled by adjusting the critical weights (re)allocation threshold θ. As it relaxes (increases), the (re)allocation frequency drops. (b) As the dominant task in the workflow changes (e.g. from 1 to 8), the resource allocation mechanism closely follows with a minimal latency delay (1-2 workflow executions). This shows the adaptivity to changes in workflow behavior.

An experiment exploring the stability of the resource allocation process is illustrated in Figure 12 (a). Stable allocation schemes put less loads on resource managers and also likely minimize resource shifting overheads (not considered here). It can be seen how θ can be used as a fine-tuning "knob" balancing this trade-off between high (re)allocation frequency and stability.

The experiment illustrated in Figure 12 (b) analyzes the adaptivity of the resource allocation mechanism. This is important to allow for quick turn-around times and stability in the resource allocation mechanisms. Depicted are both the actual dominant task (longest execution time) in various workflow instances and the proposed main additional resource re-allocation candidate. It can be seen that the algorithm adapts quickly to changes in the workflow behavior, with a minimal "following delay" (1-2 workflow instances). This is great news, in that it guarantees that resource allocation converges quickly and improves execution times accordingly.

7   Related Work

Existing work can be categorized into two parts: (1) QoS-aware service composition; (2) adaptive service composition. QoS-aware service composition has been extensibly studied. Existing approaches [10,11,12,13,14,15,16,17] consider mainly performance at composition time, whereas in our work we optimize performance at runtime. Moreover, various mechanisms [18,19,20,21] have been proposed to endow a web service workflow with adaptivity to its runtime environment. These proposals mainly focus on how to update a workflow at runtime in an non-intrusive way. Our runtime optimization can be introduced on top of such schemes.

8 Conclusions

In this paper we proposed a "dynamic" stochastic workflow modeling approach suited to handle workflows with concurrent paths. We then explored this approach experimentally through the design and proof of concept implementation of a novel monitoring component which transparently gathers execution statistics about the composing workflow tasks (web services). These statistics are then used in the resource (re)allocation algorithm to optimize overall workflow performance.

Various issues remain to be explored. Different (potentially composite) quality metrics and alternative wrapping solutions, minimizing overheads could be considered. It might be desirable to augment the solution with effective correlation sets handling. Additionally, deployment of such components in mainstream industry resource managers should be investigated and pursued.

References

1. Sion, R., Tatemura, J.: Dynamic Stochastic Models for Workflow Response Optimization. In: Proceedings of the International Conference on Web Services ICWS (2005)
2. Gillmann, M., Weikum, G., Wonner, W.: Workflow management with service quality guarantees. In: Proceedings of the 2002 ACM SIGMOD International Conference on Management of Data, pp. 228–239. ACM Press, New York (2002)
3. Broberg, M., Lundberg, L., Grahn, H.: Performance optimization using extended critical path analysis in multithreaded programs on multiprocessors. Journal of Parallel and Distributed Computing 61(1), 115–136 (2001)
4. BEA, IBM, Microsoft: BPEL4WS: Business Process Execution Language for Web Services Version 1.1 (2003)
5. W3C: Web Services Definition Language (WSDL) 1.1 (2001)
6. Gillmann, M., Weissenfels, J., Weikum, G., Kraiss, A.: Performance and availability assessment for the configuration of distributed workflow management systems. In: Zaniolo, C., Grust, T., Scholl, M.H., Lockemann, P.C. (eds.) EDBT 2000. LNCS, vol. 1777, p. 183. Springer, Heidelberg (2000)
7. Son, J.H., Kim, M.H.: Analyzing the critical path for the well-formed workflow schema. In: Proceedings of the 2001 DASFAA. IEEE, Los Alamitos (2001)
8. Lawrence, P.: Workflow Handbook. John Wiley and Sons, Chichester (1997)
9. Sion, R., Atallah, M., Prabhakar, S.: On-the-fly intrusion detection for web portals. In: Proceedings of IEEE ITCC 2003 (2003)

10. Alrifai, M., Risse, T.: Combining global optimization with local selection for efficient qoS-aware service composition. In: Quemada, J., León, G., Maarek, Y.S., Nejdl, W. (eds.) WWW, pp. 881–890. ACM, New York (2009)
11. Mukherjee, D., Jalote, P., Gowri Nanda, M.: Determining qoS of WS-BPEL compositions. In: Bouguettaya, A., Krueger, I., Margaria, T. (eds.) ICSOC 2008. LNCS, vol. 5364, pp. 378–393. Springer, Heidelberg (2008)
12. Baligand, F., Rivierre, N., Ledoux, T.: A declarative approach for qoS-aware web service compositions. In: Krämer, B.J., Lin, K.-J., Narasimhan, P. (eds.) ICSOC 2007. LNCS, vol. 4749, pp. 422–428. Springer, Heidelberg (2007)
13. Sato, N., Trivedi, K.S.: Stochastic modeling of composite web services for closed-form analysis of their performance and reliability bottlenecks. In: Krämer, B.J., Lin, K.-J., Narasimhan, P. (eds.) ICSOC 2007. LNCS, vol. 4749, pp. 107–118. Springer, Heidelberg (2007)
14. Cardellini, V., Casalicchio, E., Grassi, V., Presti, F.L.: Flow-based service selection forweb service composition supporting multiple qoS classes. In: ICWS, pp. 743–750. IEEE Computer Society, Los Alamitos (2007)
15. Li, Y., Huai, J., Deng, T., Sun, H., Guo, H., Du, Z.: QoS-aware service composition in service overlay networks. In: ICWS, pp. 703–710. IEEE Computer Society, Los Alamitos (2007)
16. Nguyen, X.T., Kowalczyk, R., Phan, M.T.: Modelling and solving qoS composition problem using fuzzy disCSP. In: ICWS, pp. 55–62. IEEE Computer Society, Los Alamitos (2006)
17. Berbner, R., Spahn, M., Repp, N., Heckmann, O., Steinmetz, R.: Heuristics for qoS-aware web service composition. In: ICWS, pp. 72–82. IEEE Computer Society, Los Alamitos (2006)
18. Moser, O., Rosenberg, F., Dustdar, S.: Non-intrusive monitoring and service adaptation for WS-BPEL. In: Huai, J., Chen, R., Hon, H.W., Liu, Y., Ma, W.Y., Tomkins, A., Zhang, X. (eds.) WWW, pp. 815–824. ACM, New York (2008)
19. Harney, J., Doshi, P.: Speeding up adaptation of web service compositions using expiration times. In: Williamson, C.L., Zurko, M.E., Patel-Schneider, P.F., Shenoy, P.J. (eds.) WWW, pp. 1023–1032. ACM, New York (2007)
20. He, Q., Yan, J., Jin, H., Yang, Y.: Adaptation of web service composition based on workflow patterns. In: Bouguettaya, A., Krüger, I., Margaria, T. (eds.) ICSOC 2008. LNCS, vol. 5364, pp. 22–37. Springer, Heidelberg (2008)
21. Mosincat, A., Binder, W.: Transparent runtime adaptability for BPEL processes. In: Bouguettaya, A., Krüeger, I., Margaria, T. (eds.) ICSOC 2008. LNCS, vol. 5364, pp. 241–255. Springer, Heidelberg (2008)

Adaptive Parallelization of Queries Calling Dependent Data Providing Web Services

Manivasakan Sabesan and Tore Risch

Uppsala DataBase Laboratory
Department of Information Technology
Uppsala University, Sweden
{Manivasakan.Sabesan,Tore.Risch}@it.uu.se

Abstract. A common pattern in queries calling web services is that the output of one web service call is the input for another. The challenge addressed in this chapter is to develop methods to speed up such *dependent* calls by paralleliza-tion. We developed a system, *WSMED*, to provide a *web service query service*. WSMED automatically parallelizes the web service calls by starting separate *query processes,* each managing a parameterized sub-query, a *plan function.* The parallel plan is defined in terms of an operator, *FF_APPLYP,* to ship in parallel to other query processes the same plan function for different parame-ters. By using FF_APPLYP we first investigated ways to set up different proc-ess trees manually to find a best one. To automatically achieve the optimal process tree we modified FF_APPLYP to an operator *AFF_APPLYP* that adapts a parallel plan locally in each query process until an optimized performance is achieved. The query execution time obtained with AFF_APPLYP is shown to be close to the best process tree obtained with FF_APPLYP.

Keywords: Adaptive parallelization, Dependent web service calls, Web service querying service, Search computing.

1 Introduction

Web services are often used for search computing [5] where data is retrieved from servers providing information of different kinds. Such *data providing web services* [2] return a set of objects for a given set of parameters without any side effects. As an ex-ample, consider a query to find *USAF Academy's Zip code* and the *State* where it is located. Three different data providing web services can be used for answering this query, using the operations *GetAllStates* from the web service *GeoPlaces* [6] to re-trieve all the states, *GetInfoByState* from *USZip* [27] to get all the Zip codes within a given state, and *GetPlacesInside* from *ZipCodes* [7] to provide all the places having a given Zip code. The Web Service MEDiator (WSMED) system [21] [23] provides a web service to compose any data providing web service operations. It can automatically define a relational view for any data providing web service operation, which can then be queried and joined using SQL. For a given SQL query, it dynamically composes the web services and optimizes the web service calls. Querying data providing web services with SQL is quite natural.

D. Agrawal et al. (Eds.): Information and Software as Services, LNBIP 74, pp. 132–154, 2011.

A naïve implementation of the query above where these web services are called in sequence makes 5000 operation calls and takes nearly 2400 seconds to execute. The reason is that each web service call incurs high latency and message set-up costs. Queries calling data providing web services often have a similar pattern where the output of one web service call (e.g. *GetAllStates*) is the input for another one (e.g. *Get-InfoByState*), i.e. the second call is dependent on the first one, etc. A challenge here is to develop methods to speed up queries requiring such *dependent* data providing web service calls. In general such speed-ups are based on the web service properties. However, those properties are not explicitly available and depend on the network and run-time environments when and where the queries are executed. It is very difficult to base execution strategies on a static cost model in such scenarios, as is done in relational databases, since the functioning of a web service operation is normally unknown and the cost to execute an operation varies over time because of network and system loads.

In our approach a web service call is considered as an expensive function call where the result is a nested data collection. It is likely that making parallel invocations of such calls will speed up the performance of queries with several dependent web service calls. To improve the response time, we present an approach to parallelize the web service calls while keeping the dependencies among them. With the approach separate *query processes* are started in parallel, each calling a parameterized sub query plan, called a *plan function*, for given parameters. Each plan function encapsulates one web service call and makes data transformations such as flattening nested results, filtering, and data conversions.

The WSMED implementation extends a main memory functional DBMS [19]. The system can import any WSDL file and store in its local database. The local database is used for representing automatically generated relational views where the result collections are flattened and can be queried with SQL. The system includes an algebra operator *cwo* that can call any web service operation and operators to construct and flatten the nested structures used in web service operation arguments and results.

The performance is often improved by setting up several web service calls to the same operation in parallel rather than to call the operation in sequence for different parameters. For a given query the WSMED optimizer first produces a non-parallel plan where web service operations are called using *cwo*. The query processor then automatically reformulates the non-parallel plan into a parallel one where web service operations are called in parallel while keeping the required dependency among the calls. The algebra operator, *FF_APPLYP* (First Finished Apply in Parallel), first ships a plan function in parallel to other child query processes. It takes a stream of parameter tuples as input and ships them as parameters to the shipped plan functions. Then, it asynchronously receives and emits the result tuples from the parallel calls to the plan functions in the children. .

Multi-level execution plans are generated with several layers of parallelism in different query processes. This forms the *process tree* for the query. The number of child processes below a parent query process is called its *fanout*. At any point in time every process in the tree executes one plan function for a specific parameter.

Normally there is an optimal number of parallel calls for a given web service operation. It is therefore important to figure out an optimized process tree for an execution plan by automatically arranging the available query processes for best performance. We first evaluated FF_APPLYP for different balanced process trees by setting different fanouts manually per tree level. We tested flat and bushy process trees over publicly available web services. By experiments we manually determined the best fanout on each level.

Each level in the optimal process tree need not have the same fanout i.e. the tree need not be balanced. Therefore WSMED adaptively achieves an optimized process tree by local run-time monitoring of each plan function call. For the adaptation it uses a modified FF_APPLYP, called *AFF_APPLYP* that dynamically modifies a parallel plan locally and greedily in each query process. The adaptation may produce a non-balanced tree. We compare the operator AFF_APPLYP to the balanced process tree with best effort manual process arrangement using FF_APPLYP.

In summary the contributions of our work are:

1. The WSMED system is developed to automatically provide general relational query capabilities over data providing web services by reading WSDL meta-data description. Queries are expressed in SQL.
2. WSMED provides a web service query service that dynamically composes and optimizes joins over any data providing web services.
3. The algebra operator FF_APPLYP dynamically distributes a plan to enable parallel calls to sub-plans that encapsulate web service operations over a stream of different parameter values.
4. An algorithm is implemented to transform a non parallel plan into a parallel plan by introducing FF_APPLYP operators and generating plan functions encapsulating each web service call. With FF_APPLYP the fanouts on each level are specified at query compilation time.
5. To automatically and adaptively optimize the parallel plan, we developed another algebra operator AFF_APPLYP that locally adjusts adaptively an initial balanced binary process tree until best performance is obtained without any static cost model. We show that the performance of AFF_APPLYP is close to the best experimental plan with manually set fanouts obtained with FF_APPLYP.

Section 2 explains the service oriented architecture of WSMED, its query web service, WSMED server components, the web service schema, and the automatic flattening of web service operations into SQL views. In section 3 we present an example of SQL queries with dependent web service calls, the functionalities of FF_APPLYP operator, and the structure of the parallel process tree. Section 4 describes the query optimization and parallelization algorithms are used, the functionalities of the adaptive operator AFF_APPLYP, and analysis of experimental results. Section 5 addresses related work. Finally, Section 6 concludes our approach and discusses future directions.

2   The WSMED System

Following the *Everything as a Service* (XaaS) paradigm [14] [26], WSMED is providing a web service query service to query arbitrary data providing web services. The WSMED web page [30] demonstrates its functionality. It allows a user to query any data providing web service and issue SQL queries without installing any software. In the web page a JavaScript program directly invokes the WSMED web service to query any data providing web services.

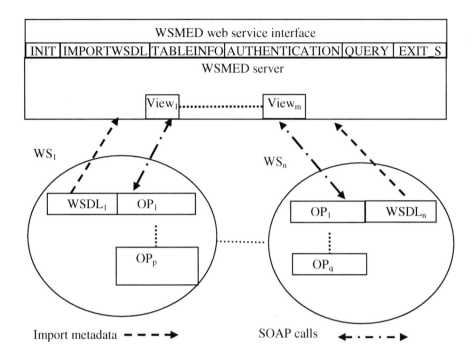

Fig. 1. Service Oriented Architecture of WSMED

Fig. 1 illustrates the service oriented architecture of WSMED. A number of web service operations are provided through the *WSMED web service interface*. The SOAP protocol is used for all web service calls.

The WSDL file [31] exports six web service operations:

- The *INIT* operation registers a WSMED user session.
- For a given URL the *IMPORTWSDL* operation imports WSDL meta-data information and automatically creates SQL views $View_i$ for every operation OP_j provided by a web service WS_k described by an imported WSDL document $WSDL_k$.
- The *AUTHENTICATION* operation provides authentication information for web service operations that so require.
- The system accepts general SQL queries to the generated views by the *QUERY* operation.
- The *TABLEINFO* operation provides information about an SQL view of a given web service operation. For example some table attributes must always be known when querying the service, since they provide the arguments for the underlying web service operation. The results from querying data providing web service operations are automatically flattened and post processed by WSMED in order to deliver the results back to the *QUERY* operation as a flat relation.
- Finally, the operation *EXIT_S* terminates a user session.

WSMED's service capabilities fulfill the major characteristics of XaaS [26]:

- *No dependency on hardware and software*: The user just needs a computer with internet connection to access a public web page to use any data providing web service.
- *No specific location*: user can access the service from anywhere.
- *Improved Tenancy* – access of the service is not limited to a fixed number of users.
- *Extension to Consumers*: service consumption is not limited to a particular domain. Any user could access the service.

2.1 The Web Service Query Service

Fig. 2 shows the processes involved in the WSMED web service. The *WSMED web server* is a standalone SOAP web server using the library, *Quick Server* [18], to send and receive SOAP messages using the HTTP protocol. The *user WSMED server* implements the WSMED functions, *IMPORTWSDL, AUTHENTICATION, TABLEINFO,* and *QUERY*, which are provided as WSMED web service operations and described by the document *wsmed.wsdl* [31]. Each user is assigned a private user WSMED server to manage the session of the data providing web services she is querying. The *coordinator* implements the WSMED operations *INIT* and *EXIT_S* to manage the user WSMED servers. When new users are registered with WSMED by operation *INIT* the coordinator starts a user WSMED server session. Analogously the WSMED server session is terminated by the operation *EXIT_S*. The web page in [30] demonstrates the functionality of the WSMED web services.

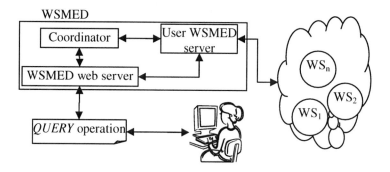

Fig. 2. Web service query service

2.2 WSMED Server Components

Fig. 3 illustrates the system components of a WSMED server. The system stores WSDL meta-data in the *web service meta-store* in terms of the *web service schema*. The *WSDL importer* can populate the web service descriptions by reading a specific WSDL document using the Java tool kits *WSDL4J* [29] and *Castor* [4]. It parses the retrieved WSDL document, converts it to the format used by the web service schema, and stores the extracted meta-data in the web service meta-store.

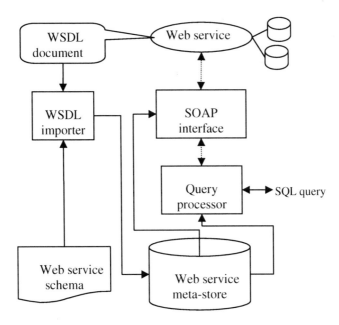

Fig. 1. WSMED System Components

The *query processor* exploits the web service meta-store and the Amos II query engine [19] to process queries. The query processor calls the *SOAP Interface* component, which is implemented using the *SAAJ* library [20]. The SOAP interface invokes web service operations using SOAP to retrieve the result for a user query.

2.3 The Web Service Schema

Fig. 4 shows an ER-diagram of WSMED's *web service schema* that represents WSDL descriptions. It represents the WSDL core elements *service, operation,* and *element.* The *service* entity type describes a particular web service. Each web service has a *name,* and a *wsdlurl.* The *ports* relationship represents the association between a service and its operations. Each entity type *operation* represents a procedure that can be invoked through the web service. The *style* indicates whether the operation is RPC-oriented or document-oriented. The attribute *authenticationstr* stores authentication information for an operation. The *encodingstyle* is a URL that indicates the encoding rules for data in SOAP messages to the operation. The *targeturl* determines the address of the operation. The *soapactionurl* identifies the task to be performed on the server side.

Each operation has a number of *input, output* and *authentication* elements. An *element* is an abstract definition of some data structure being transmitted and is associated with an XML Schema data *type.* The input and output elements define the *signature* of the operation. Complex data elements may consist of other *sub_elements* where each sub-element has a data type and the number of maximum occurrences, *maxoccurs,* within the super element.

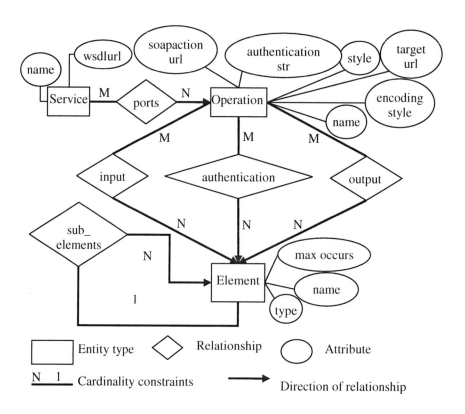

Fig. 4. Web Service Schema

2.4 Operation Wrapper Function

For a given web service WSMED automatically generates *operation wrapper functions* (OWFs) based on the WSDL definitions of the web service operations. The OWF defines an SQL view of a web service operation. SQL queries can be made over these views with the restriction that the input values of the OWFs must be known in the query. Each OWF encapsulates a data providing web service operation for given parameters and emits the result as a flattened stream of tuples.

For example, the OWF *GetAllStates* defines the result from the web service operation with the same name [6] as a relational view, *GetAllStates(Name, Type, State, LatDegrees, LonDegrees, LatRadians, LonRadians)*. Fig. 5 shows an SQL query to the view.

Fig. 6 shows the automatically generated OWF #GetAllStates, which flattens the result from the web service operation *GetAllStates* and defines a corresponding SQL view called *GetAllStates*. A unique OWF is generated for each operation in each imported web service. The OWF #*GetAllStates* presents information of US states as a set of tuples <*Name, Type, State, LatDegrees, LonDegrees, LatRadians, LonRadians*>. Any web service operation can be invoked by the built-in function *cwo* (line 14). Its parameters are the URL of the WSDL document that describes the service, the name of the service, the operation name, and the input parameter list for the operation. The web service operation *GetAllStates* has no input parameters ({ })

```
select   Name,State, LatDegrees
from     GetAllStates
where    State like 'A*'
```

Fig. 5. SQL Query

```
1   create function #GetAllStates()-> Bag of
                    Charstring Name, Charstring Type,
                    Charstring State, Real LatDegrees,
                    Real LonDegrees, Real LatRadians,
                    Real LonRadians> as
2     select  GeoPlaceDetails['Name'],
3             GeoPlaceDetails['Type'],
4             GeoPlaceDetails['State'],
5             GeoPlaceDetails['LatDegrees'],
6             GeoPlaceDetails['LonDegrees'],
7             GeoPlaceDetails['LatRadians'],
8             GeoPlaceDetails['LonRadians']
9     from    Sequence out,
10            Record GetAllStatesResult ,
11            Record GetAllStatesResult1,
12            Sequence GetAllStateResult2,
13            Record GeoPlaceDetails
14    where   out=
                CWO('http://codebump.com/services/PlaceLookup.wsdl',
                    'GeoPlaces', 'GetAllStates', {}) and
15            GetAllStatesResult1 in out and
16            GetAllStatesResult2 =
                GetAllStatesResult1['GetAllStatesResult']and
17            GetAllStateResult in GetAllStatesResult2 and
18            GeoPlaceDetails=
                GetAllStatesResult['GeoPlaceDetails'];
```

Fig. 6. Automatically generated OWF #GetAllStates

The result from *cwo* is bound to the query variable *out* (line 14). It holds an object representing the output from the web service operation temporarily materialized in WSMED's local store. The OWF converts the output XML element from the SOAP call into records and sequences. The result *out* is here a sequence from which elements are extracted (line 15) into the *GetAllStatesResult1* record structure using the *in* operator. The records have only one attribute named *GetAllStatesResult* whose values are assigned to another sequence structure *GetAllStatesResult2* (line 16). An attribute *a* of a record *r* is accessed using the notation *r[a]*. Each element record from the sequence *GetAllStatesResult2* is bound to the variable *GetAllStateResult* (line 17). The values of the attribute *GeoPlaceDetails* are assigned to the *GeoPlaceDetails* record with attributes *Name, Type, State, LatDegrees, LonDegrees, LatRadians*, and *LonRadians* (line 18).

3 Queries over Dependent Web Service Calls

Queries calling data providing web services often have a similar pattern where the output of one web service call is the input for another web service call. A naïve implementation of such queries making web service calls sequentially is very time consuming. The reason is that each web service call incurs high latency and message set-up costs. A major challenge addressed here is to develop methods to speed up queries requiring such dependent web service calls. Our solution for this research problem is to parallelize dependent data providing web service operation calls by starting several query processes and arrange them in a process tree efficiently.

3.1 Motivating Scenario

The class of queries we consider here is dependent-join [10] queries, which in their simplest form can be expressed as:

$$f(x-,y+) \ \Lambda \ g(y-,z+)$$

The predicate f binds y for some input value x and passes each y to the predicate g that returns the bindings of z as result. Thus, g depends on the output of f. The predicates f and g represent calls to parameterized sub queries, which in our case are execution plans encapsulating data providing web service operations. Inputs parameters are annotated with '-' and outputs with '+'.

We made experiments with two different queries calling different web service operations provided by different publicly available service providers.

3.1.1 Query1

In the first test case we used the SQL *Query1* in Fig. 7 that finds information about places located within 15 km from each city whose name starts with 'Atlanta' in all US states. In the query we utilize the web service operations *GetAllStates*[6], *GetPlacesWithin*[6], and *GetPlaceList*[25]. In Fig. 7 the three SQL views *GetAllStates, GetPlacesWithin,* and *GetPlaceList* define views encapsulating web service operations with the same names. The query returns a stream of 360 result tuples. An execution plan invokes more than 300 web service calls.

The generated SQL view *GetAllStates* presents information of US states as a set of tuples <*Name, Type, State, LatDegrees, LonDegrees, LatRadians, LonRadians*>. However, we are only interested in the values of the attribute *State*. The generated SQL view *GetPlacesWithin* returns a set of tuples <*ToCity, ToState, GeoPlaceDistance_Distance*> for given place (*'Atlanta'*), state (*gs.State*), distance (*15.0*), and kind of place type to find (*'City'*). The generated SQL view *GetPlaceList* retrieves a set of places <*placename, state, country, placeLon, placeLat, availableThemeMask, placeTypeId, population*> given a specification of a place (concatenate *ToCity+','+ToState*), the maximum number result tuples (*100*), and a flag indicating whether places having an associated map are returned.

```
select      gl.placename,gl.state

from        GetAllStates gs, GetPlacesWithin gp,
            GetPlaceList gl

where       gs.State=gp.state and
            gp.distance=15.0 and
            gp.placeTypeToFind='City' and
            gp.place='Atlanta' and
            gl.placeName=gp.ToPlace+' ,'+gp.ToState and
            gl.MaxItems=100 and
            gl.imagePresence='true'
```

Fig. 7. Query 1 defined in SQL

3.1.2 Query2

The second case, *Query2* in Fig. 8, finds the zip code and state of the place '*USAF Academy*'. A naïve sequential plan invokes more than 5000 web service calls. Here also three different dependent web services are involved. *GetAllStates* is the same as in *Query1*. *GetInfoByState* is provided by the USZip [27] web service to retrieve all zip codes for a given state as a single comma separated string (*gi.GetInfoByStateResult*). *getzipcode* is an helping function defined in WSMED that extracts the set of zip codes (*gc.zipcode*) given a string of zip codes (*gc.zipstr*). The generated SQL view *Get-PlacesInside* is defined by the Zipcodes [7] web service and returns for a given zip code a set of tuples <*ToPlace, ToState, Distance*> where *ToPlace* is a place located within the zip code area, *ToState* is the state of the place, and *Distance* is the distance from the place to the origin of the given zip code area.

```
select      gp.ToState, gp.zip

from        GetAllStates gs, GetInfoByState gi,
            getzipcode gc, GetPlacesInside gp

where       gs.State=gi.USState and
            gi.GetInfoByStateResult=gc.zipstr and
            gc.zipcode=gp.zip and
            gp.ToPlace='USAFAcademy'
```

Fig. 8. Query2 defined in SQL

3.2 The Parallel Process Tree

The web service metadata in a WSDL document is first imported and stored in the WSMED's web service meta-store (Fig. 3). A query is processed by a coordinator process *q0*. Fig. 9 gives an example of a process tree generated by the WSMED query optimizer. Every query process on each level can be connected with a number of child processes and all the processes on the same level execute the same plan function but with different parameters.

In Fig. 9, *q1* is connected with *q3, q4,* and *q5.* The plan function in the coordinator *q0* encapsulates the web service operation *GetAllStates,* while the plan functions of the processes in level one encapsulate the operation *GetPlacesWithin* for different states. On level two the plan function calls the operation *GetPlaceList* for different place specifications.

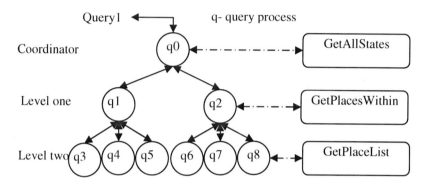

Fig. 9. Process tree

The coordinator *q0* first generates a non parallel plan containing calls to the plan functions encapsulating the web service operations. It then automatically reformulates the non parallel plan to incorporate parallel web service calls by inserting algebra operators FF_APPLYP in the execution plan whenever an a call to *cwo* is encountered. The operator FF_APPLYP enables parallel invocation of a plan function for parameter tuples delivered as an input stream to FF_APPLYP. For each *cwo* call a plan function is generated that encapsulates a fragment of the non parallel execution plan embodying the web service operation call.   When the algebra operator FF_APPLYP is executed in process *q0*, it first ships in parallel to its children in level one (*q1* and *q2*) the same plan function definition that encapsulates *GetPlacesWithin.* Then it ships in parallel a stream of parameter tuples to the shipped plan function installed in the children processes ready for execution. Analogously, the FF_APPLYP operators executing in the level one processes each send another plan function definition to the level two processes (*q3, q4, q5, q6, q7,* and *q8*). Each query process initially receives its own plan function definition once before execution. When the level two processes receive data from the wrapped web service operation *GetPlaceList,* the results will be returned asynchronously as streams to the processes in level one, and finally the results are streamed to the coordinator process.

3.3 FF_APPLYP

FF_APPLYP has the signature:

```
FF_APPLYP(Function  pf,   Integer  fo,  Stream  pstream)  →
                                         Stream result
```

It ships in parallel to *fo* number of child query processes the definition of the same plan function *pf*. Then it ships one by one parameter tuples from *pstream* to each of the children. The result stream from a call to *pf* for a given parameter tuple is sent back to FF_APPLYP asynchronously as a stream of tuples, *result*.

In our first experiments the fanout *fo* is set manually for each level. This allows us to analyze different process trees. In Fig. 9 the fanout on level one is $fo_1=2$ and on level two $fo_2=3$. The coordinator *q0* at level zero first initializes the two child processes *q1* and *q2*. Then *q0* ships the plan function encapsulating the web service operation *GetPlacesWithin* to the children (*q1 and q2*). When all plan functions are shipped it starts picking parameter tuples one by one from *pstream*, to send down to the plan functions started in the children. In *q0* the stream *pstream* is a stream of state names produced as the result of the plan function that encapsulates the web service operation *GetAllStates*. When the first round of parameter tuples are shipped to all children, FF_APPLYP will broadcast to the children that it is ready to receive results. Whenever a result tuple is received from some child it is directly emitted as a result of FF_APPLYP. When a child completed the processing of a plan function for a given parameter tuple it sends an *end-of-call* message to FF_APPLYP. When the parent receives an end-of-call message from a child it will ship the next pending parameter tuple from *pstream* to the idle child process. When there are no pending parameter tuples in *pstream* and no pending results from the child processes, FF_APPLYP is finished.

4 Query Parallelization in WSMED

Fig. 10 illustrates the query processor in WSMED [23]. It parallelizes the queries in two phases. In *Phase1* a non parallel plan is created from the given SQL query. The parallel plan is produced in *Phase2* using the non parallel plan. The calculus generator produces from the SQL query an internal calculus expression in a Datalog dialect [16].

For example, *Query1* is transformed into the following calculus expression:

```
Query1(pl,st)  :- GetAllStates()AND
                  GetPlacesWithin('Atlanta',_,15.0,'City') AND
                  GetPlaceList(_, 100,'true')
```

The symbol '_' represents an anonymous result variable.

With non parallel query optimization the calculus expression is translated by the non-parallel plan optimizer into the algebra expression in Fig. 11 . The algebra expressions contains calls to the *apply* operator γ [9], which applies a plan function for a given parameter tuple. The non parallel query execution plan with γ can be directly interpreted but with very bad performance, since many web service operations are applied in sequence.

The plan first calls the operation *GetAllStates* returning a stream of tuples *<st1>*. Each of these tuples are fed to the next operation *GetPlacesWithin* called by the apply operator with the given argument tuple *('Atlanta', st1, 15.0, 'City')* returning a stream of tuples *<city, st2>*. The built in function *concat* is then applied on each argument tuple *(city,',',st2)* producing a stream of strings *str*. Finally the operation *GetPlaceList* is applied on each argument tuple *(str,100,'true')* returning a stream of tuples *<pl,st>*.

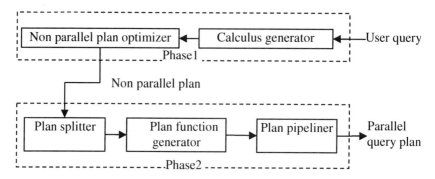

Fig. 10. Query Processor

In Fig. 10 the *plan splitter* takes as input a non parallel plan (e.g. the one in Fig. 11) and identifies there the parallelizable calls to *cwo*. Since the parallelization is based on parameter streams, *cwo* calls not having input parameters are not considered.

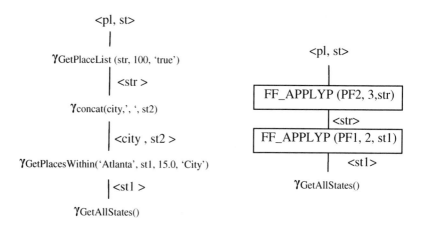

Fig. 11. Non parallel query plan - Query1   **Fig. 12.** Parallel query plan-Query1

For example, the plan in Fig. 11 can be parallelized for the operations *Get-PlacesWithin* and *GetPlaceList*, but not for *GetAllStates*. The plan splitter splits the plan into one section for each parallelizable *cwo* call starting from the bottom. The first section, flattening the result from the call to the web service operation *GetAll-States*, is executed in the coordinator. The next section contains the calls to *Get-PlacesWithin* and *concat*. The final section contains only the call to *GetPlaceList*.

For each parallelizable section the *plan function generator* creates a plan function that encapsulates a parallelizable *cwo* call. For example, the plan function *PF1* in Fig. 13 encapsulates the operation *GetPlacesWithin*. It has the signature:

```
PF1(Charstring st1) → Stream of Charstring str
```

Analogously *PF2* in Fig. 14 flattens the web service operation *GetPlaceList* to return a stream of tuples $<pl, st>$ and has the signature:

```
PF2(Charstring str)  →  Stream of <Charstring pl,
                                   Charstring st>
```

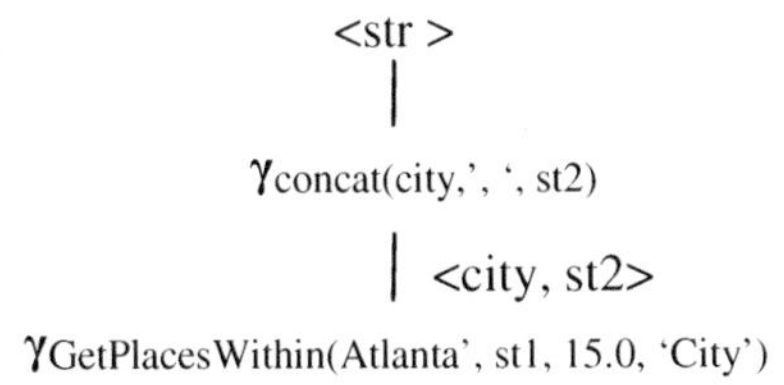

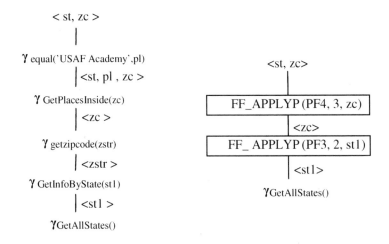

Fig. 13. Plan function PF1 wrapping GetPlacesWithin

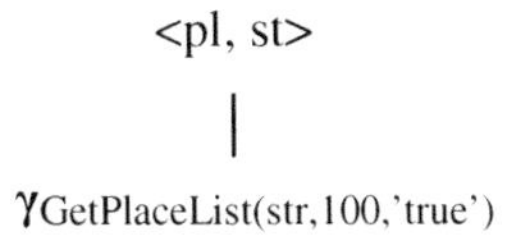

Fig. 14. Plan function PF2 wrapping GetPlaceList

Finally, the *plan pipeliner* transforms the non parallel query by inserting the algebra operator FF_APPLYP for each generated plan function. Fig. 12 shows the final parallelized execution plan with two calls to FF_APPLYP.

Fig. 15. Non parallel query plan- Query2

Fig. 16. Parallel execution plan Query2

Analogously *Query2* is initially compiled into the non parallel plan in Fig. 15. The non parallel plan first executes the operation *GetAllStates* to return a stream of tuples $<stl>$. These outputs are fed to the next operation *GetInfoByState* returning a stream of single comma separated strings *zstr*. For each *zstr* the γ operator applies the user defined helping function *getzipcode* to extract a zipcode *zc* from each string *zstr*. Then the operation *GetPlacesInside* is applied for each *zc* returning a stream of tuples $<st, pl, zc>$. Finally the *equal* function is applied to check if *pl* is equal to '*USAF Academy*' and returns stream of valid tuples $<st, zc>$.

The plan splitter splits the first parallelizable section (call to *GetAllStates*) to execute in the coordinator. The next parallelizable section contains the calls to *GetInfoByState* and *getzipcode*. The final section contains only the call to *Get-PlacesInside* and *equal*. Then the plan function generator creates plan functions to encapsulate the parallelizable *cwo* calls. The plan function *PF3* in Fig. 17 encapsulates *GetInfoByState*. It has the signature:

PF3(Charstring st1) → Stream of Charstring zc

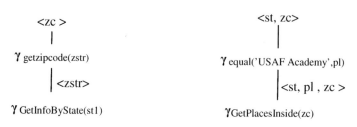

Fig. 17. Plan function *PF3* wrapping *GetInfoByState*

Fig. 18. Plan function *PF4* wrapping *GetPlacesInside*

PF4 in Fig. 18 wraps the operation *GetPlacesInside* and returns *<st,zc>*. It has the signature:

PF4(Charstring zc) → <Charstring st, Charstring zc>

Finally, the plan pipeliner transforms the non parallel query by inserting FF_APPLYP for each generated plan function as illustrated in Fig. 16.

4.1 FF_APPLYP Performance

We compared the query execution times for *Query1* using the non parallel execution plan in Fig. 11 with the parallel plan in Fig. 12 (for *Query2* we compared the plans in Fig. 15 and Fig. 16). To analyze different process trees, we assigned manually a *fanout vector* to the fanouts for the different process tree levels to evaluate the query execution times. The tests were run on a computer with a 3 GHz single processor Intel Pentium 4 with 2.5GB RAM.

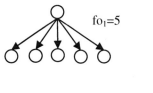

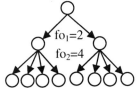

Fig. 19. Flat tree

Fig. 20. Heterogeneous fanouts

We evaluated the following process trees:

- *Flat tree* (Fig. 19): The fanout vector has $fo_2=0$ ($\{fo_1,0\}$) in which case both *cwo* calls are combined into the same plan function executed at the same level.
- *Heterogeneous fanouts* (Fig. 20): the fanouts are not equal, i.e. $fo_1 \neq fo_2$
- *Homogeneous fanouts*: the fanouts are equal, i.e. $\{fo_1,fo_2\}$, $fo_1 = fo_2$

The total number of query processes N needed to execute the parallel queries is:

$$N = fo_1 + fo_1 * fo_2$$

In general, there should be an optimum shape of the process tree based on properties of the web service calls. The experiments investigate the optimum tree topology for our example queries with up to 60 query processes.

Fig. 21 illustrates the execution times in seconds for *Query1* by varying the values of fo_1 and fo_2. It shows the lowest execution time region is achieved within the range 50 - 60 sec. The fastest execution time 56.4 sec for fanout vector $\{5,4\}$ outperformed with speedup 4.3 the parallel plan (244.8 sec).

Fig. 22 shows that the best execution time for *Query2* is achieved within the range of 1200-1400 sec. The best execution time 1243.89 sec for fanout vector $\{4,3\}$ outperformed with speed up of nearly 2 the parallel plan (2412.95 sec).

The best execution time for these specific queries is achieved for the balanced fanout trees, (*Query1*: $fo_1=5$, $fo_2=4$, *Query2*: $fo_1=4$, $fo_2=3$). Since web service calls have high latency, the optimal fanout of each level of a process tree is different and depends on the execution time of the web service operation executed at that level.

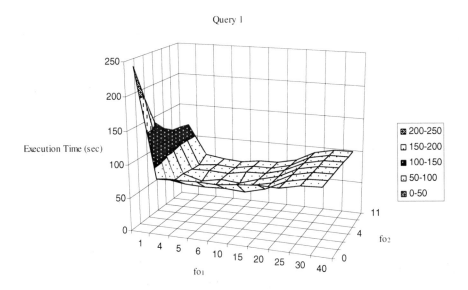

Fig. 21. Execution time for Query1

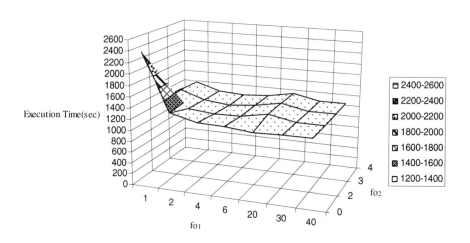

Fig. 22. Execution time for Query2

4.2 Adaptive Apply in Parallel - AFF_APPLYP

In general the properties of the data providing web services are not known explicitly and highly dependent on the network and runtime time environments when and where the queries are executed. This requires adaptive query process arrangement. To automatically achieve an optimized process tree, we developed another algebra operator *AFF_APPLYP* (Adaptive First Finished Apply in Parallel) [22] to replace FF_APPLYP that requires no explicit fanout argument. The signature of AFF_APPLYP is:

```
AFF_APPLYP (Function pf, Stream pstream) → Stream result
```

As for FF_APPLYP, the operator ships in parallel to child query processes the definition of the same plan function *pf*. Then it ships one by one parameter tuples from *pstream* to each of the children. The result stream from a call to *pf* for a given parameter tuple is sent back to AFF_APPLYP asynchronously as a stream of tuples, *result*.

Based on the observation that the best parallelization is achieved with a bushy tree, AFF_APPLYP adapts the process plan at run time starting with a binary tree. Each node locally monitors the execution times of its children to dynamically modify its sub-trees until no more performance improvement is expected. AFF_APPLYP does the following:

1. It initially forms a binary process tree (Fig. 23) by always setting fanout to 2, the *init stage*.

2. A *monitoring cycle* for a non-leaf query process is defined as when AFF_APPLYP has received the same number of end-of-call messages as its number of children. After the first monitoring cycle AFF_APPLYP adds p new child processes. Adding new processes is called an *add stage*. In Fig. 24, $p=1$ and therefore query process $q0$ adds one new process $q7$ at level 1, while $q1$ and $q2$ add $q10$ and $q11$ at level 2, respectively.
3. When an added node has several levels of children the init stages of the children's AFF_APPLYs will produce balanced binary sub–trees. That is, $q7$ adds $q8$ and $q9$.
4. AFF_APPLYP records per monitoring cycle i the average time t_i to produce an incoming tuple from the children.
   a. If t_i decreases more than a threshold (set to 25%) the add stage is rerun.
   b. If t_i increases no more children are added. As an option a *drop stage* is run that drops one child and its children.

In Fig. 25 , $q2$ adds $q12$, while $q0$ drops $q7$, and $q7$ drops $q8$ and $q9$.

We experimented with different values of p and different change thresholds, with and without the drop stage. The results for 25% change are shown in Fig. 26 and Fig. 27. The fanout values are exact for FF_APPLYP which produces a balanced tree, while fo_1 and fo_2 for the unbalanced AFF_APPLYP process trees are average fanouts. The measurements include the adaptation times.

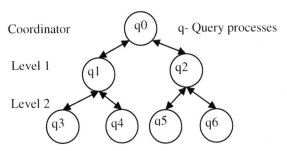

Fig. 23. Binary process tree

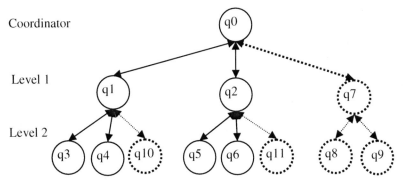

Fig. 24. Adding processes

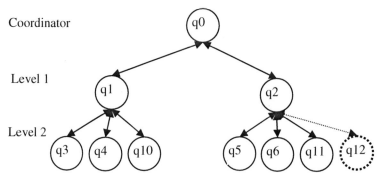

Coordinator

Level 1

Level 2

Fig. 25. Adding and removing processes

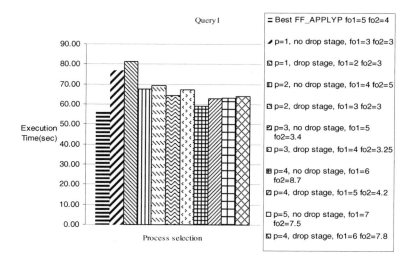

Fig. 26. AFF_APPLYP- Query1

We notice that for *Query1* the execution time with *p*=4 and no drop stage (Fig. 26) comes close to the execution time of the best manually specified balanced process tree, while for *Query2* the execution with *p*=2 and no drop stage (Fig. 27) is the closest one.

We concluded in both cases that execution time with *p*=2 and no drop stage is close to the execution time of the best manually specified process tree (*Query1* 80%, *Query2* 96 %) and further dropping processes make insignificant changes in the execution time.

The adaptive AFF_APPLYP obtained close to the best execution times obtained by manually setting the fanout vectors with FF_APPLYP. In general the execution time of a web service operation is not known in prior. AFF_APPLYP is therefore the realistic approach as it reaches the optimal execution time at run time without having any static cost model.

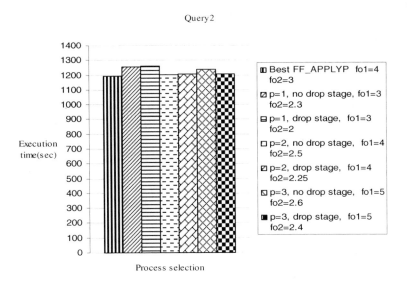

Fig. 27. AFF_APPLYP- Query2

5 Related Work

BPEL [3] proposes workflow primitives to manually invoke parallel web service calls. It requires a lot of effort on the part of the programmer to manually identify sections of the code to run in parallel, and to specify dependencies among the calls. In contrast, WSMED automatically compiles a given query over composed data providing web services by generating an adaptive, parallel, and optimized workflow.

In [1] an approach is described for statically optimizing web service compositions by procedurally traversing ActiveXML documents to select embedded web service calls. It demonstrates the gain obtained by maximizing parallelism achieved by invoking calls to *independent* web services in a query. Conversely, WSMED adaptively parallelizes *dependent* web service calls.

WSQ/DSQ [11] handles high-latency calls to wrapped web search engine interfaces by launching asynchronous materialized dependent joins in a central execution plan by using a special operator. In contrast, WSMED produces non-blocking, multi-level, and parallel plans based on streams of parameter tuples passed to parallel sub plans without any materialization.

WSMS [24] proposed an approach for pipelined parallelism among dependent web services to minimize the query execution time based on a static cost model. WSMS didn't propose any adaptive parallelization, lacked support for code shipping, and couldn't make parallel calls to the same web service. By contrast, we parallelize adaptively at run time by partitioning parameter tuple streams and invoke parameterized plans calling web services in parallel.

Two-phase parallel query optimization [13] generates a static parallelized query execution plan from an initial non parallel one. WSMED also optimizes in two phases, but adaptively parallelizes dependent joins at run time.

The plan function and parameter tuple shipping phase of FF_APPLYP is similar to the map phase of *MAPREDUCE* [8]. However, *MAPREDUCE* is more of a programming model than a query operator and is not dynamically rearranging query execution plans as AFF_APPLYP.

In [12] run time adaptation of buffer sizes in web service calls is investigated, not dealing with adaptive parallelism on web service calls at the client side.

The formal basis for using views to query heterogeneous data sources is reviewed in [28], without dealing with web services or providing adaptive parallelization.

Chocolate [15] extends the federated database capabilities of *DB2/UDB* by automatically creating views of web services from WSDL descriptions, similar to the plan function generation in WSMED, without adaptive parallelization of the web service calls.

Query as a Web Service [17] is an application that allows users to create queries over federated data and publish them as web services. In contrast WSMED provides a web service to make any data providing web services queryable with SQL using adaptive parallelization.

6   Conclusion

WSMED provides a general query web service over data providing web services given their WSDL meta-data description. Queries are expressed in SQL without any further programming. The web service query service is accessible through the web page [30] from anywhere without installing any software and hardware.

WSMED automatically parallelizes queries with dependent web service calls for scalability. A static algebra operator FF_APPLYP was first defined to parallelize calls to parameterized sub plans partitioned for different parameter tuples. FF_APPLYP was used in experiments where process trees with different fanouts were manually constructed to obtain an optimal balanced process tree. Then we developed an algebra operator AFF_APPLYP to automatically and adaptively find the best process tree. AFF_APPYP starts with a balanced binary process tree and then each non-leaf process node locally adapts the process sub-trees by adding and removing children until a local optimum is reached, based on monitoring the flow of result tuples from the children. The adaptive method obtained performance close to the best manually specified process tree with FF_APPLYP.

Our algebra operator AFF_APPLYP can handle parallel query plans for a query with any number of dependent joins. As future work the strategy should be generalized to handle queries mixing both dependent and independent web service calls. This requires investigating different kinds of process arrangement strategies.

Acknowledgments. This work is supported by Sida and the Swedish Foundation for Strategic Research under contract RIT08-0041.

References

1. Abiteboul, S., Benjelloun, O., Cautis, B., Manolescu, I., Milo, T., Preda, N.: Lazy query evaluation for active XML. In: ACM SIGMOD International Conference on Management of Data, pp. 227–238. ACM, New York (2004)
2. Barhamgi, M., Benslimane, D., Ouksel, A.M.: Composing and optimizing data providing web services. In: 17th International World Wide Web Conference, pp. 1141–1142. ACM, New York (2008)
3. Business Process Execution Language for Web Services version 1.1., http://www.ibm.com/developerworks/library/specification/ws-bpel/
4. Castor, http://www.castor.org/index.html
5. Ceri, S.: Search Computing. In: International Conference on Data Engineering, pp. 1–3. IEEE, Los Alamitos (2009)
6. codeBump- GeoPlaces web service, http://codebump.com/services/PlaceLookup.asmx
7. codeBump- Zipcodes web service, http://codebump.com/services/ZipCodeLookup.asmx
8. Dean, J., Ghemawat, S.: MAPREDUCE: Simplified Data Processing on Large Clusters. Communications of the ACM 51(1), 107–113 (2008)
9. Fahl, G., Risch, R.: Query Processing over Object Views of Relational Data. The VLDB Journal 6(4), 261–281 (1997)
10. Florescu, D., Levy, A., Manolescu, I., Suciu, D.: Query Optimization in the Presence of Limited Access Patterns. In: ACM SIGMOD International Conference on Management of Data, pp. 311–322. ACM, New York (1999)
11. Goldman, R., Widom, J.: WSQ/DSQ: a practical approach for combined querying of databases and the Web. In: ACM SIGMOD International Conference on Management of Data, pp. 285–296. ACM, New York (2000)
12. Gounaris, A., Yfoulis, C., Sakellariou, R., Dikaiakos, M.D.: Robust Runtime Optimization of Data Transfer in Queries Over Web Services. In: International Conference on Data Engineering, pp. 596–605. IEEE, Los Alamitos (2008)
13. Hasan, W., Florescu, D., Valduriez, P.: Open Issues in Parallel Query Optimization. SIGMOD Record 25(3), 28–33 (1996)
14. HP Labs Innovation Research Program, http://www.hpl.hp.com/open_innovation/irp/2008_HPL_IRP_Research_Topics_Americas.pdf
15. Josifovski, V., Massmann, S., Naumann, F.: Super-Fast XML Wrapper Generation in DB2: A Demonstration. In: International Conference of Data Engineering, pp. 756–758. IEEE, Los Alamitos (2003)
16. Litwin, W., Risch, T.: Main Memory Oriented Optimization of OO Queries using Typed Datalog with Foreign Predicates. IEEE Transactions on Knowledge and Data Engineering 4(6), 517–528 (1992)
17. Query as a Web Service, http://help.sap.com/businessobject/product_guides/boexir31/en/xi3-1_query_as_a_web_service_en.pdf
18. Quick Server, http://www.quickserver.org/

19. Risch, T., Josifovski, V., Katchaounov, T.: Functional Data Integration in a Distributed Mediator System. In: Gray, P., Kerschberg, L., King, Poulovassilis, P. (eds.) Functional Approach to Data Management - Modeling, Analyzing and Integrating Heterogeneous Data, pp. 211–238. Springer, Heidelberg (2003)
20. SAAJ, https://saaj.dev.java.net/
21. Sabesan, M.: Querying Mediated Web Services. Licentiate Thesis, Department of Information Technology, Uppsala University (2007)
22. Sabesan, M., Risch, T.: Adaptive Parallelization of Queries over Dependent Web Service Calls. In: First IEEE Workshop on Information & Software as Services, pp. 1725–1732. IEEE Computer Society, Los Alamitos (2009)
23. Sabesan, M., Risch, T.: Web Service Mediation through Multi-level Views. In: Frasincar, F., Houben, G., Thiran, P. (eds.) Fourth International Workshop on Web Information System Modeling, pp. 755–766. Tapir, Trondheim (2007)
24. Srivastava, U., Widom, J., Munagala, K., Motwani, R.: Query Optimization over Web Services. In: Very Large Database Conference, pp. 355- -366. VLDB Endowment (2006)
25. TerraServer, TerraService, http://terraservice.net/webservices.aspx
26. The Next Wave: Everything as a Service, http://www.hp.com/hpinfo/execteam/articles/robison/08eaas.html
27. USZip web service, http://www.webservicex.net/uszip.asmx
28. Ullman, J.D.: Information Integration Using Logical Views. In: Afrati, F.N., Kolaitis, P.G. (eds.) ICDT 1997. LNCS, vol. 1186, pp. 19–40. Springer, Heidelberg (1997)
29. Web Services Description Language for Java Toolkit, http://sourceforge.net/projects/wsdl4j
30. WSMED Demo, http://udbl2.it.uu.se/WSMED/wsmed.html
31. WSMED WSDL, http://udbl2.it.uu.se/WSMED/wsmed.wsdl

Data-Utility Sensitive Query Processing on Server Clusters to Support Scalable Data Analysis Services*

Renwei Yu, Mithila Nagendra, Parth Nagarkar,
K. Selçuk Candan, and Jong Wook Kim

CIDSE, Arizona State University, Tempe, AZ, 85287, USA
{renwei.yu,mnagendra,pnagarkar,candan,jong}@asu.edu

Abstract. The observation that a significant class of data processing and analysis applications can be expressed in terms of a small set of primitives that are easy to parallelize has resulted in increasing popularity of batch-oriented, highly-parallelizable cluster frameworks to support data analysis services. These frameworks, however, are known to have shortcomings for certain application domains. For example, in many data analysis applications, the utility of a given data element to the particular analysis task depends on the way the data is collected (e.g. its precision) or interpreted. However, since existing batch oriented data processing frameworks do not consider variations in data utility, they are not able to focus on the best results. Even if the user is interested in obtaining a relatively small subset of the best result instances, these systems often need to enumerate entire result sets, even if these sets contain low-utility results. `RanKloud` is an efficient and scalable utility-aware parallel processing system for ranked query processing over large data sets. In this paper, we focus on the `uSplit` data partitioning and work-allocation strategies of `RanKloud` for processing top-k join queries to support data analysis services. In particular, we describe how `uSplit` adaptively samples data from *"upstream"* operators to help allocate resources in a work-balanced and wasted-work avoiding manner for top-k join processing. Experimental results show that the proposed sampling, data partitioning, and join processing strategies enable `uSplit` to return top-k results with high confidence and low-overhead (up to $\sim 9\times$ faster than alternative schemes on 10 servers).

1 Introduction

Today, many applications, including e-commerce, web, and social media, generate very large amounts of data that need to be continuously analyzed. This massive influx of data necessitates *highly scalable* services for efficient analysis of these large data collections. Recently, the observation that – while not all [31] – a significant class of data processing applications can be expressed in terms of a small set of primitives that are in many cases easy to parallelize, has led to popularity of batch-oriented, highly-parallelizable cluster frameworks (such as MapReduce [19,3], Dynamo [20], Scope [11], PNUTS [18], HadoopDB [4]). These systems have been successfully applied in data processing, mining, and information retrieval domains [28,33] Given an atomic task, these rely on the simple semantic properties of the task to partition the work onto many machines.

---

* This work is partially funded by a HP Labs Innovation Research Program Grant "Data-Quality Aware Middleware for Scalable Data Analysis".

D. Agrawal et al. (Eds.): Information and Software as Services, LNBIP 74, pp. 155–184, 2011.

Example 1 (MapReduce). MapReduce is a functional *list processing* language [19] where a data processing workflow is constructed using *map* and *reduce* primitives. The user-provided *map* primitive takes a set of input key/value pairs and produces a set of intermediate key/value pairs. In essence, the *map* function extracts a set of *features* from the input data. The intermediate values from the *map* primitive are often supplied to a *reduce* function. The *reduce* function takes these intermediate key/value pairs (i.e., features) and produces its output by applying an aggregate function on all input values with the same key. The user-provided *map* and *reduce* primitives can be combined into more complex workflows.

These systems achieve high degrees of scalability by carefully allocating resources to available processing elements and leveraging any opportunities to parallelize basic processing tasks. Significant savings in execution times are obtained by independently parallelizing each step of the workflow and executing them (except for some very recent efforts, such as [17]) in a *batched manner* over a cluster of servers. It is important to note that such batch-oriented processing is not limited to systems based on MapReduce, but also to most parallel DBMSs (such as Vertica [2]) which rely on row- or column-based data partitioning to support parallelism.

1.1   RanKloud: Scalable Middleware for Utility-Sensitive Data Processing on Server Clusters

In many analysis applications, the utility of the elements in the data collection to a particular task varies from data instance to data instance, based on many factors including the way the data is collected (e.g. its precision), its relevance to the analysis goals, or how discriminating a particular data element and its features/attributes are. Applications that involve such varying data and feature utilities include decision support and text and media analysis (in the case of text, the popular TF/IDF keyword score is an example). When the utility assessments of the data vary, consumers are often interested not in all the data, but the ones that are best suited for the given task. Locating and using such high utility data is known as *top-k* or *ranked* query processing.

Naturally, when dealing with such data varying utilities, it would be more effective to take into account *utilities* when partitioning the data and assigning them on to the available servers. In particular, focusing the computation on to high-utility work and avoiding the production of unpromising candidates would help avoid waste and achieve better scalability. Unfortunately, most existing frameworks today are not sensitive in their operations to the underlying data utilities.

RanKloud (first introduced in [7]) is a utility-aware parallel processing framework for efficient and scalable execution of ranked queries over large data sets (Figure 1). RanKloud assumes a key/value pair extended with a utility score, u, between 0 and 1: $\langle key, value, u \rangle$. This simple model is sufficiently powerful to cover a large class of analysis tasks. For example, in an image analysis application, the triple can be used to represent the features extracted from images, $\langle image\_id, feature\_id, feature\_score \rangle$. Similarly, in a collaborative analysis application, the user ratings can be encoded as triples, $\langle user\_id, movie\_id, rating \rangle$. Given this extension, the goal of RanKloud is to support data analysis applications that heavily rely on the following query types:

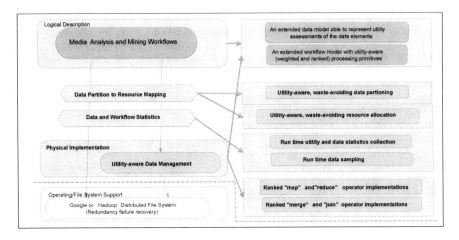

Fig. 1. Overview of the `RanKloud` architecture [7]

- *k-nearest neighbor search:* Let us be given a data set D of objects and a query object q. In addition, let us be given a similarity (or distance) function that quantifies how similar (or dissimilar) a pair of objects are. The k-nearest neighbor search involves identifying the k objects in D that are most similar (or least dissimilar) to q.

- *k-nearest neighbor and k-best-nearest neighbor joins:* Let us be given two object data sets, D_1 and D_2, and a similarity or distance function. The k-nearest neighbor join operation identifies k object pairs (each pair containing one pair from D_1 and another from D_2) that have the shortest distance from each other among all object pairs. The k-best-nearest neighbor join query not only considers distances between the objects, but also their overall utilities.

- *top-k joins:* Let us be given a data set D of objects and a preference criterion which can be described as a monotonic function of the m different properties (e.g. features) of the objects.[1] The top-k join operation identifies the k most preferred objects by considering (or *joining*) the m different properties of the objects.

- *skylines and top-k skylines:* Let us be given a set D of objects, each described using m different properties (e.g. features). Let us also assume that the domain of each property or feature is ordered. The skyline of the object set D consists of the set of objects that are not *dominated* by any other object in D when all properties are considered together. Top-k skylines are the best k objects in the skyline set of D.

- *top-k group and top-k co-group operations:* Let us be given a set D of objects, each described using m different properties (e.g. features), and a grouping or clustering criterion. Let us also be given a preference measure that quantifies the utility of each cluster based on the properties of the objects contained within. The top-k group operation identifies the best k groups of objects among all possible groups. Given data sets D_1 and D_2, the top-k co-group operation, on the other hand, identifies the best pairs of groups (each pair containing one group from the data set D_1 and

---

[1] A monotonic preference function guarantees that an object that is as good as another one in all individual features is also better than the other object when these features are considered simultaneously.

another from the data set D_2) based on a preference criterion involving individual group utilities, as well as the degree of matching between the group members.

Below, we present a set of sample RanKloud queries from a social media analysis application, all requiring some form of ranked retrieval:

Example 2 (Ranked Queries to Support Social Media Analysis)

- In a social media analysis application, given a data set, user_ratings (user_id, movie_id, rating), users can search for the top 10000 users that gave the highest rankings to the movie with ID '5632' with the query

```
top_raters = top_k_filter user_ratings
   by movie_id = '5632',
   decreasing rating, 10000, 0.95
```

Here, decreasing is the ordering criterion, 10000 is the number of elements that is being sought. The optional value 0.95 is the confidence lower bound, which means that there should be less than 5% chance that the result will include less than 10000 users.
- A more complex query using the same data involves grouping and aggregation functions:

```
highly_rated = top_k_group user_ratings
   by movie_id, decreasing avg(rating),
   100, 0.95
```

Using the same data, the user can identify the top 100 highly rated movies using the following query:
- Given the two intermediary data sets color_match_results(imageID, color_match, c_score) and texture_match_results(imageID, texture_match, t_score) describing the pre-computed color and texture matching scores for a given image collection, the user can locate the best 1000 matching images (based on the product of pre-computed color and texture matching scores) using the following query:

```
combined_results = top_k_join
   color_match_results by imageID,
   texture_match_results by imageID,
   decreasing (c_score * t_score),
   1000, 0.95
```

- Given the two intermediary data sets in the previous example, the query

```
skyline_results = skyline
   color_match_results by imageID,
   texture_match_results by imageID,
   decreasing c_score,
   decreasing t_score, 0.95
```

would return those images that are not dominated by any other images in terms of their color and texture matching scores. Moreover, the query

```
best_sl_results = top_k_skyline
    color_match_results by imageID,
    texture_match_results by imageID,
    decreasing c_score,
    decreasing t_score,
    decreasing (c_score * t_score),
    100, 0.95
```

can be used to pick best 100 among these *skyline* images.

RanKloud, implemented over Hadoop, parallelizes the ranked processing operations listed above by building on the MapReduce paradigm. It is important to note that MapReduce framework, in of itself, is not any more scalable than other data-driven application programming models. Under certain conditions its simplicity provides opportunities for significant degrees of share-nothing, batched parallelism. Implementing the ranked operations described above over a system that partitions the data and processes the partitions in batches, however, requires care: naive partitioning of the data onto servers (a) will increase the data replication cost, (b) the cost of indexing and accessing these index structures will be unnecessarily high, and (c) the system will use time and resources for producing large number of (local) candidates that will eventually be eliminated during the final result integration stage due to their lower (global) utilities. Thus, RanKloud uses novel utility-based partitioning and resource allocation schemes, referred to as uSplitstrategies. uSplit relies on two main criteria:

- *(a) wasted work criterion:* this takes into account how much of the system resources are allocated to produce results that are not in the top-k.
- *(b) partition work balance criterion:* any imbalance in the work assignment means that certain system resources will stay under-utilized, while others are over-utilized.

Based on these criteria, uSplit partitions input data on the fly (during their assignment to the servers for processing) in terms of data utilities. To support this, uSplit collects relevant statistics to estimate the utility score distribution of the output result and to avoid allocating processing resources to those data combinations that will produce results which will be pruned anyway.

In the rest of this paper, we focus on the waste-avoiding uSplit partitioning strategy for ranked top-k join processing in RanKloud. While we do not further discuss in this paper, RanKloudrequires similar waste-avoidance strategies for other operations, such as nearest neighbor search and joins as well as skyline joins.

2   uSplit: Utility-Sensitive Data Partitioning for Parallel Top-k Join Processing

When data utility is non-uniform, users are often not interested in obtaining all possible results to a query, but only the k best results. While batch-based systems promise large

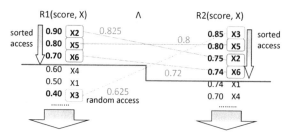

Fig. 2. Typical top-3 join processing: a sorted access phase provide initial candidate results; a random access phase contributes additional candidates tat may have been missed during sorted access; the monotonicity of the combination function (average in this example) makes it possible to stop without having to consider all the data

scale parallelism, since they do not consider variations in data utility, they are unable to scale most effectively by focusing on the data that is likely to produce the best results. To avoid waste, data processing systems need to employ data structures and algorithms that can prune unpromising data objects from consideration without having to evaluate them. This is often referred to as ranked or top-k query processing [5,9,12,21,22,25]. As we mentioned above, in this paper we focus on data partitioning strategy, called uSplit, for partitioning data and processing top-k joins over these partitions in parallel without wasted work.

Top-k Join Queries. As introduced earlier, a top-k join query integrates two or more data sets based on a join attribute, ranks the results based on a given criterion, and returns the most highly ranked k results to the user. For example, in a video recommendation application, the query

```
top_pairs = top_k_join
            male_actors by movieID,
            female_actors by movieID,
            avg(m_actScore,f_actScore), 100
```

on two tables male_actors(m_actorID, movieID, m_actScore) and female_actors(f_actorID, movieID, f_actScore), would locate "highest scoring male/female actor pairs who have played together in at least one movie" by equi-joining the two tables on movieID and identifying the top 100 results on avg(m_actScore, f_actScore). More generally, we consider *two-way*, top-k join operations of the form $R_1 \bowtie_C R_2$, where C is the join condition. Each data element, t, in R_1 and R_2 has an associated utility score between 0 and 1; i.e., $t.u \in [0, 1]$. There is also a monotonic utility combination function, $\Phi()$, associated with the join operation. Given two elements, $t_1 \in R_1$ and $t_2 \in R_2$, possible combination functions include *Euclidean*, $\Phi_{Euc}(t_1, t_2) = \sqrt{(t_1.u)^2 + (t_2.u)^2}$, *Average*, $\Phi_{avg}(t_1, t_2) = \frac{t_1.u + t_2.u}{2}$, *Product*, $\Phi_{prod}(t_1, t_2) = t_1.u \times t_2.u$, *Min*, $\Phi_{min}(t_1, t_2) = min(t_1.u, t_2.u)$, and *Max*, $\Phi_{max}(t_1, t_2) = max(t_1.u, t_2.u)$ functions [6,21]. Given a target score, these functions define different utility boundaries on the utility space of results.

Prior Work in Top-k Joins and Difficulties in Parallelizing Top-k Joins. Most existing ranked join processing algorithms, including Fagin's algorithm (FA) [21,22],

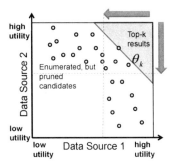

Fig. 3. Relying on sorted- and random-access operations, top-k algorithms focus their processing to the *high-utility* corner of the utility space: here, the curve represents the threshold, θ_k, defined by the lowest of the scores of the best k results; consequently, and results below this threshold will be pruned (small circles under the threshold correspond to enumerated but pruned results due to random accesses)

threshold algorithm (TA) [23], (NRA) [23], and others (such as [13,29,24,27]) assume that one, or both, of the following data access strategies is available: (a) *streaming/pipelined access* to the sorted data to identify a set of candidates, and (b) *index based* random access to verify if these are good matches or not. Given monotonic[2] queries on the data, these help identify good candidates and prune non-promising ones quickly (Figure 2). Figure 3 graphically represents the portion of the utility space covered during the top-k join operation. Here, the curve represents the threshold, θ_k, defined by the lowest of the scores of the best k results to be returned to the user (the shape of the curve depends on the combination function. Consequently, all the join work to produce the results above this curve is useful. Note that, as shown in Figure 3, top-k join algorithms may also identify candidate results below this threshold and these need to be pruned during post-processing.

In systems which partition data and process them in batches, however, top-k query processing cannot be efficiently supported. A critical difficulty with parallelizing the top-k algorithms, such as FA, TA, and NRA, is that the process is inherently sequential: as shown in Figure 2, in the first *sorted-access* phase one pointer per data source is used for scanning each data stream in decreasing order of utility. This prevents efficient parallel implementations of these algorithms. Consider for example a naive parallelization scheme where the join space is randomly split among U servers such that each server produces its own k results to be combined into a final candidate set from which the top-k results will be selected. Since, top-k join algorithms have $O(k^{\frac{1}{m}} J^{1-\frac{1}{m}})$ complexity with high probability for m-way joins, where J is the number of all potential join results [22], in this approach, each server would need to perform $O(k^{\frac{1}{m}} \left(\frac{J}{U}\right)^{1-\frac{1}{m}})$ work to produce its local top-k results. When for example $m = 2$, the amount of per server work would be $O(\frac{1}{\sqrt{U}} \sqrt{kJ})$. In other words, given U servers, the per-server work is $\frac{1}{\sqrt{U}}$ of the total

---

[2] An object that is as good as another one in all individual features is also better than the other object when these features are considered simultaneously.

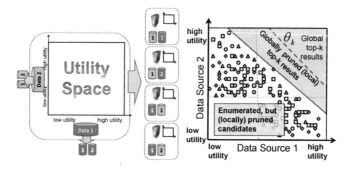

Fig. 4. Random partitioning of the data will waste resources for producing large number of candidates that will be eventually pruned (points with different shapes correspond to enumerated but pruned results in different servers)

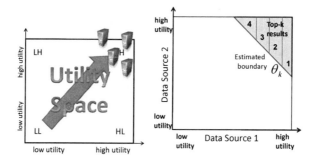

Fig. 5. The proposed algorithm estimates the cut-off θ_k to prevent redundant work and partitions the useful join work above the threshold to available servers to speed up the join processing. This enables utility-aware resource allocation for top-k join processing.

2-way top-k join operation, not close to $\frac{1}{U}$ that would be the case if there were no wasted work[3] (Figure 4).

Utility-Sensitive Data Partitioning. In this paper, we develop utility-based partitioning and resource allocation schemes based on two major criteria: *(a) wasted work criterion:* this takes into account how much of the system resources are allocated to produce results that are not in top-k and *(b) partition work balance criterion:* any imbalance in the work assignment means that certain system resources will stay under-utilized, while others are over-utilized. uSplit repartitions input data sets on the fly (during their assignment to the servers for join processing) in terms of data utility. To support this, uSplit collects relevant statistics to estimate the utility score, θ_k, of the kth output result, and avoids allocating processing resources to those data combinations that will produce results with utilities less than θ_k.

---

[3] Note that this naive partitioning strategy could provide close to $\frac{1}{\sqrt{U}}$ gain when m is large; however, top-k algorithms are often avoided for large m, because this would result in a total of $O(J)$ work. I.e., a full join would need to be done anyhow (this is known as the *curse of dimensionality*).

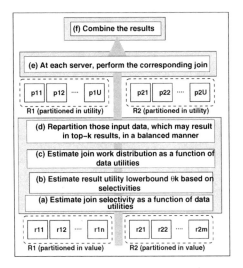

Fig. 6. Top-k join processing with uSplit

Note that, since the results may not be uniformly distributed in the utility space, both the shape of the utility boundary and statistics about the result distribution as a function of the input data utilities are needed to estimate the θ_k lower bound. Intuitively, this is similar to the *filtering* strategy that has been successfully applied for top-k query processing in relational databases [15,8,9,10]. In the context of batched data processing, however, existing *filtering* techniques cannot be directly applied due to the lack of index structures that provide efficient filtering, and the lack of prior statistics about the intermediary data produced and consumed within a workflow.

Confidence Target Parameter. Since we are relying on statistics to estimate the θ_k lower bound, we also take a *confidence target* as a query processing parameter from the user. For example, $\geq 95\%$ confidence target would mean that the user allows for up to 5% chance that the system may return less than k top results. In other words, high confidence target indicates that the user wants the system return closer to k (top) results with high probability, whereas a low target indicates that the user might be satisfied with less than k matches in most cases. Otherwise, the query model is deterministic in that the system will not return any results that are not in top-k. As we will see in Section 4, this confidence target helps the system to choose tighter or looser θ_k thresholds based on the available statistics. Tighter thresholds means less wasted work, but may result in some misses.

Summary. Figure 6 visualizes the steps of the uSplit top-k join processing. (a) uSplit first estimates the join selectivity as a function of the input data utilities and then (b) computes the lower bound, θ_k, on the utilities of the top-k results based on these selectivities. Next, (c) uSplit estimates the amount of (useful) work needed for computing the top-k results, and based on this estimate, (d) it repartitions the input data in a *work-balanced* manner, before assigning these partitions onto the available servers for processing. (e) Each server creates the necessary data structures and performs the assigned join task. Finally, (f) the results from the individual servers are combined to select the best k results.

3   Runtime Statistics Collection

Note that we cannot assume independence of join selectivities from the score distribution. Therefore, we need statistics to identify the join selectivities as a function of
the input utilities: this enables that (given the confidence limit) the cutoff can be estimated as tightly as possible. Since we cannot assume that statistics about the intermediary, transient data within the workflow are available in advance, uSplit first collects
any statistics needed to estimate the join selectivities as a function of the data utility[4].
uSplit performs this by sampling intermediary data along the utility scores.

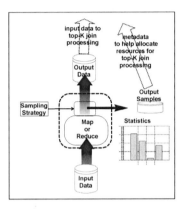

Fig. 7. Piggy-backed sampling: Given a sampling strategy, each (upstream) operator produces
samples to support down-stream operations

Since the input data to the top-k join operation itself may be produced using a
parallel-executing operator, we have three alternative runtime sampling options:

- *Piggy-backed sampling:* For intermediary data generated within a workflow, in order
  to eliminate unnecessary passes over the data, one option is to piggy-back the sampling work on the "*upstream*" operators: each pararellel instance of the "*upstream*"
  operator produces a set of samples (using reservoir sampling technique [36]) as it
  produces its output data, as shown in Figures 7 and 8.
- *Partial-output sampling:* In this alternative, each upstream machine produces samples on its local output and later these individual samples are combined to obtain
  the full set of samples (Figure 9). Note that in this method, a full scan of the data is
  required, but each upstream machine can sample its data in parallel with the others.
- *Combined-output sampling.* In this option, after the outputs of the upstream operators
  are merged, one server node samples the full combined data set (Figure 10). Note
  that, also in this method, a full scan of the data is required.

---

[4] Note that this is especially important when the join attributes and the utilities are not completely independent.

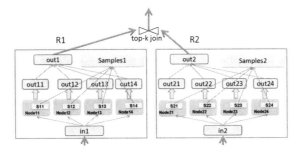

Fig. 8. Piggy-backed sampling at the upstream operators

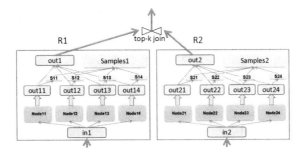

Fig. 9. Partial-output sampling at the upstream operators

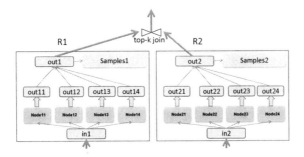

Fig. 10. Combined-output sampling at the upstream operators

Note that piggy-backed sampling is the most efficient alternative as it avoids an extra scan of the data and allows each upstream machine to sample its own output data in parallel to the others. Partial-output sampling is faster than combined-output sampling, since it also allows the data sampling process to be run in parallel in upstream operators. The combined-output sampling option requires a full, sequential scan of the combined data; however, this option may be necessary to avoid bias in sampling when the data partitioning attributes for the upstream operator and the data utilities relevant for the down-stream top-k operator are not independent.

It is important to note that obtaining samples from joins is extremely difficult. In [16], Chaudhuri *et al.* showed the need for non-oblivious and non-uniform sampling strategies. [16] also showed that there are lower-bounds on the sizes of the samples even when these samples are generated in a non-oblivious manner. Here, we propose to address this difficulty by budgeting the samples for top-k processing intelligently where they matter the most.

3.1   Allocation of the Data Sampling Budget

Let us reconsider the ranked join operation, $R = R_1 \bowtie_C R_2$, where C is the join condition, $|R_1| = N$, and $|R_2| = M$. Each data element, t, in R_1 or R_2 has an associated utility score, $t.u \in [0, 1]$. The first task of uSplit is to sample R_1 and R_2 to estimate the join selectivities as a function of data utilities. Since the overall goal of the sampling process is to support top-k joins, it is most important that the selectivities are estimated with higher precision towards the higher end of the utility spectrum. Therefore, instead of sampling R_1 and R_2 uniformly across the utility space to obtain histograms that are equally precise in all regions (as is commonly done in traditional databases [14,30,32]), uSplit targets higher precision for higher utilities. Thus, uSplit segments the utility range and allocates samples to different ranges: in particular, as shown in Figure 11, the higher the utility of the segment, the larger the number of samples allocated.

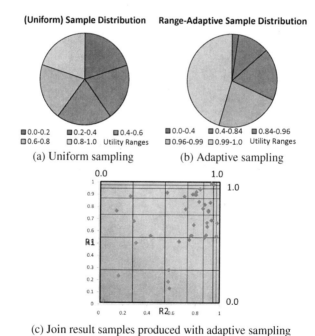

(a) Uniform sampling   (b) Adaptive sampling

(c) Join result samples produced with adaptive sampling

Fig. 11. Utility-range adaptive sampling of input data ensures that more join result samples are collected at the high utility range of the utility space

Let $0 = x_0 < x_1 < \ldots < x_{n-1} < x_n = 1$ and $0 = y_0 < y_1 < \ldots < y_{m-1} < y_m = 1$ denote the x- and y-boundaries[5], which are used for segmenting the two dimensions of the utility space: i.e., $\mathbf{x}_i = (x_{i-1}, x_i]$ and $\mathbf{y}_j = (y_{j-1}, y_j]$ are the utility segments corresponding to the two dimensions of the utility space[6]. For $1 \leq i \leq n$ and $1 \leq j \leq m$, let $R_{1,i}$ and $R_{2,j}$, be the subsets of R_1 and R_2 in the corresponding utility ranges, and let $r_{1,i} = |R_{1,i}|$ and $r_{2,j} = |R_{2,j}|$ denote the number of data elements in each segment.

In addition, let $s_{1,i}$ and $s_{2,j}$, where

$$\sum_{1 \leq i \leq n} s_{1,i} = s_1 \text{ and } \sum_{1 \leq j \leq m} s_{2,j} = s_2,$$

denote the number of samples uSplit allocates to the utility segments $\mathbf{x}_i$ and $\mathbf{y}_j$. Here, $s_1 \ll N$ is the overall sampling budget for R_1, and $s_2 \ll M$ is the sampling budget for R_2. Given this sampling budget, uSplit estimates the join selectivities across the utility space by (a) first sampling the input data sets R_1 and R_2, for each segment $\mathbf{x}_i$ ($1 \leq i \leq n$) and $\mathbf{y}_j$ ($1 \leq j \leq m$), for $s_{1,i}$ and $s_{2,j}$ data elements, respectively, and then (b) joining all resulting pairs of sample sets, $S_{1,i} = \{u_1, u_2, \ldots, u_{s_{1,i}}\}$ and $S_{2,j} = \{v_1, v_2, \ldots, v_{s_{2,j}}\}$ (where $|S_{1,i}| = s_{1,i}$ and $|S_{2,j}| = s_{2,j}$). This provides a count, $C_{i,j} = |S_{1,i} \bowtie_C S_{2,j}|$, of results for each pair of utility segments $\mathbf{x}_i$ and $\mathbf{y}_j$, $1 \leq i \leq n$ and $1 \leq j \leq m$. $C_{i,j}$ is then used for estimating the number of results in $R = R_1 \bowtie_C R_2$:

$$|R_{1,i} \bowtie_C R_{2,j}| \sim C_{i,j} \times \frac{r_{1,i} \times r_{2,j}}{s_{1,i} \times s_{2,j}}.$$

In other words, the join selectivity for a given pair, $\mathbf{x}_i$ and $\mathbf{y}_j$, of segments is $\sim \frac{C_{i,j}}{s_{1,i} \times s_{2,j}}$.

3.2 Impact of the Sample Size on the Quality of Join Selectivity Estimates

When $s_{1,i} \ll r_{1,i}$ and $s_{2,j} \ll r_{2,j}$, the total cost of the sample based selectivity estimation process will be much less than the cost of the full join of the data. Despite these savings, however, it is important that the samples are allocated to the segments in such a way that the sampling errors are minimized at the higher end of the utility range. To achieve this in a systematic way, uSplit quantifies the error margins associated with the selectivity estimates and identifies a sampling strategy that minimizes these margins.

Let us consider a pair, $\mathbf{x}_i$ and $\mathbf{y}_j$, of utility segments and the corresponding sets, $S_{1,i} = \{u_1, u_2, \ldots, u_{s_{1,i}}\}$ and $S_{2,j} = \{v_1, v_2, \ldots, v_{s_{2,j}}\}$, of samples. When a sample $v_l \in S_{2,j}$ joins with $u_h \in S_{1,i}$, we denote this as $match_{h,l} = 1$. Similarly, a mismatch between $v_l \in S_{2,j}$ and $u_h \in S_{1,i}$ is denoted as $match_{h,l} = 0$. Let us assume that $u_h \in S_{1,i}$ matches with $count_h$ many samples out of the $s_{2,j}$ samples in $S_{2,j}$. The *mean likelihood*, μ_h, of a match to $u_h \in S_{1,i}$ by data in $S_{2,j}$ can be computed as

$$\mu_h = \frac{1}{s_{2,j}} \sum_{1 \leq l \leq s_{2,j}} match_{h,l} = \frac{count_h}{s_{2,j}}.$$

---

[5] We discuss how to set segment boundaries in Section 3.3.

[6] The segments $\mathbf{x}_1 = [0, x_1]$ and $\mathbf{y}_1 = [0, y_1]$, which are closed in both sides, are minor exceptions.

uSplit similarly computes the standard deviation, std_h, of the matches to u_h as

$$std_h^2 = \frac{1}{s_{2,j}} \sum_{1 \leq l \leq s_{2,j}} (match_{h,l} - \mu_h)^2.$$

Lemma 1 (Selectivity of a Single Entry). *Given the above definitions of mean likelihood of match, μ_h, and the standard deviation, std_h, if we want to be $100 \times (1 - \alpha)\%$ confident of the rate of match we are computing for u_h, then (assuming that the likelihood of matches are normally distributed[7], samples are randomly selected, and the number of samples are much smaller than the amount of data in the utility segment – i.e., $s_{2,j} \ll r_{2,j}$)[8] we can associate the following confidence interval for the true likelihood of match, μ_h^*:*

$$\mu_h - \frac{t_{(s_{2,j}-1),\alpha/2}}{\sqrt{s_{2,j}}} \times std_h \ \leq \mu_h^* \leq \mu_h + \frac{t_{(s_{2,j}-1),\alpha/2}}{\sqrt{s_{2,j}}} \times std_h.$$

◇

Here, the value $t_{(s_{2,j}-1),\alpha/2}$ is the t distribution, with $(s_{2,j} - 1)$ degrees of freedom and corresponding to $100 \times (1 - \alpha)$ percent confidence [35]. This confidence interval implies that the margin of error, $\mathcal{E}_h$, in the expected rate of matches for u_h is

$$\mathcal{E}_h = 2 \times \frac{t_{(s_{2,j}-1),\alpha/2}}{\sqrt{s_{2,j}}} \times std_h.$$

Since the t values tend to be relatively constant for degrees of freedom greater than 5, in general, for a given confidence target α, the error margin is inversely proportional to $\sqrt{s_{2,j}}$.

Theorem 1 (Join Selectivity Estimate). *Given tuples $t_1 \in R_{1,i}$ and $t_2 \in R_{2,j}$, the likelihood of the combined tuple $[t_1, t_2]$ being in $R_{1,i} \bowtie_C R_{2,j}$ is*

$$\mu_{i,j} = \frac{1}{s_{1,i}} \sum_{1 \leq h \leq s_{1,i}} \mu_h$$

$$= \frac{1}{s_{1,i}} \sum_{1 \leq h \leq s_{1,i}} \frac{count_h}{s_{2,j}} = \frac{C_{i,j}}{s_{1,i} \times s_{2,j}}.$$

The error margin, $\mathcal{E}_{i,j}$, corresponding to this rate of match at $100 \times (1 - \alpha)$ percent confidence is

$$\mathcal{E}_{i,j} = 2 \times \frac{t_{(s_{1,i}-1),\alpha/2}}{\sqrt{s_{1,i}}} \times std_{i,j}.$$

◇

---

[7] It is empirically known that the confidence intervals for μ based on normality is highly reliable, in the sense of providing good coverage, even when the real distribution of the data is much different from normal [35].

[8] When $\frac{|S_{2,j}|}{|R_{2,j}|} = \frac{s_{2,j}}{r_{2,j}} \geq 0.05$, the confidence interval can be corrected by reducing the margin of error with a *finite population correction* factor, $f = \sqrt{\frac{r_{2,j}-s_{2,j}}{r_{2,j}-1}}$ [35].

Proof Sketch. Let us consider a pair, x_i and y_j, of utility segments and the corresponding sets, $S_{1,i} = \{u_1, u_2, \ldots, u_{s_{1,i}}\}$ and $S_{2,j} = \{v_1, v_2, \ldots, v_{s_{2,j}}\}$, of samples. When a sample $v_l \in S_{2,j}$ joins with $u_h \in S_{1,i}$, we denote this as $match_{h,l} = 1$. Similarly, a mismatch between $v_l \in S_{2,j}$ and $u_h \in S_{1,i}$ is denoted as $match_{h,l} = 0$. Let us assume that $u_h \in S_{1,i}$ matches with $count_h$ many samples out of the $s_{2,j}$ samples in $S_{2,j}$.

Now, let us consider a set of samples, $S_{1,i} = \{u_1, u_2, \ldots, u_h, \ldots, u_{s_{1,i}}\}$, from the segment x_i, and the corresponding rate, μ_h, of matches with the tuples in y_j, we can compute the average rate of matches of tuples in $S_{i,1}$ with the tuples in y_j as

$$\mu_{i,j} = \frac{1}{s_{1,i}} \sum_{1 \leq h \leq s_{1,i}} \mu_h.$$

Similarly, the corresponding standard deviation, $std_{i,j}$, is computed as

$$std_{i,j}^2 = \frac{1}{s_{1,i}} \sum_{1 \leq h \leq s_{1,i}} (\mu_h - \mu_{1,i})^2.$$

Thus, once again, if the likelihood of matches are normally distributed[9], samples are randomly selected, and $s_{1,i} \ll r_{1,i}$, then, targeting a statistical confidence rate of $100 \times (1 - \alpha)\%$, we can associate the confidence interval

$$\left[\mu_{i,j} - \frac{t_{(s_{1,i}-1),\alpha/2}}{\sqrt{s_{1,i}}} \times std_{i,j} \,,\; \mu_{i,j} + \frac{t_{(s_{1,i}-1),\alpha/2}}{\sqrt{s_{1,i}}} \times std_{i,j} \right]$$

to the true rate of matches of tuples in x_i with the tuples in y_j. Here, the value $t_{(s_{1,i}-1),\alpha/2}$ is the t-distribution, with $(s_{1,i}-1)$ degrees of freedom and corresponding to $100 \times (1-\alpha)$ percent confidence [35].

Note that, this true rate of matches (of tuples in x_i with the tuples in y_j) is nothing but the *selectivity* of the join between the tuples in partitions x_i and y_j. Thus, the theorem follows. □

Theorem 2 (Sample Allocation). *Given parameters* $\rho_1, \rho_2 > 1.0$ *allocation of the sample budget such that*

$$\forall_{i,j} \quad s_{1,i} = \rho_1^2 \times s_{1,(i-1)} \quad \text{and} \quad s_{2,j} = \rho_2^2 \times s_{2,j-1},$$

subject to the overall sampling budget constraints $\sum_{1 \leq i \leq n} s_{1,i} = s_1$ *and* $\sum_{1 \leq j \leq m} s_{2,j} = s_2$, *ensures that the margins of errors decrease exponentially with increasing segment index (i.e., with rates* ρ_1^{-i} *and* ρ_2^{-j} *for partitions* x_i *and* y_j, *respectively).* ◇

Proof Sketch. As Theorem 1 implies, for a given statistical confidence target $100 \times (1 - \alpha)\%$, higher sampling rates $s_{1,i}$ and $s_{2,j}$ will lead to lower margins of errors. More specifically, since the t values tend to be relatively constant for degrees of freedom greater than 5, for a given confidence target α, this error margin is inversely proportional

---

[9] See Footnote 7.

to $\sqrt{s_{1,i}}$. From this, it follows that if we allocate more samples at the higher end of the utility spectrum; i.e., $\forall_{i,j}\; s_{1,i} > s_{1,(i-1)}$ and $s_{2,j} > s_{2,j-1}$ such that the ratio of the samples for consecutive segments are proportional with ρ_1 and ρ_2, respectively, the margins of errors decrease exponentially with increasing segment index.   □

3.3   Selecting the Utility Partition Boundaries

The sample allocation scheme described above considers the order of the segments, but is agnostic to where the segment boundaries are actually located in the utility space. This, however, can pose two difficulties: (a) Firstly, since our goal is to compute selectivities more precisely at the upper end of the utility spectrum, setting the boundaries of the segments, x_i and y_j, tighter for those segments that are nearer to 1.0 should help reduce errors at the high utility spectrum. (b) Secondly, the error margin computation in Theorem 2 assumes that μ_h and std_h properly model the distribution of the likelihood of matches. This assumption will often hold for sufficiently large segments, but will be more likely to be violated if the segment contains a small number of elements. Consequently, for extremely biased data distributions, such as the Zipfian [35], where there are only few high utility elements, naively selected segment boundaries can result in high-utility segments with too few elements to support sampling with predictable error margins.

Therefore, segment boundaries need to be selected carefully. To ensure tighter segments closer to 1.0, we adjust the segment boundaries, $0 = x_0 < x_1 < \ldots < x_{n-1} < x_n = 1$ and $0 = y_0 < y_1 < \ldots < y_{m-1} < y_m = 1$, using two segment scaling factors, $\pi_1, \pi_2 > 1.0$, such that

$$\forall_{2 \le i \le n}\; \pi_1 \times \Delta x_i = \Delta x_{i-1}$$

$$\forall_{2 \le j \le m}\; \pi_2 \times \Delta y_j = \Delta y_{j-1},$$

subject to the constraints,

$$\sum_{1 \le i \le n} \pi_1^{n-i} \Delta x_n = 1 \quad \text{and} \quad \sum_{1 \le j \le m} \pi_2^{m-j} \Delta y_m = 1,$$

where $\Delta x_i = x_i - x_{i-1}$ and $\Delta y_j = y_j - y_{j-1}$. For data sets where the utilities are highly biased (such as normal or Zipfian, where there are insufficiently many high utility data) sampling irregularities need to be prevented. We refer to this as the *de-biasing of the utilities*. In general, scores in a biased distribution can be de-biased[10] by considering high-level data distribution parameters.

Theorem 3 (De-biasing). *Let Ω_D denote the utility distribution of a given data set, D. Given a utility score, u, let us replace it with u', such that*

$$u' = CDF(\Omega_D, x) = \frac{|\{a \mid a \in D \land a.u \le u\}|}{|D|},$$

---

[10] De-biasing is used only when determining the partition boundaries; during query processing and ranking, the actual utilities are used.

where CDF is the cumulative distribution function of Ω_D. For any two ranges, $(v'_\perp, v'_\top]$ and $(w'_\perp, w'_\top]$, in the transformed utility space, if $(v'_\top - v'_\perp) = (w'_\top - w'_\perp)$, then the number of data entries within these two ranges are the same. $\diamond$

Proof Sketch. Given $(u'_\perp, u'_\top]$ in the transformed utility space, it is easy to see that $u'_\top - u'_\perp = \frac{|\{a \mid a \in D \wedge u_\perp < a.s \leq u_\top\}|}{|D|}$, for some $u_\perp$ and $u_\top$. Similarly, $v'_\top - v'_\perp = \frac{|\{a \mid a \in D \wedge v_\perp < a.s \leq v_\top\}|}{|D|}$, for some $v_\perp$ and $v_\top$. Thus, if $(u'_\top - u'_\perp) = (v'_\top - v'_\perp)$ then it follows that

$$|\{a \mid a \in D \wedge u_\perp < a.s \leq u_\top\}| = |\{a \mid a \in D \wedge v_\perp < a.s \leq v_\top\}|.$$

$\square$

Note that in a Zipfian data set with N' elements, if the number of elements above a given utility score, u, is proportional to $\frac{1}{u}$, then $N' - \frac{c}{u}$ elements have utilities less than or equal to u, for some c. Thus, the de-biasing theorem implies that rescaling the utility scores of a Zipfian distribution as

$$u' = \frac{N' \times u - c}{N' \times u},$$

de-biases the data. Similarly, in data with normal utility distributions, rescaling the utility scores as

$$u' = CDF(Normal(avg, stdev), x) = \frac{1}{2} + \frac{1}{2}\text{Erf}\left(\frac{u - avg}{stdev\sqrt{2}}\right),$$

where avg is the mean, $stdev$ is the standard deviation, and Erf is the Gauss error function [35], de-biases the data.

In uSplit, extreme bias in the data utilities is detected and high-level distribution parameters are estimated by a partial pre-sampling step in the upstream operator, carried out before the overall data sampling strategy is decided. For example, whether a data set is normal is validated through statistical tests, such as the Kurtosis test which measures the peakedness or flatness of a distribution relative to the normal distribution, applied on a small initial sample.

3.4 Discussion

In practice, the sampling budget needs to be selected in such a way that the cost of statistics collection (scan + sample join) is below a maximum target sampling cost. This can be achieved using standard scan and join cost models.

There are two concerns in selecting segment and sampling scaling factors (π and ρ, respectively). Firstly, as Figures 16 and 18 in the Experiments section (Section 6) show, these cannot be too close to 1.0 (since *uniform sampling* introduces higher errors). Similarly, values that are much larger than 1.0 can negatively impact performance by requiring too many samples in too small regions of the utility space. Experiments have shown good results for $\pi \sim 1.15$ and $\rho \sim 2.0$.

Finally, again experiments reported in Section 6 show de-biasing ensures that the confidence targets on the estimation of Θ_k can be matched even if the underlying distributions are significantly skewed. Therefore, despite its minor additional cost, the pre-sampling step should not be skipped.

4   Computing the Lower Bound, Θ_k

In the previous section, we discussed how uSplit segments the utility space and samples the input data sets in a way that enables the join selectivities to be estimated with small margins of error, closer to the high-utility portion of the utility space. In this section, we discuss how to compute the utility score, θ_k, associated with the kth best result of the join operation based on these selectivities. In the literature, this problem has been considered under different assumptions [15,16,26]. In the most related work [26], authors have proposed a method to estimate the depth of a top-k join query based on sample-based estimators; however, none of these provide guarantees as to the error rate, while our goal is to match user provided confidence targets.

Let us consider two data sets, $R_{1,i}$ and $R_{2,j}$ (where $|R_{1,i}| = r_{1,i}$ and $|R_{2,j}| = r_{2,j}$). Let us also consider a set, P, of utility segment pairs (or *utility cells*) and ask the question, "What is the probability that the cells in P will, collectively, return exactly k results?". This requires modeling the probability distribution of the sums of independent, but not identical, random variables, which themselves are distributed in a binomial fashion. While this is not straightforward, a reasonable approximation can be obtained by approximating each $p_{i,j}(k)$ with a Poisson distribution, $poisson(\alpha, k)$.

Theorem 4 (Probability of Having k Results). *The probability, $p_P(k)$ with which the set P of utility cells returns exactly k tuples is*

$$p_P(k) \simeq poisson(\alpha_P, k) = e^{-\alpha_P} \frac{(\alpha_P)^k}{k!},$$

where

$$\alpha_P = \sum_{\langle \mathbf{x}_i, \mathbf{y}_j \rangle \in P} \mu_{i,j} \times (r_{1,i} \times r_{2,j}).$$

$\Diamond$

Proof Sketch. Let us consider two data sets, $R_{1,i}$ and $R_{2,j}$ (where $|R_{1,i}| = r_{1,i}$ and $|R_{2,j}| = r_{2,j}$) , and a pair of utility segments, $\mathbf{x}_i$ and $\mathbf{y}_j$, from each data set. In the previous section, we computed the likelihood of a match between a given $t_1 \in R_{1,i}$ and $t_2 \in R_{2,j}$, and represented this likelihood as $\mu_{i,j}$. Here, we note that, for each pair $t_1 \in R_{1,i}$ and $t_2 \in R_{2,j}$, the corresponding likelihood of match can be modeled as a Bernoulli trial with a success probability of $\mu_{i,j}$, and a failure probability of $(1 - \mu_{i,j})$ [35]. Based on this, uSplit describes the probability, $p_{i,j}(k)$, that the pair of segments, $\mathbf{x}_i$ and $\mathbf{y}_j$, will result in exactly k results relying on a binomial model:

$$p_{i,j}(k) = \binom{r_{1,i} \times r_{2,j}}{k} \times \mu_{i,j}^k \times (1 - \mu_{i,j})^{r_{1,i} \times r_{2,j} - k}.$$

Now, let us also consider a set, P, of utility segment pairs (or *utility cells*) and ask the question, "What is the probability that the cells in P will, collectively, return exactly k results?". This requires modeling the probability distribution of the sums of independent, but not identical, random variables, which themselves are distributed in a binomial fashion. While this is not straightforward, a reasonable approximation can be obtained by approximating each $p_{i,j}(k)$ with a Poisson distribution, $poisson(\alpha, k)$.

A commonly used statistical rule of thumb [35] is that it is possible to approximate a given binomial distribution, $binom(a, b, p) = \binom{a}{b} p^b (1 - p)^{a-b}$, with a Poisson distribution, $poisson(\alpha, k) = e^{-\alpha} \frac{(\alpha)^b}{b!}$, where $\alpha = ap$, as long as $a \geq 20$ and $p \leq 0.05$. Therefore, if $r_{1,i} \times r_{2,j} \geq 20$ (which is often the case), and the join selectivity, $\mu_{i,j}$, is relatively small, we can approximate $p_{i,j}(k)$ using Poisson distributions[11]. Since the sum of independent Poisson processes with g parameters, $\alpha_1, \ldots, \alpha_g$, itself is a Poisson process with parameter $\alpha = \sum_{1 \leq i \leq g} \alpha_i$ [35], the theorem follows. $\square$

Given this, the probability, $p_{\overline{P}}^{\geq}(k)$, with which "$P$ will return *at least* k tuples" can be computed as

$$p_{\overline{P}}^{\geq}(k) = \sum_{k \leq h} p_P(h) = 1 - \left(\sum_{0 \leq h < k} p_P(h) \right).$$

Let p_ϵ be the maximum probability of error the user can accommodate in the estimation of θ_k (in other words, the confidence lowerbound for the estimation of θ_k is $1 - p_\epsilon$). Let $p_{\overline{P},\theta}^{\geq}(k)$ denote the probability with which the set P of utility cells will collectively return *at least* k tuples above the utility threshold θ. Given these, if $C = \{x_1, \ldots x_n\} \times \{y_1, \ldots y_m\}$ denotes the set of all cells in the utility space, then we are looking for a utility score θ_k, where

$$\theta_k = arg \max_\theta \; p_{\overline{C},\theta}^{\geq}(k) \geq 1 - p_\epsilon.$$

Since, given θ, we are interested in only those results with utility scores above θ, we normalize the Poisson distribution parameter, $\alpha_{C,\theta}$, in a way that takes into account the likelihood of the results having scores above θ.

Given the above definition of $p_{\overline{C},\theta}^{\geq}(k)$, the algorithm for computing $\theta_k = arg \max_\theta \; p_{\overline{C},\theta}^{\geq}(k)$ is shown in Figure 12. Note that, when the while loop of Step 5 of the algorithm ends, the final value of $\theta_\perp$ is within θ_Δ of the true value of θ_k (with confidence $1 - p_\epsilon$), and thus, for sufficiently small values of θ_Δ, $\theta_\perp$ can be used as an approximation of θ_k. Also, note that the Poisson distribution parameter, $\alpha_{C,\theta}$, is computed assuming that the results are uniformly distributed in each utility cell, $\langle x_i, y_j \rangle \in C$. The utility-space partitioning strategy presented in Section 3 which results in smaller cells nearer to the high-utility region of the utility space, helps ensure that the assumption is more likely to hold at more critical (high-utility) parts of the utility space.

---

[11] If the join selectivity is higher than 0.05, the Poisson approximation of the binomial distribution may not be appropriate. In that case, we compute the expected number of results, $\mu_{i,j} \times (r_{1,i} \times r_{2,j})$, that the pair, x_i and y_j, will return and we deduct this amount from the target, k.

Inputs:

- The set, $\mathcal{C} = \{x_1, \ldots x_n\} \times \{y_1, \ldots y_m\}$, of utility-cells.
- The error upper bound, p_ϵ.

1. given the segment boundaries, $0 = x_0 < x_1 < \ldots < x_{n-1} < x_n = 1$ and $0 = y_0 < y_1 < \ldots < y_{m-1} < y_m = 1$, compute the utility score, $\theta_{i,j}$, corresponding to each segment boundary intersection, (x_i, y_j).
2. compute the confidence, $p^{\geq}_{P_{i,j}, \theta_{i,j}}(k)$, for each segment boundary intersection, (x_i, y_j), where $P_{i,j} \subseteq \mathcal{C}$ is the set of utility cells to the north-east of the segment boundary intersection, (x_i, y_j).
3. find the largest $\theta_{i,j}$, such that $p^{\geq}_{P_{i,j}, \theta_{i,j}}(k) \geq 1 - p_\epsilon$, and let $\theta_\perp = \theta_{i,j}$;
4. let $\theta_\top$ be the next larger utility score of a segment boundary intersection (*at this point we have* $\theta_\perp \leq \theta_k < \theta_\top$).
5. while $\theta_\top - \theta_\perp > \theta_\Delta$, do

   (a) let $\theta = \frac{\theta_\top - \theta_\perp}{2}$

   (b) if $p^{\geq}_{P_{i,j}, \theta}(k) \geq 1 - p_\epsilon$, then let $\theta_\perp = \theta$

   else let $\theta_\top = \theta$
6. $\theta_k = \theta_\perp$
7. return θ_k

Fig. 12. Algorithm for estimating θ_k

5   Balanced Work Allocation

Once the target utility lowerbound, θ_k, is computed within an acceptable error bound, the next step in the process is to partition the (sufficiently high-utility) portions of the input data, and to assign the resulting work quanta onto the available servers for join processing. In the simplest *random split* strategy, the data elements can be assigned to the available servers randomly (e.g., hash partitioning). This approach is obviously very easy to implement, and could, in fact, ensure that the amount of input data assigned to the servers is balanced. On the other hand, in general, there is no guarantee that the useful workload (i.e., workload for candidate input pairs with utility score greater than or equal to θ_k) will be balanced across different servers in the system. In contrast, a *boundary-aware, utility-driven split* strategy would rely on the utility statistics (which were already collected for obtaining the utility-boundary θ_k – see Section 3) to estimate the distribution of the workload in the utility-space above θ_k, and partition the data along the utility dimensions in such a way that the useful workload (consisting of candidate input pairs, with utility score greater than or equal to θ_k) is balanced, and non-useful workload is avoided as much as possible.

As described in Section 3, uSplit segments the two dimensions of the utility space (corresponding to data sources R_1 and R_2), for helping with the allocation of the sampling budget for estimating the join selectivities. For work partitioning, uSplit considers a second set of utility boundaries, $0 = \chi_0 < \chi_1 < \ldots < \chi_{u-1} < \chi_u = 1$ and $0 = \gamma_0 < \gamma_1 < \ldots < \gamma_{v-1} < \gamma_v = 1$, which are *uniformly spaced*; i.e., , $\forall 1 \leq i \leq u$ and $\forall 1 \leq j \leq v$

$$(\chi_i - \chi_{i-1}) = \Delta x_n \quad \text{and} \quad (\gamma_j - \gamma_{j-1}) = \Delta y_m.$$

where Δx_n and Δy_m denote the sizes of the smallest segments for which statistics are available (see Section 3.3). During the statistics collection phase (see Section 3

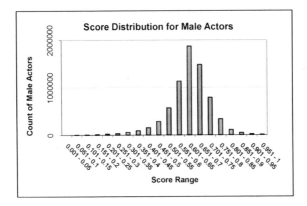

Fig. 13. Score distribution for male actors; the distribution for the female actors is similar

and Figure 7), for each data partition, $\Xi_i = (\chi_{i-1}, \chi_i]$ or $\Upsilon_j = (\gamma_{j-1}, \gamma_j]$, uSplit collects additional statistics including the numbers, $\eta_{1,i}$ and $\eta_{2,j}$, of data elements in these partitions.

uSplit selects one of the two sources, R_1 or R_2, as the pivot to drive the partitioning process. Without loss of generality, let us assume that the dimension corresponding to the utility partitions, $\Xi_i = (\chi_{i-1}, \chi_i]$, is selected as the pivot. The work above the utility boundary (defined by θ_k and the combination function, Φ) for each pivot partition, $\Xi_i = (\chi_{i-1}, \chi_i]$, is estimated using the selectivities that have been computed in Section 3. Let $W = \sum W(\Xi_i)$ denote the total work above the utility threshold for all partitions. If U servers are available for processing, we expect that each server will be assigned roughly $\frac{W}{U}$ units of work. Thus, uSplit aggregates the utility partitions into U roughly equi-work, *contiguous* groups (or *slices*), each with $\sim \frac{W}{U}$ workload. The data corresponding to each slice are then allocated for one of the servers for join processing.

6   Experiments

In this section, we evaluate the effectiveness of uSplit in (a) predicting join selectivities, (b) estimating the utility threshold θ_k, and (c) end-to-end query processing time.

For evaluation purposes, we used data sets with different characteristics and sizes: (a) We have created synthetic data sets with up to $500M$ data elements (14GB) per source. We considered *uniform*, *normal* ($mean = 0.5$, $var = 0.15$), and *Zipfian* utility distributions. (b) We have also run experiments using the *Internet Movie Database* (IMDB) data set [1]; we focused on *male* and *female* actors (1M entries each), and used the average rating of the movies a given actor played in as the corresponding utility. Figure 13 shows that these ratings show a normal distribution.

On the synthetic data set, we considered an equijoin (with ~ 10 matches per data entry). For the actors data, we considered the following top-k join query: "*find the K highest scoring male-female actor pairs who have played in at least one movie together.*"

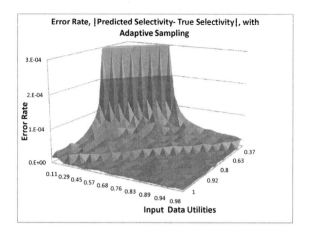

Fig. 14. With adaptive sampling, errors in selectivity estimation are lower at high utility ranges – the true selectivity is ∼ 0.001 (Uniform 10K data set, 20 segments, segment scaling factor = 1.1, sampling scaling factor = 1.05, sampling budget = 1000)

Number of Elements above a Threshold			
Range	Real Count	Adaptive Seg.	Uniform Seg.
≥ 0.95	877	891	953
≥ 0.9	3393	3440	3704
≥ 0.8	22356	22402	23301
≥ 0.7	90965	92059	91696

Fig. 15. Especially for high utility thresholds, adaptive segmentation provides highly precise predictions of the number of results (1M data set, segment scaling factor = 1.1, num. of segments = 23)

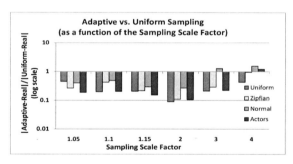

Fig. 16. Effect of sampling scale factor (1M data, Euclidean combination, segment scaling factor = 1.1, 20 segments, sampling budget = 1% of data)

In order to observe the impact of de-biasing, we de-biased the data sets with *Zipfian* distributions (which has extreme bias), but left the *actors* and *normal* data sets intact.

We used *average*, *product*, and *Euclidean* combinations.

The experiments were executed over the Amazon EC2 platform with up to 20 RedHat CentOS 5.2 machines; each machine had 7.5 GB memory, 4 EC2 64-bit Compute Units

(2 virtual cores with 2 EC2 compute units each), with *high* I/O performance option. Once the data is sampled and partitioned, the actual joins on the servers were done using Vertica [2] DBMS (Vertica Analytic Database 3.5.10-0). Unless specified otherwise, the results are averages of three runs.

6.1 Effectiveness of the Adaptive Sampling

Impact of Non-Uniform Sampling. We first provide a high-level overview of the impact of the adaptive approach to sampling, presented in Section 3. As Figure 15 and Figure 14 show, the proposed strategies ensure that the selectivity estimation errors are very close to zero for the high utility region (which is the only region that matters for top-k joins), instead of being uniform across the utility space.

Figure 16 quantifies the benefits of using non-uniform sampling rates by varying the sampling scale parameter, ρ, between 1.05 and 4.0 and comparing the errors in the estimation of the number of results above a given threshold ($\theta = 1.33$) to the errors resulting when uniform sampling is used. As the figure shows, when $\rho \sim 2$ adaptive sampling leads to errors that are only 10% to 50% of the errors that occur with uniform sampling. Note also that using too large a ρ does not help as it concentrates too large a number of samples to a too small a portion of the utility space, resulting in degradations elsewhere.

Impact of the Sampling Budget. Figure 17 verifies that, as expected, a higher sampling budget helps reduce the amount of errors; but a relatively small number of samples

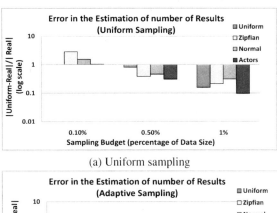

(a) Uniform sampling

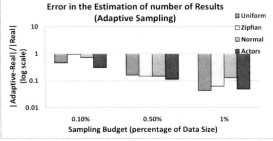

(b) Adaptive sampling

Fig. 17. Effect of the sampling budget (1M data, Euclidean comb., $\theta_k = 1.33$, segment scaling factor = 1.1, sampling scaling factor = 1.05, 20 segments)

are sufficient for accurate estimates. Moreover adaptive sampling provides significantly better result estimates.

Impact of Using Non-Uniform Utility Segments during Sampling. Figure 18(a) shows the benefits of using non-uniform segment boundaries during sampling; in the figure, the segment size scale parameter, π, is varied between 1.05 and 2.0 and the corresponding errors in the estimation of the number of results above $\theta = 1.33$ are compared against the errors that occur when using uniform partition boundaries (i.e., $\pi = 1.0$). When the segment size scale parameter is 1.15, non-uniform segmentation results in sampling errors that are only 10% to 40% of the errors that occur when using uniform boundaries. Further increasing the segment scaling factor however is not useful: while the very high utility region gets finely segmented, the granularity drops quickly for values slightly lower than 1.0, resulting in degradations in accuracy.

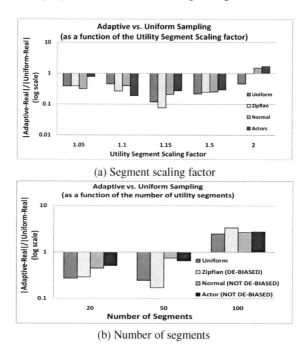

(a) Segment scaling factor

(b) Number of segments

Fig. 18. Effects of (a) segment size scaling factor and (b) the number of segments (1M data, Euclidean combination, sampling scaling factor = 1.05, 20 segments, sampling budget = 1%)

Figure 18(b) shows that using a larger number of segments does not imply better sampling: this is because, as discussed in Section 3.3, when the number of data elements in a segment is too small, this may negatively effect the estimation of error margins. This is confirmed by Figure 18(b) which shows that the problem is more pronounced when the utilities are biased.

Impact of the De-biasing. Figure 19 tracks the success rate of obtaining top-k results using different target confidence rates, $1 - p_\epsilon$, over 100 runs. As the figure shows, for the uniform and the *de-biased* Zipfian data sets (despite the initial extreme bias of

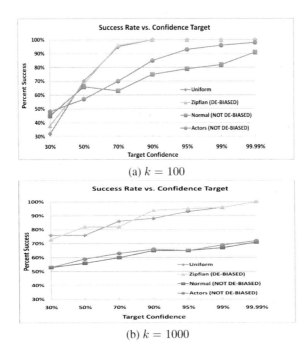

(a) $k = 100$

(b) $k = 1000$

Fig. 19. Effect of de-biasing (10K data, average, sampling scaling factor = 1.05, 50 segments, segment scaling factor = 1.1, sampling budget = 10%)

the Zipfian distribution) the algorithm is able to provide success rates larger than or almost equal to the target confidence. For non-de-biased data sets (Normal and Actors), on the other hand, the success rates are lower, especially for large ks and high target confidences. This is because, when the utilities are skewed, this increases the chances of having sampling errors. The problem is compounded for large k values, which lead to relatively lower θ_k values, thus moving into the regions of the utility space where sampling errors are relatively larger. This highlights the importance of de-biasing the input data sets through an initial high-level utility distribution analysis.

Target Number of Results vs. Obtained Number of Results. Figure 20 shows the relationship between the target number of results (k) and the obtained number of results. As shown in this figure, uSplit is highly accurate in matching the target number of results and this is true for different data distributions (Figure 20(a)) and combination functions (Figure 20(b)).

6.2   Impact of uSplit on Processing Times

After the above experiments in which we have explored the impact of uSplit based sampling on the success rate in top-k result enumeration, in this section, we consider the execution time and scalability. In these experiments, we use two data sources, each with 500M entries. Each entry joins with $\sim$ 10 entries in the other source. The score merge function is *average* and the data utilities are uniformly distributed.

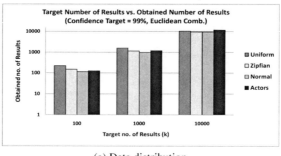

(a) Data distribution

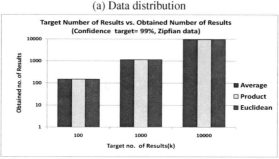

(b) Combination function

Fig. 20. Targeted vs. obtained results (1M data, sampling scaling factor = 1.05, 20 segments, segment scaling factor = 1.1, sampling budget = 1%)

Experiments are run on EC2. In implementing uSplit partitioning, we used the combined-output sampling strategy (the costliest –i.e., worst-case– of the sampling strategies, which requires a full-scan over the data (see Section 3).

Cost of top-k Retrieval w/o uSplit. As Figure 21(a) shows, the full join of these two sources using the Vertica [2] column DBMS (Vertica Analytic Database 3.5.10-0) on 10 EC2 machines takes 20.2 hours. Even using the "limit k" option with an order by clause, the execution time drops only to 358mins for $k = 100M$ and to 56mins for $k = 1000$.

Cost of Retrieval using uSplit based Thresholding. As described in Section 3, uSplit piggy-backs the data sampling process on the up-stream operator. Neverthe-less, for 500M entries, collecting 0.1% samples partitioned into 20 segments from each source and (once the samples are collected) joining these 20×20 segment pairs using a single EC2 machine running Vertica to collect join statistics costs 14.6 minutes of extra overhead.

Once the Θ_k values are computed by uSplit using these statistics (Section 4), one possible query processing strategy is to formulate a threshold query that can be executed using a standard parallel query processing engine, such as Vertica. As shown in Figure 21(b), given Θ_k corresponding to the target k, performing the threshold joins using Vertica on 10 EC2 machines took, even accounting for the cost of statistics collec-tion and data loading, only 72 minutes for $k = 100M$ and 152 minutes for $k = 900M$. These are significant savings over naive "limit k" based retrieval results in Figure 21(a).

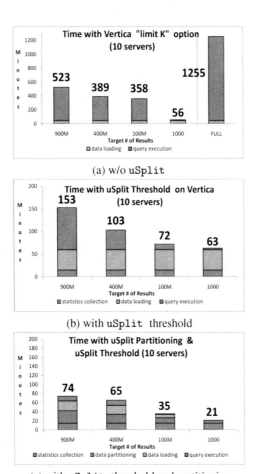

(a) w/o uSplit

(b) with uSplit threshold

(c) with uSplit threshold and partitioning

Fig. 21. Impact of the uSplit on retrieval times(500M per source, sampling scaling = 1.05, 20 segments, segment scaling = 1.1, sampling budget = 0.1%, 10 servers)

Only the $k = 1000$ case fares slightly worse than the case without uSplit, because in that case the statistics collection time is not amortized with gains in processing time.

Cost of Retrieval using uSplit Data Partitioning. Alternatively, uSplit can directly partition the data and assign the partitions onto the available servers using the collected statistics (Section 5). As Figure 21(c) shows, with uSplit partitioning (performed using Vertica on 10 EC2 servers), the total execution times have been pushed all the way down to only 35 minutes for $k = 100M$ and 74 minutes for $k = 900M$. Importantly, with uSplit partitioning, data loading and query execution times for $k = 1000$ are negligible (thus much fewer than 10 servers would probably be sufficient) and, thus, top-k processing costs only 21 minutes.

Note that with uSplit partitioning, the standard deviation of the work on the 10 machines was less than 3 minutes.

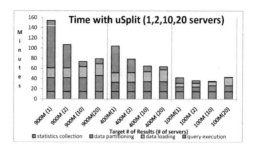

Fig. 22. Impact of the number of servers (500M per source, sampling scaling = 1.05, 20 segments, segment scaling = 1.1, sampling budget = 0.1%)

Impact of the Number of Servers. Finally, Figure 22 shows the impact of the number of servers. Using more servers tend to reduce the final query processing time. However, the linear drop does not continue forever: this is because uSplit eliminates wasted work and thus reduces the need for large number of servers[12], the overheads of statistics collection, data partitioning, and data loading start becoming dominant and the end-to-end processing times start suffering beyond 10 servers for these experiments. Note that, since in general join processing is much costlier than statistics collection, partitioning, and data loading, as the data sizes or k increase, allocating more servers to the join operation will be helpful and the system will continue scaling linearly for a larger number of servers.

7   Conclusions

In this paper, we first noted that top-k query processing (a core operation in many data analysis operations) over current batch-oriented data processing systems, such as MapReduce, or parallel DBMSs, such as Vertica, can waste resources. To address this shortcoming, we developed and presented a novel data partitioning framework, called uSplit which processes top-k queries in a work-balanced and waste-avoiding manner. uSplit includes novel techniques for predicting join selectivities as a function of data utilities and estimating a utility lowerbound, θ_k, for the kth result using these selectivities. A sampling strategy which adaptively allocates the data sampling budget and also adapts the partition boundaries helps ensure that selectivity estimates are especially precise for high-utilities; consequently θ_k estimation can be done with high confidence. In the experiments, uSplit provided up to $\sim 9\times$ gains.

References

1. Internet Movie Database, http://www.imdb.com/interfaces
2. Vertica, http://www.vertica.com
3. Yahoo! "Hadoop", http://hadoop.apache.org

---

[12] A task that requires 300 to 500 minutes on 10 machines without uSplit Figure 21(a) may need only ~ 150 mins with uSplit even using only 1 server (Figure 22).

4. Abouzeid, A., Bajda-Pawlikowski, K., Abadi, D.J., Silberschatz, A., Rasin, A.: HadoopDB: An Architectural Hybrid of MapReduce and DBMS Technologies for Analytical Workloads. Proceedings of the Very Large Data Bases Endowment 2(1), 922–933 (2009)

5. Arai, B., Das, G., Gunopulos, D., Koudas, N.: Anytime Measures for Top-k Algorithms. In: Proceedings of the 33rd International Conference on Very Large Data Bases, pp. 225–237 (2007)

6. Candan, K.S., Li, W.-S.: On Similarity Measures for Multimedia Database Applications. Knowledge and Information Systems 3(1), 30–51 (2001)

7. Candan, K.S., Kim, J.W., Nagarkar, P., Nagendra, M., Yu, R.: RanKloud: Scalable Multimedia Data Processing in Server Clusters. To appear in IEEE MultiMedia (2010)

8. Carey, M.J., Kossmann, D.: On Saying "Enough Already!" in SQL. In: Proceedings of the ACM SIGMOD International Conference on Management of Data, pp. 219–230 (1997)

9. Carey, M.J., Kossmann, D.: Processing Top N and Bottom N Queries. IEEE Data Engineering Bulletin 20(3), 12–19 (1997)

10. Carey, M.J., Kossmann, D.: Reducing the Braking Distance of an SQL Query Engine. In: Proceedings of the 24th International Conference on Very Large Data Bases, pp. 158–169 (1998)

11. Chaiken, R., Jenkins, B., Larson, P., Ramsey, B., Shakib, D., Weaver, S., Zhou, J.: SCOPE: Easy and Efficient Parallel Processing of Massive Data Sets. Proceedings of the Very Large Data Bases Endowment 1(2), 1265–1276 (2008)

12. Chakrabarti, K., Ganti, V., Han, J., Xin, D.: Ranking Objects by Exploiting Relationships: Computing Top-K over Aggregation. In: Proceedings of the ACM SIGMOD International Conference on Management of Data, pp. 371–382 (2006)

13. Chang, K., Hwang, S.-W.: Minimal Probing: Supporting Expensive Predicates for Top-k Queries. In: Proceedings of the ACM SIGMOD International Conference on Management of Data, pp. 346–357 (2002)

14. Chaudhuri, S., Motwani, R., Narasayya, V.: Random Sampling for Histogram Construction: How much is enough? In: Proceedings of the ACM SIGMOD International Conference on Management of Data, pp. 436–447 (1998)

15. Chaudhuri, S., Gravano, L.: Evaluating Top-k Selection Queries. In: Proceedings of the 25th International Conference on Very Large Data Bases, pp. 397–410 (1999)

16. Chaudhuri, S., Motwani, R., Narasayya, V.: On Random Sampling over Joins. In: Proceedings of the ACM SIGMOD International Conference on Management of Data, pp. 263–274 (1999)

17. Condie, T., Conway, N., Alvaro, P., Hellerstein, J.M., Elmeleegy, K., Sears, R.: MapReduce Online. Technical Report, EECS Department, University of California, Berkeley (2009)

18. Cooper, B., Ramakrishnan, R., Srivastava, U., Silberstein, A., Bohannon, P., Jacobsen, H., Puz, N., Weaver, D., Yerneni, R.: PNUTS: Yahoo!'s Hosted Data Serving Platform. Proceedings of the Very Large Data Bases Endowment 1(2), 1277–1288 (2008)

19. Dean, J., Ghemawat, S.: MapReduce: Simplified Data Processing on Large Clusters. In: Proceedings of the 6th Conference on Symposium on Opearting Systems Design and Implementation, pp. 137–150 (2004)

20. DeCandia, G., Hastorun, D., Jampani, M., Kakulapati, G., Lakshman, A., Pilchin, A., Sivasubramanian, S., Vosshall, P., Vogels, W.: Dynamo: Amazon's Highly Available Key-Value Store. Proceedings of the 21st ACM SIGOPS Symposium on Operating Systems Principles 41(6), 205–220 (2007)

21. Fagin, R.: Combining Fuzzy Information from Multiple Systems. In: Proceedings of the 15th ACM SIGACT-SIGMOD-SIGART Symposium on Principles of Database Systems, pp. 216–226 (1996)

22. Fagin, R.: Fuzzy Queries in Multimedia Database Systems. In: Proceedings of the 17th ACM SIGACT-SIGMOD-SIGART Symposium on Principles of Database Systems, pp. 1–10 (1998)
23. Fagin, R., Lotem, A., Naor, M.: Optimal Aggregation Algorithms for Middleware. Journal of Computer and System Sciences 66(4), 614–656 (2003)
24. Güntzer, U., Balke, W.-T., Kiessling, W.: Towards Efficient Multi-Feature Queries in Heterogeneous Environments. In: Proceedings of the International Conference on Information Technology: Coding and Computing, pp. 622–628 (2001)
25. Kim, J.W., Candan, K.S.: Skip-and-Prune: Cosine-based Top-k Query Processing for Efficient Context-Sensitive Document Retrieval. In: Proceedings of the 35th SIGMOD International Conference on Management of Data, pp. 115–126 (2009)
26. Schnaitter, K., Spiegel, J., Polyzotis, N.: Depth Estimation for Ranking Query Optimization. In: Proceedings of the 33rd International Conference on Very Large Data Bases, pp. 902–913 (2007)
27. Li, C., Chang, K.C.-C., Ilyas, I.F., Song, S.: RankSQL: Query Algebra and Optimization for Relational Top-k Queries. In: Proceedings of the ACM SIGMOD International Conference on Management of Data, pp. 131–142 (2005)
28. Lin, J.: Brute Force and Indexed Approaches to Pairwise Document Similarity Comparisons with MapReduce. In: Proceedings of the 32nd International ACM SIGIR Conference on Research and Development in Information Retrieval, pp. 155–162 (2009)
29. Marian, A., Bruno, N., Gravano, L.: Evaluating Top-k Queries over Web-Accessible Databases. ACM Transactions on Database Systems 29(2), 319–362 (2004)
30. Matias, Y., Vitter, J., Wang, M.: Wavelet-based Histograms for Selectivity Estimation. In: Proceedings of the ACM SIGMOD International Conference on Management of Data, pp. 448–459 (1998)
31. Pavlo, A., Paulson, E., Rasin, A., Abadi, D., DeWitt, D., Madden, S., Stonebraker, M.: A Comparison of Approaches to Large-Scale Data Analysis. In: Proceedings of the 35th SIGMOD International Conference on Management of Data, pp. 165–178 (2009)
32. Poosala, V., Haas, P., Ioannidis, Y., Shekita, E.: Improved Histograms for Selectivity Estimation of Range Predicates. In: Proceedings of the ACM SIGMOD International Conference on Management of Data, pp. 294–305 (1996)
33. Singh, S., Kubica, J., Larsen, S., Sorokina, D.: Parallel Large Scale Feature Selection for Logistic Regression. In: Proceedings of the SIAM International Conference on Data Mining, pp. 1171–1182 (2009)
34. Thusoo, A., Sarma, J.S., Jain, N., Shao, Z., Chakka, P., Zhang, N., Antony, S., Liu, H., Murthy, R.: Hive A Petabyte Scale Data Warehouse Using Hadoop. In: Proceedings of the 26th International Conference on Data Engineering, pp. 996–1005 (2010)
35. Trivedi, K.S.: Probability and Statistics with Reliability, Queuing and Computer Science Applications, 2nd edn. John Wiley and Sons Ltd., Chichester (2002)
36. Vitter, J.S.: Random Sampling with a Reservoir. ACM Transactions on Mathematical Software 11(1), 37–57 (1985)

Multi-query Evaluation over Compressed XML Data in DaaS

Xiaoling Wang[1], Aoying Zhou[1], Juzhen He[1], Wilfred Ng[2], and Patrick Hung[3]

[1] Shanghai Key Laboratory of Trustworthy Computing,
East China Normal University, Shanghai 200062, China
`xlwang@sei.ecnu.edu.cn,ayzhou@sei.ecnu.edu.cn`
[2] Department of Computer Science,
Hong Kong University of Science and Technology, Hong Kong
`wilfred@cs.ust.hk`
[3] Faculty of Business and Information Technology,
University of Ontario Institute of Technology, Canada
`patrick.hung@uoit.ca`

Abstract. This paper addresses the problem of evaluating a heavy load of sub-scribed queries (or simply multi-queries) over compressed XML data in a distributed service-oriented DaaS (Database as a Service) environment. We pro-pose a holistic approach that evaluates complex queries over a compressed doc-ument and forwards the compressed results directly to the data requestor (DR). Firstly, we review the data management issues in DaaS, and then we will address the multi-queries optimization problem. Secondly, we introduce a new rewriting translation technique to decompose and reorganize a complex query into its cor-responding Structure of complex XPath (SXP). Following this, multi-query eval-uation is performed based on the containment relationships between the queries. The containment relationships are exploited by a global data structure, the Structural-Query-Index Tree (SQIT), which supports prefix sharing among the submitted queries. The experimental results demonstrate that the proposed ap-proach obtains higher query processing efficiency than traditional ones.

Keywords: XML, Database as a Service, Multi-query processing, XML queries, XML compression.

1 Introduction

With the popular use of service-oriented technology, various computing functionality modules as different services are developed and provided. Database as a Service (**DaaS**) becomes one of the hottest research topics in SOA (Service-Oriented-Architecture) ap-plications. **DaaS** can provide data management services such as data storage, query processing, data backup, access control, capacity planning, and can avoid data owners (**DO**) from managing and maintaining the hardware (computer) and software (database products and application programs). In the industrial aspect, the increasing number of applications are multi-tenant [1] rather than single-tenant. Multi-tenant techniques are key in the literature of **DaaS**. Former work [4,5] has studied the data partition and

D. Agrawal et al. (Eds.): Information and Software as Services, LNBIP 74, pp. 185–208, 2011.

data placement strategies in distributed environment, and the security considerations, including data encryption and access control mechanism, has been studied by [2,6,7].

However, most former work [2,3,6,8] in DaaS focus on relational data. In the real applications, XML has already become a de-facto standard for data representation and exchange, and there are increasing applications which create XML data. In this paper, our goal is to explore the multi-query processing techniques for XML data. The repeated tags and redundant structures give rise to the well-known data verbosity problem, and this problem hinders the development of applications that involve intensive use of XML in practice, given the fact it may lead to a substantial increase in the costs of storing, processing, and exchanging service data. In order to tackle this problem, many XML-specific compression systems have recently been proposed. Some of these methods [11,17,19,23] are able to support direct access to compressed documents and avoid expensive decompression in the query evaluation stage.

In the multi-tenant applications, the **DSP** (Database Service Provider) needs to provide services for multiple users, so, only supporting single-query processing is not adequate in **DaaS** applications, this is due to the fact that the number of queries from data requester (**DR**) maybe very huge, as a result processing queries one at a time is time consuming and is not practical for handling the heavy load of subscribed queries for the **DSP**. More importantly, parsing compressed documents for many **DR**s imposes much burden on the **DSP**. With the rapid increase in both the number and size of XML documents over the Internet in SOA (Service-Oriented Architecture) applications, equipping the **DSP** with queryable XML compression technologies [20,21] is a reasonable solution that deserves further investigation. A **DSP** can be dedicated to handling documents in a compressed format. Thus, processing of multi-queries over compressed documents has emerged as a practical and meaningful issue. In order to support the XML applications that involve multiple query processing and high volumes of result dissemination in **DaaS** applications, we developed a succinct structure to organize queries and efficient techniques to evaluate multi-queries over large-scale compressed XML documents.

We will now describe a **DaaS** application scenario of processing multi-queries over compressed XML documents. In Fig. 1, there are three roles in **DaaS**:

- The data owner (DO) put his/her data and access control table (ACT) to database service provider (DSP). The ACT describes the access control information for each data requestor;
- The DSP is responsible to manage data. The data management tasks include data storage, query processing, access control, data security issues, and so on.
- The DR submits queries to the DSP and obtains query results from the DSP.

In such a scenario, it is important to adopt XML compression techniques in order to save both on the storage cost in the DSP, bandwidth in the result delivery, and the query optimization technique to avoid the heavy query processing burden at the DSP. In this paper, we focus on studying effective solutions to query processing over compressed XML data at the DSP side.

There are several challenges to develop an efficient approach for the above application. First of all, unlike the usual distributed query processing [16], it is not feasible to process all of these queries simultaneously, given that the number of queries is extremely large. Secondly, XML documents are compressed in order to save storage

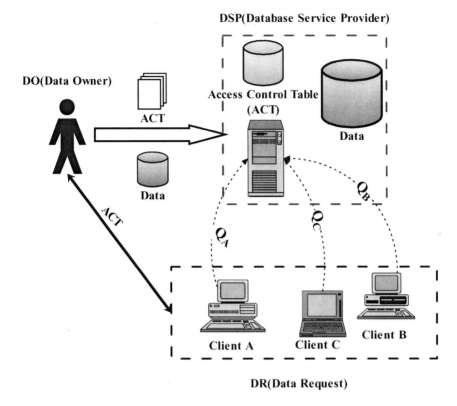

Fig. 1. The Architecture of DaaS

and bandwidth, and multi-queries need to be evaluated directly without performing full decompression of the documents. Next, using existing methods, evaluating complex queries over compressed documents is still a time-consuming process. In this paper, we do not only consider the efficient evaluation of single complex queries, but also explore the containment relationships among the queries to improve the efficiency of the multi-query evaluation. In order to address the above challenges, a novel query decomposition and organization strategy, called the Structure of complex XPath (SXP), is proposed. This will serve as the basis of Structural-Query-Index Tree (SQIT), which is the kernel structure in query processing. The main contributions of this paper are highlighted as follows:

1. We propose a DaaS framework and we address the problem of multi-query processing over compressed XML documents at the DSP side.
2. We develop a new query translation technique that organizes complex XPath queries into the Structure of XPath (SXP). SXP is a data structure that allows us to analyze a complex XPath query and evaluates the method on compressed documents.
3. We present a novel Structural Query Index Tree (SQIT), which takes advantage of containment relationships among queries. The SQIT is a global data structure.

This will organize all subscribed queries as a whole. Based on the SQIT, we will develop an efficient query evaluation strategy.

4. We conduct an experimental study on the evaluation of the XPath queries on compressed XML data. Compared with existing approaches, our results show that the proposed approach is significantly more efficient.

The remaining part of this paper is organized as follows: in the next three sections we (1) overview the related work, (2) give the preliminaries and background knowledge of our approach, and (3) present a decomposition model for an XPath query. Then it follows two sections on core technical issues. The first section is about the definition of the SQIT and algorithms for building and maintaining the SQIT. The second section describes how we evaluate multi-queries over compressed data based on the SQIT. After that, it follows a section in which an experimental study is presented. In the last section we give our concluding remarks.

2   Related Work

Most related work on this topic is from the areas of XML query processing, XML filtering and XML compression techniques. First, several indexing techniques have been proposed for query optimization over an XML document. For example, the structure index [10,14,22] offers an efficient support for path or structure queries. Amer-Yahia [9] combines the structure index and keyword search in XML document retrieval. However, these methods are not applicable to processing heavy loads of subscribed queries over compressed XML documents. Second, XML filtering techniques are related to our work. However, most XML filtering systems developed by [12,13] compute queries by navigating XML documents through query structures, including the prefix tree or Non-Deterministic Finite Automaton (NFA). For example, Diao [12] employs a single NFA to represent all path queries by sharing the common prefixes. Third, there are several emerging XML compression techniques and strategies [17,23], which can be classified into two categories of queryable or unqueryable compression. We will only discuss the first category, since it is more relevant to this work. XGrind [23] and XPress

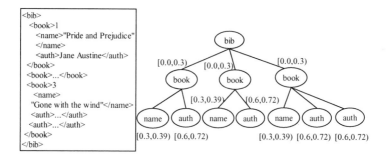

Fig. 2. An XML snippet and its corresponding tree structure with encoded tags

are two examples of homomorphic compressors in the first category; they both support direct querying of compressed data by retaining the document structure. XGrind uses dictionary-encoding and Huffman-encoding for tags and data. XPress adopts reverse arithmetic encoding for tags, and diverse encoding methods for text according to the data types. The encoding techniques enable XPress to achieve better compression ratios and higher query performance than XGrind. However, these methods do not support the evaluation of multi-queries.

3   Preliminaries

In this section, the scope of XML queries, the notion of XPath containment, and the interval encode technique [19] are introduced.

3.1   XPath Containment

As shown in Fig. 2, an XML document is represented as an ordered labeled tree with the root node, where the node corresponds to an element or a value in the XML document. The value pairs in Fig. 2 is the interval encodes for tags. The detailed encoding method is described in Section 3.2.

In the subsequent discussion, only the XPath queries in $XP^{\{/,//,*,[]\}}$ are considered. The grammar of $XP^{\{/,//,*,[]\}}$ is described by the following expression:

$$q \rightarrow l \mid * \mid . \mid q/q \mid q//q \mid q[q] \tag{1}$$

where "l" is a node label, "$*$" is a wildcard and "." denotes the context node. We use "/" and "//" mean the child and the descendant axes.

We assume that all XPath queries or path expressions are $XP^{\{/,//,*,[]\}}$ queries throughout. Furthermore, the $XP^{\{/,//,*,[]\}}$ queries containing only "/" are called *simple path queries*. Otherwise, they are called *complex path queries* as illustrated in Example 1.

Example 1. $Q1 = $ "$//closed_auctions[*[personID = 1]]/date[text = $ "12/15/ 1999"]" is a *complex query*.

Containment relationships may exist among different queries in $XP^{\{/,//,*,[]\}}$.

Definition 1 (Containment of XPath). *For XPath Q_1 and Q_2, if the result of Q_1 is contained in the result of Q_2 for any given XML document, we say that Q_1 is contained by Q_2, and this fact is denoted as $Q_1 \subset Q_2$.*

The containment relationship helps to avoid some extensive and repetitive evaluation of contained queries on the original document. However, the containment of the $XP^{\{/,//,*,[]\}}$ expression is a co-NP problem. Miklau and Suciu [18] present a sufficient but incomplete PTIME algorithm to compute the containment, whose underlying idea is that each XPath expression can be expressed as a one-arity pattern tree, and vice versa. XPath expressions can then be translated into pattern trees, and following this, the containment is evaluated

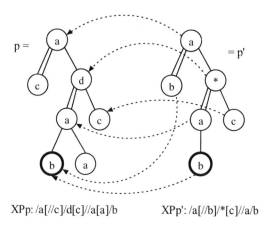

XPp: /a[//c]/d[c]//a[a]/b   XPp': /a[//b]/*[c]//a/b

Fig. 3. A pattern homomorphism from p' to p

based on finding the homomorphism relationships of the pattern trees (or simply the pattern homomorphisms). Informally, a pattern homomorphism is a mapping, h, from the nodes in a pattern, p, to the nodes in another pattern tree, such that h is root-preserving, respects node labels, and obeys edge constraints. The formal definition of h can be consulted from [18]. When there is a pattern homomorphism between two pattern trees, there also exists a containment relationship between the same two XPath queries [18]. For example, Fig. 3 shows a pattern homomorphism from one pattern tree to another pattern tree p. In this case, the XPath query XP_p, which is translated into the pattern tree p, is contained by the XPath query XP'_p, which is translated into the pattern tree.

3.2   XML Compression Technique

XML compression has the benefits of reducing the cost of both storage and result delivery incurred by a network. We compress XML documents by using dictionary encoders for text and interval encoders for tags. The Interval Encoding method is applied for encoding tags by [19]. The underlying idea is as follows: before compression, we collect the statistical information of tags by parsing the document. Assume the name of the ith tag is $t(i)$, where i are in $(1, \ldots, m)$ and m is the number of different tags in the document. The probability of $t(i)$ is $prob_{t(i)}$ and then $t(i)$ is allocated with an initial region encode $[MIN^0{}_{t(i)}, MAX^0{}_{t(i)}]$ in $[0, 1)$ based on the probability information of $t(k)$ and $1 \leq k \leq i$. Then, each tag in the document is encoded as an interval computed according to Equation (2).

$$MIN^j_{t(i)} = \sum_{k=1}^{i-1} prob_{t(k)}; MAX^j_{t(i)} = \sum_{k=1}^{i} prob_{t(k)} \tag{2}$$

For each simple path $p_0/p_1/ \ldots /p_n$, the jth tag for $j \in 0, 1, 2, \ldots, n$, corresponds to the tag name p_j. This path is encoded as an interval computed according to Equation (3).

$$MIN^j_{p_j} = MIN^0_{p_j} + prob_{p_j} * MIN^{j-1}_{p_{j-1}}; MAX^j_{p_j} = MIN^0_{p_j} + prob_{p_j} * MAX^{j-1}_{p_{j-1}}; \tag{3}$$

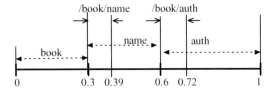

Fig. 4. An Example of Interval Encoding

As shown in Fig. 4, the frequency of the tag $< book >$ is 3 and the frequency of all of the tags (i.e. $< book >$, $< name >$ and $< auth >$) is 10. Thus, the tag $< book >$ has the probability of 0.3. Because "$< book >$" is the first element in the document, it will be allocated with a given initial interval, $[min_{book}^0, max_{book}^0) = [0.0, 0.3)$, the first range fragment in $(0, 1]$. The initial intervals of $< name >$ and $< auth >$ are $[0.3, 0.6)$ and $[0.6, 1.0)$, respectively. During compression, $< book >$ is the first element and is encoded into a value in the range of $[0.0, 0.3)$. The tag $< name >$ of the path "/book/name" is compressed into a value in the range of $[0.3 + (0.6 - 0.3) * 0.0, 0.3 + (0.6 - 0.3) * 0.3)$, which is equal to $[0.3, 0.39)$. And $< auth >$ with path "/book/auth" has the interval of $[0.6 + (1.0 - 0.6) * 0.0, 0.6 + (1.0 - 0.6) * 0.3)$, which is equal to $[0.6, 0.72)$. All the intervals are marked with their corresponding tags in Fig. 4.

To evaluate queries within a compressed document, all the queries have to be translated into intervals and directly compared with the compressed tags. Based on the computing rules given by Equations (2) and (3), the reverse arithmetic encoding method has a useful feature of suffix-containment, as shown in Fig. 4. If the XPath expression of Q_A is the suffix of that of Q_B, then Q_A's interval contains Q_B's. Thus, to evaluate the query "/auth", we are only required to find the tag whose value is in $[0.6, 1.0)$ (i.e. the initial value of $< auth >$). As for the query "/book/auth", we only need to find the tags within the range $[0.6, 0.72)$, but do not need to cache the element $< book >$ in the query evaluation.

However, the above technique is only applicable for the cases consisting of simple paths of only child axes. The complex queries that contain "*", "[ ]" and "//" cannot be directly translated into intervals. Thus, we develop a new query translation technique and some sophisticated data structures, the SQIT, for handling complex queries, which will be presented in the next section.

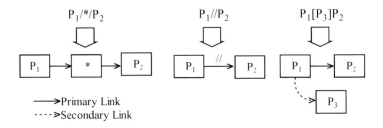

Fig. 5. Query Decomposition and Reorganization

4   Structural Query Index Tree

In this section, some techniques are presented to process complex queries over the compressed documents. The multi-query processing strategy is based on translating methods that transform complex queries into efficient tree structures.

4.1   Query Translation

For a complex query containing "*", "//" or "[ ]", our approach is to split the query into several simple paths or predicate expressions, called split components, which can be encoded into intervals. Following this, the components are connected by wildcard "*", descendant "//" or predicate "[ ]". Each complex query may be split into several components. For example, suppose there are three components P_1, P_2 and P_3 as shown in Fig 5, we reorganize the components in order to express the following three queries, "$P_1/*/P_2$", "$P_1//P_2$" and "$P_1[P_3]/P_2$".

The dotted and solid directed edges in Fig.5 represent two different kinds of relationships between the components. A primary link specifies the components linked on the main path, which ends with the last requested element specified in an XPath expression; whereas a secondary link is a link between the branch or predicate component and a primary link. Components coming from links marked by "//" indicate the descendant matching. This depicts the "ancestor/descendant" relationship between the component and its succeeding component (e.g. the query $P1//P2$ shown in Fig. 5). Otherwise, the relationship is assumed to be "parent/child". Based on these two kinds of links and the relevant split components, a complex XPath query is translated into a data structure called SXP as defined in Definition 2.

Definition 2   (Structure of Complex XPath (SXP)). *Given an XPath query Q, the structure of the components of Q, denoted as SXP, is a tree structure defined by* (V, E_j, E_n), *where (i) V is a set of components, which are the split component of Q; (ii) E_j is a set of primary links, which are directed edges composed of the main path except for the branches of this SXP. The ending tag on a primary link is the requested tag; and (iii) E_n is a set of secondary links, which are directed edges connecting the predicates to corresponding branch components on primary links.*

The query Q_1 that is given in Example 1 is decomposed into five components represented as P_1 to P_5, and reorganized into an SXP as shown in Fig. 6.

In an SXP, each component except the root has its preceding component, and each component except the leaves have subsequent components, including components on its primary links and secondary links. Fig. 6 shows the SXP of Q_1 and its components, where a primary link running from P_1 to P_4 is the main path of Q_1. Besides, there are three secondary links: P_1 to P_2, P_2 to P_3, and P_4 to P_5. These three secondary links stand for the branch queries located at the ending element of their corresponding components. For example, the secondary link from P_1 to P_2 indicates the fact that there is a predicate expression for the branch element "closed auctions" of P_1.

P_1: //closed_auctions
P_2: *
P_3: personID=1
P_4: /date
P_5: text ="12/15/1999"

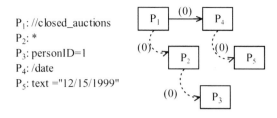

Fig. 6. Components and the SXP of the complex query Q1 in Example 1

Now, we present the algorithm of transforming a complex query into SXP in Algorithm 1, where the input query Q is first decomposed into several components. The components are then reorganized into a SXP as output. According to the level of branches, the algorithm parses the complex query and splits it recursively. In this algorithm, P_i stands for the path of the ith component appearing in the main path of the input query. We use Cxp_i to indicate the ith component of P_i. For each component on the main path, we check whether it has secondary links (Lines 6-9) and then attach each component with secondary links to the resulting SXP (Line 10). When applied to Q_1, we first find P_1, and then its secondary link P_2 (with P_3) is attached. The final result of the SXP is illustrated in Fig 6.

4.2 Structural Query Index Tree

We now introduce the strategy of processing multi-queries over compressed data based on SXPs. The essence of this strategy is that all submitted queries are composed into a Structural Query Index Tree (SQIT) by exploiting the containment relationship and shared prefixes among SXPs. This strategy helps to minimize the processing times. The definition of the SQIT is now given as follows:

Algorithm 1. TransSXP (Query Q)

Input: An XPath query Q
Output: The SXP of Q

1: Initiate t_{sxp} as the result SXP
2: Set m_{end} pointing to the end of the primary link of t_{sxp}
3: Partition the main path of Q into a set of components, $P_1, \ldots, P_n$, by "*" and "//"
4: **for** each component P_i **do**
5:     Create a C_{xpi} for P_i
6:     **if** P_i has a secondary link $[Pred_i]$ **then**
7:         Set SXP $min_i = TransSXP(Pred_i)$
8:         Add min_i into the secondary link of Cxp_i
9:     **end if**
10:     Add Cxp_i into t_{sxp}
11:     Change m_{end} into C_{xpi}
12: **end for**
13: Return t_{sxp}

Definition 3 (Structural Query Index Tree (SQIT)). *Given a set of subscribed XPath queries* $S_Q = Q_1, Q_2, \ldots, Q_n$, *the Structural Query Index Tree (SQIT) of* S_Q *is defined by the triplet* (V_Q, E, R), *where each component is given as follows.*

1. V_Q *is a finite set of query nodes, in which each node corresponds to a unique query in* S_Q. *E includes the set of edges representing the parent-child relationship in the tree. R is the (virtual) root of the tree. We will use the terms "query" and "query node" interchangeably in our subsequent discussion.*
2. *Each query node is defined by* $(Q_{cid}, SXP_Q, begin[], end[])$, *where* "$Q_{cid}$" *is the corresponding identity of the DR client,* "SXP_Q" *is the SXP of the original query* Q, *and* "$begin[]$" *and* "$end[]$" *keep the beginning and ending positions of the fragments of the query result in the compressed document.*
3. *All query nodes constitute the descendant set of R. E is the set of edges that represent the containment relationship between the nodes in* V_Q.

Example 2. (SQIT) Fig. 7 shows an example of SQIT. The set of queries, $S_Q = Q_A, Q_B, \ldots, Q_I$ listed in the box are submitted queries which are organized into the tree as shown. It can be observed that when Q_B is contained by Q_A, the node for Q_B is a descendant node of Q_A.

In brief, the SQIT is a global data structure that organizes all subscribed queries as a whole. The SXP provides a local data structure to deal with a single complex XPath query as discussed in the subsection of query translation. The SQIT reveals the containment relationship of query results among the ancestor and descendant nodes. Thus, if an XML fragment as a result cannot be satisfied by any node, there is no need to check its children or descendant queries in the sub-trees of the SQIT. Consequently, the whole search space for all queries is greatly reduced.

Sharing in the SQIT. With containment relationships, the SQIT and SXP provide a method to explore shared prefix components among queries. As shown in Fig. 7, when a tag "$< a >$" comes, the first component "$/a$" of Q_D can be satisfied, as can the second child Q_H. Thus, the first components of Q_F and Q_H should be evaluated together; otherwise, the path information of each element in Q_D's result will be lost after it is satisfied. To avoid repeatedly comparing tag "$< a >$" with the first components of Q_D and Q_H, or recursively comparing it to another component at even deeper level, we assign a sharing index to the directed edge connecting from the branch node to the SXP child. Once Q_H has a child also starting with a "$/a$" component, returning to Example 2, the sharing index "(1)" on the edge from Q_D to Q_H means that Q_H shares the first component with its parent. For Q_F, the interval of "$/a/b$" is not equal to that of "$/a$", thus the sharing index of Q_D and Q_F is "(0)".

4.3   Building the SQIT

The SQIT is generated by comparing the containment relationship among queries in a recursive manner. First, complex queries are decomposed and reorganized into SXPs by using Algorithm 1, since complex queries cannot be directly translated and evaluated over the compressed document. Then, a stack structure may be used to store the

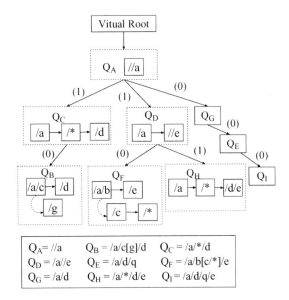

Fig. 7. An Example of the Structural Query Index Tree (SQIT)

query nodes of a branch, and the nodes in a stack are recursively classified based on the containment relationship. The details of the procedure are shown in Algorithm 2.

Initially, an empty stack is built and the first query is pushed into the stack (Line 1). When a new query arrives, it is compared to the queries on the top of all current stacks. If this query is contained by the top query of a stack, it is then pushed into the stack after the original top is popped out. At this point, the original stack top is pushed back and the stack top remains unchanged (Lines 11-14). If this query contains the top query of a stack, it should be put on the top of the stack. The query is also compared to other stacks, since there may exist other stack whose top queries are contained by this query. In this case, these two stacks are combined and the query is assigned as the new top (Lines 7-10). If there is no stack whose top query has the containment relationship with the new arriving one, we will have to set up a new stack in order to accommodate this (Lines 17-18). After all the queries have been processed, each stack will stand for a separate class. For those classes that have more than one query, we recursively classify the queries and build the hierarchy according to the containment relationships (Lines 23-27) until the whole the SQIT is constructed. A query may be contained by two or more branches of the SQIT as a result of containment computing. Thus, the containment relationship of queries may be a graph instead of a tree. For example, the query expression, Q_H = "$/a/ * /d/e$", is contained by both query expressions, Q_C = "$/a/ * /d$" and Q_D = "$a//e$". A basic approach to tackle this ambiguity is to adopt some heuristic rules, such as choosing the branch which maintains fewer nodes (i.e. Q_D in the example). An alternative is to classify this query into the class represented by the first generated stack which contains the query as our algorithm does.

Algorithm 2. `BuildingSQIT(Query Set $S$, node $R$)`

Input: S is a set of queries; node R is current root of the SQIT tree
Output: the SQIT tree

```
 1:  Set up a new stack and add the first query into it;
 2:  for each query Q in S do
 3:     if Q is a complex query then
 4:        Decompose and reorganize Q into the SXP by Algorithm 4
 5:     end if
 6:     for each existing stack S do
 7:        if S.top is contained by Q then
 8:           S.push(Q)
 9:           Continue to check whether other stack tops are contained by Q
10:           Combine all such stacks and push Q in the combined stack as its top
11:        else if Q is contained by S's top then
12:           tempQ = S.pop
13:           S.push(Q); S.push(tempQ)
14:           Break
15:        end if
16:     end for
17:     if Q has not classified into existing stacks then
18:        Set up a new stack and push Q into it
19:     end if
20:     Calculate the prefix sharing index between tops of current stacks and R
21:     Set the tops of current stacks as the children of R, make sharing index on the edges
22:  end for
23:  for each stack S' do
24:     if S' has other elements except the top T' then
25:        Set S' as the query set of elements except T'
26:        BuildingQIT (S', T')
27:     end if
28:  end for
29:  Return R
```

5   Multi-query Evaluation at the DSP

For both the SQIT and the SXP, the subscribed queries can be evaluated across compressed XML data. We first discuss the evaluation of a single query over the compressed document and then present the approach for processing multi-queries.

5.1   Single Query Evaluation over the SXP

Given the SXP of an XPath query, the evaluation of the query over a compressed document is done by traversing the SXP, where each component is translated into an interval and evaluated over the compressed document directly. During this procedure, the link types in relation to the components of an SXP should also be considered. If the link type is a descendant one, say $C_P//C_S$, then once the preceding component C_P is satisfied by a coming compressed XML element E, the subsequent component C_S should be compared with all descendant elements in the XML fragment rooted at E. If the link type is a child one, for example, $C_P/*/C_S$, once the preceding component C_P is satisfied by the element E, the subsequent component (such as C_S) needs to be compared only to the sub-elements in the second level of E's fragment.

In addition to the relationship between the SXP and its preceding component, the type of the link where the component comes from should also be considered for its evaluation. When a component C_M comes after a secondary link, this means that it is a branch component. The goal is to check if there is any match in the fragment where its preceding component C_P is satisfied. If C_M is linked to a primary link of the SXP in the result fragment of its preceding C_P, all C_M's matching results should be cached until C_P's fragment ends. To simplify this point, for an unsatisfied component, the locations and times of its evaluation depend on its link to its preceding component and the link type it comes from.

5.2 Multi-query Evaluation over the SQIT

We will now explain how the SQIT is used to support multi-query processing. We first introduce the evaluation rules and then demonstrate an example to illustrate the entire process.

Evaluation Rules. Let $n_i \in V_Q$ be a node corresponding to the query $q_i \in S_Q$ in a SQIT and T_i be the sub-tree rooted at n_i. We use "SXP children" to indicate n_i's children whose queries are complex ones and have been translated into their corresponding SXPs.

During the query evaluation, if q_i is a complex query, it can be partially satisfied when parts of its components are satisfied or fully satisfied when the whole query is satisfied. For example, the query "$//a$" is fully satisfied by the tag "$< a >$", but the query "$/a[c]/b$" is only partially satisfied by this tag. In general, for an element E in the compressed document, we consider the following rules applied for the two cases:

- Case (1): if q_i is partially satisfied, it is possible that some of the SXP children of n_i can also be partially satisfied at E, thus the SXP children of n_i should be checked. However, there is no need to check the children with a simple path when q_i is not fully matched, since q_i contains all the query of its children.
- Case (2): if q_i is fully satisfied at E, all children of n_i should be checked simultaneously.

If any child of q_i is partially or fully satisfied, the above rules are recursively applied to this child node according to Cases (1) and (2).

In Fig. 7, Q_A is fully satisfied by the tag "$< a >$", and its children Q_C and Q_D are partially satisfied. Thus, Q_B, Q_F and Q_H, as the SXP children, should also be checked.

5.3 Evaluation Strategy

During the process of query evaluation, the compressed document is parsed as a SAX stream. For each coming compressed XML tag, each query in the SQIT has one and

---

Algorithm 3. QueryEvaluation(Compressed doc Doc, SQIT S_{qit})

Input: Doc is the compressed XML document, S_{qit} is the SQIT containing all queries
Output: The stack containing the results for the queries in S_{qit}

  1: Create a path structure PS_r for the root of Doc /*PathStack is the stack for holding path structures for coming tags*/
  2: Insert children of S_{qit}'s root into PS_r.UnsatNodes
  3: Push PS_r into $PathStack$
  4: **for** each coming tag T with interval I_T **do**
  5:     Set PS_T as the path structure of T
  6:     Set PS_P as the top of **PathStack**
  7:     TestChildren(I_T, PS_P.UnsatNodes, false, PS_T)
  8:     **for** each Cxp_w in PS_P.WaitCXPs **do**
  9:         **if** I_T is contained by $Interval_{Cxp_w}$ **then**
10:             **if** Cxp_w's query node Q_w is fully satisfied **then**
11:                Add Q_w into PS_T.SatNodes
12:                TestChildren(I_T,Q_w's children, true, PS_T)
13:             **else**
14:                Add children of Cxp_w into PS_T's WaitCXPs
15:                TestChildren(I_T, Q_w's children, Cxp_w's No., PS_T)
16:             **end if**
17:         **end if**
18:         **if** (I_T is not contained by $Interval_{Cxp_w}$) or (Cxp_w's type is "Descendant") **then**
19:             Add Cxp_w into PS_T.WaitCXPs
20:         **end if**
21:     **end for**
22:     Push PS_T into $PathStack$
23:     Return PS_T.SatNodes
24: **end for**

---

only one of the following three states: satisfied, unsatisfied and partially satisfied. Thus, three respective data structures are designed for each tag T of the compressed document. First, the structure **UnsatNodes** keeps the roots of the sub-trees in the SQIT whose nodes have not been satisfied after the tag T comes. Second, the structure **Wait-CXPs** keeps the subsequent components of the components that are satisfied at T, but their query is partially satisfied by T. Third, the structure **SatNodes** keeps those nodes that are satisfied when parsing the tag T. From now on, these three structures are collectively called the **path structure** for a compressed XML tag.

For a coming compressed XML tag T, if a query in the SQIT cannot be satisfied, there is no need to check any of its descendants. We only keep the unsatisfied state of those nodes (i.e. the roots of the unsatisfied states) in the stack. Because there exists a containment relationship between the ancestor query and the descendant queries, once the root of this sub-tree and T are not matched, all the descendant nodes and T are not matched either. As shown in Fig. 8, when the tag "$< a >$" comes, the sub-tree rooted at Q_G is an unsatisfied sub-tree, and therefore Q_G will be inserted into **UnsatNodes** of the tag "$< a >$".

Algorithm   4. `TestChildren(Interval` I`, QueryNodeSet` $QNodes$`,`
`Boolean` B`, Structure` PS`)`

Input: I is the given interval; $QNodes$ is a set containing the query nodes which have not been tested; B indicates the query is a simple one (true) or complex one (false); PS is the structure of I's tag
Output: PS.SatNodes with matched children and PS.WaitNodes with partially matched children

```
 1: for each query node Q_c in QNodes do
 2:    if Q_c's query is a simple path then
 3:       if B = true and I ⊂ Interval_Q_c then
 4:          Add Q_c into PS.SatNodes
 5:          TestChildren( I, Q_c.children, true,PS)
 6:       else
 7:          Add Q_c into PS.UnsatNodes
 8:       end if
 9:    else
10:       Set Cxp_f as the first CXP of Q_c
11:       if I ⊂ Interval_Cxp_f then
12:          Add CXP children of Cxp_f into PS.WaitCXPs
13:          TestWaitCXPs( I,Q_c, 1, PS)
14:       else
15:          Add Q_c into PS.UnsatNodes
16:       end if
17:    end if
18: end for
```

There also exist some nodes that are partially satisfied in Fig. 8, such as Q_C when the tag "$< a >$" comes into the system. These queries in the figure are complex ones and are expressed as SXPs. For each partially satisfied SXP, we keep the state of "waiting to be compared to the subsequent components of the satisfied components" in **WaitCXPs**.

The query evaluation algorithm based on the path structure is shown in Algorithm 3. Initially, for the root element of the queried document, the path structure is constructed to contain all the children of the root query node in the SQIT (Lines 1-3). When a new compressed tag T comes, suppose the parent tag of T is P, each query node Q_u in P's **UnsatNodes** and each CXP in P's **WaitCXPs** should be checked (Lines 4-24).

For any node Q_u in P's **UnsatNodes**, Algorithm 4 is employed to test the node against the current tag. If Q_u's query is a simple path, its interval value will be compared with the coming interval value directly in order to check whether or not they are matched (Lines 2-8). Otherwise, Q_u's path expression is transformed into an SXP, and its root component should be checked against the tag T (Lines 9-17). If it is satisfied, the subsequent components of the root component become waiting components for the next coming tag by inserting them into the **WaitCXPs** (Lines 11-13). If Q_u's root component is fully satisfied, all SXP children of Q_u in the SQIT are checked, which is implemented by the procedure *TestWaitCXPs* in Algorithm 5. If Q_u's root CXP and T are not matched, it is added into **UnsatNodes** of T (Line 15).

Algorithm 5. `TestWaitCXPs(Interval` I, `QueryNode` Q, `Integer` N_{cxp}, `Structure` PS`)`

Input: I is the interval of the current compared tag; Q is the query node whose children with com-plex queries should be evaluated; $N_{c}xp$ is the number of the considered component of Q; PS is the structure of the current tag
Output: PS.WaitCXPs with added CXP subsequences

1: **for** each SXP child Q_i of Q **do**
2:    Set S_i as the sharing index from Q to Q_i
3:    Set Cxp_f as the first CXP of Q_i
4:    **if** $S_i \geq N_{cxp}$ **then**
5:       TestWaitCXPs(I, Q_i, N_{cxp}, PS)
6:    **else if** ($S_i = N_{cxp}$) **then**
7:       Add CXP children of the N_{cxp}^{th} CXP of Q_i into PS.WaitCXPs
8:       TestWaitCXPs(I, Q_i, N_{cxp}, PS)
9:    **else if** (S_i=0) and (I is contained by $Interval_{Cxp_f}$) **then**
10:       Add CXP children of Cxp_f into PS.WaitCXPs
11:       TestWaitCXPs($I, Q_i, 1, PS$)
12:    **end if**
13: **end for**

Algorithm 5 is designed for testing the SXP children of the input query node over the current interval I. A sharing index, S_i, is to exploit the sharing prefixes between any two queries and used to skip some evaluation in the algorithm. Once the number of the current component is smaller than S_i, this child component is skipped. However, if the number is equal to S_i, the subsequent components of the current component are added into **WaitCXPs** (Lines 7-8) in order to evaluate this part with the next tags. For those SXP children that share nothing with its parent query, all the first components are evaluated (Lines 10-11).

The following example helps illustrate the multi-query evaluation with the SQIT.

Example 3. (Evaluation Procedure) In Fig. 7, Q_A, Q_C, Q_D, Q_B, Q_F and Q_H are complex queries submitted by their respective DR. These queries are inserted into the SQIT and are transformed into SXPs. The components of a query are denoted by Q_{ij}, where $i \in \{A, B, \ldots, H\}$, and j is an index to represent the identity of a component in the query. As the evaluation procedures illustrated in Fig. 8, Q_A being the children of the root is initially put into an **UnsatNodes** within the root element of the document. When the compressed tag "$< a >$" comes, in **UnsatNodes** of the root element, Q_A is checked and found to be qualified, thus its child nodes in the SQIT should also be checked. Clearly, the first components of Q_C and Q_D can be satisfied by "$< a >$", the SXP children of Q_C and Q_D and the root component of Q_H are checked if they are satisfied by "$< a >$". For the satisfied components, the subsequent components (Q_{C_2}, Q_{D_2} and Q_{H_2}) are inserted into the **WaitCXPs** of the current tag "$< a >$". Although Q_G is a simple path, there is no containment with an interval of "$< a >$" after comparing the encoded interval value. Thus, Q_G is inserted into **UnsatNodes** and we can skip checking its children. Similar actions are conducted for other new coming tags until the tag named "$< d >$" comes. Consequently, Q_C, as an SXP, is fully satisfied and inserted into **SatNodes**, whereas its child node Q_B, as an unsatisfied SXP, is inserted into **UnsatNodes**.

In our multi-query evaluation algorithm, the worst-case outcome occurs when the SQIT is a flat tree, where no sharing and containment can be utilized, and our approach is reduced to the single query evaluation. However, the case of a flat SQIT rarely occurs. For example, the average level of the SQIT is from 4 to 6, and DR's queries are closed in the common datasets, such as XMark [24] and NITF (New Industry Text Format)[15].

6   Experiments

The algorithms discussed in the previous sections are implemented and extensive experiments are carried out on synthetic and real data sets as shown in Table 1. All the experiments were conducted on a PC with Pentium IV 3.2 GHz CPU and 2 GB of RAM.

6.1   Experimental Setting

The synthetic data is a set of XML documents generated by using IBM's XMLGenerator and the real data is a commonly used XML benchmark dataset called XMark [24]. The synthetic documents generated with NITF (New Industry Text Format) DTD are attribute-abundant, text-few and structure-complex. XMark documents have relatively simple structures with heavy textual content and deeply nested levels for some elements.

Both synthetic and real queries are used in our experiments. The real query set is obtained from the XMark query benchmark, which provides about 40 queries for auction data. The synthetic query set is obtained from YFilter XPath generator [12], which generates queries according to the parameters of query lengths, wildcard probabilities, predicate probabilities, and other options. In our experiment, we set a group of default parameters to generate different queries, in which the probabilities of "*", "//", "[]" and "[[...]]" are 0.1, 0.1, 0.05 and 0.05, respectively. We also generate 100 to 3000 queries with respect to XMark DTD and NITF DTD. In our system, the average compression

Table 1.

Data Set	XMark	NITF
Data Type	Auction data	New industry text format
Characteristics	Simple structure; Few attributes; Large element content; Deep nested level;	Complex structure; Many attributes; Few element content; Deep nested level;
Data Size	1MB to 5MB	1KB to 1MB
Compression Ratio	47.3%	65.4%
Query Number	500 to 1000	1000 to 3000
Example Query	/site/regions/*/item [@id=0]/description/keyword	/nitf/body/*[tagline/pronounce //q[@id=8]]//bibliography

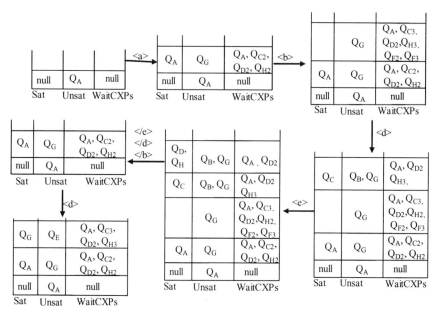

Sat: the set of satisfied query node
Unsat: the set of query nodes that are not satisfied for the coming tag
WaitCXPs: the subsequent components of partially satisfied queries

Fig. 8. An Example of Query Evaluation Using the Path Structure

ratio of XMark and NITF XML documents are 47.3% and 65.4%, respectively. The features of these two kinds of documents are summarized in Table 1.

The objectives of our experiments are twofold. The first is to study the performance of building the SQIT and processing queries in our system. These results are presented in the next two subsections. The second is to evaluate the advantage of processing queries directly on compressed data, and our approach is compared with SAXON [25] in other subsection following the previous results. The comparison is based on the time spent on evaluation and result compression for SAXON, and the time spent on building the SQIT and the query evaluation in our approach.

6.2   The Building Performance of the SQIT

This experiment is designed to study the performance of Algorithm 2 with respect to the synthetic queries. We first generate queries by YFilter path generator with default parameters and then test the CPU cost of the algorithm with different numbers of queries. The building time includes the cost of checking the containment relationship between subscribed queries, transforming complex queries into the SXP and constructing the structure of the SQIT trees. The results are given in Fig. 9. The time for building the SQIT is roughly linearly scalable to the number of subscribed queries. In addition, the building time is less than 2.5 seconds, regardless of whether the number of queries reaches 1000.

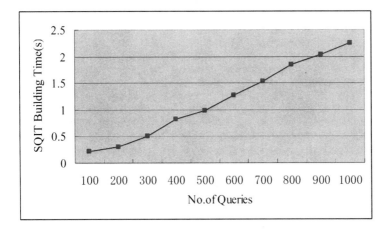

Fig. 9. Building Time of the SQIT

6.3 Performance of Query Evaluation

This experiment is designed to study the performance of the query evaluation with respect to different data sets and a variety of queries. The performance of the query evaluation on both NITF and XMark documents are tested against a range of significant parameters of document size, query type, query number and query length.

Query Evaluation over NITF. Over the NITF document four groups of queries are generated by the YFilter Query Generator. Each group has 1000 queries. The query type of the first group is called "Linear", which contains only "*" and "//". The second one is called "Nested", which contains "*", "//" and nested "[ ]". The third one is called "Predicates", which contains "*", "//" and predicate expressions such as "[@id = 1]". The fourth one is referred to as "Mixed", which consists of the above three query types.

When evaluating queries over compressed documents, the branch queries require lots of intermediate results to be cached. Descendant components will be evaluated repeatedly in each fragment that is satisfied by its preceding components. Predicates require not only structure matching, but also the value validation, which requires checking the text compressed by the dictionary encoder.

Fig. 10 presents the Hit-Ratio (HR), determined by the Equation (4), and the query processing time T (bar charts) on four groups of queries.

$$HR = \frac{\#MatchedQueries}{\#Queries} \qquad (4)$$

Note that the queries are generated by YFilter query generator, and some of these queries do not match input documents. Thus, HR has an impact on T and the evaluation efficiency will be influenced by the document size, query type, and hit-ratio. "Linear" queries have the highest HR (denoted as Linear HR) and the processing time is the longest one because the descendant components in linear queries are checked repeatedly. Although "Mixed" queries are more complex than "Predicates" and "Nested"

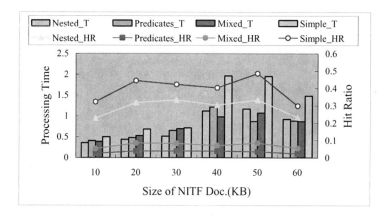

Fig. 10. Performance on Four Queries

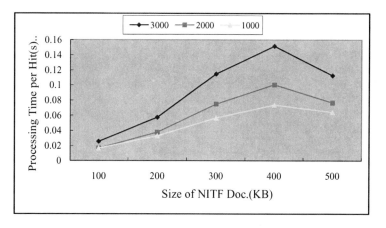

Fig. 11. Performance for Different Query Number

queries, the HR value for "Mixed" queries (denoted as Mixed HR) is not much higher than its counterparts. In a nutshell, the time spent on evaluating 1000 mixed queries with a $10\% HR$ is limited into 1.5 seconds for all documents.

In Fig. 11, we use 1000, 2000, and 3000 complex queries to evaluate NITF documents ranging from $100KB$ to $500KB$. In this experiment, we use the metric, $PTH = \frac{ProcessTime}{\#Hit}$, to observe the impact of query length and document size on performance of our SQIT approach. The PTH indicates the time spent on matching one query out of different groups and across different-size documents. As Fig. 11 shows, the PTH value for the group of 3000 queries is the highest, and that for the group of 2000 queries takes the second place. When the document size doubles, the PTH is roughly twice of the original one. However, with a double number of queries, the time spent on evaluating a query is far less than twice of the processing time. The efficiency of our approach is affected less by the query number than by the document size. This finding is encouraging, since

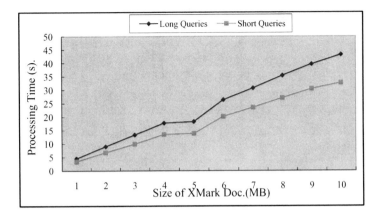

Fig. 12. Performance on Query Length

our main goal is to process a heavy load of subscribed queries as a whole on compressed documents.

Query Evaluation over XMark. This experiment is to study the impact of query length of an XMark document, which has a larger size than an NITF document. The group with four tags on average is classified as "Short" queries, and the one with ten tags is classified as "Long" queries. Each group has 1000 queries. The short queries get results from the document and the long queries get a 90% match.

Fig. 12 illustrates the impact of query length on query processing. The processing time of the long queries is comparable to the processing time of the short queries. Our approach is found to be scalable to document size for both short and long queries. The time required for evaluating 1000 queries within the two groups on a 10MB compressed document takes less than 50 seconds. This is acceptable since the system returns the exact and compressed results for the queries.

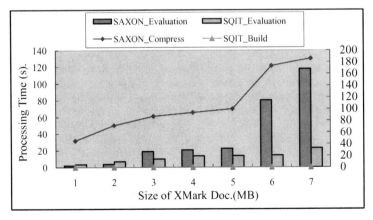

Fig. 13. SQIT vs. SAXON

6.4 Comparison with SAXON

SAXON [25] is one of the commonly used XPath processors. We now compare the processing time of our approach with the processing time of SAXON. The processing time of our approach, T_{SQIT} , can be defined as follows.

$$T_{SQIT} = T_{SQIT_{Building}} + T_{SQIT_{Evaluation}} \qquad (5)$$

We also test 100 complex mixed queries and the following Equation (6) is used to compute the processing time of SAXON.

$$T_{SAXON} = T_{SAXON_{Evaluation}} + T_{result_{compression}} \qquad (6)$$

Then the output results obtained from SAXON and the SQIT are both under compression. The size of the XMark documents ranges from 1MB to 7MB. As shown in Fig. 13, the SQIT has a stable performance on both query evaluation and its building cost is very small for various document sizes. For the processing time of small size documents, the SQIT is comparable to SAXON, since our approach needs to traverse the SQIT tree. However, the system greatly outperforms SAXON when the document size increases.

7 Conclusion

In this paper, a holistic approach is presented for processing a heavy load of queries efficiently over compressed XML documents in a **DaaS** application. Efficient query evaluation techniques are proposed to process multi-queries in a dynamic environment. The underlying idea is to utilize XML compression technologies to process the queries as a whole directly across the compressed data; this is instead of processing the queries with a demand-driven decompression.

From technical perspective, we exploit containment relationships between queries in order to publish compressed XML results and to reduce the required bandwidth. We develop two efficient data structures, SXP and SQIT, to evaluate XPath queries. From the empirical perspective, we have conducted comprehensive experiments, which show that our approach is efficient for compressed XML query processing. There are two interesting extensions that can be further investigated based on this paper. One is the scope of queries could be further extended to include more expressive XML queries such as XPath/XQuery Full-Text. Another is to exploit the security issues at the Database Service Provider side.

Acknowledgements

We would like to thank the reviewers for their helpful comments. This work is supported by NSFC grants (No. 60925008 and No. 60773075), National Hi-Tech 863 program under grant 2009AA01Z149, Shanghai Education Project(No. 10ZZ33) and Shanghai Leading Academic Discipline Project(Project NumberB412).

References

1. Salesforce.com. The Force.com Multitenat Architecture(WhitePage), 1–26 (2009)
2. Mouratidis, K., Sacharidis, D., Pang, H.: Partially materialized digest scheme: an efficient verification method for outsourced databases. The VLDB Journal 18(1), 363–381 (2009)
3. Pang, H., Tan, K.: Verifying Completeness of Relational Query Answers from Online Servers. ACM Transactions on Information and System Security 11(2), 1–50 (2008)
4. Yui, M., Miyazaki, J., Uemura, S., Kato, H.: Xbird/d: distributed and parallel xquery processing using remote proxy. In: Proceedings of ACM Symposium on Applied Computing, pp. 1003–1007 (2008)
5. Machdi, I., Amagasa, T., Kitagawa, H.: GMX: an XML data partitioning scheme for holistic twig joins. In: Proceedings of Information Integration and Web-based Application and Services, pp. 137–146 (2008)
6. Li, F., Hadjieleftheriou, M., Kollios, G., Reyzin, L.: Dynamic authenticated index structures for outsourced databases. In: Proceedings of the 2006 ACM SIGMOD international conference on Management of data, pp. 121–132 (2006)
7. Ge, T., Zdonik, S.B.: Answering aggregation queries in a secure system model. In: Proceedings of the International Conference on Very Large Data Bases, pp. 519–530 (2007)
8. Damiani, E., De Capitani, V., Foresti, S., Jajodia, S., Paraboschi, S., Samarati, P.: Selective Data Encryption in Outsourced Dynamic Environments. Electronic Notes in Theoretical Computer Science 168, 127–142 (2007)
9. Amer-Yahia, S., Koudas, N., Marian, A., Srivastava, D., Toman, D.: Structure and Content Scoring for XML. In: Proceedings of the 31st International Conference on Very Large Data Bases, pp. 361–372 (2005)
10. Bruno, N., Gravano, L., Koudas, N., Srivastava, D.: Navigation- vs. Index-Based XML Multi-Query Processing. In: Proceedings of the 19th International Conference on Data Engineering, pp. 139–150 (2003)
11. Cheng, J., Ng, W.: XQzip: Querying Compressed XML Using Structural Indexing. In: 9th International Conference on Extending Database Technology, pp. 219–236 (2004)
12. Diao, Y., Altinel, M., Franklin, M.J., Zhang, H., Fischer, P.: Path Sharing and Predicate Evaluation for High Performance XML Filtering. ACM Trans. Database Sys. 28(4), 467–516 (2003)
13. Gong, X., Qian, W., Yan, Y., Zhou, A.: Bloom Filter-based XML Packets Filtering for Millions of Path Queries. In: Proceedings of the 21st International Conference on Data Engineering, pp. 890–901 (2005)
14. Jiang, H., Lu, H., Wang, W., Ooi, B.: XR-Tree: Indexing XML Data for Efficient Structural Joins. In: Proceedings of the 19th International Conference on Data Engineering, pp. 253–263 (2003)
15. Karben, A.: NITF, http://www.nitf.org/index.php
16. Khan, L., McLeod, D., Shahabi, C.: An Adaptive Probe-Based Technique to Optimize Join Queries in Distributed Internet Databases. International Journal of Database Management by Idea Group Publishing 12(4), 3–14 (2001)
17. Liefke, H., Suciu, D.: XMill: An Efficient Compressor for XML Data. In: Proceedings of the 2000 ACM SIGMOD International Conference on Management of Data, pp. 153–164 (2000)
18. Miklau, G., Suciu, D.: Containment and Equivalence for an XPath Fragment. Journal of the ACM 51(1), 2–45 (2004)
19. Min, J., Park, M., Chung, C.: XPRESS: A Queryable Compression for XML Data. In: Proceedings of the 2003 ACM SIGMOD International Conference on Management of Data, pp. 22–33 (2003)

20. Ng, W., Lam, Y.W., Cheng, J.: Comparative Analysis of XML Compression Technologies. World Wide Web Journal 9(1), 5–33 (2006)
21. Ng, W., Lam, W.Y., Wood, P., Levene, M.: XCQ A Queriable XML Compression System. Knowledge and Information Systems 10(4), 421–452 (2006)
22. Qun, C., Lim, A., Win, K.: D(k)-Index: An Adaptive Structural Summary for Graph-Structured Data. In: Proceedings of the 2003 ACM SIGMOD International Conference on Management of Data, pp. 134–144 (2003)
23. Tolani, P.M., Haritsa, J.R.: XGRIND: A Query-Friendly XML Compressor. In: Proceedings of the 18th International Conference on Data Engineering, pp. 225–234 (2002)
24. Xmark, http://www.xml-benchmark.org/
25. Kay, M.: SAXON, http://saxon.sourceforge.net

The HiBench Benchmark Suite:
Characterization of the MapReduce-Based Data Analysis

Shengsheng Huang, Jie Huang, Jinquan Dai, Tao Xie, and Bo Huang

Intel China Software Center, Shanghai, P.R. China, 200241
{shengsheng.huang,jie.huang,jason.dai,tao.xie,
bo.huang}@intel.com

Abstract. The MapReduce model is becoming prominent for the large-scale data analysis in the cloud. In this paper, we present the benchmarking, evaluation and characterization of Hadoop, an open-source implementation of MapReduce. We first introduce HiBench, a new benchmark suite for Hadoop. It consists of a set of Hadoop programs, including both synthetic micro-benchmarks and real-world Hadoop applications. We then evaluate and characterize the Hadoop framework using HiBench, in terms of speed (i.e., job running time), throughput (i.e., the number of tasks completed per minute), HDFS bandwidth, system resource (e.g., CPU, memory and I/O) utilizations, and data access patterns.

1 Introduction

The transition to cloud computing is a disruptive trend, where most users will perform their computing work by accessing services in the cloud through the clients. There are dramatic differences between delivering software as a service in the cloud for millions to use, versus distributing software as bits for millions to run on their PCs. First and foremost, services must be highly scalable, storing and processing an explosive size of data in the cloud. For instance, big websites can generate terabytes of raw log data every day. The sheer size of its data set has led to the emergence of new cloud infra-structures, characterized by the ability to scale to thousands of nodes, fault tolerance and relaxed consistency. In particular, the MapReduce model [1] proposed by Google provides a very attractive framework for large-scale data processing in the cloud.

At a high level, a MapReduce program essentially performs a group-by-aggregation in parallel over a cluster of nodes. In the first stage a Map function is applied in parallel to each partition of the input data, performing the grouping opera-tions; and in the second stage, a Reduce function is applied in parallel to each group produced by the first stage, performing the final aggregation. The MapReduce model allows users to easily develop data analysis programs that can be scaled to thousands of nodes, without worrying about the details of parallelism.

Consequently, having moved beyond its origins in search indexing, the MapRe-duce model is becoming increasingly attractive to a broad spectrum of large-scale data analysis applications, including machine learning, financial analysis and simulation, bio-informatics research, and etc. In particular, its popular open source implementation, Hadoop [2], has been used by many companies (such as Yahoo and Facebook) in production for large-scale data analysis in the cloud. In addition, many

D. Agrawal et al. (Eds.): Information and Software as Services, LNBIP 74, pp. 209–228, 2011.

new systems built on top of Hadoop (e.g., Pig [3], Hive [4], Mahout [5] and HBase [6]) have emerged and been used by a wide range of data analysis applications.

Therefore, it is essential to quantitatively evaluate and characterize the Hadoop framework through extensive benchmarking, so as to optimize the performance and total cost of ownership of Hadoop deployments, and to understand the tradeoffs of new computer system designs for the MapReduce-based data analysis using Hadoop. Unfortunately, existing Hadoop benchmark programs (e.g., GridMix [7] and the Hive performance benchmark [9]) cannot properly evaluate the Hadoop framework due to the limitations in their representativeness and diversity. For instance, Yahoo has resorted to the simplistic sorting programs [10] to evaluate their Hadoop clusters [11].

In this paper, we first propose HiBench, a new, realistic and comprehensive benchmark suite for Hadoop, which consists of a set of Hadoop programs including both synthetic micro-benchmarks and real-world applications. We then evaluate and characterize the Hadoop framework using HiBench, in terms of speed (i.e., job running time), throughput (i.e., the number of tasks completed per minute), the Hadoop distributed file system [12] (HDFS, an open source implementation of GFS [13]) bandwidth, system resource utilizations, as well as data access patterns.

The main contributions of this paper are:

- The design of HiBench, a new, realistic and comprehensive benchmark suite for Hadoop, which is essential for the community to properly evaluate and characterize the Hadoop framework.
- The quantitative characterization of different workloads in HiBench, including their data access patterns, system resource utilizations and HDFS bandwidth.
- The evaluation of different deployment (both hardware and software) choices using HiBench, in terms of speed, throughput and resource utilizations.

The rest of the paper is organized as follows. We first introduce the Hadoop and its existing benchmarks in section 2, and then describe the details of the HiBench suite in section 3. We present the experimental results in section 4, and finally we conclude the paper in section 5.

2   Related Work

In this section, we first present an overview of Hadoop, and then describe existing Hadoop benchmark programs and discuss their limitations.

A. Overview of Hadoop

In Hadoop, the input data are first partitioned into splits, and then a distinct map task is launched to process each split. The intermediate map output (that is divided into several partitions) are then optionally combined (by the Combiner) and stored into a temporary file on the local file system. (However, if no reduce tasks are specified, the map task directly writes its output to HDFS as the final results.)

A distinct reduce task is launched to process each partition of the map outputs. The reduce task consists of three phases (namely, the shuffle, sort and reduce phases). The shuffle phase fetches the relevant partition of all map outputs, which are merged by the sort phase. Finally the reduce phase processes the partition and writes the final results to HDFS.

B. Existing Benchmarks

In practice, several benchmark programs are often used to evaluate the Hadoop framework. However, they are mainly micro level benchmarks measuring specific Hadoop properties.

1) Sort Programs: The sorting program has been pervasively accepted as an important performance indicator of MapReduce (e.g., it is used in the original MapReduce paper [1]), because sorting is an intrinsic behaviour of the MapReduce framework. For instance, the Hadoop Sort program [10] is often used as a convenient baseline benchmark for Hadoop, and is the primary benchmark for evaluating Hadoop optimizations in Yahoo [11]. In addition, both Yahoo and Google have used TeraSort [14] (a standard sort benchmark) to evaluate their MapReduce cluster [17] [18].

2) GridMix: GridMix [7] is a synthetic benchmark in the Hadoop distribution, which intends to model the data-access patterns of a Hadoop cluster by running a mix of Hadoop jobs (including 3-stage chained MapReduce job, large data sort, reference select, indirect read, and API text sort). In practice, the total running time of GidMix is almost always dominated by the large data sort job.

3) DFSIO: The DFSIO [19] is a file system benchmark in Hadoop that tests how HDFS handles a large number of tasks performing writes or reads simultaneously. It is implemented as a Hadoop job, in which each map task i just opens an HDFS file to write or read sequentially, and measures the data size (S_i) and execution time (T_i) of that task. There is a single reduce task followed by a post-processing task, which aggregates the performance results of all the map tasks by computing the following two results (assuming there are totally N map tasks):

- Average I/O rate of each map task $= \sum_N (S_i / T_i) / N$

- Throughput of each map task $= \sum_N S_i / \sum_N T_i$

4) Hive Performance Benchmark: The Hive performance benchmark [9] is adapted from the benchmark first proposed by Pavlo et. al [8], which is used to compare the performance of Hadoop and parallel analytical databases. The benchmark consists of five programs, the first of which is the Grep program taken from the original MapReduce paper [1]; the other four analytical queries are designed to be representative of traditional structured data analysis workloads, including selection, aggregation, join and UDF aggregation jobs [8].

C. Discussions

Benchmarking is the quantitative foundation of any computer system research. For a benchmark suite to be relevant, its workloads should represent important applications of the target system, and be diverse enough to exhibit the range of behaviour of the target applications. Unfortunately, micro level Hadoop benchmarking programs as described above are limited in their representativeness and diversity, and consequently cannot properly evaluate the Hadoop framework.

In particular, though these synthetic kernels (such as Sort, Grep or GridMix) attempt to model the behavior of real world Hadoop applications and clusters, they do not exhibit some important characteristics of real world Hadoop applications. First, as these kernels intend to simulate the data access patterns, they contain almost no computations in the map or reduce tasks, while many real world applications (e.g. machine learning [5]) have complex computations. Second, real world Hadoop applications may have data access patterns outside the original MapReduce model that is strictly followed by these kernels; for instance, the index system of Nutch [20] (a popular open source search engine) needs to read/write a lot of temporary files on local disks in its reduce tasks.

In addition, the workloads contained in the Hive performance benchmark can only represent traditional analytical database queries; in a sense, these workloads are more about what queries that Hadoop/MapReduce is not good at (e.g., random access using index and join using partitioning key), rather than evaluating Hadoop over a broad spectrum of large-scale data analysis.

On the other hand, the HiBench suite is a more realistic and comprehensive benchmark suite for Hadoop, including not only synthetic micro-benchmarks, but also real-world Hadoop applications representative of a wider range of large-scale data analysis (e.g., search indexing and machine learning). We plan to include more workloads representing additional data analysis applications (e.g., traditional structured data analysis such as those in the Hive performance benchmark) in the future version of HiBench.

3 The Hibench Suite

In this section we describe the HiBench suite, which consists of a set of Hadoop programs including both synthetic micro-benchmarks and real-world applications. Currently the benchmark suite contains eight workloads, classified into four categories, as shown in Table 1. The first seven are directly taken from their open source implementations, and the last one is an enhanced version of the DFSIO benchmark that we have extended to evaluate the aggregated bandwidth delivered by HDFS.

A. Micro Benchmarks

The Sort [10], WordCount [21] and TeraSort [15] programs contained in the Hadoop distribution are three popular micro-benchmarks widely used in the community, and therefore are included in the HiBench suite. Both the Sort and WordCount programs are representative of a large subset of real-world MapReduce jobs – one class of programs transforming data from one representation to another, and another class extracting a small amount of interesting data from a large data set [1].

The Sort program relies on the Hadoop framework to sort the final results, and both its map and reduce functions are simply identity functions (that is, directly emitting the input key-value pairs as output). In the WordCount program, each map task

Table 1. Constituent Benchmarks

Category	Workload
Micro Benchmarks	Sort
	WordCount
	TeraSort
Web Search	Nutch Indexing
	PageRank
Machine Learning	Bayesian Classification
	K-means Clustering
HDFS Benchmark	EnhancedDFSIO

simply emits (word, 1) for each word in the input, the combiner computes the partial sum of each word in a map task, and the reduce tasks simply compute the final sum for each word. In HiBench, the input data of Sort and WordCount are generated using the RandomWriter and RandomTextWriter programs contained in the Hadoop distribution respectively. The TeraSort program sorts 10 billion 100-byte records generated by the TeraGen program [16] contained in the Hadoop distribution.

B. Web Search

The Nutch Indexing and PageRank workloads are included in HiBench to evaluate Hadoop, because they are representative of one of the most significant uses of MapReduce (i.e., large-scale search indexing systems).

The Nutch Indexing workload is the indexing sub-system of Nutch [20], a popular open-source (Apache) search engine. We have used the crawler sub-system in Nutch to crawl an in-house Wikipedia mirror and generated about 2.4 million web pages as the input of this workload, which gathers the web links from input and converts the link information into inverted index files. The map function of NutchIndexing is simply an identity function, and the reduce function generates the inverted index files using the Lucene [22] plug-in.

The PageRank workload is taken from a test case in SmartFrog [23], an open source framework for managing distributed systems. It is an open source implementation of the page-rank algorithm [24], a link analysis algorithm used widely in web search engines that calculates the ranks of web pages according to the number of reference links. The PageRank workload consists of a chain of Hadoop jobs, among which several jobs are iterated until the converge condition is satisfied. We have used the Wikipedia page-to-page link database [25] as the input of this workload.

C. Machine Learning

The Bayesian Classification and K-means Clustering implementations contained in Mahout [5], an open-source (Apache) machine learning library built on top of Hadoop, are included in HiBench, because they are representative of one of another important uses of MapReduce (i.e., large-scale machine learning).

The Bayesian Classification workload implements the trainer part of Naive Bayesian [26] (a popular classification algorithm for knowledge discovery and data mining). It consists of four chained Hadoop jobs, which extract the terms using the N-Gram algorithm [27] from input web page text, calculate the Tf-Idf (term frequency–inverse document frequency) [28] for each term, and perform the weighting and normalization. The input of this benchmark is extracted from a subset of the Wikipedia dump [29]. The Wikipedia dump file is first split using the built-in WikipediaXmlSplitter in Mahout, and then prepared into text samples using the built-in WikipediaDatasetCreator in Mahout. The text samples are finally distributed into several files as the input of the benchmark.

The K-means Clustering workload implements K-means [30] (a well-known clustering algorithm for knowledge discovery and data mining). Its input is a set of samples, and each sample is represented as a numerical d-dimensional vector. The workload first computes the centroid of each cluster by running one Hadoop job iteratively, until different iterations converge or the maximum number of iterations (set by the user) is reached. After that, it runs a clustering job that assigns each sample to a cluster. We have developed a random data generator using statistic distributions to generate the workload input.

D. HDFS Benchmark

We have extended the DFSIO program contained in the Hadoop distribution to compute the aggregated bandwidth delivered by HDFS. As described in Section 2, the original DFSIO program only computes the average I/O rate and throughput of each map task. Because DFSIO is tightly coupled to the Hadoop framework, it is not straightforward how to properly sum up the I/O rate or throughout of all the map tasks if some map tasks are delayed, re-tried or speculatively executed by the Hadoop framework.

The Enhanced DFSIO workload included in HiBench computes the aggregated bandwidth by first disabling the speculative execution of map tasks, and then sampling the number of bytes read/written at fixed time intervals in each map task. Consequently, when a map task is complete, a series of samples is obtained, with each sample presented in the format of (map id, timestamp, total bytes read/written).

Assuming that the time on each server is synchronized (e.g., using a time server), during the reduce and post-processing stage, the samples of each map task are linear interpolated and re-sampled at a fixed plot rate, so as to align the time series between map tasks. The re-sampled points at the same timestamp of all map tasks are then summed up to compute the total number of bytes read/written by all the map tasks at that timestamp, and finally the aggregated throughput curve can be computed using that number (as illustrated in Fig. 1).

As shown in Fig. 1, the aggregated throughput curve has a warm-up period and a cool-down period where map tasks are launching up and shutting down respectively. Between these two periods, there is a steady period where the aggregated throughput values are stable across different time slots. Therefore, the Enhanced DFSIO workload computes the aggregated HDFS throughput by averaging the throughput value of each time slot in the steady period. In Enhanced DFSIO, when the number of concurrent map tasks at a time slot is above a specified percentage (e.g., 50% is used in our benchmarking) of the total map task slots in the Hadoop cluster, the slot is considered to be in the steady period.

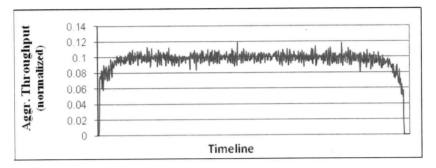

Fig. 1. Normalized aggregated throughput curve of Enhanced DFSIO (write)

4 Evaluation and Characterization

In this section, we present the experimental results, which evaluate and characterize the Hadoop framework using HiBench, in terms of speed (i.e., job running time), throughput (i.e., the number of tasks completed per minute), aggregated HDFS bandwidth, system resource (e.g., CPU, memory and I/O) utilizations, and data access patterns. The baseline Hadoop cluster that we have used consists of one master (running JobTracker/NameNode) and several slaves (running TaskTracker/DataNode), all connected to a gigabit Ethernet switch. The detailed hardware and software configurations of the servers are shown in Table 2.

Table 2. Hardware and Software Configurations of Slaves

Processor	Dual-socket quad-core Intel® Xeon® X5500 processor
Hard disk drive	5 SATA 7200RPM HDDs (one for system and log files, and the other 4 for HDFS files)
Memory	16GB ECC DRAM
Network	1 Gigabit Ethernet NIC
Operation system	Redhat Enterprise Linux 5.2
JVM	jdk1.6.0_02
Hadoop version	Hadoop 0.19.1 with patch 5191[33]

A. Hadoop Workload Characterization

In this experiment, there are four slaves in the Hadoop cluster. Table 3 summarizes the data access patterns of MapReduce model for all workloads (except Enhanced DFSIO that has no relevant input and output) in the experiment, in terms of the sizes of job input, map output, shuffle data and job output; and Table 4 summarizes the ratio of map execution time vs. reduce execution time of each workload. In addition, Fig. 2 – 9 shows the timeline-based CPU, memory and disk I/O utilizations of each workload. (Network I/O is never a bottleneck in the experiment, since the scale of the cluster used is small and all the nodes are arranged in one rack. Therefore the network utilization is not presented in this part.)

Table 3. Workload Data Access Patterns

Workload	Job	Job/Map Input	Map Output (Combiner Input)	Shuffle Data (Combiner Output)	Job/Reduce Output
Sort	Sort	60G	60G	60G (no combiner)	60G
Word Count	WordCount	60G	85G	3.99G	1.6G
TeraSort	TeraSort	1T	139G [b]	139G (no combiner)	1T
Nutch Indexing	Nutch Indexing	8.4G [b]	26G	26G (no combiner)	6.3G
PageRank [a]	Dangling-Pages	1.21G	81.7K	672B	30B
	Update-Ranks	1.21G	5.3G	5.3G (no combiner)	1.21G
	SortRanks	1.21G	86M	86M (no combiner)	167M
Bayesian Classification	Feature	1.8G	52G	39.7G	35G
	TfIdf	35G	26G	22.8G	13.3G
	Weight-Summer	13.3G	16.8G	8.7G	8.2G
	Theta-Normalizer	13.3G	5.6G	163K	8.6K
K-means Clustering [c]	Centroid-Computing	66G	67G	303K	4.6K
	Clustering	66G	66.3G	no combiner	no reducer

[a] PageRank runs 3 chained jobs iteratively. The data access patterns vary slightly between different iterations and the data here show one such iteration.
[b] The data size is the compressed result.
[c] We synthesized 160 million samples (each with 20 dimensions), to be clustered into 10 groups as input of K-Means Clustering workload.

Since the Sort workload transforms data from one representation to another, the shuffle data and the job output of Sort are of the same size as the job input, as shown in Table 3. Consequently, the Sort workload is mostly I/O bound, having moderate CPU utilization and heavy disk I/O, as shown in Fig. 2. In addition, considering the large amount of shuffle data, it is expected to have network I/O bottlenecks in the shuffle stage when running on large (multi-rack) clusters.

On the other hand, since the WordCount workload extracts a small amount of interesting data from a large data set, the shuffle data and the job output of WordCount are much smaller than the job input, as shown in Table 3. Consequently, the Word-Count workload is mostly CPU bound (especially during the map stage), having high CPU utilization, light disk/network I/O, as shown in Fig. 3. In addition, its behavior is expected to remain somewhat the same even on larger clusters.

In essence, the TeraSort workload is similar to Sort and therefore is I/O bound in nature. However, we have compressed its shuffle data (i.e., map output) in the experiment so as to minimize the disk and network I/O during shuffle, as shown in Table 3. Consequently, TeraSort have very high CPU utilization and moderate disk I/O during the map stage and shuffle phases, and moderate CPU utilization and heavy disk I/O during the reduce phases, as shown in Fig. 4.

Table 4. Workload Execution Time Ratio

Workload	Job	Avg. Map Task vs. Avg. Reduce Task Execution Time Ratio[a]	Map Stage vs. Reduce Stage Execution Time Ratio[b]
Sort	Sort	2.00%	33.36%
WordCount	WordCount	55.98%	94.67%
TeraSort	TeraSort	0.26%	70.71%
Nutch Index	Nutch Indexing	6.22%	31.16%
PageRank	DanglingPages	15.36%	124.12%
	UpdateRanks	49.90%	66.81%
	SortRanks	5.74%	49.50%
Bayesian	Feature	14.33%	57.93%
Classification	TfIdf	7.86%	75.57%
	WeightSummer	19.32%	72.64%
	ThetaNormalizer	29.37%	87.75%
K-means	CentroidComputing	5.67%	102.58%
Clustering	Clustering	no reduce tasks	no reduce tasks

[a] Average Map Task execution time is defined as the average of execution time of all Map Tasks. Average Reduce Task is defined similarly.
[b] The Map Stage is defined as the period between when the first Map Task starts and when the last Map Task ends. The Reduce Stage is defined similarly.

In the experiment, the NutchIndexing workload first decompresses the crawl data to about 26GB intermediate results in the map tasks, and then the reduce tasks convert them to about 6.3GB inverted index files. As shown in Fig. 5, NutchIndexing is CPU bound during map stage and more disk I/O bound (with about 60% CPU utilizations) in the reduce stage.

The PageRank workload spends most of its time on the iterations of several jobs, and these jobs are generally CPU bound, with low to medium disk I/O and memory utilizations, as shown in Fig. 6.

The Bayesian Classification workload contains four chained Hadoop jobs, and the first job is the most time consuming (taking about half of the total running time in the experiment). As shown in Fig. 7, the four jobs are all mostly disk I/O bound, except that the map tasks of the first job also have high (over 80%) CPU utilizations.

The K-means Clustering workload spends most of its time on job iterations for the centroid computation. In the experiment, we have set the max iteration limit to five so as to make sure that the test finishes in a reasonable time period. As shown in Fig. 8, the centroid computation in K-means Clustering is mostly CPU bound, because its combiner swallows most of the map outputs and consequently the shuffle data are relatively small, as shown in Table 3. On the other hand, the clustering job is I/O bound, mostly due to the output to HDFS of the map tasks (as there are no reduce tasks in the clustering job).

Finally, since the Enhanced DFSIO workload only tests the HDFS throughput, it is completely disk I/O bound. Fig. 9 shows the resource utilizations of Enhanced DFSIO read workload (the utilizations of the write workload are similar).

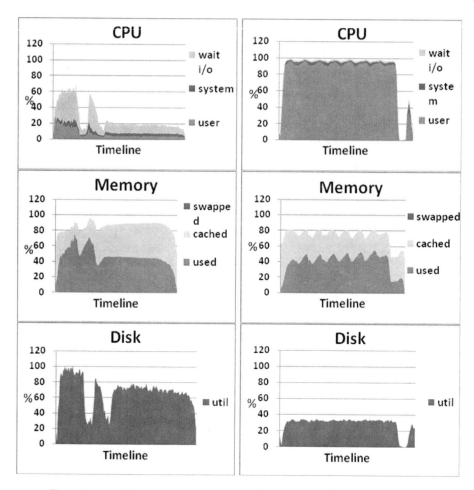

Fig. 2. System Utilization of Sort   **Fig. 3.** System Utilization of WordCount

As described in the above characterization, the Hadoop workload usually has very heavy disk and network I/O, unless the map output size is (or can be combined to be) very small (e.g., as in the case of WordCount and K-means Clustering). The best performance (total running time) of Hadoop workloads is usually obtained by accurately estimating the size of the map output, shuffle data and reduce input data, and properly allocating memory buffers to prevent multiple spilling (to disk) of those data [32]. In the experiment, we have tuned the workloads to keep these data in memory as much as possible, and consequently, as shown in Fig. 2 – 9, all of them have high memory consumptions (over 80% memory utilization), except PageRank that performs a lot of computations on a relatively small data set.

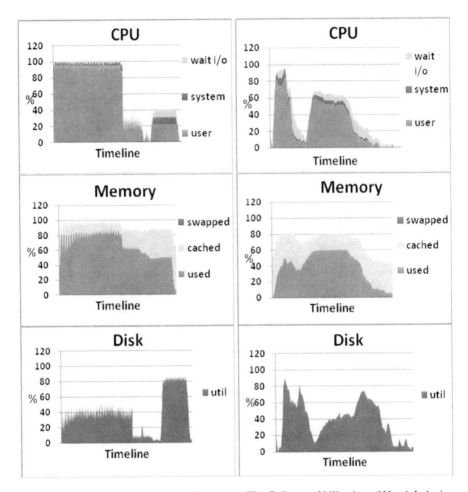

Fig. 4. System Utilization of TeraSort   **Fig. 5.** System Utilization of Nutch Indexing

B. HDFS Bandwidth

In this experiment, we examine the results of Enhanced DFSIO workload and the original DFSIO benchmark, using the same-load-per-cluster, same-load-per-node and same-load-per-map configurations (as shown in Table 5), and for different numbers of slaves and different map slots (i.e. the maximum number of parallel map tasks that can run on each server). We have normalized the y-axis values of all the figures in this section (i.e. Fig. 10-14) as fraction of a certain value for clearer representation and easier comparison.

Fig. 10 and 11 show the average I/O rate & throughput of DFSIO for different numbers of slaves (with 4 map slots per node) in the cluster and different numbers of map slots per node (in a 16-slave cluster) respectively. Similarly, Fig. 12 and 13 show the aggregated throughput of Enhanced DFSIO for different numbers of slaves in the cluster and map slots per node respectively. As shown in Fig. 10 and 11, the DFSIO

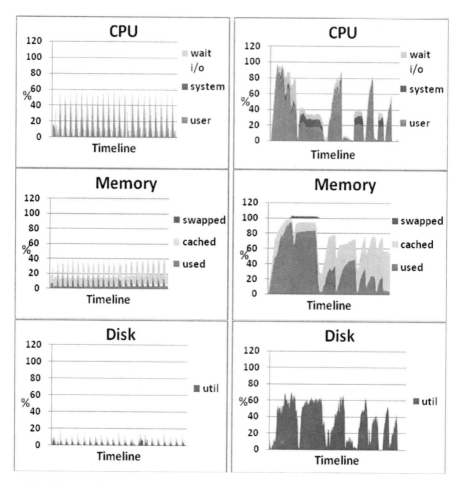

Fig. 6. System Utilization of PageRank

Fig. 7. System Utilization of Mahout Bayesian Classification

average I/O rate and throughput results remain the same or decrease slightly as the number of slaves or map slots increases; the aggregated throughput of HDFS actually increases as the number of slaves increases, as shown in Figure 12 and 13. Therefore, DFSIO is not appropriate for the evaluation of the aggregated bandwidth delivered by HDFS, which is the design goal of HDFS and GFS. As shown in Figure 12, the aggregated write throughput of HDFS scales almost linearly with the number of slaves in the experiment; on the other hand, the aggregated read throughput in the 4-slave cluster is about the same as or even slightly higher than that in the 8-slave cluster. The reason for that poor scalability of read is, since the HDFS replication factor is set to 3 in the experiment (i.e. each HDFS file block is replicated on 3 nodes), the possibility that a HDFS read request is served from the local node in the 4-slave cluster is much higher than that in the 8-node cluster. However, the benefit of locality

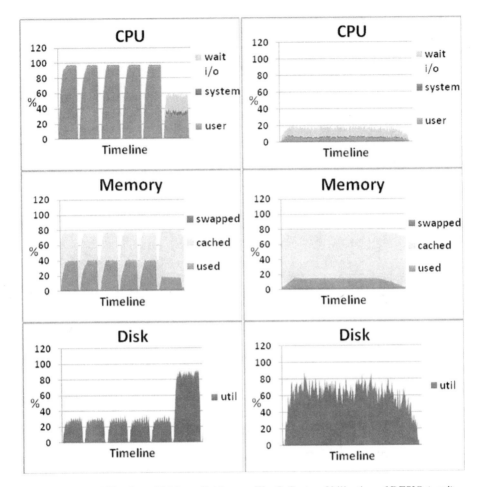

Fig. 8. System Utilization of Mahout K-Means Clustering

Fig. 9. System Utilization of DFSIO (read)

quickly diminishes as the number of slaves in the cluster increases, and therefore it can be expected that the aggregated read throughput scales linearly with the number of slaves when the scale of cluster is large enough. In addition, as shown in Figure 13, the aggregated throughput will also increase with number of map slots in the 16-node cluster until the cluster is saturated.

Both workloads measure the number of bytes read/written at the application level; however, in HDFS write operations are buffered and performed asynchronously. Fig. 14 compares the aggregated throughput measured at the application level by Enhanced DFSIO and that measured at the HDFS level (i.e., when the bytes to be written are acknowledged by HDFS), and those two results are almost the same. Hence, the aggregated throughput measured at the application level by the Enhanced DFSIO can be used to properly evaluate the aggregated throughput of the HDFS cluster.

C. Evaluation of Hadoop Deployments

1) Comparison of processor platforms: In this experiment, we use HiBench to compare the baseline cluster with 4 slaves (referred to as the current cluster) and a 4-slave old cluster that is configured using the same configuration as shown in Table 2, except that the slave uses the Xeon X5400 processor (older than the Xeon X5500 processor). Fig. 15 compares the speed (i.e., job running time) of the Sort and WordCount workloads in these two clusters, and Fig. 16 compares the throughput (i.e., the number of tasks completed per minute measured when the Hadoop cluster is at 100% utilization processing multiple Hadoop jobs).

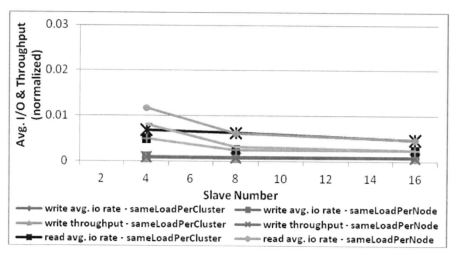

Fig. 10. DFSIO: normalized average I/O rate & throughput as function of slave number

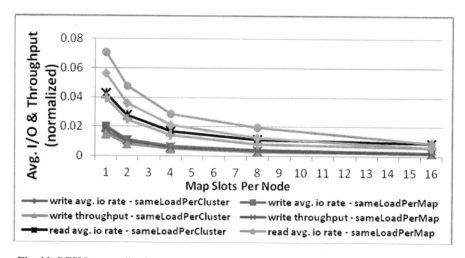

Fig. 11. DFSIO: normalized average I/O rate & throughput as function of map slots per node

In terms of speed, the current cluster has 48% and 66% speedup over the old cluster for Sort and WordCount respectively; on the other hand, in terms of throughput, the current cluster has 86% and 65% speedup over the old cluster for Sort and Word-Count respectively. Therefore, both speed and throughput are important performance metrics in evaluating Hadoop deployments.

Table 5. Test Configuration of Enhanced DFSIO Benchmarking

Workload Configuration	Size of Each File to Be Read/Written (MB)	Total Number of Files to Be Read/Written
Write – sameLoadPerCluster	360	256
Write – sameLoadPerNode	360	16 x number of slave nodes
Write – sameLoadPerMap	360	16 x number of map slots per node
Read - sameLoadPerCluster	720	256
Read - sameLoadPerNode	720	16 x number of slave nodes
Read - sameLoadPerMap	720	16 x number of map slots per node

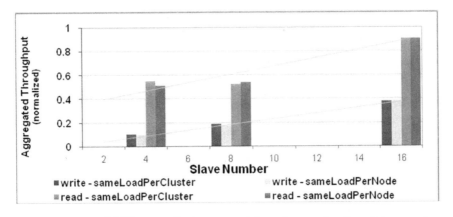

Fig. 12. Enhanced DFSIO: normalized aggregated throughputs as function of slave number

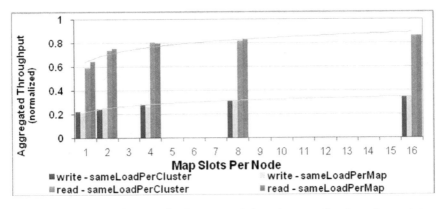

Fig. 13. Enhanced DFSIO: normalized aggregated throughputs as function of map slots per node

In addition, because the current cluster is more powerful than the old cluster in processors, the Nutch Indexing and Bayesian Classification workloads have different characteristics on these two clusters. NutchIndexing, which is CPU bound during the map stage and more disk I/O bound during the reduce stage in the current cluster (as shown in Fig. 5), becomes completely CPU bound during both stages in the old cluster (as shown in Fig. 17). All the four jobs in Bayesian Classification are mostly disk I/O bound in the current cluster (as shown in Fig. 6), while become CPU bound during the map stage in the old cluster (as shown in Fig. 18).

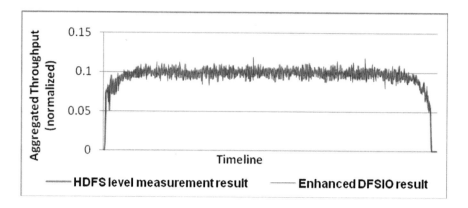

Fig. 14. Normalized aggregated throughput of Enhanced DFSIO vs. HDFS level measure result

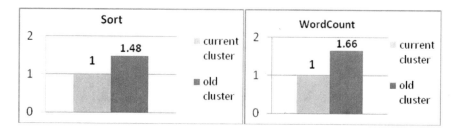

Fig. 15. Normalized Sort, WordCount job running time (lower is better)

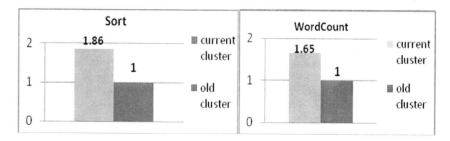

Fig. 16. Normalized Sort, WordCount throughput (higher is better)

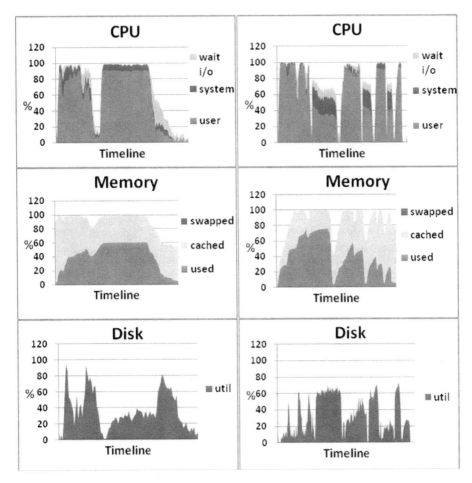

Fig. 17. NutchIndexing in the old cluster   **Fig. 18.** Bayesian Classification in the old cluster

2) Comparison of Hadoop versions: In this experiment, we use HiBench to compare Hadoop 0.19.1 and Hadoop 0.20.0 (using Yahoo! distribution of Hadoop [31]) in the baseline cluster with 4 slaves. Fig. 19 shows the running time of the Sort and WordCount workloads using Hadoop 0.19.1 and 0.20.0. As shown in Fig. 19, the Map stage in v0.20.0 is slower (and uses more memory) than v0.19.1, but the overall job running time is about the same or even slightly faster in v0.20.0. This is mostly due to the improved task scheduling (i.e., multi-task assignment) in v0.20.0.

Fig. 20 shows the timeline-based execution breakdown for the second Hadoop job in Bayesian Classification using Hadoop 0.19.1, in which most of reduce tasks cannot start until after all the map tasks are done. This is because in Hadoop 0.19.1, the Job-Tracker can only schedule one task in a heartbeat (every 5 seconds by default) to a TaskTracker and map tasks have higher priority. When there are a lot of map tasks that finish very fast (e.g., less than 5s), the scheduling of reduce tasks is significantly delayed. On the other hand, in Hadoop 0.20.0, the JobTracker can schedule multiple tasks in a heartbeat and this performance issue is no long there (as shown in Fig. 21).

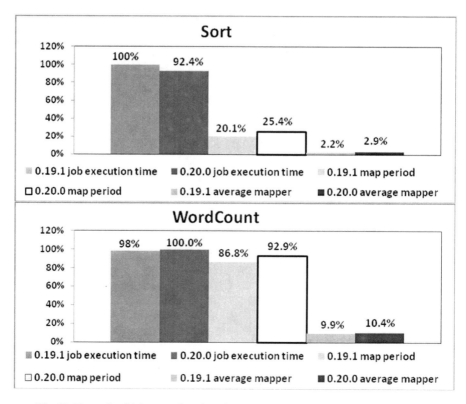

Fig. 19. Normalized job execution time & map period & average mapper comparison

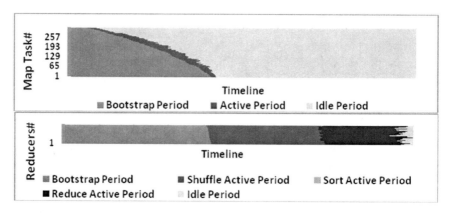

Fig. 20. Timeline-based MapReduce breakdown on Hadoop 0.19.1 for the 2nd job of the Bayesian Classification workload

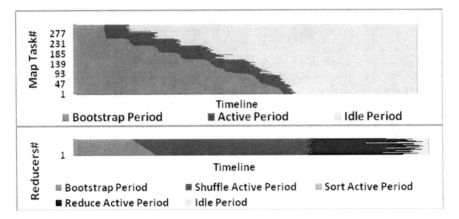

Fig. 21. Timeline-based MapReduce breakdown on Hadoop 0.20.0 for the 2nd job of the Bayesian Classification workload

5 Conclusion and Future Work

In this paper, we first introduce HiBench, a new, realistic and comprehensive benchmark suite for Hadoop, which consists of a set of Hadoop programs including both synthetic micro-benchmarks and real-world applications (e.g., web search and machine learning). We then use experimental results to evaluate and characterize the Hadoop framework using HiBench, in terms of speed (i.e., job running time), throughput (i.e., the number of tasks completed per minute), HDFS bandwidth, system resource (e.g., CPU, memory and I/O) utilizations, and data access patterns.

The HiBench suite is essential for the community to properly evaluate and characterize Hadoop, because its workloads not only represent a wide range of large-scale data analysis using Hadoop, but also exhibit very diverse behaviors in terms of data access patterns and resource utilizations, as shown by the experimental results.

We plan to continuously evolve the HiBench suite to represent an even broader spectrum of large-scale data analysis using the MapReduce model, such as financial analysis and bio-informatics research. In addition, we plan to quantitatively evaluate more Hadoop deployment choices using HiBench, including the scale of the cluster, the capacity of memory and disks, and the impacts of processor micro-architecture.

References

[1] Dean, J., Ghemawat, S.: MapReduce: Simplified Data Processing on Large Clusters. USENIX OSDI (December 2004)
[2] Hadoop homepage, http://hadoop.apache.org/
[3] Pig homepage, http://hadoop.apache.org/pig/
[4] Hive homepage, http://hadoop.apache.org/hive/
[5] Mahout homepage, http://lucene.apache.org/mahout/
[6] HBase homepage, http://hadoop.apache.org/hbase/
[7] GridMix program. Available in Hadoop source distribution: src/benchmarks/gridmix

[8] Pavlo, A., Rasin, A., Madden, S., Stonebraker, M., DeWitt, D., Paulson, E., Shrinivas, L., Abadi, D.J.: A Comparison of Approaches to Large-Scale Data Analysis. SIGMOD (June 2009)

[9] Jia, Y., Shao, Z.: A Benchmark for Hive, PIG and Hadoop, http://issues.apache.org/jira/browse/HIVE-396

[10] Sort program. Available in Hadoop source distribution: src/examples/org/apache/hadoop/examples/sort

[11] Zaharia, M., Konwinski, A., Joseph, A.D., Katz, R., Stoica, I.: Improving MapReduce Performance in Heterogeneous Environments. In: OSDI 2008 (December 2008)

[12] HDFS homepage, http://hadoop.apache.org/hdfs/

[13] Ghemawat, S., Gobioff, H., Leung, S.: The Google File System. In: 19th ACM Symposium on Operating Systems Principles (October 2003)

[14] TeraSort., http://sortbenchmark.org/

[15] Hadoop TeraSort program. Available in Hadoop source distribution since 0.19 version: http://src.examples.org/apache/hadoop/examples/terasort

[16] TeraGen program. Available in Hadoop source distribution since 0.19 version: http://src.examples.org/apache/hadoop/examples/terasort/TeraGen

[17] O'Malley, O., Murthy, A.C.: Winning a 60 Second Dash with a Yellow Elephant, http://sortbenchmark.org/Yahoo2009.pdf

[18] Sorting 1PB with MapReduce, http://googleblog.blogspot.com/2008/11/sorting-1pb-with-mapreduce.html

[19] DFSIO program, Available in Hadoop source distribution: http://src.test.org/apache/hadoop/fs/TestDFSIO

[20] Nutch homepage, http://lucene.apache.org/nutch/

[21] WordCount program. Available in Hadoop source distribution: http://src.examples.org/apache/hadoop/examples/WordCount

[22] Lucene homepage, http://lucene.apache.org

[23] SmarFrog project homepage, http://www.smartfrog.org

[24] Castagna, P.: Having fun with PageRank and MapReduce. Hadoop User Group UK talk, http://static.last.fm/johan/huguk-20090414/paolo_castagna-pagerank.pdf

[25] Haselgrove, H.: Using the Wikipedia page-to-page link database, http://users.on.net/~henry/home/wikipedia.htm

[26] Mahout Naïve Bayesian, http://cwiki.apache.org/MAHOUT/naivebayes.html

[27] N-Gram, http://en.wikipedia.org/wiki/N-gram

[28] Tf-Idf, http://en.wikipedia.org/wiki/Tf%E2%80%93idf

[29] Wikipedia Dump, http://en.wikipedia.org/wiki/index.php?curid=68321

[30] Mahout K-means, http://cwiki.apache.org/MAHOUT/k-means.html

[31] Yahoo! distribution of Hadoop, http://developer.yahoo.com/hadoop/distribution/

[32] Coskun, N.: Optimizing Hadoop Deployments. Hadoop World, Presentation (2009)

[33] Hadoop-5191, http://issues.apache.org/jira/browse/HADOOP-5191

Enabling Migration of Enterprise Applications in SaaS via Progressive Schema Evolution

Jianfeng Yan[1] and Bo Zhang[2,*]

[1] SAP Research China Center, 1001 Chenghui Road, Shanghai, 201203, China
jianfeng.yan@sap.com
[2] University of Shanghai for Science and Technology,
519 Jungong Road, Shanghai, 200093, China
zhangbo@fudan.edu.cn

Abstract. Update of applications in SaaS is expected to be a continuous efforts and cannot be done overnight or over the weekend. In such migration efforts, users are trained and shifted from one existed version to another new version successively. There is a long period of time when both versions of applications co-exist. Maintenance of two systems with both existed and new version at the same time is not a cost efficient option and such two systems may suffer from slow response time due to continuous synchronization with each other. In this paper, we focus on how to enable the migration of enterprise applications in SaaS via progressive evolved schema. Instead of maintenance with two systems, our solution is to build a multi-version applications supported system by designing an series of intermediate schemas which are optimized for mixed workloads from both existed and emerging users. With an application migration schedule, an genetic algorithm is used to find out the more effective intermediated schema as well as migration paths and schedule. A key advantage of our approach is optimum performance during the long migration period while maintaining the same level of data movement required by the migration. We evaluated the proposed progressive migration approach on a TPCW benchmark and experimental results validated its effectiveness of across a variety of scenarios. They demonstrate that the schema evolution based application migration could bring about 200% performance gain comparing to the systems with either existed old version or targeted new version.

Keywords: multi-version system, progressive migration, enterprise application, schema evolution, genetic algorithm, intermediate schema, TPCW benchmark.

1 Introduction

Update of applications in SaaS is expected to be a continuous efforts and cannot be done overnight or over the weekend. In such migration efforts, users are trained and shifted from one existed version to another new version successively: the workloads for new version of application are incrementally applied along with the decreasing of those for old version. Furthermore, it means that there is a long period of time when both versions of applications co-exist. Maintenance of two systems with both existed and new version

---

* Work done while with SAP.

D. Agrawal et al. (Eds.): Information and Software as Services, LNBIP 74, pp. 229–256, 2011.

at the same time is not a cost efficient option. From the point view of database system, two systems means that two dependant database schema instances with redundant data storage. Especially, to keep the data consistency between them, such two systems may suffer from slow response time due to continuous synchronization with each other.

One desirable solution is to design a unified system which is able to execute workloads for multi-version requests and optimized for them. With such property, even during update process, system can provide online services to users for both old version and new version of application with stable and acceptable response time. For database system, in order to do so, during the migration of enterprise applications, the database server should support several intermediate schemas, which are expected to be designed by the business priorities and schedules. By optimized schemas to the temporal workload distributions and data statistics, the system provides users the choice to update their business step by step.

Besides of how to choose such intermediate schemas, one big challenge for this solution is data migration. Along with the accumulation of new users, it is generally expected that the data can be migrated into an optimized schema smoothly.

Traditional approach for database system update follows the rule of *shutdown-migration-restart*, which needs the planned downtime to accomplish the reconfiguration, data migration and application transformation, which is unacceptable for multi-version applications software systems in SaaS. Especially for the systems with large volume of data, the cost of data migration is too high to accept. It will take the system several days to complete the system update, meanwhile, the customer business will be blocked during such process.

In this paper, we focus on how to enable the migration of enterprise applications in SaaS via progressive evolved schema. Instead of maintenance with two systems, our solution is to build a multi-version applications supported system by designing an series of intermediate schemas which are optimized for mixed workloads from both existed and emerging users. With an application migration schedule, an genetic algorithm is used to find out the more effective intermediated schema as well as migration paths and schedule. Instead of *shutdown-migration-restart* rule, we applies the incremental data migration which is much friendly for users. The risks for system update, even including the training cost, can be decreased dramatically. A key advantage of our approach is optimum performance during the long migration period while maintaining the same level of data movement required by the migration.

Figure 1 illustrates the scenario of progressive migration for system updating. The system update starts from one existed schema (defined as *Source Schema* in this paper). The workload changes following the rule of decreasing users for old application and increasing users for new application. Accordingly, several intermediate schemas are created and data are migrated partially to fit for the better database performance and system response. At the end of system update, with the termination of old application completely, the schema of database achieves a stable schema (defined as *Target Schema*). For the single version applications, it is the responsibility for system architects or DBAs to design a proper database schema instance according to the requirements. It means, we can suppose that both source and target schema have high performance and quick response for old application users and new application users respectively.

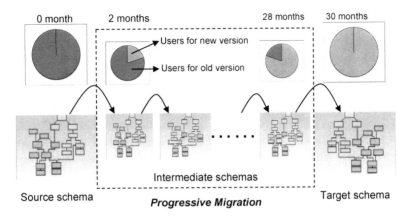

Fig. 1. A scenario of schema evolution in the process of application migration. At the beginning of system update, all the workloads running on the source schema belong to old version. And then, several workloads for new version are added, which causes the database schema unsuitable to provide the best performance. Then, the schema is updated to an intermediate schema according to current system status (mainly including glossary workload distribution and data statistic). This action is repeated several times until all the users for old version are updated to new version application.

The problem this paper aims to is, how to implement the evolution from source schema instance to target one with the reasonable performance guaranteed.

To the best of our knowledge, our work is the first effort to provide an incremental data migration solution for *multi-version* software systems. The key contributions of this paper including:

- Identify the challenge of incremental data migration in the update process for large scale enterprise software systems. That is, along with the trend updating to target schema, how to find out the best intermediate schemas, which are adaptive for the gradual changing workload distribution and data statistics. The answer of this challenge also provides a reference solution for performance guaranteed *multi-version* systems.
- Propose the basic operators to decompose the above process into several atomic steps. In each step, the query cost can be estimated by statistic data.
- Provide two cost models for progressive migration, which are local optimization and global optimization. The local optimization chooses the best intermediate schema according to the status of current snapshot. The global optimization finds it with the consideration of prediction.
- Evaluate our data migration algorithm by migrating from a typical TPCW schema to designed target schema with several steps. The results show that our approach is adaptive to variant conditions.

The rest of the paper is organized as following: Section 2 analyze the complexity and category of problem addressed in this paper, and, present a proposed framework to handle it. Section 3 describes our new automated, dynamic schema evolution approach from source schema to target schema. Section 4 gives our experimental results which is based on well-known TPCW benchmark and a real database system. Section 5 summarizes the related work and compares them with our approach. Finally, section 6 concludes this paper and shows our future work.

2   Scope of Problem

From source schema to target schema, to support the migration of applications continuously by a series of intermediate schemas, one big dilemma we have to face to. That is, how to balance the choice between improving performance by optimal schema and reducing the data migration cost. To understand the complexity of this problem, we definite two kinds of intermediate schemas which can be chosen in progressive evolution accordingly.

- **Optimal intermediate schema:** Which has the best performance for current workload distribution and data statistic among all possible reorganized schemas from previous intermediate schema. In the other word, it is the best physical schema for system status, and independent with the limitation of both source and target schema.
- *Target-driven* **intermediate schema:** It also has the best performance for current workload distribution and data statistic, but only among the *target-driven* reorganized schemas from previous intermediate schema. Here, *target-driven* means that the schema change is just for the necessary evolution limited by the target schema. The direction of such evolution is close to it.

As mentioned in [1], current enterprise computing systems store tens of terabytes of active, online data in dozens to hundreds of disk arrays, which are interconnected by storage area networks. It is time consuming to migrate data from one schema to another. So, first of all, in order to keep system performance, we propose our solution based on partial data migration instead of "shutdown-migration-restart" one. Here, the "partial" means that such migration involves just a partial of the whole database instance, for example, a few tables in a large scale schema. But even in this approach, since the migration processes have to be executed by off-line the related database tables, the workloads which relates to will be blocked. Obviously, the *optimal intermediate schema* solution takes no consideration about what the data scope impacted within its model, so the data migration is out of control. In the worst cases, each intermediate requires a whole system off-line to migrate data. However, the second solution limited the number of migration steps and the scope of migration data by predefined sets of basic operators, and hence minimized migration scope is guaranteed.

Another reason for choosing the second intermediate is its target schema oriented property. Besides of the consideration of high performance, schema design for both source and target should also considerate other aspects, such as manageability, expendability, readability, and so on. Without the directional schema evolution with *target-driven*, it is possible to apply intermediate schemas which differ from the target schema greatly. The result is, user has to apply another big off-line migration at the end of progressive process. On the contrary, target-driven schema migration will always drive the intermediate schema to the target schema with relatively high performance.

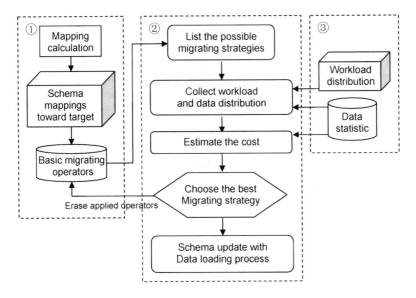

Fig. 2. A framework for progressive schema migration. (1) A schema mapping calculation tool is used to find out all the mappings from source schema to target schema. (2) At one *check point* which is the predefined time point to begin one step of progressive migration, the possible schema reorganizations are virtually listed by composite of the mappings which are not applied. After the one which has the best performance to fit for system status is chosen, the new intermediate schema is physically created in database instance and then following by data loading process. After that, the mappings what have been used are erased. (3) Maintain the data to describe the system status. Workload distribution is counted by a collector or predefined by customers, and data statistic is refreshed by DBMS in real time.

In the rest of this paper, we use the *intermediate schema* to express the *target-driven intermediate schema* only.

Figure 2 shows the framework of our approach. The key components of the system consist of searching the basic operator set and finding the best intermediate schema to evolve.

In order to separate data migration into several incremental steps, we propose basic migrating operators, which describe the schema evolution in atomic way. Three basic operators are proposed for progressive migration.

– **Creating table.** When new columns should be added into the source schema, this operator is applied to create a new table by the dependency between some columns in existing table and new columns.
– **Combining table.** When there is a combination in schema mapping set, this operator is applied to combine two tables by the reference within them.
– **Splitting table.** When one table have to be split according to schema mapping set, this operator is applied to split the table into two tables, and a new reference is also created to keep the constraint.

Previous researches [2] [3] provide us many approaches to construct the schema mapping between two schemas. Based on the generated schema mapping set, it is easy to construct the corresponding set of migration operators. The source schema could be migrated to target schema step by step by progressively applying these operators once and only once.

In order to choose the proper intermediate schema for current workload distribution and data statistic, the workload cost on this schema in current snapshot should be estimated. Such functionality is provided by SAP MaxDB, which provides the cost estimation of workload based on I/O throughput. We use these data in our experiment.

If the system is complicated, there are always numerous mappings between the source schema and the target schema. Furthermore, a big amount of possible operators will be generated for creating the intermediate schemas. Corresponding, the huge number of intermediate schemas should be estimated. The system have to make an adaptive tradeoff between choosing the best intermediate schema and saving the running time for cost estimation. Moreover, to get the higher performance of system in global performance analysis, a more complex process for cost estimation with predictive steps should also be executed. A Genetic Algorithm (GA) based approach is proposed in this paper to cope with this problem.

In this paper, we propose two models for selecting the proper intermediate schema from all possible candidates.

- **Local adaptive model.** The proper intermediate schema is selected according to current status, that is, to make the system performance better than other candidate schemas.
- **Global adaptive model.** The proper intermediate schema is selected according to current status and all possible future intermediate schema. This is to ensure that the strategy selected archives best performance in global way.

After selecting one proper intermediate schema in a migration point, the previous schema should be update to it and data should also be loading into it. Usually, only a part of choosing schema is different from previous one, it is reasonable to block only the workloads which need access the partial schema.

Another necessary component is **query rewriter**, which rewrites the mixed queries both of old version and new version to adapt with the intermediate schema. Many previous works were related to this problem[4] [5]. Here, we just figure out a straightforward method which is to find out the identifications from original query data access units, such as tables and attributes. Then, rewrite them for intermediate schema. During this, the schema mapping from previous schema to current one is necessary to be maintained. This process may spend extra system resource. But with the predictive of intermediate schemas, the queries can be rewritten in advance of runtime environment, and then the system performance is not affected anymore.

In general, our approach for progressive migration has the following characteristics:

- To the best of our knowledge, this is the first work to identify the beneficial use for the update of large scale enterprise system. It makes possible for system to update incrementally.

- As the basic operator set is limited to a transformation of schema mapping from source schema to target one, our approach ensures the migration process working toward target schema.
- Our work applied to not only get the proper incremental migration to get the best system response adaptive to current system status, but also provide the model for global optimization, which is proper to be applied in the well-known workload trend changing scenario.
- The implementation of each step in progressive migration approach is only related to a part of whole schema changing, so the applications which are independent with this part can be executed without block. In some word, partial online update of system is achieved.

3   Design Approach

In this section, we describe the basic operators, adaptive models and cost estimation algorithms for our progressive schema evolution approach in framework above.

3.1   Basic Migration Operators

In the relational model, a relation schema consists of a head for all relations and the constraints that should hold for every relation. A database schema is composed by all the relation schemas and the constraints between them, for example, foreign key dependencies. Thus, the database schema presents the semantic information of a data set one database instance stored. Furthermore, schema evolution is the process of assisting and maintaining the changes to the schematic information and contents of a database. To maintain the change of data presentation in logical level, we extend a set of atomic operators in schema manipulation.

Creating Table. This operator is used to add new columns into one existing schema. Functional dependency which describe the relationship between new columns with existing data should be predefined before applying this operator. For example, if source schema contains a table to describe the information of books, and the abstract of each book should be added as a new column in target schema, then a new column with type of string value will be added by creating a new table. For example, if it is reasonable to apply the functional dependency as the key *bookID* of *book* table to *abstract* column, a new table should be created with two column *bookID* and *abstract*. Figure 3 shows the corresponding schema mapping of creating table.

No operator is defined for deleting table, because it is generally hard to predicate whether some information is not necessary before the migration process is finished. So, after progressive migration is finished, an additional work is to delete all the unnecessary tables.

Combining Table. This operator is used to combine two tables in source schema into one table. The reference to determine the relationship between these tables should be predefined before applying this operator. For example, if source schema contains table *book* for the information of books, and table *author* for the information of book authors,

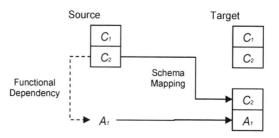

Fig. 3. Creating Table Operator. According to the functional dependency from C_2 to new information A_1, a new table with columns C_2 and A_1 is created.

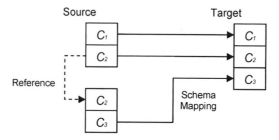

Fig. 4. Combining Table Operator. According to the reference between C_2, the two tables are combined.

then these two tables could be combined into table *glossary* for presenting all the information related to each book. And, it is reasonable to employ the column *author name* in both tables as the reference. Figure 4 shows the corresponding schema mapping of combining table.

This operator is defined for combining just two tables into one table. When combining n $(n \geq 2)$ tables, this operator should be called for $n - 1$ times.

Splitting Table. This operator is used to split one table in source schema into two tables. A reference to determine the relationship between the result tables should be created before applying this operator. For example, source schema contains *user* table for the information about users, and if we want to split the general information such as birthday and name from it, we can just split it into two tables, one for general information, the other for the rest information. It is reasonable to create the foreign key by user ID between two new tables as the new reference. Figure 5 shows the corresponding schema mapping of splitting table.

This operator is defined to split one table into just two tables. When splitting one table into n $(n \geq 2)$ tables, this operator should be called for $n - 1$ times.

Generally, the definition of operators above provide the basic methods to manipulate the schema evolution from one perspective to another. While, since the schema changed, one important issue is to provide evolution transparency to the users, whereby they would be able to pose queries to the database based on a (possibly old) version of the

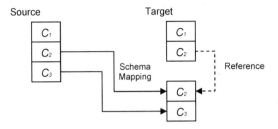

Fig. 5. Splitting Table operator. One table is split into two tables, and the reference of C_2 is created to maintain the dependency.

schema they are familiar with, even if the schema has evolved to a different state. This will make the front-end to the user more declarative, as users are no longer bothered about the details of the database schema.

A possible approach would be to assume that the users have the knowledge of a particular "schema" which is upper on our schema evolutions and let them use this to formulate queries against the database, even after the database schema has been modified. The idea is to shield the modifications to the schema of the database from the users as much as possible. As a consequence, it should be possible to maintain currency and relevance of application programs with very little modifications to account for the changes to the schema. Thus, the framework affords the possibility of schema-independent querying and programming. In this paper, we do not discuss this issue in depth. Instead, we propose that a smart query rewriter can provide a unified data presentation for applications.

3.2   Cost Estimation for One Snapshot

Cost estimation is much critical to determine the selection of intermediate schema. We provide a concept formula to express the cost estimation for one snapshot. The cost value for one snapshot S is shown in the following:

$$CostValue = C(TargetSchema) - C(S)$$

The $CostValue$ is the performance benefit by changing the schema to current snapshot S. The $C(TargetSchema)$ is the evaluation cost with workload on target schema, and the $C(S)$ is the evaluation cost on current snapshot S. With increase of $CostValue$, more benefit we can get from migration.

Both $C(TargetSchema)$ and $C(S)$ can be with following formula. The C_i is the cost of the i_{th} query estimated by the query engine. The F_i is the frequency of the i_{th} query.

$$C(Schema) = \sum C_i F_i$$

3.3   Check Point Selection

During the migration of applications via schema evolution, *Check Point* is defined as the time point to start a schema cost estimation and decide whether and how to evolve the schema. Though the database performance is changed between different check points, the schema itself and even the cost estimation process does not information to determine the distribution of check points. Thus, the selection of check points is independent with our solution on intermediate schema determination. Here, we recommend three kinds of strategies which are classified by customer requirements.

- *Predefined Mode:* all the check points are predefined by system administrators or DBAs according to the utilization of applications. For example, if the system was relatively idle in the weekend, such time slots can be arranged for the intermediate schema estimation and evolution in advance.
- *On-demand Mode:* the start of each check point is determined by system administrators or DBAs by the demand. This mode is much flexible for applications, especially, for the status of system which is hard to be predicated.
- *Trigger Mode:* the check points are triggered by some p kinds of predefined thresholds, such as transaction throughput, response time, etc. When performance of system achieves such limitations, one check point starts to evolve the schema. As a result, new quality of system performance may under the predefined thresholds. Note that, improper setting of thresholds may bring too many check points.

The mode of check point is selected by the by the property of application environment. For example, if the system is working under the environment which is sensitive with the partial off-line migration, that is, workloads are critical to be blocked by the schema evolution, predefined mode may proper to provide a "lazy" progressive migration strategy. Or, if the system is performance sensitive, the check points should be selected as much as possible to keep the schema match the real time system status. So, on-demand mode is proper to be applied when the monitor of system found the slow response of workloads. And, if the monitoring component of system can provide fluent and reliable performance sampling data, an automatic trigger mode to start the check points can be implemented to provide more sophisticated services to users.

The formal relation between the selection of check points and system performance is hard to be formalized since they are separated in different aspects of system execution. Here we just figure out a conceptual relationship between them as below. Generally, Since the checking process is based on cost estimation with real time workload distribution and data statistic, the check point means the adjustment of database schema to provide the optimal performance response. While, on the contrary, the checking process needs lock some tables to finish the off-line schema evolution, as a result, the workloads related have to be blocked. Even if such locking actions are only related with a partial of database schema, some transactions need to be cached or rollback, which damages the performance of system critically. Thus, the number of check points should be controlled under an acceptable scope, which is also related to the requirements of real systems.

3.4 Local Adaptive Model

In this section, we present the model of progressive migration to adapt local system status. The main idea of this approach is to select the proper intermediate schema just according to the cost estimation of current system status. It can be regarded as the method how to find the best intermediate schema for one snapshot among several migration points.

- Source schema contains 3 tables
- m is the new column which should be added
- Target schema integrates them into 4 tables

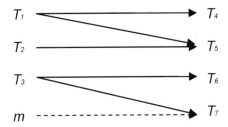

Fig. 6. An example for schema mapping relationship between source schema and target schema. Additionally, how to add a new column is also presented.

Operator Set Calculation. We employ the single direct mappings between two sets as the description of schema mapping relationship, an example is shown in Fig. 6.

From the schema mapping relationship, the minimal basic operator set can be peeled off by applying a straightforward method as below.

- Each new column, which should be added into target schema, corresponds to one create table operator.
- Each table in target schema, which has two mappings from two tables in source schema, corresponds to one combining table operator.
- Each table in source schema, which has mappings to tables in target schema, corresponds to one splitting table operator.

Schema Evaluation Based on Operator Set. According to the schema mapping relationship, it is obviously that, by applying each operator in operator set once, the source schema could evolve into target schema. Here, the problem is what operators and how many operators should be applied at one migration point to evolve to a proper new intermediate schema. From a certain snapshot, all the different selections deduce several different potential intermediate schemas for this snapshot. According to the cost estimation of them, one effective intermediate schema could be selected. Correspondingly, the applied operators are erased from operator set. And then, the system finishes the data loading and waits for next migration point until target schema achieves.

Figure 7 shows the schema evolution is time dimension.

In each migration point, **LAA** *(Local Adaptive Algorithm)*, shown in Algorithm 1 is executed to construct a subset of operator set. Line 14 lists all possible sub operator subset for current snapshot. From line 17 to line 19, one of them is picked up and the cost of coresponding schema is estimated. A method to estimate the cost of schema is given in next subsection. Line 21 to Line 24 is used to record the operator subset to create the best intermediate schema. Line 26 erases the checked operator subset from superset of all operators. After checking all the operator subset, this funtion returns one for constructing the minimum cost intermediate schema.

By utilizing all the operators in the output set, the intermediate schema with the best performance for current query distribution and data statistic will be migrated. After schema migration and data loading, all the operators in this subset should be erased from original operator set, because each operator can be used only once.

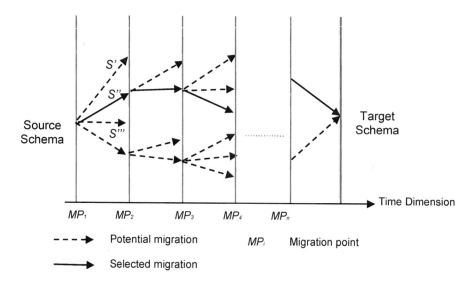

Fig. 7. The process that source schema migrates to target schema in a progressive way. In each migration point, some of basic operators can be selected according to the cost of the intermediate schema created after applying them.

Suppose that at one migration point, there is m operators left in operator set. Since every subset of the operator set should be tested, we have 2^m possible intermediate schemas to estimate for one migrating snapshot. So, if we have c migration points predefined and n operators found from schema mappings, in the worst scenario, there are $c \times 2^n$ intermediate schemas to be estimated among the whole migration process. It is the scenario which the source schema is always the best intermediate one, no operators is applied in each migration point. But every time, the cost estimation should be applied for all possible intermediate schemas.

Even in the best scenario, there are still 2^n intermediate schemas to be estimated. It is cause by applied all operators in the migration point, that is, from the cost estimation for all possible intermediate schemas, the target schema which applies all the operators is the best one. Then, after that, the operator set is empty and schema evolution is also finished.

Obviously, the resulting combinatorial search against this solution space is in exponential size. As **LAA** is based on the exhausted search strategy, it is not proper to be used in complex schema mapping environment. In the next subsection, we describe our heuristic genetic search algorithm for finding the optimum intermediate schema.

Figure 8 shows one kind of progressive migration process as an example. It is based on the schema mapping shown in Figure 7. There are three migration points in this scenario. The first one applies two operators from operator set. After that, three operators are still left in this set. The second one applied another two operators, and the last one applied the left one operator. And, finally, the target schema achieved.

Algorithm 1. Best operator set selecting

```
 1: FUNCTION OpSet Select
 2: IN: W, workload distribution
 3: IN: D, data statistic
 4: IN: S, current schema, at the first time, it is just the source schema
 5: IN: OpSet, current operator set which contains all un-applied operators
 6: OUT: Applied, the operators should be applied in this snapshot
 7: BEGIN
 8: Cost Min := ∞
 9: Set Applied := ∅
10:
11: Set TempOps
12: SuperSet SupperOpSet
13:
14: SupperOpSet := ListAllSubSet(OpSet)
15:
16: while (SupperOpSet is not ∅) do
17:     TempOps := PickOneSet(SupperOpSet)
18:     Schema TempSchema := ApplyOperators(S, TempOps)
19:     Cost TempCost := CostEstimate(TempSchema, W, D)
20:
21:     if (Min ≥ TempCost) then
22:         Min := TempCost
23:         Applied := TempOps
24:     end if
25:
26:     Erase TempOps from SupperOpSet
27: end while
28: return Applied
29: END
```

3.5 Global Adaptive Model

Last section gives the strategy to find out the best intermediate schema which is matching the system status in each migration point. But it is not the best solution for global migration process. In this section, a global optimization model with the forward scan is described.

Estimation with forward scan. Under the precondition that the trend of workload distribution and data statistic is predicted, a global optimization method can be applied. That is, in each migration point, calculating the performance information on all the possible future snapshots instead of only current on. (usually, it is reasonable, since customers always have the plan to define the migration process and proper migration points. For example, if the update of system is begun from financial department to sales one and than product one, a simple tool can be applied to count the trend of workloads by the business frequency of each department. And, if every weekend evening, the system can be blocked for update, it can be regarded as the migration points).

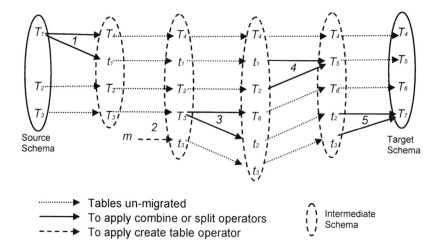

Fig. 8. An example with three migration points and two intermediate schemas. It is based on the schema mapping example at the beginning of this section.

Actually, in the first migration point, the best strategy is selected by the idea above. The reason we still prefer to check the forward scan in several migration point is, that the predictive workload trend may not very precise. If we trust it in complex system update, such imprecision may be accumulated and affect the whole performance migration plan.

Suppose we have c migration points and n operators. In the worst scenario, $2^{c \times n}$ intermediate schemas should be estimated in the first migration point. And, the whole process has to check the number of $\sum_{i=0}^{c} 2^{i \times n}$ schemas. It is also the scenario which the source schema is always the best intermediate one, no operators is applied in each migration point.

To search this solution space, we use **GAA** *(Global Adaptive Algorithm)* which is based on general genetic algorithm (GA) search heuristic [6], [7] that finds a tradeoff between finding the high performance intermediate schema and minimizing the estimation of intermediate schemas. The **GAA**'s output is the subset of operators that should be used to create new intermediate schema.

Implementation of the global adaptation with a genetic algorithm. A GA emulates Darwinian natural selection by having population members compete against one another over successive generations in order to converge toward the best solution. As shown in Algorithm 2, chromosomes evolve through multiple generations of adaptation and selection.

We note that we use a GA as a tool to find a solution in the combinatorial problem. There are many possible approaches to finding a good solution, such as local-search stochastic hill-climbers and global-search simulated annealing, but we chose a GA due to our familiarity with the algorithm. Since we are trying to find an subset of basic operators, potential solutions can be naturally formed as a string of integers, a well-studied representation that allows us to leverage prior GA research in effective chromosome recombination (e.g. [8]). Furthermore, it is known that a GA provides a very good

Algorithm 2. Genetic algorithm

```
 1: FUNCTION GA
 2: BEGIN
 3: Time t
 4: Pop P(t)
 5:
 6: Evaluate(P(t))
 7: while ! done do
 8:     Recombine/Mutate P(t)
 9:     t := t + 1
10:
11:     select the best P(t) from P(t − 1)
12:     evaluate(P(t))
13: end while
14: END
```

tradeoff between exploration of the solution space and exploitation of discovered maxima [7].

The method we present the chosen operators as string of integers in each migration point is described as following. The length of string is the number of all operators which are not applied yet. Each position in the string responds one operator in the operator set. Suppose we have c migration points from current stage to the target schema, the integer i in each position of string is limited in the range of $(0, c)$, which means, the corresponding operator should be applied in migration point i.

GA execution. A GA proceeds as follows. Initially a random set of chromosomes is created for the population. The chromosomes are evaluated (hashed) to some metric, and the best ones are chosen to be parents. In our problem, the evaluation produces the cost estimation of intermediate schema with the current workload distribution and data statistic. The parents recombine to produce children, simulating sexual crossover, and occasionally a mutation may arise which produces new characteristics that were not available in either parent. In our work, we further implemented an adaptive mutation scheme whereby the mutation rate is increased when the population stagnates (i.e. fails to improve its workload benefit metric) over a prolonged number of generations. The children are ranked based on the evaluation function, and the best subset of the children is chosen to be the parents of the next generation, simulating natural selection. The generational loop ends after some stopping condition is met; we chose to end after 1000 generations had passed, as this value was empirically the best tradeoff between execution time and thoroughness of the search. Note that converging toward and finding the global optimum is not guaranteed because the recombination and mutation are stochastic.

GA recombination and mutation. As mentioned, the chromosomes are permutations of unique integers. Figure 9 shows a recombination of chromosomes applied to two parents will produce a new child using a two-point crossover scheme [8]. Using this approach, a randomly chosen contiguous subsection of the first parent is copied to the

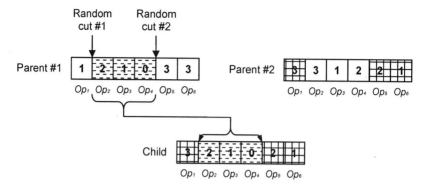

Fig. 9. An example showing how the GA produces a child chromosome from parent chromosomes using a two-point crossover recombination. Each chromosome represents a permutation string. To maintain the requirement that all the integers must be unique in the string, the recombination first takes a contiguous subsection of the first parent (chosen to be the piece between two randomly chosen slices), places this subsection at the start of the child, and then picks up all remaining values in the second parent not included from the first parent.

child, and then all remaining items in the second parent (that have not already been taken from the first parent's subsection) are then copied to the child in order of appearance. The uni-chromosome mutation scheme chooses two random items from the

---

Algorithm 3. GA evaluation function

1: **FUNCTION** Select
2: **IN:** *checkpoints*, the number of remained check points
3: **IN:** $W(c)$, array of workload distribution on each check point
4: **IN:** $D(c)$, array of data statistic on each check point
5: **IN:** S, current schema, at the first time, it is just the source schema
6: **IN:** *OpArrange*, chromosome which contains the arrangement of operators in each check-point
7: **OUT:** *Estimation*, cost of the intermediate schema
8: **BEGIN**
9: Schema *TempSchema*
10: Set *TempOps*
11: Cost *Estimation*
12:
13: **for** *checkpoints* ≥ 0 **do**
14:     *TempOps* := Choose the operators from *OpArrange*
15:     *TempSchema* := ApplyOperators(S, *TempOps*)
16:     *TempCost* := CostEstimate(*TempSchema*, $W(i)$, $D(i)$)
17:
18:     *checkpoints* := *checkpoints* - 1
19:     *Estimation* := *Estimation* + *TempCost*
20: **end for**
21: **return** *Estimation*
22: **END**

---

chromosome and reverses the elements between them, inclusive. We will look at other recombination and mutation schemes from the GA community in the future.

GA evaluation function. An important GA component is the evaluation function. Given a particular chromosome representing one selection of operators, the function deterministically calculates the cost estimation of intermediate schema by applying these operators with the current query distribution and data statistic. The evaluation function follows the pseudocode in Algorithm 3.
For loop in line 13 means the migration points. One number of the loop variable is

mapping to one migration point. Line 14 is used to pickup the arrangement operators for tested migration point. For example, if current loop variable is 3, all operators which chromosome integer is just 3 will be picked up. Line 15 and 16 is used to create intermediate schema and estimate its cost. By line 18, the algorithm turns to check next migration point. Line 19 accumulates the glossary cost.

According to the operator arrangement in chromosome, **GAA** selects all the operators which should be applied in this stage and estimates the performance of system. After finishing the loop, the evaluation of one migration strategy is achieved.

4   Experimental Evaluation

In this paper, we use the schema in TPCW benchmark to test our method on MaxDB. TPCW specifies a book store for customers to browse and buy products from a website. Based on simplified schema in TPCW, we design source schema and target schema as shown in Appendix 6.

4.1   Query Workload

We test two sets of queries in our experiments, namely old queries and new queries. Each set includes ten different queries. The old queries corresponds to source schema with decreasing frequency, while new queries corresponds to target schema with increasing frequency. Notice the queries can be executed on corresponding schema directly, and both old and new queries are executed on intermediate schemas with a rewriting process during migration. In in Appendix 6, we shows the experimental setting for the workload.

4.2   Situations for Comparison

We compare three kinds of situations with same workload: **(a) Opt-Schema**: the source schema coexists with target schema at same time, and the old queries and new queries are executed on source schema and target schema respectively; **(b) Pro-Schema**: the schema is changed after a period of time according to both frequent workload and basic operators of migration, both old queries and new queries are rewritten and executed on intermediate schema during migration; **(c) Obj-Schema**: both the old and new queries are rewritten and executed on target schema.

Hence the performance of Obj-Schema gives the upper bound of three situations. Opt-Schema is the optimal situation for both old queries and new queries, it is the baseline of the three situations. Pro-Schema is the situation with incrementally schema evolution according to both workload performance and migration operators. Measuring the performance of Obj-Schema and Opt-Schema give us a better picture of how Pro-Schema performs in incremental migration.

4.3   Experimental Parameters

In order to better test and understand the characteristics of our method, we design a set of parameters which include: data size, query frequency and migration frequency. As shown in Table 1, the data size refers to the size of data base, we use the data size of 100MB and 1GB respectively.

With our method, the schema is changed in incremental manner, which begins from source schema, reaches to target schema after several migration points. We test three and five migration points respectively.

During the migration process, the frequency of old queries are decreasing and the new queries increasing. We use two kinds of query frequency in this paper. The first one is regular frequency, within which the old(new) queries are decreasing(increasing) with determinate rate. The second one is irregular frequency which means the frequency of old(new) queries decreases(increases) at random rate.

Table 1. Parameters

	Parameters	Values
1	Data Size	100MB, 1GB
2	Query Frequency	Regular, Irregular
3	Migration Frequency	3, 5

4.4   Performance Measurements

We compare **Pro-Schema** with **Opt-Schema** and **Obj-Schema** with LAA and GAA methods in terms of the following two performance indicators: Phase-Cost and Overall-Cost.

The Phase-Cost is the query cost calculated on migration point, it collects the cost of queries between two migration points in the form of I/O number. The Overall-Cost is the sum of Phase-Cost, and it reflects the overall performance.

For three kinds of situations, we test Phase-Cost to examine the local optimization of LAA method. At each migration point, we multiply the cost of each query with its frequency, then by summing up the cost for each query. For testing the overall optimization with GAA method, we do the experiment with the migration points number from two to five.

4.5   Performance Results

In this subsection, we study the performance of different situations by various parameters. We classify the test into two sets of irregular frequency and regular frequency. Within each set, we further varies the data size and migration frequency. This enables us to test our methods from different dimensions.

Irregular Frequency. In this subsection, we test the situation that the frequency of queries changes at random rate. In Figure 10, we list the workload frequency between different migration points. We only list the situation where there are five migration points as an example, and omit other situations for simplicity.

Workload	P0-P1	P1-P2	P2-P3	P3-P4	P4-P5
O1	50	40	30	20	10
O2	12	8	5	3	2
O3	40	35	30	10	5
O4	7	6	5	1	1
O5	30	28	12	6	4
O6	22	20	10	6	2
O7	70	30	25	15	10
O8	30	10	5	3	2
O9	45	43	41	40	11
O10	40	38	35	32	15
Workload	**P0-P1**	**P1-P2**	**P2-P3**	**P3-P4**	**P4-P5**
N1	10	20	30	40	50
N2	2	3	5	8	12
N3	5	10	30	35	40
N4	1	1	5	6	7
N5	4	6	12	28	30
N6	2	6	10	20	22
N7	10	15	25	30	70
N8	2	3	5	10	30
N9	11	40	41	43	45
N10	15	32	35	38	40

Fig. 10. Workload Frequency between Migration Points

In Figure 11(a) and Figure 11(b), we test Phase-Cost of LAA method with five migration points, on the data size of 100MB and 1GB respectively. We can see that the Pro-Schema performs between the Obj-Schema and Opt-Schema, Opt-Schema provides the optimal scenario, and Pro-Schema achieves averagely 1.5 times performance gain over Obj-Schema. The advantages of Pro-Schema over Obj-Schema demonstrate that our incremental migration method can acquire an optimization at each migration point, this is because the Pro-Schema evolves according to the frequent queries at each migration point, so we get an optimized schema for executing queries after each incremental migration, and the optimized schema can improve the Phase-Cost between migration points.

In Figure 12(a) and Figure 12(b), we test Phase-Cost with LAA method with three migration points, on the data size of 100MB and 1GB respectively. The same results can

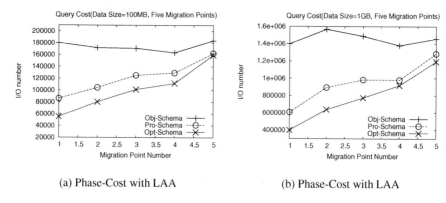

(a) Phase-Cost with LAA   (b) Phase-Cost with LAA

Fig. 11. Experiment Results

be obtained since Obj-Schema and Opt-Schema define the bounds for Pro-Schema. For the above figures with five migration points, the Pro-Schema is more closer with Opt-Schema compared with the situations with three migration points. This is because with more migration points, the queries are partitioned into more groups, and each group of queries are between two migration points. Thus the changing rate of queries is more smooth, we can make an better exploration for workload distribution than the situation with less migration points, thus the Pro-Schema can be more sensitive to the workload changing, this enables the Pro-Schema progress to Opt-Schema smoothly and closely.

regular Frequency. In this subsection, we compare the Overall-Cost with LAA and GAA methods. We test the situations with migration points from two to five, and collect the Overall-Cost for each number of migration points. Also we consider the scenario that frequency of new(old) queries are increasing(decreasing) at determinate rate during the migration process, this enables the execution of GAA method.

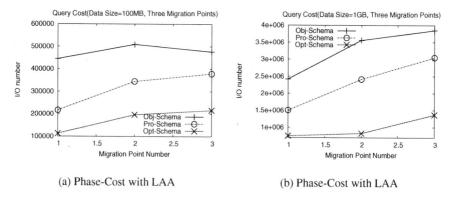

(a) Phase-Cost with LAA   (b) Phase-Cost with LAA

Fig. 12. Experiment Results

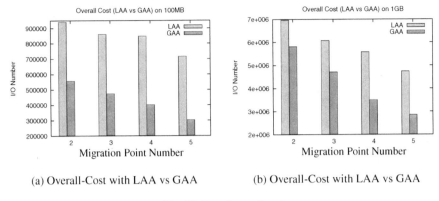

(a) Overall-Cost with LAA vs GAA   (b) Overall-Cost with LAA vs GAA

Fig. 13. Experiment Results

In Figure 13(a) and Figure 13(b), we test the Overall-Cost with LAA and GAA methods on the data size of 100MB and 1GB respectively. We can see the Overall-Cost of both methods decreases with the increasing number of migration points. This benefit comes from the more refined analysis of workload. Also, GAA is more efficient than the LAA method. This is because GAA explores not only historical workload distribution, but also further workload at each migration point, aiming at changing schema according to more queries, and this enables the global optimization during migration process.

5   Related Works

Data integration is a pervasive challenge faced in applications that need to query across multiple autonomous and heterogeneous data sources. Data integration is crucial in large enterprises that own a multitude of data sources [9]. Such projects typically involve two phases [10]. The first phase aims at establishing the schema and data mappings required for transforming schema and data. The second phase consists of developing and executing the corresponding schema and data transformations.

Such projects typically involve two phases [10]. The first phase aims at establishing the schema and data mappings required for transforming schema and data. The second phase consists of developing and executing the corresponding schema and data transformations.

Several tools have been designed to assist the discovery of appropriate schema mappings [2], P. Bernstein and S. Melnik demonstrated a tool that circumvents the schema matching by doing it interactively. The tool suggests candidate matches for a selected schema element and allows convenient navigation between the candidates [11].

Y. Velegrakis, C. Yu and L. Popa provides a framework and a tool (ToMAS) for automatically adapting mappings as schemas evolve [12] [13]. The development of the corresponding schema and data transformations is usually an ad-hoc process that comprises the construction of complex programs and queries. Recently, such work has been

in the road towards creating an industrial-strength tool [3]. The research of schema matching is still made by usage of new techniques [14] and domain knowledge [15].

The research of schema matching is still made by usage of new techniques [14] and domain knowledge [15].

The problem of data migration has also been extensively studied (e.g. [16] [17]) in the context of system integration, storage system, schema evolution and ETL tool chains. Various industrial tools have even been developed for the Data Migration process, such as components ProfileStage, QualityStage and DataStage in IBMs WebSphere Information Integration Suite [18], Data Fusion, which utilizes a domain specific language to conveniently model complex data transformations and provides integrated development environment [10]. Since it is always ineffective to move data from one data storage to another, and during the process, system is usually blocked for the service. Numerous algorithms have been proposed for effective or even online data migration [19] [1] [20] [21] [22]. However, none of them addresses the issue of progressive data migration. Since it is always ineffective to move data from one data storage to another, and during the process, system is usually blocked for the service. Numerous algorithms have been proposed for effective or even online data migration [19] [1] [20] [21] [22]. However, none of them addresses the issue of progressive data migration.

M. Tresch and M. H. Scholl provided the reasons why schema reorganizations should be avoided in [23], that is, (1) Updates to the schema must propagate to physical updates of existing instances; (2) Compatibility of the transformed schema with existing applications must be guaranteed. They gave a solution to avoid it by the data independence helps to avoid reorganizations in case of capacity preserving and reducing schema transformations. But it can be used only in object oriented system.

M. Ronstrom [24] presents a method to handle schema changes which is based on a transaction oriented change with the aid of triggers. The old and the new schema can be used concurrently so it is never necessary to block any transactions. This feature of the method is easy to integrate into an already existing DBMSs.

Based on the usage of log for change propagation, J. Loland and S. Hvasshovd [22] provides a method for performing non-blocking full outer join and split transformations. Their solution can be integrated into existing DBMSs and running as a low priority background process. As a result, the transformation has little impact on concurrent user transactions.

Generally, previous industry and academic research efforts in this area concentrated on constructing the schema mapping between source scheme and target schema automatically, and, some of them pay attention to eliminate the cost of data migration. Our approach for data migration is based on the definition of basic schema evolution operators and the cost estimation for them under different workload distribution and data statistic. In order to minimize the total migration cost, a heuristic rule and a genetic algorithm are proposed to construct the effective intermediated schemas. our solution provides more advanced techniques to solve the problem in schema evolution and data migration. Schema matching related works implement the relationship between multiversion systems, effective and online data migration support system to provide service even during data loading process.

6   Conclusion and Further Work

Data migration is an important problem in many domains, especially in multi-version applications in SaaS. In this paper we present progressive migration, an incremental framework for migrating data for the scenario of system update. Based on the definition of basic schema mapping operators and the cost estimation for them under different workload distribution and data statistic, a framework of incremental evolution schema is presented. In order to provide optimized intermediate schemas during system updating, we employ both local and global optimized algorithms to implement the progressive migration.

To evaluate our system, we used TPCW benchmark [25] and a reasonable new version of TPCW-liked schema as the target schema in our experiments. Our results validate the utilization of incremental migration for system updating can bring a substantial performance improvement. Although we have focused on schema updating during our experiments, our approach can be applied to multi-version enterprise softwares and on-line data migration.

In the future, we plan to work on the optimization of schema design for more general purpose, not under the limitation on target schema driven, but the best physical design of schema for system workload distribution and data statistic.

References

1. Lu, C., Alvarez, G.A., Wilkes, J.: Aqueduct: online data migration with performance guarantees. In: Proceedings of the 1st USENIX Conference on File and Storage Technologies, Monterey, CA, pp. 219–230 (2002)
2. Rahm, E., Bernstein, P.A.: A survey of approaches to automatic schema matching. The VLDB Journal 10(4), 334–350 (2001)
3. Haas, L.M., Hernandez, M.A., Ho, H., Popa, L., Roth, M.: Clio grows up: From research prototype to industrial tool. In: Proceedings of the 2005 ACM SIGMOD International Conference on Management of Data, Baltimore, Maryland, pp. 805–810 (2005)
4. Pirahesh, H., Hellerstein, J.M., Hasan, W.: Extensible/rule based query rewrite optimization in starburst. In: Proceedings of the 1992 ACM SIGMOD International Conference on Management of Data, San Diego, California, United States, pp. 39–48 (1992)
5. Krishnaprasad, M., Liu, Z., Manikutty, A., Warner, J.W., Arora, V., Kotsovolos, S.: Query rewrite for xml in oracle xml db. In: Proceedings of the 30th VLDB Conference, Toronto, Canada, pp. 1134–1145 (2004)
6. Holland, J. (ed.): Adaptation in Natural and Artifcial Systems: An Introductory Analysis with Applications to Biology, Control, and Artifcial Intelligence. MIT Press, Cambridge (1992)
7. Goldberg, D. (ed.): Genetic Algorithms in Search, Optimization and Machine Learning. Kluwer Academic Publishers, Dordrecht (1989)
8. Davis, L.: Job shop scheduling with genetic algorithms. In: Proceedings of 16th International Conference on Genetic Algorithms, Mahwah, NJ, USA, pp. 136–140 (1985)
9. Halevy, A., Rajaraman, A., Ordille, J.: Data integration: The teenage years. In: Proceedings of the 32nd VLDB Conference, Seoul, Korea, pp. 9–15 (2006)
10. Carreira, P., Galhardas, H.: Efficient development of data migration transformations. In: Proceedings of the 2004 ACM SIGMOD International Conference on Management of Data, Paris, France, pp. 915–916 (2004)

11. Bernstein, P.A., Melnik, S.: Incremental schema matching. In: Proceedings of the 32nd VLDB Conference, Seoul, Korea, pp. 1167–1170 (2006)
12. Velegrakis, Y., Miller, R.J., Popa, L.: Mapping adaptation under evolving schemas. In: Proceedings of the 29th VLDB Conference, Berlin, Germany, pp. 584–595 (2003)
13. Yu, C., Popa, L.: Semantic adaptation of schema mappings when schemas evolve. In: Proceedings of the 31th VLDB Conference, Trondheim, Norway, pp. 1006–1016 (2005)
14. Agrawal, H., Chafle, G., Goyal, S., Mittal, S., Mukherjea, S.: An enhanced extractctransformcload system for migrating data in telecom billing. In: Proceedings of 24th International Conference on Data Engineering, Cancun, Mexico, pp. 1277–1285 (2008)
15. Elmeleegy, H., Ouzzani, M., Elmagarmid, A.: Usage-based schema matching. In: Proceedings of 24th International Conference on Data Engineering, Cancun, Mexico, pp. 20–29 (2008)
16. Hall, J., Hartline, J., Karlin, A.R., Saia, J., Wilkes, J.: On algorithms for efficient data migration. In: Proceedings of the Twelfth Annual ACM-SIAM Symposium on Discrete Algorithms, Washington, D.C., United States, pp. 620–629 (2001)
17. Dasgupta, K., Ghosal, S., Jain, R., Sharma, U., Verma, A.: Qosmig: Adaptive rate-controlled migration of bulk data in storage systems. In: Proceedings of 21st International Conference on Data Engineering, Tokyo, Japan, pp. 816–827 (2005)
18. "Information integration, IBM,
    http://www-306.ibm.com/software/data/integration/
19. Khuller, S., Kim, Y.-A., Wan, Y.-C.: Algorithms for data migration with cloning. SIAM Journal on Computing 33(2), 448–461 (2004)
20. Sundaram, V., Wood, T., Shenoy, P.: Efficient data migration in self-managing storage systems. In: Proceedings of the 2006 IEEE International Conference on Autonomic Computing, Dublin, Ireland, pp. 297–300 (2006)
21. Soundararajan, G., Amza, C.: Online data migration for autonomic provisioning of databases in dynamic content web. In: Proceedings of the 2005 Conference of the Centre for Advanced Studies on Collaborative Research, Toronto, Ontario, Canada, pp. 268–282 (2005)
22. Løland, J., Hvasshovd, S.-O.: Online, non-blocking relational schema changes. In: Ioannidis, Y., Scholl, M.H., Schmidt, J.W., Matthes, F., Hatzopoulos, M., Böhm, K., Kemper, A., Grust, T., Böhm, C. (eds.) EDBT 2006. LNCS, vol. 3896, pp. 405–422. Springer, Heidelberg (2006)
23. Tresch, M., Scholl, M.H.: Schema transformation without database reorganization. ACM SIGMOD Record 22(1), 21–27 (1993)
24. Ronstrom, M.: On-line schema update for a telecom database. In: Proceedings of 16th International Conference on Data Engineering, San Diego, CA, USA, pp. 329–338 (2000)
25. The tpcw benchmark, http://www.tpc.org/tpcw

Appendix

TPCW Schema Instance

Figure 14 shows the original TPCW schema. Figure 15 is the new schema with reasonable update.

Workload Setting

In Figure 16, we show the query distribution for old and new queries. In Figure 17 and Figure 18, we show the query instance in our experiments.

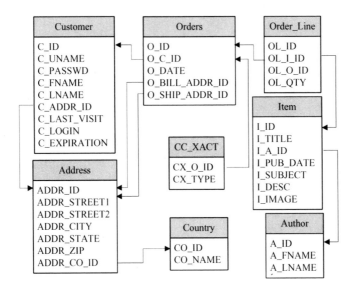

Fig. 14. Source Schema

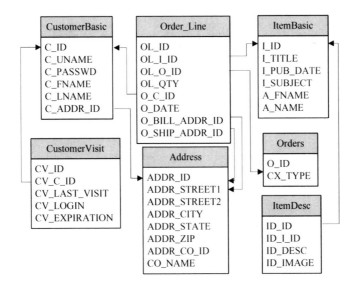

Fig. 15. Target Schema

OldQuery	NewQuery	Distributions	Frequency
O1	N1	15%	150
O2	N2	3%	30
O3	N3	12%	120
O4	N4	2%	20
O5	N5	8%	80
O6	N6	6%	60
O7	N7	15%	150
O8	N8	5%	50
O9	N9	18%	180
O10	N10	16%	160

Fig. 16. Workload Distribution

O1	Select ADDR_CITY, CO_NAME From Address, Country Where Address.ADDR_ID=Country.CO_ID
O2	Select C_FNAME, C_LOGIN From Customer Where C_UNAME ='SE'
O3	Select C_UNAME, ADDR_CITY, CO_NAME From Customer, Address, Country Where Address.ADDR_ID=Country.CO_ID And Customer.C_ADDR_ID=Address.ADDR_ID And C_UNAME='SE'
O4	Select O_ID, O_BILL_ADDR_ID From Orders, Order_Line Where Orders.O_ID=Order_Line.OL_O_ID
O5	Select O_ID, CX_TYPE From Orders, CC_XACTS Where Orders .O_ID= CC_XACTS.CX_O_ID
O6	Select * From Item, Author Where Item.I_A_ID=Author.A_ID and Item.I_SUBJECT='HISTORY' Order by I_PUB_DATE desc, I_TITLE
O7	Select * From Address, Country Where Address.ADDR_ID=Country.CO_ID
O8	Select C_ID, C_PASSWD, C_FNAME, C_LAST_VISIT From Customer where C_UNAME='RI' and C_PASSWD='ri'
O9	Select * From Item, Author Where Item.I_A_ID=Author.A_ID and Item.I_SUBJECT='SPORTS'
O10	Select O_ID, O_DATE, CX_TYPE From Orders, CC_XACTS Where Orders .O_ID= CC_XACTS.CX_O_ID

Fig. 17. Workload Example(Old Queries)

N1	Select CV_ID, CV_LAST_VISIT, CV_LOGIN, CV_EXPIRATION
	From CustomerVisit
N2	Select C_UNAME, C_EMAIL
	From CustomerBasic
N3	Select I_TITLE, A_LNAME , A_FNAME
	From ItemBasic
N4	Select I_TITLE, OL_QTY, ADDR_CITY
	From Itembasic, FinalOrder_Line, CountryAddress
	Where Itembasic.I_ID=finalOrder_Line.OL_O_ID
	And FinalOrder_line. OL_BILL_ADDR_ID=countryaddress.Addr_ID
N5	Select O_ID, CX_TYPE
	From finalOrders
N6	Select *
	From Itembasic, Itemdesc
	Where Itembasic.I_ID=Itemdesc.ID_ID
N7	Select O_ID, ADDR_CITY, CO_NAME, OL_QTY
	From finalOrders, finalOrder_Line, countryAddress
	Where finalOrder_Line.OL_BILL_ADDR_ID=countryAddress. ADDR_ID
	And finalOrders.O_ID=finalOrder_Line.OL_O_ID
N8	Select * from CustomerBasic
	Where C_UNAME='OGUL'
	And C_PASSWD='ogul'
N9	Select I_TITLE, ID_DESC, ID_IMAGE
	From Itembasic, itemdesc
	where Itembasic.I_ID=Itemdesc.ID_I_ID
N10	Select ADDR_STREET1,ADDR_STREET2,ADDR_CITY,
	ADDR_STATE,ADDR_ZIP,CO_NAME from CountryAddress

Fig. 18. Workload Example(New Queries)

Towards Analytics-as-a-Service Using an In-Memory Column Database

Jan Schaffner[1], Benjamin Eckart[1], Christian Schwarz[1], Jan Brunnert[1],
Dean Jacobs[2], and Alexander Zeier[1]

[1] Hasso Plattner Institute
University of Potsdam
August-Bebel-Strasse 88
14482 Potsdam, Germany
[2] SAP AG
Dietmar-Hopp-Allee 16
69190 Walldorf, Germany
`firstname.lastname@hpi.uni-potsdam.de`
`firstname.lastname@sap.com`

Abstract. For traditional data warehouses, mostly large and expensive server and storage systems are used. For small- and medium size companies, it is often too expensive to implement and run such systems. Given this situation, the SaaS model comes in handy, since these companies might opt to run their OLAP as a service. The challenge is then for the analytics service provider to minimize TCO by consolidating as many tenants onto as few servers as possible, a technique often referred to as multi-tenancy.

In this article, we report on three different results on our research around building a cluster of multi-tenant main memory column databases for analytics as a service. For this purpose we ported SAP's in-memory column database TREX to run in the Amazon cloud. We evaluated the relation between data size of a tenant and number of queries per second and created a formula which allows us to estimate how many tenants with different sizes and request rates can be put on one instance for our main memory database. We discuss findings on cost/performance tradeoffs between reliably storing the data of a tenant on a single node using a highly-available network attached storage, such as Amazon EBS, vs. replication of tenant data to a secondary node where the data resides on less resilient storage. We also describe a mechanism to provide support for historical queries across older snapshots of tenant data which is lazy-loaded from Amazon's S3 near-line archiving storage and cached on the local VM disks.

1 Introduction

Data warehouses are expensive from both a setup and maintenance perspective. For traditional data warehouses, mostly large and expensive server systems are used. In particular, for small- and medium size companies, it is often too expensive to run such systems. These companies might be interested in using analytics as a service. Even large companies would profit from the fact that only operational expenses, but no capital expenses occur.

D. Agrawal et al. (Eds.): Information and Software as Services, LNBIP 74, pp. 257–282, 2011.

The question is how can a service provider for analytics provide its service with a continuous high performance but at low costs even in case of load variations. A solution to overcome these challenges is to use cloud computing and to consolidate multiple customers onto few machines, a technique often referred to as multi-tenancy. With cloud computing, it is possible to start or stop instances on demand, depending on the need of computing resources, which results in an enormous flexibility. With the use of multi-tenancy, the service can be provided at lower cost, because a service provider would not have to run a dedicated instance for each customer.

Besides, the high cost of a data warehouse is caused by a) complex cube structures containing pre-aggregated values for reporting and b) materialized views to pre-compute joins between fact and dimensions tables. Memory-based column databases (MCDBs) store the whole data set in main memory, which can be accessed much faster than disk. This performance gain removes the necessity of pre-computed aggregates and makes it possible to calculate joins on-the-fly without relying on materialized views.

In this paper, we report on some initial results around building an OLAP cluster of multi-tenant MCDBs on the Amazon EC2 cloud computing environment, for which purpose we ported SAP's in-memory column database TREX to run in the Amazon cloud. We report on three isolated results that are part of the overall solution.

In a multi-tenant environment, only a limited number of tenants can be served by one instance. This number of tenants is dependent on the size and request rate of each tenant. We analyze the relation between tenant size and request rate and define a read workload model for TREX and our used test queries. It turns out that this relation is close to but not exactly linear. However, if a tenant is larger, the analytical queries have to scan more rows to calculate aggregates and produce a higher workload than queries of smaller tenants. In future work, we will use this workload model to decide whether a tenant needs to be migrated and if there are enough resources on the instance available to which a tenant should be migrated. Additionally, we present a cost model which makes us able to calculate the cost of a tenant depending on its size and request rate and Amazon AWS infrastructure costs.

Cloud computing providers like Amazon with its Elastic Computing Cloud, in general, only guarantee the availability of the whole cloud, but not of single instances. Therefore, an applications provider has to implement an own strategy to keep the availability and reliability of a service running in EC2. Availability for databases in a cloud computing network can be achieved by replicating data across multiple nodes or by increasing the resilience of individual nodes, e.g. by logging all updates to a local or remote disk. We discuss findings on cost/performance tradeoffs between reliably storing the data of a tenant on a single node using a highly-available network attached storage, such as Amazon EBS, vs. replication of tenant data to a secondary node where the data resides on less resilient storage.

Having one specialized OLAP database management system explicitly aimed at performing ad-hoc queries on an ever-growing database requires the capability of an MCDB to retain historical states so that applications can calculate consistent values based on previous states of the database. Generally, MCDBs store the complete data set in main memory. However, since main memory is limited and older snapshots might be used rarely, it might become necessary to use less expensive storage mediums for older snapshots. Consequently, we evaluate the concept of lazy loading older snapshots of tenant data from local VM disks.

This paper is organized as follows: Section 2 presents our multi-tenant OLAP cluster: the Rock framework. Section 3 shows how a cost model depending on tenant size and request rate can be developed for an in-memory column store providing analytics. Section 4 discusses the cost and performance of several options to provide high availability in Rock. In Section 5 we make the case for historical query support and describe our archiving solution for historic database snapshots. Section 6.1 discusses related work and Section 7 concludes the paper.

2   The Rock Framework

Rock is a multi-tenant database framework based on Amazon EC2[1] that supports load balancing, scaling and versioning. Rock is built around SAP's in-memory column database TREX ([12,8]), which is the engine at the core of SAP's Business Warehouse Accelerator.

The Rock clustering framework runs in front of a collection of TREX servers and provides multi-tenancy, replication of tenant data, and fault tolerance. Figure 1 illustrates the architecture of the Rock framework. Read requests are submitted to the cluster by the analytics application. Write requests are submitted by the batch importers, which periodically pull incremental updates of the data from transactional source systems. The Rock framework itself consists of three types of processes: the *cluster leader*, *routers*, and *instance managers*. Each instance manager ("node") is paired one-to-one with a TREX server to which it forwards requests.

The cluster leader exists only once in the landscape and assigns tenant data to instance managers. Each copy of a tenant's data is assigned to one instance manager and each instance manager is responsible for the data from multiple tenants. The cluster leader maintains the assignment information in a *cluster map*, which it propagates to the routers and instance managers so all components share a consistent view of the landscape. The cluster leader tracks changes to the cluster state based on information it collects from the Amazon EC2 API such as IP addresses, instance states, and geographic location. The cluster leader is not directly involved in request processing.

The routers accept requests from outside the cluster and forward them to the appropriate instance managers. Routing is based on the tenant who issued the query and the chosen load balancing strategy. Our current implementation supports round-robin, random, and server-load-based load balancing. The tests in this paper use the latter algorithm. Load is taken to be the CPU idle time of the TREX server averaged over a 10 second window. The small window size is crucial for the router's ability to re-direct queries to the least utilized replica during a load burst. Load information is piggy-backed onto query results as they are returned to the router.

2.1   Update Propagation Model

The Rock framework can be configured so that write requests must be written to i out of n nodes in a ring before the node that originally received the write request from a

---
[1] http://aws.amazon.com/ec2

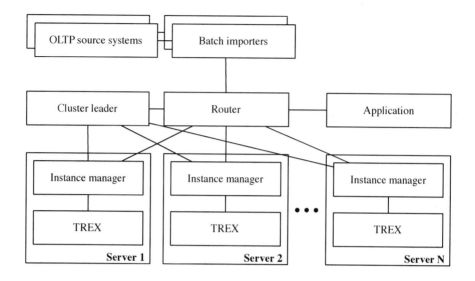

Fig. 1. The Rock Analytic Cluster Architecture

router reports the write successful. The update is then asynchronously replicated to the nodes $i + 1$ to n.

Fine-granularity writes are supported to facilitate real-time analytics, where changes to operational data are rapidly integrated into reporting. We assume writes come from a single source per tenant, such as a batch process that extracts changes from an external transactional system. This model is used, for example, by SAP BusinessObjects BI On-Demand to provide analytical services for Salesforce.com[2]. We require that writes be sequentially numbered for each tenant at the source. Rock allows a write to be applied at any replica and propagates it to the other replicas. Out-of-order writes at a server are delayed until all previous writes have been received. Read consistency, which is required to support multi-query drill down into a data set, is implemented using snapshot isolation.

2.2   TREX Database

The TREX database is an in-memory column store and as such has different characteristics than an usual row based relational database management system (RDBMS) which must be taken into consideration. In the remainder of this section we will discuss the most important particularities of TREX for our project.

Write-Optimized vs. Read-Optimized Storage. The logical database tables in TREX are physically split into a so-called main table and delta table. Since the main table is column oriented and highly optimized for read access, TREX holds a delta table to

[2] http://www.ondemand.com/solutions/salesforce/

allow fast data retrieval while concurrently updating its data set. All updates and inserts coming into TREX are collected in the delta table. When responding to a query, data in the delta table as well as the main table is accessed and the results are merged together in order to provide a consistent view of the entire data. With an increasing number of updates, the delta table reduces the read performance because of its structure and thus must be optimized in regular intervals. During this optimization the data structure of the delta is transferred into the structure of the main table and both are merged together. To avoid write locks during the merge process additional inserts and updates are written to a new delta table.

Transaction Support and Versioning. In order to support basic transactions and multi-version concurrency control (MVCC), TREX has a special type of storage engine codenamed *Newton*. This engine adds transaction IDs to individual records in a fashion similar to POSTGRES [14] to keep track of their older versions.

To increase query performance for the retrieval of the current version of the data, each Newton table is partitioned into two parts, one part for the currently valid data and another one for historical data. Each of those two parts has his own delta and main table. While a dataset is updated, all new versions are stored inside the current delta until it gets merged into the current main. During this process all outdated datasets from the current table are written to the history delta and last there, until it gets merged into the historical main separately.

Horizontal Partitioning and Parallel Query Processing. Due to the fact that TREX is limited by the amount of available main memory, it supports multiple algorithms for horizontal partitioning to split data across multiple machines, such as range partitioning, round-robin or hash partitioning. When running multiple partitions on a single host, TREX is able to use multiple CPUs to process queries in parallel against the different partitions and in a second step assembles the sub-results on the individual partitions into a result set.

3   Estimating OLAP Workload for an MCDB

Before we can build a cost model for read only workloads, we characterize the performance we want to achieve for all queries. Analogue to the performance guarantee of Amazon Dynamo [3], we define the guarantee that 99% percent of all queries shall have a sub-second response time. The query with the highest response time among 99% of all queries with the lowest response time is called the 99% *percentile value*.

The question is how much tenants with different sizes and different request rates can be consolidated onto one server while our response time goal of one second within the 99% percentile is not violated. Processing aggregation queries of larger tenants takes longer than processing queries of smaller tenants because more data needs to be scanned. Therefore, we describe the workload as a function of request rate and size for each tenant.

To get to know the maximum possible workload depending on request rate and tenant size, we conducted several tests. In these tests, we used the Star Schema Benchmark [11] to estimate the maximum possible workload. The Star Schema Benchmark is a modified version of the TPC-H benchmark [17] which has been adjusted for OLAP workloads. At the level of the data model, the most important differences between TPC-H and SSB are the following:

1. The TPC-H tables `lineitem` and `orders` are combined into one table called `lineorders`. This change transforms the TPC-H data model from 3rd Normal Form (3NF) into a star schema, which is common practice for data warehousing applications.
2. The TPC-H table `partsupp` is dropped because it contains data on the granularity of a periodic snapshot, while the `lineorder` table contains data on the finest possible granularity: the individual line items. It is sufficient to store the data on the most fine-grained level available and to obtain numbers on a more coarse granularity by aggregation.

To produce data for our tests, we use the data generator of SSB, which is based on the TPC-H data generator. We give each tenant their own private tables, thus there is one instance of the SSB data model per tenant. The fact tables vary in size from 600,000 to 6,000,000 rows across tenants and the dimension tables increase linearly with the size of the fact tables. As a point of comparison, a typical Fortune 500 enterprise produces about 120 million sales order line items per year, which is a factor of 20 greater than our largest tenant. Using TREX's standard dictionary compression, the fully-compressed data sets consume between 25 and 204 MB in main memory.

While TPC-H has 22 independent data warehousing queries, SSB has four *query flights* with three to four queries each. A query flight models a drill-down, i.e. all queries compute the same aggregate measure but use different filter criteria on the dimensions. This structure models the exploratory interactions of users with business intelligence applications. We modified SSB so all queries within a flight are performed against the same TREX transaction ID to ensure that a consistent snapshot is used. Different queries might impact the workload differently. However, we assume that the workload of each tenant would contain the same type of queries as all tenants use similar analytical services.

All tests are run on *large memory* instances on Amazon EC2, which have 2 virtual compute units (i.e. CPU cores) with 7.5 GB RAM each.

3.1 Analyzing Relation between Request Rate and Tenant Size

The workload is defined as a function which depends on the size of a tenant and its request rate. In our setup, we tested different tenant sizes with an increasing request rate. In particular, we increased the request rate until our response time goal of 1000 ms for the 99% percentile value was violated. Figure 2 shows the maximum achieved request rate per tenant for different tenant sizes which did not violate our response time goal.

The 99% percentile value was calculated for a test run lasting ten minutes and additionally averaged for three test runs with the same parameters. The landscape in each test contained several tenants of a particular tenant size so that approximately 20% of the available main memory have always been used for tenant data. All data has been preloaded into main memory before each test run and a six minute warm-up time has been performed before each run. The test data has been generated by the Star Schema Benchmark Data Generator [11].

Figure 3 shows the same graph using a logarithmic scale. This graph shows a straight line which means that the relation can be described as

$$log(f(t_{Size})) = m \cdot log(t_{Size}) + n$$

where n is $f(0)$ and m is the gradient. n and m can be calculated using the measured numbers. The gradient for this graph is $m \approx -0.945496$ and $f(0) = n \approx 3.6174113$. This equation can then be rearranged to (1).

$$t_{RequestRate} = f(t_{Size}) = (10^{log(t_{Size})})^m \cdot 10^n \tag{1}$$

$$f(t_{Size}) = t_{Size}^m \cdot 10^n \tag{2}$$

$$f(t_{Size}) = \frac{1}{t_{Size}^{-m}} \cdot 10^n \tag{3}$$

$$f(t_{Size}) = \frac{1}{t_{Size}^{0.945496}} \cdot 4143.92 \tag{4}$$

The maximum workload $w_{max}(t_{RequestRate}, t_{Size}) = 1$ can be defined as the point where the 99% percentile value reaches the response time goal of 1000 ms depending on request rate and size of a tenant. Using the formula above the maximum workload is then defined as:

$$t_{RequestRate} = \frac{1}{t_{Size}^{-m}} \cdot 10^n \tag{5}$$

$$1 = \frac{t_{RequestRate} \cdot t_{Size}^{-m}}{10^n} \tag{6}$$

$$w_{max}(t_{RequestRate}, t_{Size}) = 1 = \frac{t_{RequestRate} \cdot t_{Size}^{-m}}{10^n} \tag{7}$$

Normally, more than one tenant size occurs in a landscape and thus the workloads of different tenants have to be aggregated to a total workload. The total sum of the workload of all tenants depending on request rate and size is defined as

$$w(T) = \sum_{t \in T} \frac{t_{RequestRate} \cdot t_{Size}^{-m}}{10^n} \tag{8}$$

where $m \approx -0.945496$ and $n \approx 3.6174113$ and T is the set of all tenants.

3.2 Analyzing Relation between Read Workload and 99% Percentile Value

To analyze the relation between workload and 99% percentile value, four different landscape settings with a varying number of tenants with multiple different sizes have been tested. The 99% percentile value for each test has been calculated. The measurements have been conducted without writes with a single instance only. The number of users

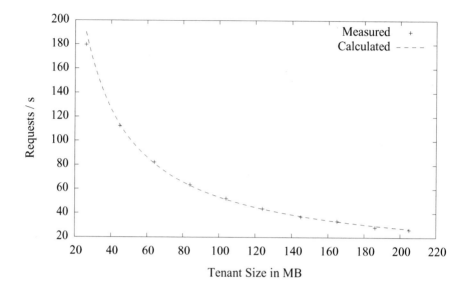

Fig. 2. Maximum Request Rate for Several Tenant Sizes

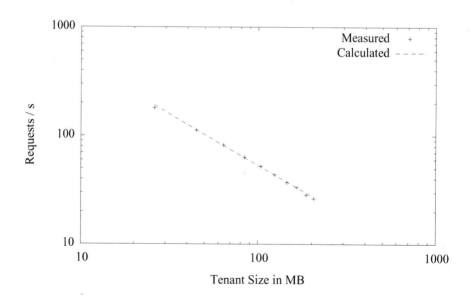

Fig. 3. Maximum Request Rate for Several Tenant Sizes (Logarithmical Scale)

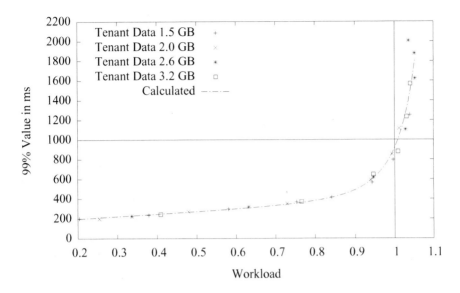

Fig. 4. Capacity of a Single Instance with Read Only Workload

has been increased for each landscape configuration. The results are shown in Figure 4. It shows the 99% percentile value for different workloads.

The workload mentioned in Figure 4 has been calculated as shown in equation (8). Up to a workload of 0.9, the graph is increasing linearly. Afterwards, it is increasing exponentially. Therefore, the graph can be described as shown in equation (9) with the parameter a, b, c, d and e.

$$f(w) = a \cdot w + b \cdot e^{c \cdot w^d} + e \tag{9}$$

Using the *Levenberg-Marquardt-Algorithm* and a start parameter $e = 200$ and $d = 7$ the parameters can be estimated to the following values: $a \approx 242.106$; $b \approx 68.9128$; $c \approx 2.15925$; $d \approx 7$; $e \approx 80.1237$. This function can now be used, to check whether the response time goal is really achieved at $w_{max} = 1$:

$$f(w_{max} = 1) = a \cdot w + b \cdot e^{c \cdot w^d} + e \tag{10}$$
$$= a + b \cdot e^c + e \tag{11}$$
$$\approx 242.106 + 68.9128 \cdot e^{2.15925} + 80.1237 \tag{12}$$
$$\approx 919.2 \tag{13}$$

Compared to the response time goal of 1000 ms, this results in a deviation of 8.7%.

In Section 3.1, we have shown that the equation of workload is valid in case of our maximum 99% percentile value. However, as can be seen in Figure 4, even for lower 99% percentile values, different landscapes with different data sizes form the same graph. Within a set of tenants which contains less data but is used with higher request rates, we can achieve the same 99% percentile value for a particular workload as with a landscape which contains more data but is used with a lower request rate. This means that our definition of workload as shown in equation (8) is also valid for other 99% percentile values than the maximum allowed value of 1000 ms.

For larger tenants, more data needs to be scanned for an OLAP query and there-fore queries for a larger tenant are causing more workload than tenants with less data. However, as shown in (8), the relation is close to but not exactly linear. Smaller tenants with the same size produce a marginally higher workload than one large tenant with the same request rate, because each single query causes overhead which is independent of the data size.

Analyzing Relation Between Read Workload and 99% Percentile Value with added Writes. No writes have been conducted in the last tests. In our use case, we assume that a batch importer inserts new rows every 5 minutes on average. For each tenant 0.05% rows of the initial size of the main fact table are added.

Adding those writes to the test results in a reduction of the highest possible read workload as shown in Figure 5.

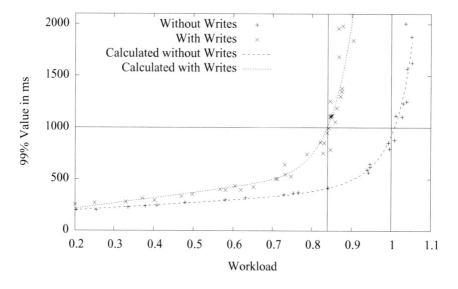

Fig. 5. Capacity of a Single Instance with Read Only Workload

The shape of the graph is similar to the graph without writes but has different param-eters $a \approx 527.712; b \approx 22174.7; c \approx 0.337272; d \approx 16; e \approx -22067.7$. The maximum possible read workload with concurrent writes is reduced to $w_{max} \approx 0.84$.

3.3 Calculating Costs

With the formula mentioned above, it is also possible to estimate the costs for one tenant in case of a maximum workload. An instance per hour with 7.5 GB memory costs 0.34 $

per hour on Amazon. This calculation does not include costs for transferring data and running a separate Router instance. Besides, the workload of an instance is also limited by the total data size. In our tests, we could only use 40% of the available RAM for data, because the same amount of data is used for additional indexes for that data. The remaining 20% are used for intermediate results, program data, and the operating system.

The cost for a tenant specified as $C(t)$ would be as shown in (14) where C_i specifies the costs per hour and $w(t)$ the utilization for a tenant.

$$C(t) = \frac{C_i}{w_{max}} \cdot w(t) \tag{14}$$

$$= \frac{C_i}{w_{max}} \frac{t_{RequestRate} \cdot t_{Size}^{-m}}{10^n} \tag{15}$$

For this calculation we assume that we can achieve an average workload of 0.8. This would mean that a tenant with 6.000.000 Rows with a compressed size of 205 MB and 50 concurrent users which conduct a query every 5 seconds would lead to monthly costs of 113.25 \$:

$$C(t) = \frac{C_i}{w_{max}} \frac{t_{RequestRate} \cdot t_{Size}^{-m}}{10^n} \tag{16}$$

$$= \frac{0.34 \cdot 24 \cdot 30}{0.8} \cdot \frac{50/5 \cdot 205^{0.945496}}{4143.92} \tag{17}$$

$$= 113.25\$/month \tag{18}$$

With our definition of read workload $w(t_{RequestRate}, t_{Size})$, we can perform capacity planning for OLAP queries and our used MCDB and decide how many tenants can be put on one instance where sub-second response times for 99% of all requests are still guaranteed. We can also estimate the 99% percentile value for a given set of tenants containing different tenant sizes and different request rates. Besides, we can estimate the costs depending on request rate and size for each tenant. Additionally, the workload function can be used to decide whether a tenant should be migrated and if there is enough space on the target instance to which the tenant should be migrated.

4   Cost/Performance Tradeoffs for High Availability

In a cloud computing environment, resources are shared between different customers, which may lead to security issues or varying access to resources, like varying I/O throughput. Further, cloud computing providers like Amazon with its Elastic Computing Cloud, in general, only guarantee the availability of the whole cloud, but not of single instances[3]. Therefore, the application provider has to implement an own strategy to ensure the availability and reliability of a service running in EC2.

Availability for databases in a cloud computing network can be achieved by either replicating data across multiple nodes or by either increasing the resilience of individual

---

[3] http://aws.amazon.com/ec2-sla/

nodes, e.g. by logging all updates to a local or remote disk. Using EC2, there are three options to store data with different security levels: in local memory, on local disk of each node, or remotely in Amazons Elastic Block Storage (EBS). Local memory is the fastest possible storage medium. However, if the process or even the complete EC2 instance (a node) fails, the data is lost. The storage is not durable. It is safer to log incoming data synchronously to a local or remote disk. Data on the local disk remains, even if the process fails, but it is still lost if a node fails. Therefore, a safer storage option is a remote storage, which provides durability even beyond the lifetime of instances. On Amazon, EBS can be used for this purpose. EBS provides highly available and reliable storage volumes, which can be attached to any running EC2 instance.

To achieve data security for local memory, the data can be distributed to local memory of k nodes to realize k-safety [6]. This implies that data has to be replicated to at least $k+1$ different nodes. Synchronous logging and synchronous replication negatively affect throughput of updates, because it takes some time to replicate data to another node or write a log to disk. Consequently, the throughput of the different storage options is evaluated. The following paragraphs aim to analyze these different storage regarding availability and reliability level, performance, and costs.

4.1 Test Setup

All tests have been executed in EC2 using *Large Instances*. Each instance, called *node*, has 7.5 GB of RAM, runs on a 64 bit Linux operation system, and has two virtual EC2 compute units. One EC2 compute unit is similar to a 1.0–1.2 GHz Opteron 2007 / Xeon CPU. Unfortunately, one does not get equivalent instances every time. Especially I/O performance might vary. To avoid this problem, only instances with the same underlying hardware (AMD Opteron 270 Processors with 2.0 GHz clock speed per core) have been used in all tests.

Depending on the storage option, updates are synchronously logged either to local disk, to Elastic Block Storage (EBS), or only stored in main memory. According to Amazon, the annual failure rate of EBS is 0.1%–0.5% (compared to 4% for normal disks). However, it is possible to create snapshots of EBS volumes and store them in S3 to achieve an even higher reliability.

TREX is used to perform the test. All updates are stored in an in-memory delta table and depending on the test setup also logged to a persistent storage, which resides on local disk or EBS. In each write, 5000 rows (132 KB CSV data) have been added to the database. This simulates an OLAP environment where updates come in large batches and in general no single updates occur.

The measurements were performed using both, single node and multiple node configurations. For each setup, all storage options (in memory, local disk and remote storage on EBS) are analyzed. In case of in-memory storage, the data is stored in main memory only. Even with local disk or EBS storage, the data is stored in main memory as well. However, additionally, all updates are logged to disk.

4.2 Comparing Throughput Using One Single Node

In the first test setup, only one node and different logging strategies were used. Each run was performed 600 times using an increasing number of concurrent client threads.

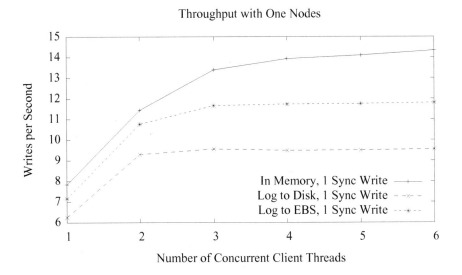

Fig. 6. Comparing Throughput of Storage Options with One Node

The data had been purged prior to each run. For every number of concurrent client threads, this was repeated five times and the average response time and throughput per number of threads was calculated. Figure 6 shows the write throughput with one node for an OLAP workload.

With an increasing number of threads, the throughput increases up to a number of four threads and, then, remains relatively constant. As can be seen, the highest throughput can be achieved by turning synchronous logging to disk completely off. However, the throughput of synchronous writes to EBS is on average only up to 15% less than the throughput, that can be achieved without logging. Surprisingly, the remotely stored EBS is even faster than the local disk. A possible explanation is the use of a Software RAID for EBS and the small size of the blocks written to disk.

In the above test, only one node was used. However, running the system with only one node cannot provide high availability, because the service will not be available in the event of a system or process failure. There is no second server, which can immediately respond to all queries in that case. The question is how long it will take to recover the system. This shall be investigated in the following.

4.3   Recovery from Log

There are different types of failures, which require different recovery processes. If the TREX process fails, it has to be restarted and the data has to be read the from log file of the local disk or EBS into main-memory again. With one node, it is not possible to recover the data using the in-memory storage option. The recovery times are shown in Table 1. The data in the preloaded table has been stored in the delta table.

Table 1. Recovery Times

	Process Failure	Instance Failure
Instance Start Up	-	6 min
EBS Attach & Mount	-	6.5 s
TREX Startup	3s or 30s	30 s
Preload Table (132 MB)	41.86 s (Disk) 41.84 s (EBS)	41.86 s (Disk) 41.84 s (EBS)

The mentioned times are averaged values of at least five runs. The TREX startup takes only approximately 3 seconds in the case that only the core engine process has failed, but needs about 30 seconds for a complete start of all components. If the complete instance fails, a new EC2 instance has to be started, which takes up to 6 minutes or a stand-by instance has to take over the workload. In both cases, the EBS volume has to be mounted at the new volume, which takes 6.5 seconds on average. Using one node only, the data can only be restored if the log file has been written to EBS.

Because of the long start up time of instances it is likely that pooled instances, which are already up and running should be used. These instances can then be used to replace failed instances. Therefore, the instance start up time can be avoided.

It is noteworthy that the recovery time is hardly affected by the used storage option. A reason for this behavior may be that TREX spends most of the time to replay the log file, whereas reading the log file from disk or EBS is comparably fast. Reading a file of 132 MB size with 5 million rows should only take a few seconds with normal disk.

Within TREX, unmerged files are stored in a separate delta table. As can be seen in Figure 7, restoring rows from a merged table without log files is significantly faster. The diagram shows the time in seconds it took to preload rows from local disk if they have

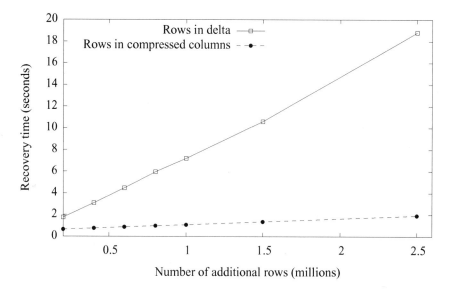

Fig. 7. Loading Times from Local Disk

been stored in a delta table or have been merged. Large delta table should therefore be avoided as they negatively impact the time needed for recovery.

TREX is already able to answer request, even if the data has not been completely preloaded into main-memory. However, it will not achieve its highest possible performance, until the data has completely been preloaded into main-memory. In the last test setup, the data could not be distributed synchronously to further nodes, because only one node was active. Therefore, a multiple number of nodes is used in the next test setup.

4.4 Comparing Throughput Using Multiple Nodes

In this test setup, two nodes were used. This time, all updates were distributed synchronously or asynchronously to the next node. As in the previous test, each run was again performed 60 times using an increasing number of concurrent client threads and the data has been purged prior to each run. This measurement was performed 10 times for each number of concurrent client threads and the response time and corresponding throughput has been averaged.

The result is shown in Figure 8. With logging to Elastic Block Storage, all writes were synchronously written to the first node and asynchronously distributed to the second node only, because synchronous logging to a second node with EBS should not longer be necessary.

With logging to local disk or without logging to a persistent disk, all writes were distributed synchronously or asynchronously to the second node. Using main memory or local disk, updates were also distributed synchronously to a second node, because they represent the unsafest storage option. Distributing updates synchronously to another node means that k=1 safety is achieved (see above).

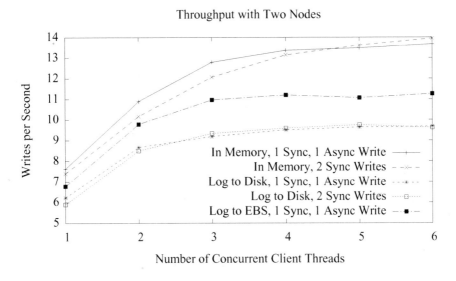

Fig. 8. Comparing Throughput of Storage Options with Two Nodes

As can be seen in Figure 8, the option without persistent logging and synchronous distribution is the fastest variant, but it is also the unsafest option. The throughput of each variant is similar to the measurement with one node in Figure 6. This is not surprising, although two nodes are available; each update has to be written to both nodes and this can be done in parallel. Another interesting point is that there is almost no difference if the data is written synchronously or asynchronously to the second node. However, this can be explained quite easily. After the data was transferred to the first instance it is sent in parallel to the next instance and inserted into TREX. Transferring the data is relatively fast, however inserting the data into TREX takes most of the time. The time of a write to be processed for one synchronous write is the sum of transferring the data to the first node and inserting it at the first node: The time of a write to be processed for two synchronous writes is the sum of transferring the data to the first node, the maximum of inserting it at the first node or the second node, and the time to transfer the data to the second node.

4.5   Evaluation

With one node, there are two possible storage variants: local disk and EBS. Storing data on local disk is not safe in case of instance failures, but can, at least, handle process failures. The Harvard Research Group defined different levels of availability [4]. Storing data on local disk with one node falls into the conventional class, which means that the service can be interrupted and that data integrity it not essential.

Storing data on EBS is safe in case of process or instance failures, but cannot guarantee high availability, since it takes some time until the service is restored and it is unavailable within that time frame. Thus, high availability cannot be achieved unless at least two nodes are in use. With two nodes, a second node can still handle the complete workload if failures on one node occur. As with one node, the reliability increases with the use of a more resilient storage medium. Using only one node, a high consistency and tolerance to network partitioning can be easily achieved, because no updates need to be propagated to further instances. With two nodes, consistency and tolerance to network partitioning depends whether updates are propagated synchronously or asynchronously. In case of synchronous propagation, consistency can be guaranteed, but this comes of course with the drawback of less tolerance to network partitioning.

There is no significant difference in the average performance of the different storage options. The highest possible throughput can be achieved with storing the data in main memory. Using two nodes with main memory storage only is 9% faster on average than storing the data on one node on EBS and 33% faster than storing the data on one node on local disk. Nevertheless, there is a major difference regarding availability level and costs of the storage variants. Using only one node costs only 0.40 $ per hour, but carries the tradeoff of a reduced availability. Using one node only makes sense if EBS is used, because it achieves a higher reliability level. Additional costs are incurred with the use of EBS volumes. 1 GB of space costs 0.10 $ per month + 0.10 $ for 1,000,000 read or wrote I/O blocks. TREX accessed 620,000 blocks while adding 5,000,000 rows with 132 MB CSV data. This would cost 0.062 $. Adding 1 GB of data to TREX would, therefore, cost approximately 0.50 $ on Amazon.

If high availability is required two nodes must be used, which doubles the costs to 0.80 $ per hour. Using only one node is the cheapest option, although it can only achieve high reliability with EBS, but not high availability. This is due to the fact that query processing will be impossible within the recovery time window in the event of process or instance failures. The use of two nodes hardly affects the measured write throughput, since all data must be written to both nodes. However, the read performance would naturally be much higher since requests can be load-balanced across two instances. Read throughput is, however, not the focus of this article and thus not discussed any further.

As mentioned above, in all test setups only instances running on AMD Opteron 2.0 GHz CPUs were used. On EC2 instances with different CPUs, which might also be provisioned from time to time, the throughput of local disk is much higher. On these instances, the performance of the local disk is consequently higher than on EBS. However, the benchmarks were only performed on the 2.0 GHz CPUs, because they happen to be started most of the time when a *Large Memory Instance* is requested. By always running on instances with the same CPU underneath it was possible to reproduce the measured results, although one should note that I/O performance varies with the type of virtual machine that is provisioned by Amazon.

5   Support for Historical Data

In a business environment there exist multiple reasons for management of historical data. The history is required for auditing purposes, as well as to monitor changes to produce more precise forecasts.

In order to enable a database to be aware of older versions of the requested data, multiple strategies exist. One well known strategy is the usage of change documents. If an entry in the database is changed, the value is updated in its original place and so called change document is written to a different location, which contains the valid value before the update occurs together with some meta information about the update. This solution minimizes the time required to retrieve the current version of the data, while it makes it much more expensive to retrieve older versions of the same dataset, because the evaluation of all change documents for a data entry since the requested version have to be evaluated and must be applied to the dataset. This makes is especially expensive to report on the data based on a specified timeframe.

To improve auditing support TREX implements an transaction ID based "insert-only" approach which makes reconstruction of old data unnecessary, as described in Section 2.2. If the data is enhanced by combining the transaction ID with a physical timestamp, it would also be possible to report on the data and to monitor the changes inside the database. The main drawback of this solution is, that the table size increases depending on the amount of updates to the database.

Using the TREX Newton engine with support for historic versions of a tuple, it is possible that the size of the tables grows beyond the capacity of a server. Therefore, techniques must be developed to ensure that historical queries would be possible with reasonable overhead for query processing and data loading from different storage layers. In order to increase throughput special declustering methods will be introduced to reduce the amount of data that has to be processed while a query is executed.

5.1   Concepts for Archiving on Top of Rock

To introduce a long-term solution for the increasing amount of data, while a history table is used, we reapplied the multi-layered storage approach proposed by Stonebraker [15]. The database automatically vacuums older versions of the data to a slower but much cheaper storage medium as more current data is added to the system. In POST-GRES this concept was based on moving records from the main disk structure to a Write Once Read Many (WORM) medium, in that time an optical disk, for archiving purposes. This archiving could then be extended with an intermediate, cheap disk layer, compared to a more expensive, high-performance disk layer for the current database.

In the case of Rock with TREX, such a multi-layer approach would have main memory as the highest, fastest layer of the system, which contains both the most up-to-date version of the data and the historical versions in memory. Local disk of the cluster nodes holds a copy of these in-memory database for the purpose of passivating unused tables to conserve main memory and to allow recovery of the main-memory database upon failure. As there is plenty of disk storage available compared to main memory, many tenants' databases and archives of old states can be held available on the individual cluster nodes' local disk storage read for usage by the engine. The lowest layer is S3 storage, being the cheapest yet slowest available storage option for long-term archiving.

Upon receiving a snapshot request, the tables for the given tenant are merged and then a snapshot is exported from the system. The resulting snapshot of the main database including the main table and history table is uploaded to S3, and a local cache of these copies can be held on multiple cluster nodes on otherwise unused transient storage space. After creating a snapshot of the database, an internal record is created in a snapshot database in the router component of the Rock framework. This record contains the S3 URL of the snapshot as well as the high water mark transaction ID of the snapshot. After snapshot creation and registration, the currently active history table in TREX is cleared to free up memory. The router keeps an updated record of which nodes in the cluster have copies of the snapshot on their local disk to load past states on a node that has unused resources at the request time.

The TREX engine itself does not provide functionality for long-term management of this historical data at the moment. The Rock framework could therefore provide a long-term storage mechanism of these historic states, which remain available for querying, on the middleware level. The high cost of main memory in the cloud relative to disk storage gives a clear motivation to archive infrequently used historical states of the database to such a lower-cost archive.

Subsequent requests to records with transaction IDs not available on active nodes automatically trigger re-activation of an old snapshot from the local disk. The database tracks the availability of snapshots in the nodes' caches and the system has to download snapshots from S3 to nodes with unused ephemeral storage capacity during times of low system activity and not during query processing. As the snapshots are then available to the database engine and TREX supports lazy loading of table data, queries to archived states can be answered, but with a performance penalty compared to full in-memory operation. A node for loading of archived tables can be selected at random, but once the required information is available within the Rock framework, this decision is based on the memory usage and load situation on the nodes in order to optimize response time and overall cluster load.

5.2 Test Setup

When working with archives there are two main performance questions related to the TREX engine that need to be answered. First, how fast can a previous state be queried compared to querying the main state, when the table containing the historical data is completely in main memory? This is the case when working with the most recent version that is not loaded from a snapshot, or when submitting subsequent queries to a snapshot that has been completely loaded. Second, how fast can a snapshot from disk be loaded into main-memory by the engine, which is the case when accessing a snapshot from the local disk-cache. This defines how quickly answers to queries to unloaded snapshots can be generated compared to active tables, which are already in memory. The performance of S3 is only relevant, when the cache is not fresh and no node with a cached snapshot is available. S3 performance varies greatly and is limited to the maximum network bandwidth, and therefore the caching mechanism should prevent prevalent use of this transfer method, with most transfers from S3 being conducted in the background during normal operations, when loading the local disk cache.

Querying Historical States on Completely-Loaded Tables. To evaluate the performance of queries against past states, a test was conducted. An empty table is created and the transaction ID is initialized with 1. It is then populated with five million rows, loaded in batches of one million rows. Each of these batches creates a new transaction ID, which can be queried. After the initial load, 100,000 records are updated in each iteration, which are written to the delta table as described in Section 2.2. After each write

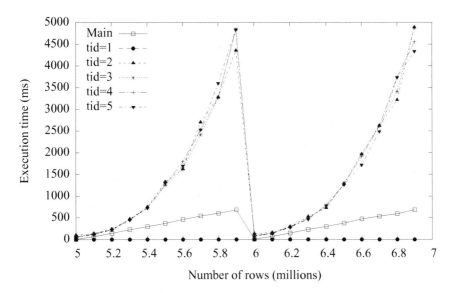

Fig. 9. Response Times for History Table Access

ten aggregation queries are run on the entire table, which are conducted for the current version and each of the five first transaction IDs of the database in order to query against historical versions of the data. The query response times are averaged and graphed, as seen in Figure 9. After ten iterations, the table is merged, which results in a sharp drop in query response times, and the above procedure is repeated.

Figure 9 shows the response times resulting from the test, with different series indicating access to different previous states in the database and the x-axis showing the number of records in the table at the time of querying, which increases as the test writes more data to the table. As more rows are added to the table the delta table is filled with the updated data and requests to the current state of the database show a linear response time increase, from an initial 10 ms for aggregation the 5 million rows on the merged initial state to 675 ms after 900,000 updates. When querying for historical states, the query times rise much faster. The response time rises apparently exponentially for historic queries from a low of about 50 ms reaching up to 4.75 seconds of response time for historical queries on 5,9 million rows. After the merge has been performed, the response times drop again to almost the initial level. Concluding one can say, that querying for historical data which still resides in the delta table, takes much longer than querying for historical data in the historical table.

The initial query ranges from 50ms for queries to historic transaction ID 5 to 100 ms for queries for historic transaction ID 2. Transaction ID 1 is the initial, empty database state, which always shows the same response time of close to 0 as no data is to be aggregated. This supports the general assumption that querying for earlier states in the timeline requires access to more data and therefore yields higher response times even on the merged historical table, which yields the highest performance since the delta table is not used.

Performance of Lazy Loading from Disk. The second key performance characteristics is the required time to make data available from disk which are not yet loaded into memory. Because of its column-based data structure, TREX is able to load attributes, that are required for query processing separately instead of loading the whole table with all its attributes at once.

To determine, how long it would take to read the attributes of a table into memory we used TREX preload feature, which loads the requested attributes of a table without executing an actual query. If the preload is not used, the preload time has to be added to the query execution time. In our test we loaded different attributes from disk and compared the required time with the time, the hard disk needs to send the data to the CPU, as shown in Figure 10.

Loading Newton Tables from disk takes two times longer, than the actual disk speed allows it to read data. If the attributes contain optimizations like indexes, loading is 7 times slower. As future work we will thus address two possible optimizations: on the one hand, TREX could be enhanced to store indexes along with the data structures on the hard disk. On the other hand, the data could be partitioned as described in Section 2.2 and a parallel preload algorithm could be implemented. This would shorten the recovery time since optimizations such as index creation or partitioning would have been already applied to the stored data and multiple processors or servers could be used for the preload. Early results indicate that preloading could indeed be sped up by the

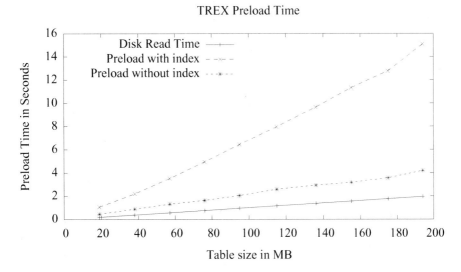

Fig. 10. Preload Time in Seconds

Table 2. Parallel Preloading with Two Partitions

	Non-Parallel	Parallel	Non-Parallel w/ Indexes	Parallel w/ Indexes
Data size (MB)	175	175	207	207
HDD Loading Time (s)	1.77	1.89	2.17	2.32
Preload Time (s)	3.57	3.24	12.77	8.62
HDD Time / Preload Time	2.01	1.71	5.88	3.71

use of declustering. These results are shown in Table 2. If the data is partitioned into two parts, the preload process with creating indexes is 1.4 times faster on a server with two CPU cores.

Costs of Horizontal Partitioning. While the benefit of parallel preloading is clear for loading tables, one would assume that the overall query throughput decreases when having multiple partitions of a small tenant on a server which also hosts other active tenants. The reasoning behind is that the intermediate results of the partitions must be reassembled which incurs additional computing overhead for small partitions.

To measure the cost of having multiple partitions for a single table we constructed the following test: tables of different sizes are split into multiple parts, while TREX is configured to use only one CPU core at a time to process the query. During this test, different sizes of the earlier mentioned SSB data set are used as well as the corresponding queries. Because TREX needs to scan and search the data of the different parts sequentially, the increase in response time with an increasing number of parts shows the cost of merging the intermediate results of the individual partitions. As can be seen in Figure 11, the costs of merging results of multiple partitions increase linear with

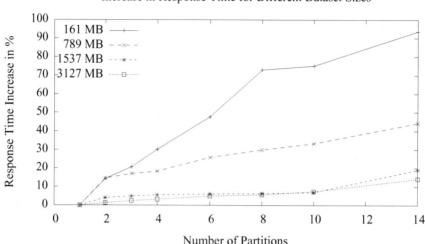

Fig. 11. Response Time Increase in Percent for Sequential Processing of Multiple Partitions

Table 3. Increasing Throughput Using Declustering

	1 Partition	2 Partitions
Concurrently active users	169	176
Max. response time in 99-th % percentile	819 ms	937 ms
Max. response time in 75-th % percentile	325 ms	402 ms

increasing number of partitions. It can also be seen that the overhead is larger for smaller tables than for large ones.

While answering queries against multiple partitions on a server becomes slower when partitions are scanned sequentially, the response times decrease if multiple cores are used for query processing. To ensure that the overall throughput is not decreased, multiple partitioning methods were benchmarked with the test described earlier in Section 3 and the throughput was measured. Each partition contained at least 2.5 million rows and no table was split into more parts than the number of available CPUs on the server. The test was run on a single EC2 large memory instance, with two 2.6GHz CPU cores and 7.5 GByte of RAM. The initial results shown in Table 3 suggest that the throughput can even be increased when using declustering without violating the maximum response time of 1 seconds in the 99% percentile.

6 Related Work

In this section, we report on related work for our three covered topics: capacity planning and workload models, highly available shared nothing architectures and temporal databases and historic queries.

6.1 Capacity Planning and Workload Models

There are different methods to model a workload: analytic modeling using queuing network models, simulation, or benchmarking [2]. Queueing network modeling is a approach where a computer systems is represented by a network of queues which is evaluated analytically [7]. In [20], Zawawy et al. developed a queueing network model for DB2 which can be used to carry out capacity planning studies for this database.

Another approach is to conduct simulations. [13] presents *CloudSim* which simulates the infrastructure of a cloud computing environment to quantify the performance of resource allocation policies and application scheduling algorithms.

In our case, benchmarking was a sufficient approach for building up a workload model. It made us able to create a cost model on top and to estimate the performance of one instance under several conditions. Our goal was to create a workload model which makes it possible to estimate the workload to find out whether another tenant can be served by a particular instance. This can be achieved by the presented model for the used set of queries.

Simulations instead of real benchmarks are normally be conducted to save costs. However, performing a benchmark on a single instance in a computing cloud is not very expensive anymore. More complex models like Queuing Network Models would give a deeper insight into the behavior of the system but require an analyzation of the steps taken by the database to process a query. This would be a very time consuming process and not necessary for estimating the maximum capacity of a single instance. If the implementation changes, the whole model might not be valid any longer. In our case, we would only have to redo the benchmarks and adjust the parameters accordingly.

In our benchmarks we continuously executed queries of different classes of the TPC-H benchmark. We did not focus or analyze the different workloads for different queries. We assumed that the workload of each tenant would contain the same type of queries as all tenants use similar analytical services. In case of more heterogenous workloads of different tenants, another possibility would be to categorize queries regarding their workload which has been done in [19].

6.2 Highly Available Shared Nothing Architectures

According to the CAP theorem [1], consistency, availability and tolerance to network partitions cannot be achieved at the same time. If updates are distributed asynchronously to multiple instances, other instances may not reply with the last updated value, because it may not have been distributed to all instances. This will not occur in case of synchronous distribution. Tolerance to network partitions means that the system can tolerate a drop of all messages and still be available. With synchronous distribution of updates this will not be possible anymore, because a write will not be committed if other nodes are not reachable anymore.

Consistency as a part of ACID [5] transactions is more important for OLTP workloads and less for OLAP workloads. In contrast to OLTP, OLAP workloads are query intensive and use mostly ad hoc, complex queries with large numbers of aggregates, but require less updates. [18] describes a tradeoff between high availability and data consistency and explains a compromise, the eventual consistency. It is a specific form of weak consistency, in which if in a specific amount of time no updates are applied to an object, all accesses will eventually return the last updated value. An example for such a system is the Domain Name System (DNS).

The storage options evaluated in Section 4 do also have different levels of availability, consistency and tolerance to network partitions and have been evaluated accordingly.

6.3   Temporal Databases and Historical Queries

A "time-travel" feature was mentioned in a description of the POSTGRES database management system [16]. Previous states of the database can be accessed by adding a time-stamp or range to the query and the engine will only consider records valid at the stated time. By implementing a new storage mechanism that retains old record versions upon updates, the two goals of multi version concurrency control and time-travel could be implemented at once. Actually, time travel in POSTGRES was mainly implemented for isolation rather than for historical queries, and many researchers conducted their research in the extension of databases to support valid-time.

In the description of the POSTGRES storage system [14] a new type of database storage was first introduced that retains old record versions in the database and merely adds new records. The store for the record enriches them with timestamps to form a transaction time validity range. Alternatively, the storage engine could add a transaction ID to the records and keep a separate mapping of transaction IDs to transaction times, which was the preferred mode of operation when time-travel queries were infrequently executed.

By keeping multiple versions of a record in a database it becomes possible to use multi-version concurrency schemes [9]. As updates to the database are conducted by means of inserting new records with a new transaction time, readers can be effectively isolated by operating only on a transaction time-span that is known to be committed.

The POSTGRES storage system also provided a vacuuming component that either deletes or moves old records to a write-once archive store. In [15], the notion of a disk-based store vacuumed to an archive medium is advanced to having multiple levels of storage characterized by decreasing cost and performance, with the highest level of main memory, which yields highest performance at the highest price.

7   Conclusion

In this paper, we made the case for a cloud-based infrastructure providing multi-tenant analytics on top of an in-memory column database. The developed workload and cost model makes us able to estimate the capacity of one instance and to calculate the costs for one tenant depending on its request rate and size. In future work, we will analyze how we can react to an unbalanced landscape by migrating tenants to other instances and how we can react to a varying request rate. The developed workload model gives us the opportunity to calculate in advance onto which instance a tenant would best be moved before migration is actually executed.

Tradeoffs between cost and performance of different storage options and replication to make system highly available have also been discussed. In summary, one can say that there is no huge difference in the performance of the different storage options. However, there is a remarkable difference of the achievable availability and reliability levels and the incurred costs. The safest option is also the most expensive one: using EBS with two replicas. Storing data on a remote file system is of particular interest in clouds like EC2, where the data on local disk is lost in case of instance failures.

We have also argued that main-memory based systems, which are more prevalently used for analytical workloads today, need a mechanism to archive infrequently used, historical data to cheaper storage facilities, while retaining the system's ability to query against these historical states. We showed that using a snapshot archiving mechanism built on top of the Rock framework, this goal could be achieved with an acceptable query time penalty for accessing old states. By adding a mapping between transaction time and transaction IDs, queries against historical states could be made based on the transaction times of the old records. We extended the framework to store the relevant metadata along with the snapshots, in order to automatically retrieve them upon query time. When analyzing the performance behavior of the system, we observed the expected particularities of a column database, where the delta table drives the query cost with increasing number of rows, as this write-optimized store is more expensive at query time than the main table. Therefore, merging is strongly advised before making multiple historical queries. Generally, the performance exhibited is such, that querying for historical states is a factor 3–5 slower than querying the main state of the database, when all data is kept in memory. The benefits of transaction isolation, a consistent view on past states and the generally fast response time of the TREX database make the solution a cost-effective option for long-term availability of analytical data. It was shown, that parallel data loading not just reduces the time required for lazy-loading of the data stored on disk, but also increases the overall throughput of the system, if the partitions have a reasonable size.

Many challenges must be addressed when multi-tenant analytics on top an in-memory column database have to be provided. In this paper, we addressed some of the most important issues which are necessary to provide such a service within a defined service level agreement.

References

1. Brewer, E.A.: Towards robust distributed systems (abstract). In: Neiger [10], p. 7
2. Carper, I.L., Harvey, S., Wetherbe, J.C.: Computer capacity planning: strategy and methodologies. SIGMIS Database 14(4), 3–13 (1983)
3. DeCandia, G., Hastorun, D., Jampani, M., Kakulapati, G., Lakshman, A., Pilchin, A., Sivasubramanian, S., Vosshall, P., Vogels, W.: Dynamo: amazon's highly available key-value store. In: SOSP 2007: Proceedings of Twenty-First ACM SIGOPS Symposium on Operating Systems Principles, pp. 205–220. ACM, New York (2007)
4. Glorioso, R.M., Desautels, R.E.: Disaster recovery or disaster tolerance: The choice is yours
5. Härder, T., Reuter, A.: Principles of transaction-oriented database recovery. ACM Comput. Surv. 15(4), 287–317 (1983)
6. Lau, E., Madden, S.: An integrated approach to recovery and high availability in an updatable, distributed data warehouse. In: Dayal, U., Whang, K.-Y., Lomet, D.B., Alonso, G., Lohman, G.M., Kersten, M.L., Cha, S.K., Kim, Y.-K. (eds.) VLDB, pp. 703–714. ACM, New York (2006)

7. Lazowska, E.D., Zahorjan, J., Graham, G.S., Sevcik, K.C.: Quantitative system performance: computer system analysis using queueing network models. Prentice-Hall, Inc., Upper Saddle River (1984)
8. Legler, T., Lehner, W., Ross, A.: Data Mining with the SAP Netweaver BI Accelerator. In: VLDB, pp. 1059–1068 (2006)
9. Majumdar, D.: A Quick Survey of MultiVersion Concurrency Algorithms (2006)
10. Neiger, G. (ed.): Proceedings of the Nineteenth Annual ACM Symposium on Principles of Distributed Computing, Portland, Oregon, USA, July 16-19. ACM, New York (2000)
11. O'Neil, P.E., O'Neil, E.J., Chen, X.: The Star Schema Benchmark, SSB (2007), http://www.cs.umb.edu/~poneil/StarSchemaB.PDF
12. Plattner, H.: A common database approach for oltp and olap using an in-memory column database. In: SIGMOD 2009: Proceedings of the 35th SIGMOD International Conference on Management of Data, pp. 1–2. ACM, New York (2009)
13. Buyya, R.R., Ranjan, R., Calheiros, R.N.: Modeling and simulation of scalable cloud computing environments and the cloudsim toolkit: Challenges and opportunities. In: Proc. of the 7th High Performance Computing and Simulation (HPCS 2009), p. 11 (2009)
14. Stonebraker, M.: The design of the Postgres storage system. In: Readings in Object-Oriented Database Systems, p. 286 (1989)
15. Stonebraker, M.: Managing persistent objects in a multi-level store. ACM SIGMOD Record 20(2), 2–11 (1991)
16. Stonebraker, M., Kemnitz, G.: The POSTGRES next generation database management system (1991)
17. TPC-H, http://www.tpc.org/tpch/
18. Vogels, W.: Eventually consistent. Commun. ACM 52(1), 40–44 (2009)
19. Wasserman, T.J., Martin, P., Skillicorn, D.B., Rizvi, H.: Developing a characterization of business intelligence workloads for sizing new database systems. In: DOLAP 2004: Proceedings of the 7th ACM International Workshop on Data Warehousing and OLAP, pp. 7–13. ACM, New York (2004)
20. Zawawy, H., Martin, P., Hassanein, H.: Supporting capacity planning for db2 udb. In: CASCON 2002: Proceedings of the 2002 Conference of the Centre for Advanced Studies on Collaborative Research, p. 15. IBM Press (2002)

At the Frontiers of Information and Software as Services*

K. Selçuk Candan[1], Wen-Syan Li[2], Thomas Phan[3], and Minqi Zhou[4]

[1] Arizona State University, Tempe, AZ, USA
candan@asu.edu
[2] SAP, Shanghai, China
wen-syan.li@sap.com
[3] Microsoft Corporation, USA
thomphan@microsoft.com
[4] Fudan University, Shanghai, China
zhouminqi@fudan.edu.cn

Abstract. The high cost of creating and maintaining software and hardware infrastructures for delivering services to businesses has led to a notable trend toward the use of third-party service providers, which rent out network presence, computation power, and data storage space to clients with infrastructural needs. These third party service providers can act as data stores as well as entire software suites for improved availability and system scalability, reducing small and medium businesses' burden of managing complex infrastructures. This is called information/application outsourcing or software as a service (SaaS). Emergence of enabling technologies, such as service oriented architectures (SOA), virtual machines, and cloud computing, contribute to this trend. Scientific Grid computing, on-line software services, and business service networks are typical examples leveraging database and software as service paradigm. In this paper, we survey the technologies used to enable SaaS paradigm as well as the current offerings on the market. We also outline research directions in the field.

1 Introduction

The high cost of creating and maintaining software and hardware infrastructures for delivering services to businesses has led to a notable trend toward the use of third-party services which provide network presence, computation power, and data storage space to clients with infrastructural needs. These third party services can act as data stores as well as entire software suites for improved availability and system scalability, thereby reducing businesses' burden of managing complex infrastructures. This provisioning is called information/application outsourcing or software as a service (SaaS).

---

* Authors are listed in alphabetical order. This is a revised and extended version of the theme paper for the first IEEE Workshop on Information and Software as Services: K. Selçuk Candan, Wen-Syan Li, Thomas Phan, and Minqi Zhou. "Frontiers in Information and Software as Services."First IEEE Workshop on Information and Software as Services, pp. 1761-1768, Shanghai, China, 2009.

D. Agrawal et al. (Eds.): Information and Software as Services, LNBIP 74, pp. 283–300, 2011.

Many companies, government agencies, and other institutions of all sizes are turning to SaaS for their key business computing needs, such as sale force automation, customer relationship management, accounting, human resources, video conferencing, email management and so on. SaaS applications offer important benefits, such as rapid deployment, instant scalability, and low cost, leveraging:

- the Web-native property of SaaS offerings, whose interfaces can be tailored for Web browsers, and
- the one-to-many form of architecture adhered to by SaaS' for application delivery; managed in a centralized manner, SaaS reduces software management costs, potentially resulting in large capital savings for the SaaS clients.

IDC, a global provider of market intelligence for the information technology sector, estimates that the worldwide revenue associated with SaaS reached $3.98 billion in 2006 and that it will reach $14.5 billion in 2011, representing a compound annual growth rate of 30% [1]. In a 2007 study by Forrester [2], 16% of respondents indicated that they were either "already using" or "currently piloting" SaaS, up from only 12% of respondents in 2006. This represents 33% growth in a year. While "interested" or "planning to pilot" responses remained the same at 46%, "not at all interested" responses declined from 41% to 37%. Another report [3], again by Forrester, indicated that most deployments of SaaS-based solutions are currently for human resources, collaboration, and customer relationship management (CRM) applications.

As an example of SaaS provisioning and the types of research issues involved, consider a software service that must host database-driven applications in a cost-efficient manner. In order to host such applications as SaaS offerings, providers commonly deploy multi-tenancy strategies, where one instance of the application is shared by many businesses (i.e. tenants). Multi-tenancy, a natural extension of hosting applications in a single-tenant configuration with a dedicated physical server or virtual machine, helps save not only capital expenditures, such as for hardware, software, and data center networking, but also operational expenditures, such as costs for people and power. However, multi-tenancy does incur higher costs software development and deployment due to the complexity of enabling service level agreements (SLA) [4] in multi-tenant environments. Therefore, the choice between hosting applications in a traditional single-tenant configuration with a dedicated physical server or virtual machine and the alternative of using a multi-tenant configuration depends on the tradeoffs between the benefits and overheads of the multi-tenant environments. Note that a hosted database application usually has two layers: an application layer running on web and application servers and a database layer running the database management system. Multi-tenancy invariably occurs at the database layer of a service; indeed, in many deployments, this layer may be the only place it occurs since application servers for highly-scalable Web applications are often already stateless [5] (i.e., each request is considered independently from all other before or concurrent with it) and do not benefit from multi-tenancy.

These types of tradeoffs between performance, scalability, and reliability are at the core of current research and development in SaaS. Our goal in this paper is to provide an overview of the state-of-the-art in critical technologies, such as multi-tenancy, that enable design and deployment of SaaS environments capable of delivering business applications and workflows as services. The rest of this paper is organized in the following manner. In Section 2, we present an overview of the SaaS types. In Section 3, we provide an overview of technologies available for describing business logic to support SaaS deployments. Section 4 discusses application servers and virtual machines technologies available for efficient SaaS implementations. In Section 5, we describe the multi-tenant database technologies critical for applications that are data-driven. In Section 6, we describe emerging data cloud technologies that are being used for large scale data management in SaaS context. We finish this paper by providing an overview of research challenges in Section 7.

2   SLAs, SaaS Types, and Current Offerings

Due to the significant demand from businesses and other institutions, Software as a Service (SaaS) technology is an important contemporary research and development topic. Pursued by many companies, SaaS has been enhanced since the late 1990s when initial SaaS offerings were made available to businesses. The key challenge in SaaS architecture development is to design a system that can reliably support service level agreements.

A service level agreement (SLA) is a contract written between a SaaS provider and the service customers. These customers may be third-parties or may belong to the same business entity as the provider, as is sometimes the case for large-scale software organizations with separately-managed teams [6]. SLAs are needed to define what the service provider is selling to the customer and what the expectations of the customer should be. The SLA is commonly a document detailing the expectations between the provider and customer, and in the context of server-side SaaS provisioning, the SLA may cover the performance of the service, its availability, the penalties for service failure, and the entity responsible for taking measurements [4]. SLAs are a common practice in current online service provisioning. For example, Amazon.com's SLA commitment is a 99.9% availability for its S3 storage service [7] and a 99.95% availability for its Elastic Compute Cloud service [8]. In addition to service availability, the SLA's language may define the minimum, maximum, and average response time to complete a transaction from the point of view of the customer as well as the turnaround time of the provider to fix critical and non-critical failures. The penalties included in the SLA may include reductions in service fee that the customer may need to pay. Therefore, to be practical in real-world scenarios, SaaS architectures have to be designed to provide not only scalability in the presence of variations in load and/or resource availabilities but also robustness against system failures.

According to Microsoft MSDN [9], SaaS architectures can be classified into four maturity levels in terms of their deployment customization, configurability, multi-tenant efficiency, and scalability, attributes. Each level is distinguished from the previous one by the addition of one of those three attributes.

2.1   Level 1: Ad-Hoc/Custom

At the first level of maturity, each customer has its own customized version of the hosted application and runs its own instance of the application on the host's servers. Migrating a traditional non-networked or client-server application to this level of SaaS typically requires the least development effort and reduces operating costs simply by consolidating server hardware deployment and administration.

2.2   Level 2: Configurable

The second maturity level provides greater program flexibility through configurable metadata, so that many customers can use separate instances of the same application code. This approach allows the vendor to meet the different needs of each customer through detailed configuration options, while simplifying maintenance of the common code base.

2.3   Level 3: Configurable, Multi-tenant-Efficient

The third maturity level adds multi-tenancy to the second level, so that a single program instance serves multiple customers. This approach enables potentially more efficient use of server resources without any apparent difference to the end user.

2.4   Level 4: Scalable, Configurable, Multi-tenant-Efficient

At the fourth and so far final SaaS maturity level, explicit scalability features are added through a multi-tier architecture supporting a load-balanced farm of identical application instances, running on a variable number of servers. The system's capacity can be increased or decreased to match demand by adding or removing servers, without the need for any further alteration of application software architecture. This fourth level of SaaS could be further categorized into three phases: infrastructure as a service (IaaS), platform as a service (PaaS), and software as a service (SaaS) [10,11].

- *Infrastructure as a Service (IaaS):* This phase provides traditional computing resources, such as servers, storage, and other forms of low level network and hardware resources in a virtual, on demand fashion. In a general sense, IaaS provides the ability to acquire resources in specific configurations at will and delivers value similar to what one might find in a traditional data center. Storage services, such as Amazon's S3 [12], Microsoft's SSDS [13], Mosso's CloudFS [14], and computation services, such as Amazon's EC2 [15] and GoGrid [16], are examples of IaaS offerings.
- *Platform as a Service (PaaS):* These provide runtime-systems and application frameworks that present themselves as execution environments and computing platforms with the sole purpose of acting as host to clients' application software. PaaS focuses on enabling SaaS applications; thus, many core issues, such as multi-tenancy need to be resolved for PaaS offerings. Appenda's SaaSGrid [17] and Google's AppEngine [18] provide PaaS.
- *Software as a Service (SaaS):* Unlike IaaS and PaaS, SaaS offerings providing specialized functionalities to augment of replace existing business software components. Salesforce's customer relationship managment (CRM) [19] SaaS deployment is a prominent example in the sphere.

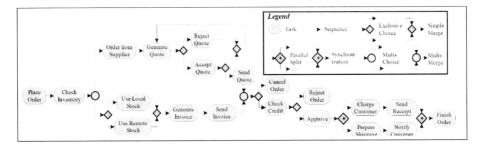

Fig. 1. A workflow example: online order fullfilment [20]

With the emergence of the *cloud computing* paradigm and rich workflow languages and platforms, SaaS extends its scalability features by inheriting the distributed and network-wide nature of cloud computing and starts to step out of this fourth level into new directions.

3   Modeling and Describing Business Logic

Workflow languages provide platforms through which enterprises can roll out new integrated services efficiently and effectively [21]. IBM's XML-based Web Services Flow Language (WSFL [22]), Microsoft's XLANG [22], the Business Process Execution Language for Web Services (BPEL4WS [23]), and the Workflow Management Coalition's (WfMC) XML Process Definition Language (XPDL [24]) all provide mechanisms for orchestrating services into an end-to-end enterprise application. A business workflow, described by a workflow language or through a visual diagram (an UML activity diagram [25] or a visual process notation standard, such as OMG's BPMN [26]) describe how to assemble separate business activities, each implemented through a different service, into a complete business process. For example, Figure 1 shows an example online order fulfillment workflow. Given a service request, each web service generates response messages based on the underlying business activity logic. The interface between the request and response of a service is usually provided using a web service definition language (WSDL). The workflow language relies on these interfaces to declare how to orchestrate a complex business application. This declarative description (as opposed to integration through software code) of the business process model enables platform independence as well as ease of adaptation and evolution of the business logic as business needs and systems change. Workflow patterns [27] help abstract commonly recurring business activity flows and thus help reduce the costs of developing and deploying new enterprise applications.

A business workflow described using a workflow language, such as WSFL, can be executed by a workflow engine leveraging Web Services as remote procedure calls endpoints or deployed in the form of a Java code to be executed within an application server. A particular challenge in the service oriented architecture (SOA) space is the amount and diversity of the workflow languages, standards, and engines. In fact, while it is commonly agreed that workflows are essential for business process modeling, re-engineering, and automation, there is little agreement about what a business workflow is and which of the many possible features a given workflow management system must provide. The various workflow languages and standards have different foci and choosing one among the many is not a trivial task. For example, while BPEL focuses on the description of interactions between web services and the control and data flow between services, WfMC's XPDL instead focuses on the exchange of business diagrams and leaves the execution to XPDL-compliant business process management (BPM) software. From a theoretical perspective, workflows can be considered from control-, data-, or resource- perspectives [28]. From the control-perspective, the various business tasks and activities are connected through control links that describe how the work flows as the individual activities complete. In the data control perspective, the data movements between individual business activities are declared through data links. The resource perspective of workflows associates human and hardware roles for executing individual workflow tasks; for example, in WSFL and BPEL4WS, each business activity is associated with a service provider that implements the corresponding web service.

Most workflow languages support sequences, iterations, AND and XOR splits/joins. A sequence is a set of business activities to be completed one at a time, in the given order. Iterations describe sequences that are repeated until the corresponding stop conditions are satisfied. Splits describe forking of control sequences into multiple paths: an AND split forks multiple paths all of which are simultaneously followed, whereas an XOR split allows only one of the outgoing paths to be followed at a given execution instance. Joins involve merging of multiple control-flows into a single control flow. An AND join requires synchronization in that all incoming flows need to completed before the workflow can proceed, while an XOR join processed as soon as one of the incoming control flows is completed. For example, BPEL (an XML based language developed in a collaboration between IBM, BEA Systems, Microsoft, SAP, and Siebel Systems) follows the basic structure of IBM's WSFL in leveraging web services and WSDL as the main messaging mechanism. Workflows are described in a hierarchical fashion, using sequence, if-then-else, while, and (parallel) flow constructs that combine individual service and sub-workflows into increasingly complex structures. While there is no standard graphical visualization of BPEL, the Business Process Modeling Language (BPML) or UML activity diagrams are commonly used as graphical notations to describe BPEL workflows.

There are many possible formalisms to formally describe a workflow (including various event algebra [29] and calculi [30] and state automata [31]). In particular, Petri nets [32] provide a reasonably expressive representation and modeling formalism to capture the most significant requirements of control flow [33]. In its simplest form, a Petri net is a bipartite, directed graph which consists of places, transitions, and arcs between places and transitions (Figure 2). Each transition has a number of input places and a number of output places. The places hold tokens and the distribution of the tokens is referred to as the marking of the Petri net. A transition is enabled when each of its input places contains at least one token. When a transition fires, it eliminates a number of tokens from its input places and puts a number of tokens to its output places. This way, the markings of the Petri net evolve over time. More formally, a Petri net can be represented as a 5-tuple (S, T, F, M_0, W), where S denotes the set of places, T denotes the transitions, and F is the set of arcs between the places and transitions.

M_0 is the initial marking (i.e., the initial state) of the system. W is the arc weights which describes how many tokens are consumed and created when the transitions fire. Petri nets allow analysis of the various properties of the system, including reachability (i.e., whether a particular marking can be reached or not), safety/boundedness (i.e., whether the places may contain too many tokens or ever reach a situation where no transition is enabled). Higher-level Petri nets also include extensions for data communication [34] and time [35,36], providing both computational completeness and relative ease of description. YAWL (Yet another Workflow Language [28]) extends Petri nets with additional constructs to allow (a) multiple instances of a task, where the number of necessary instances are determined only at the runtime based on the current context, (b) advanced synchronizations, including an OR-join, where the number of incoming workflows that need to be synchronized is determined by the number of flows that were forked earlier in the workflow, and (c) cancellation patterns, which allow for the removal of tokens from multiple places in the case of interruption of the workflows. Moreover, YAWL allows for composite and timed tasks, and as such, it is more expressive than Petri nets and other popular business workflow standards, including XPDL and BPEL4WS.

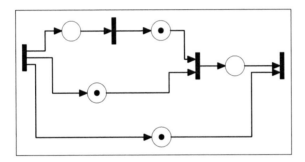

Fig. 2. A Petri net example: each circles correspond to a place (a service or a process) and each marking corresponds to a token (denoting current activity)

4   Application Servers and Virtual Machines

Application servers fill a key role in the multi-tier server-side infrastructure in which business applications and workflows are delivered: the application server contains and executes the business logic of the provisioned application and should do so in a scalable and responsive manner. In the context of a web application, an application server commonly sits between a presentation tier that formats and delivers the HTML and a database tier that stores and retrieves business and customer data. From a deployment perspective, the term application server may refer to both the software, the hardware on which the application server is running, or a virtual machine that contains it.

The business logic run at the application server drives the application and performs any necessary computing. Consider the role of such logic in an on-line commerce website. While a lower database tier may contain the data on product availability pricing, it is the responsibility of the business logic to authenticate the end user and then determine what products to show and what rules to follow as the user proceeds to purchase a product. This logic determines what is shown by the presentation layer through the Web interface.

Many commercial and open source application server products are available. Microsoft's .NET Framework [37] provides a variety of software components such as ASP.NET and Internet Information Services that allow engineers to develop in several languages that execute on the Microsoft Common Language Runtime [38]. On the Java platform, Java Enterprise JavaBeans execute business logic in Web containers and are presented through Java Server Pages and Servlets [39]. Java application server products include BEA's WebLogic Server [40], IBM's WebSphere [41], and Apache's Tomcat [42].

Since the application server must execute critical business logic, its performance is important. A common approach to attain better response time for each customer invocation is to keep the application server stateless [43], a strategy similarly taken by the stateless HTTP protocol. No information regarding a customer's current engagement with the application is maintained at the application server. Instead, small tokens for user identification or transaction record can be kept through the use of HTTP cookies that are sent as part of every HTTP invocation between the customer through the web server to the application. Larger long-lived data, such as a customer's purchase history or delivery address, can be maintained at the database tier. By keeping such state out of the application server, per-invocation response time can be reduced since the application server can tightly execute business logic instead of additionally maintaining data and its associated management issues, such as caching and consistency.

An additional approach to improving performance is to scale the application server outwards across a cluster or rack of physical machines, where invocations for the application server are directed across the machines through the direction of a load-balancing router [44]. Requests can be routed to an appropriate physical machine by inspecting application-layer cookies or IP-layer addresses. While supporting an application server across a cluster of physical machines reduces response latency by having underloaded machines execute the application server, it also increases underutilization: over-provisioning by having too many machines in the cluster or rack is wasteful of money, electricity, and needed maintenance. An increasingly popular alternative is to run these application servers in separate virtual machines that provide an isolated execution environment. Each virtual machine can be configured with different operating systems and support libraries that best fit the needs of the provisioned application. For example, a physical server can run Microsoft Windows Server and IIS in one virtual machine as well as Linux and Apache in another virtual machine. Furthermore, because a virtual machine's execution state (which includes its entire hardware and software) is serialized to disk, the virtual machine can be moved across physical machines to help improve load-balancing. The use of a virtual machine also improves fault isolation between applications while increasing server utilization and reducing the number of needed physical servers. However, execution within a virtualized environment has a performance cost; in [45] results showed an 8% to 25% decrease in request throughput compared to running multiple application servers without a virtualized environment.

5   Multi-tenant Data Management

As described earlier, the application layer is often stateless and can be scaled up by providing additional hardware. On the other hand, the data layer requires further care because different applications may share the same database and/or DBMS resources; in such cases, providing SLAs for isolation, security, and performance may require the use of multi-tenant database systems. There are three major approaches [46] to multi-tenant DBMS design:

- *Tagging:* In tagging, the host adds one extra attribute to each table to represent ownership of each row and then share tables among tenants. Tagging thus requires that applications modify their queries to add one ownership-checking condition to each table access query statement. This approach thus is suitable only for scenarios where all users run the same application. Further, it incurs both storage overhead for extra ownership columns as well as query processing overhead for extra query statement conditions to check for row ownership.
- *Integrated schema:* This approach requires mappings from single-tenant logical schemas into a multi-tenant physical schema and must trade off the amount of consolidation against performance degradation [46]. This approach is ideal for hosting applications, such as email, with simple and similar schema designs and a relatively small amount of data.
- *Database space:* Database space is a feature provided by most state-of-the-art DBMSs that allows multiple users running on the same database system while storing their data separately in separate data spaces. This approach has the advantage of user data isolation and requires no modification to the applications. Overheads, however, may be incurred for system level resources, such as systems tables and other applied processes, since these resources are required per database space.

Naturally, each of these three approaches have their pros and cons and are suitable for different scenarios. The main limitation of the first two approaches is that they cannot effectively support SLAs for reliability and performance, provide data isolation, nor enable differential user classes. The database space approach provides better security than the other two since its security is implemented within the infrastructure while the security of the other two is implemented within the users' applications. Although the data space approach to multi-tenancy has system resource overheads, it is ideal for mission critical deployments, where tenants require QoS SLAs, data isolation, and security. Especially when each server hosts a small number (e.g. less than 100) of tenants, each with sizable data and computational loads, the overhead of system tables is relatively insignificant compared with the benefits the data space approach provides.

6   Data Clouds for Large Scale Data Services

Cloud computing platforms leverage high degrees of data processing parallelism to provide scalability to applications running in the service providers' data centers. Commercial cloud computing systems started to appear by 2000, and modern distributed computing systems for data analytics (such as Google's MapReduce [47], Amazon.com's

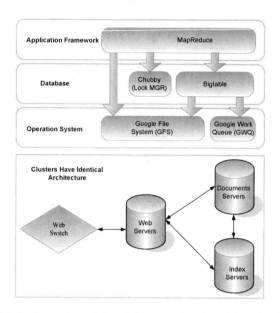

Fig. 3. A high-level overview of Google's map-reduce based data cloud framework

Dynamo [48], Microsoft's Cosmos and SCOPE [49] and the open-source Hadoop [50] serve as a foundation to build up highly scalable computation capacity through the use of commodity hardware, intelligent automation, and programmatic abstractions that provide query processing capabilities.

Based on an underlying parallel processing approach, cloud computing systems fall into three categories. With *horizontal partitioning*, data sets are partitioned, mapped, and processed by processing nodes in a mutually independent manner. In *vertical partitioning*, data is processed in a pipelined manner on the processing nodes in succession. Finally, *hybrid partitioning* combines features from both horizontal and vertical partitioning approaches.

6.1   MapReduce-Based Intensive Data Processing

Google's MapReduce [47] framework is a good example for the horizontal approach to data-intensive computing (Figure 3). The data is partitioned in a *map* phase, and the partitioned sets can then be processed and aggregated in a following *reduce* phase. This simple scheme is based on the *map-reduce* functional list-processing language construct.

While being simple, MapReduce framework is sufficiently rich for implementing many real-world tasks, including web link analysis, web access log analysis, and document clustering and retrieval. A typical task at which MapReduce excels is extract-transform-load (ETL), where data is read from a source, cleansed and pre-processed, transformed via some specific operations, and then loaded into a database or other reporting tool for further analysis [51]. This type of ETL processing is the bread-and-butter operation for modern Web-driven companies such as Google, where copious webpage information is processed and analyzed on a daily basis [52]. MapReduce systems also work well for other tasks, such as parsing semi-structured data and running queries on ad hoc datasets that would otherwise be too time-consuming to load into a database system.

MapReduce systems are highly scalable; for example, Google's cluster architecture [53] uses commodity PCs to achieve a very high performance-to-price ratio. The Google File System (GFS [54]) hosts data and maintains replicas on such distributed clusters using a master/slave scheme, resulting in high throughput in data processing and fault-tolerance. Alternatively, the BigTable data management layer [55] enables Google's framework to have some DBMS-like properties (including record formats and consistency through its lock server, Chubby [56]).

Despite being composed of commodity hardware, this MapReduce-based framework shows astonishing power in data-intensive computing, according to the latest test results released by Google [57], *one petabyte of data (10 trillion 100-byte records) can be sorted on 4,000 computers in six hours and two minutes.* One reason for this efficiency is that when data can be partitioned into independent sets which are processed separately without interaction among each other, parallel processing is easy to achieve.

MapReduce is a coarse-grained procedure division. To further leverage parallelism opportunities, business computation can be partitioned into more phases, forming complex workflows that are processed in a pipeline. This parallel processing scheme, commonly used for computation-heavy applications, is referred to as *vertical partition processing* [58]. [59] provides a decentralized example for vertical partition processing over a network. Nevertheless, pure vertical partition processing systems (especially for Internet scale data processing applications) are rare because of the difficulty in scaling the system, due to interdependencies of phases of the workflow. Thus, driven by web-scale applications, such as Google and Amazon, hybrid partition processing schemes are gaining popularity. A number of recent systems, such as Dryad [60] fromm Microsoft, Dynamo [48] form Amazon, Pig Latin [61] and PNUTS [62] from Yahoo!, Clustera [63], and the S3 database [64], fall in this hybrid category.

6.2 Beyond MapReduce

Current development trends in cloud computing for parallel processing suggest several common themes: (a) parallel processing for partioned data, (b) parallel processing with some DBMS-like functionalities, and (c) parallel processing support for full data and software as services. Early data cloud systems (such as Google's MapReduce) process divided subsets of data mutually independently with results generated separately.

While MapReduce and traditional RDBMS approaches may seem significantly different, one can in fact translate all SQL operations into the MapReduce primitives, allowing a user the flexibility to write almost any querying task with either traditional SQL or MapReduce operations [51]. User-defined functions can fulfill the role of the Map phase and system GROUP BY aggregates or user-defined aggregates can serve as the Reduce phase. While the MapReduce framework does not have an explicit join or merge primitive that combines data from different data sources, equijoins can be implemented by extending the data entries from different sources using a data-source tag and

	Key-base Access		SQL Supported				Transaction Supported		
	HBase/ Bigtable	Dynamo	Scope	Pig Latin	Dryad	Clustera	PNUTS	Database on S3	Cassandra
Data Model	Distributed column-based data store	Key-value pair only	Serialized file	Nested data model	Serialized file or file with schema	Serialized file	Simple relation model	Relational model	Distributed column-based data store
SQL	Key-based selection or scan, supports bloom filtering, map-reduce	Key-based access	Key-based selection, bloom filter	Supports limited SQL queries	Supports full fledged SQL queries	Supports full fledged SQL queries	Supports limited SQL queries	Supports full fledged SQL queries	Key-based selection, bloom filter
Data Storage	Several indexing scheme implementation in progress	Use consistent hashing to locate a record	Serialized file, hierarchical metadata	Serialized file	Serialized file, record	Serialized file, metadata in database	Table, record	B-tree indexes	Secondary indexing?
Update	Append only	Supported	Append only	Not supported	supported	Supported	supported	supported	Supported
Transaction	No concept of transaction	No concept of transaction	No concept of transaction	No concept of transaction	No concept of transaction	No concept of transaction	Application transaction but stops short of full serializability	Maximize consistency and other transactional guarantees	Single row transaction
Job Schedule	Not Supported	Supported	Supported	Supported	Supported	Supported	Not Supported	Not supported	Supported
Scalability	Highly scalable	Highly scalable	Highly scalable	Highly scalable	Highly scalable	Highly scalable	Highly scalable	Highly scalable	Highly scalable
Availability/ Consistency	Strong consistency, highly available	Eventual consistency, highly available	Eventual consistency, highly available	Read only	Eventual consistency, highly available	Eventual consistency	Pre-record consistency, highly available	Eventual consistency, highly available	Eventual consistency, highly available
Powered-by	Yahoo! & Microsoft	Amazon	Microsoft	Yahoo!	Microsoft	Wisconsin-Madison	Yahoo!	ETH Zurich	Facebook

Fig. 4. Feature comparisons among various current data cloud frameworks

applying a specialized reduce function which combines the data entries from different sources having the same key into a single entry.

This relationship between SQL operations and MapReduce primitives has led a number of different systems that look to provide a SQL-like interface on top of a modern distributed MapReduce system. For example, Microsoft's SCOPE programming language [49] closely resembles SQL and also allows users to implement user-defined C# code blocks to process their data. A user's SCOPE script is compiled into a query plan and executable primitives, which are then executed on Cosmos, Microsoft's distributed computing infrastructure on commodity hardware. The execution plan is handled by Dryad, a runtime orchestration manager. Another system with similarities to a SQL DBMS is Facebook's Hive [65], which uses a query language called QL for performing data warehousing on top of Hadoop. Hive implements a structed data store, including system catalogs and metadata that manages schemas and associates tables to physical data. Like SCOPE, Hive compiles queries into a graph of MapReduce primitives which are executed on a large-scale distributed cluster. Other SQL-like systems include IBM's JAQL [66], Yahoo's Pig [61], Greenplum [67], and Aster Data's nCluster [68].

Despite these SQL interfaces, the limited operators provided by the MapReduce primitives are far from being satisfactory to applications that require high-levels of functionality today supported by DBMSs [69]. MapReduce systems are typically schema-less, and as a result, as data is passed through a system like Hadoop, text fields must be parsed and converted to native data types, resulting in poor performance. Current MapReduce systems may also fall short in performance with respect to parallel database systems due to poorer implementations of compression, pipelining, and scheduling, topics which have been researched by the database community for several decades.

To address this problem of ad hoc, schemaless data, Google's implemention of MapReduce reads and writes data using their Protocol Buffer format, where a high-level description of inputs and outputs is compiled into executable code that manipulates binary data [70].

Current cloud computing systems may be integrated with data management systems that provide more complex data processing semantics than MapReduce offers. Other approaches include Bigtable [55], HBase [71], and Dynamo [48] (Figure 4), which store and access data solely in terms of key-value pairs (as in MapReduce) without any concept of transactions. Pig Latin, Dryad, and Clustera provide more extensive SQL functionalities. Update operators are limited to Dryad and Clustera, yet they also lack transaction support. MongoDB [72] and Apache's CouchDB [73] are document-oriented databases intended to support large corpora.

Transaction support is needed to provide reliable units of work that allow recovery from failures: when execution (completely or partially) stops and operations remain uncompleted, being able to recover the system correctly and keeping the database consistent requires some book-keeping. Moreover isolation between programs which accessing a database concurrently requires appropriate data structures and protocols that prevent interference between various data management processes. Thus, providing full ACID properties (i.e, *atomicity, consistency, isolation,* and *durability*) is expensive and many times prohibitive for Internet scale data processing. As shown in Figure 4, Cassandra, PNUTS, and Database on S3 provide limited transaction support. Cassandra supports transactions on single rows while PNUTS stops short of full consistency.

6.3   Other Applied SaaS Systems

While MapReduce and its SQL-like interfaces are modern tools for data-driven analytics, SaaS systems are available for a variety of other software domains. Traditional software applications, such as payroll and inventory management, have traditionally been sold as shrink-wrapped software packages but have found new avenues of use as SaaS offerings. For example, Workday [74] uses SaaS to sell payroll, procurement, and resource management in its Workday 9 package. Another SaaS company is Salesforce.com [19], which provides a range of traditional applications delivered over the Web, including Customer Relationship Management software for sales, support, and real-time collaboration. Their Force.com cloud service further allows users to build and run business applications in sandbox environments on top of their provisioned multi-tenant software and hardware infrastructure. Customer applications are written in a custom objected-oriented language, and business applications can be modeled and designed with a visual workflow manager.

As mentioned above, MapReduce systems are especially adept at ETL, a task typically handled in the RDBMS ecosystem by dedicated ETL software such as IBM's Infosphere [75], Informatica's Data Services [76], and Pentaho Data Integration [77]. Dedicated SaaS software for ETL include offerings from SnapLogic [78] and Cast Iron Systems [79]. Business intelligence is another software domain that has come to SaaS, including products from PivotLink [80], Cloud9 Analytics [81] , and Quantivo [82] . Data warehousing products sold through SaaS include those from Kognotio [83] and SAP [84].

6.4 Not Just Software

In this work, we have discussed Software as a Service, but other offerings are available beyond just software in the cloud. As mentioned earlier, Infrastructure as a Service (IaaS) provides computing, storage, and networking resources for customers in an on-demand manner. An important area of research in IaaS is that of power consumption minimization and power management, with many efforts to make the infrastructure become more "green." Recent work in modern data center design has produced mobile deployment containers that hold all the computing, cooling, and cabling needed to connect a large number of computing racks, such as the Sun/Oracle Solaris Containers [85]. More aggressive designs include the FAWN (Fast Array of Wimpy Nodes) project [86], which looks to put together a large number of embedded processors and flash memory nodes to form a fast, low-power aggregate computation farm.

7 Conclusions and the Future of Research and Development at the Frontier

Information and software as services is a model of software deployment where information products and applications are hosted as services provided to customers across the Internet. As described in the earlier sections, platforms that support these services must be designed in such a way that it enables multiple customers to simultaneously use the storage and computation power of a shared infrastructure (such as a a multi-tenant backend or a cloud computing system). Software as a Service (SaaS) platforms are distinguished from client/server systems or Application Service Provider(ASP) solutions in that SaaS offerings leverage enormous economies of scale in various stages of the software life cycle, including deployment and management. Emergence of enabling technologies, such as J2EE, .Net, XML, virtual machines, and web services contribute to this trend. Currently, scientific grid computing, on-line software services, and business service networks are typical examples exploiting database and software as service paradigm.

While the financial incentives are obvious and, as described in this paper, many advances are made in the description and deployment of database and software as services, convincing potential customers that outsourcing their data is a viable alternative to deploying complex infrastructures requires research and technological advances in *the business model, pricing, regulation, security and information assurance, SLA, QoS, and differential services, service class guarantees, service delivery and tracking, database support for SaaS and multi-tenant databases, dynamic service composition, service deployment and provisioning,* and *cloud computing as a service.* Thus, we can comfortably state that the paradigm of data and application as services is still in its infancy, with many key enabling results are still to come.

In this paper, we provided an overview of the challenges faced by the SaaS systems, current state-of-the-art techniques for supporting data-intensive SaaS applications, and future research directions. Being at the apex of the wish list for many small-, medium-, and large-size companies and other institutions, *data and application as services* will keep generating increasing demand and push towards innovation. It is apparent supporting richer and more expressive business workflows and improving the scalability and adaptivity of distributed/decentralized data management systems will require significant amounts of research and development and, thus, will attract further attention both from industry and academia over the coming years.

References

1. TenWolde, E.: Worldwide software on demand 2007-2011 forecast: A preliminary look at delivery model performance. IDC No. 206240, IDC Report (2007)
2. Herbert, L., Brown, E.G., Galvin, S.: Competing in the fast-growing saas market, No. 0,5110,44254,00, 2008. Forrester Report (2008)
3. Herbert, L., Martorelli, B., Ross, C.F., Parker, A., Thresher, A., Galvin, S.: Saas clients face growing complexity, No. 0,5110,45700,00, 2008. Forrester Report (2008)
4. Wustenhoff, E.: Service level agreement in the data center,
   http://www.sun.com/blueprints/0402/sla.pdf
5. Hamilton, J.R.: On designing and deploying internet-scale services. In: Proc. of the 21th USENIX Large Installation System Administration Conference, Dallas, Texas, USA, pp. 231–42 (2007)
6. DeCandia, G., et al.: Dynamo: Amazon's highly available key-value store. In: SOSP (2007)
7. Amazon.com: Amazon s3 sla (2008), http://aws.amazon.com/s3-sla/
8. Amazon.com: Amazon ec2 sla (2008), http://aws.amazon.com/ec2-sla/
9. Microsoft: Architecture strategies for catching the long tail (2008),
   http://msdn.microsoft.com/en-us/library/aa479069.aspx
10. Natis, Y.V., Gall, N., Cearley, D.W., Leong, L., Desisto, R.P., Lheureux, B.J., Smith, D.M., Plummer, D.C.: Cloud, saas, hosting and other off-premises computing models, No. G00159042, Gartner Research (2008)
11. Schuller, S.: Demystifying the cloud: Where do saas, paas and other acronyms fit in? (December 2008),
    http://www.saasblogs.com/2008/12/01/demystifying-the-cloud-where-do-saas-paas-and-other-acronyms-fit-in/
12. Amazon: S3 (2008), http://aws.amazon.com/s3/
13. Microsoft: Azure service platform (2008),
    http://www.microsoft.com/azure/data.mspx
14. Mosso: Cloudfs (2008), http://www.mosso.com/cloudfs/
15. Amazon: Ec2 (2008), http://aws.amazon.com/ec2/
16. GoGrid: Gogrid (2008), http://www.gogrid.com/index.v3.php
17. Apprenda: Saasgrid (2008), http://apprenda.com/
18. Google: Appengine (2008), http://code.google.com/appengine/
19. Salesforce, http://www.salesforce.com/
20. Ding, L., Chen, S., Rundensteiner, E.A., Tatemura, J., Hsiung, W.P., Candan, K.S.: Runtime semantic query optimization for event stream processing. In: ICDE, pp. 676–685 (2008)
21. Georgakopoulos, D., Hornick, M.: An overview of workflow management: From process modeling to workflow automation infrastructure. In: Distributed and Parallel Databases, pp. 119–153 (1995)
22. IBM: Web services flow language (wsfl) (2009),
    http://www.ibm.com/software/solutions/webservices/pdf/WSFL.pdf
23. Business process execution language for web services version 1.1 (2007),
    http://www.ibm.com/developerworks/library/specification/ws-bpel/

24. WfMC: Workflow process definition interface – xml process definition language. Document Number WFMC-TC-1025 (2001)
25. OMG: Unified modeling language (2008), http://www.uml.org
26. OMG: Bpmn 1.1: Omg specification (2008), http://www.bpmn.org
27. van der Aalst, W.M.P., ter Hofstede, A.H.M., Kiepuszewski, B., Barros, A.P.: Workflow patterns. Distrib. Parallel Databases 14(1), 5–51 (2003)
28. van der Aalst, W., ter Hofstede, A.H.M.: Yawl: yet another workflow language. Information Systems 30, 245–275 (2005)
29. Singh, M.P., Meredith, G., Tomlinson, C., Attie, P.C.: An event algebra for specifying and scheduling workflows. In: DASFAA, pp. 53–60 (1995)
30. Cicekli, N.K., Cicekli, I.: Formalizing the specification and execution of workflows using the event calculus. Information Sciences 176(15), 2227–2267 (2006)
31. Wombacher, A., Fankhauser, P., Neuhold, E.: Transforming bpel into annotated deterministic finite state automata for service discovery. In: ICWS, pp. 316–323 (2004)
32. Petri, C.: Kommunikation mit Automaten. PhD thesis, Fakultat fur Mathematik und Physik, Technische Hochschule Darmstadt, Germany (1962)
33. van der Aalst, W.: The application of Petri nets to workflow management. The Journal of Circuits, Systems and Computers 8(1), 21–66 (1998)
34. Jensen, K.: Coloured petri nets: a high level language for system design and analysis. In: Rozenberg, G. (ed.) APN 1990. LNCS, vol. 483, pp. 342–416. Springer, Heidelberg (1991)
35. Marsan, M.A., Balbo, G., Conte, G., Donatelli, S., Franceschinis, G.: Modelling with generalized stochastic petri nets. SIGMETRICS Perform. Eval. Rev. 26(2) (1998)
36. Natkin, S.: Timed and stochastic petri nets: From the validation to the performance of synchronization schemes. In: PNPM, pp. 2–3 (1985)
37. Microsoft: Microsoft .net framework (2008), http://www.microsoft.com/net/
38. Cormen, T., Leiserson, C., Rivest, R.: Introduction to Algorithms. McGraw Hill Publishers, New York (1990)
39. Sun: Java ee at a glance (2008), http://java.sun.com/javaee/index.jsp
40. BEA: Bea homepage (2008), http://www.bea.com
41. IBM: Ibm websphere homepage (2008),
    http://www.ibm.com/software/websphere/
42. Apache: Apache tomcat (2008), http://tomcat.apache.org/
43. Letizi, O.: Stateful web applications that scale like stateless ones (2008),
    http://www.ddj.com/development-tools/208403462
44. Kopparapu, C.: Load Balancing Servers, Firewalls, and Caches. Wiley, Chichester (2002)
45. Yarnall, M., Berc, L., Wang, Q.: Using vmware esx server with ibm websphere application server (2006)
46. Aulbach, S., Grust, T., Jacobs, D., Kemper, A., Rittinger, J.: Multi-tenant databases for software as a service: Schema-mapping techniques. In: Proc. of the ACM SIGMOD Int'l. Conference on Management of Data (2008)
47. Dean, J., Ghemawat, S.: MapReduce: simplified data processing on large clusters. In: Proceedings of the 6th conference on Symposium on Opearting Systems Design & Implementation-Volume 6 table of contents, pp. 10–10 (2004)
48. DeCandia, G., Hastorun, D., Jampani, M., Kakulapati, G., Lakshman, A., Pilchin, A., Sivasubramanian, S., Vosshall, P., Vogels, W.: Dynamo: amazon's highly available key-value store. In: Proceedings of Twenty-First ACM SIGOPS Symposium on Operating Systems Principles, pp. 205–220 (2007)
49. Chaiken, R., Jenkins, B., Larson, P., Ramsey, B., Shakib, D., Weaver, S., Zhou, J.: SCOPE: easy and efficient parallel processing of massive data sets. In: Proceedings of the International Conference on Very Large Databases, pp. 1265–1276 (2008)

50. Hadoop, hadoop.apache.org
51. Stonebraker, M., Abadi, D., DeWitt, D., Madden, S., Paulson, E., Pavlo, A., Rasin, A.: MapReduce and Parallel DBMSs: Friends or Foes? Communications of the ACM 53(1) (January 2010)
52. Manning, C., Raghavan, P., Schutze, H.: Introduction to Information Retrieval. Cambridge University Press, Cambridge (2008)
53. Barroso, L., Dean, J., Hölzle, U.: Web Search for a Planet: The Google Cluster Architecture. IEEE MICRO, 22–28 (2003)
54. Ghemawat, S., Gobioff, H., Leung, S.: The Google file system. In: Proceedings of the 19th Symposium on Operating Systems Principles (OSDI 2003), pp. 29–43 (2003)
55. Chang, F., Dean, J., Ghemawat, S., Hsieh, W., Wallach, D., Burrows, M., Chandra, T., Fikes, A., Gruber, R.: Bigtable: a distributed storage system for structured data. In: Proceedings of the 7th Symposium on Operating Systems Design and Implementation (OSDI 2006), pp. 205–218 (2006)
56. Burrows, M.: The Chubby lock service for loosely-coupled distributed systems. In: Proceedings of the 7th Symposium on Operating Systems Design and Implementation, pp. 335–350 (2006)
57. Google: Sorting 1pb with mapreduce (2008),
    http://googleblog.blogspot.com/2008/11/sorting-1pb-with-mapreduce.html
58. Litzkow, M., Livny, M., Mutka, M.: Condor-a hunter of idle workstations. In: 8th International Conference on Distributed Computing Systems, pp. 104–111 (1988)
59. Cavendish, D., Candan, K.S.: Distributed xml processing: Theory and applications. J. Parallel Distrib. Comput. 68(8), 1054–1069 (2008)
60. Isard, M., Budiu, M., Yu, Y., Birrell, A., Fetterly, D.: Dryad: distributed data-parallel programs from sequential building blocks. In: Proceedings of the 2007 Conference on EuroSys, pp. 59–72 (2007)
61. Olston, C., Reed, B., Srivastava, U., Kumar, R., Tomkins, A.: Pig latin: a not-so-foreign language for data processing. In: Proceedings of the 2008 ACM SIGMOD International Conference on Management of Data, pp. 1099–1110 (2008)
62. Cooper, B., Ramakrishnan, R., Srivastava, U., Silberstein, A., Bohannon, P., Jacobsen, H., Puz, N., Weaver, D., Yerneni, R.: PNUTS: Yahoo's hosted data serving platform, pp. 1265–1276 (2008)
63. DeWitt, D., Paulson, E., Robinson, E., Naughton, J., Royalty, J., Shankar, S., Krioukov, A.: Clustera: an integrated computation and data management system, pp. 28–41 (2008)
64. Brantner, M., Florescu, D., Graf, D., Kossmann, D., Kraska, T.: Building a database on S3. In: Proceedings of the 2008 ACM SIGMOD International Conference on Management of Data, 251–264 (2008)
65. Facebook: Hive (2008), http://wiki.apache.org/hadoop/Hive
66. IBM: Jaql (2008), http://www.jaql.org/
67. Greenplum: Mapreduce, http://www.greenplum.com/resources/MapReduce/
68. Aster: ncluster, http://www.asterdata.com/product/mapreduce.php
69. Pavlo, A., Paulson, E., Rasin, A., Abadi, D.J., DeWitt, D., Madden, S., Stonebraker, M.: A comparison of approaches to large-scale data analysis. In: Proceedings of the 2009 ACM SIGMOD International Conference on Management of Data, pp. 165–178 (2009)
70. Dean, J., Ghemawat, S.: MapReduce: A Flexible Data Processing Tool. Communications of the ACM 53(1) (January 2010)
71. Yahoo!: Hbase, http://hadoop.apache.org/hbase/
72. MongoDB, http://www.mongodb.org/
73. CounchDB, A., http://couchdb.apache.org/

74. Workday, http://www.workday.com/
75. Infosphere, I., http://www.ibm.com/software/data/infosphere/
76. Informatica, http://www.informatica.com
77. Pentaho, http://www.pentaho.com/
78. SnapLogic, http://www.snaplogic.com/
79. Systems, C.I., http://www.castiron.com/
80. PivotLink, http://www.pivotlink.com/
81. Analytics, C., http://www.cloud9analytics.com/
82. Quantivo, http://www.quantivo.com/
83. Kognotio, http://www.kognitio.com/
84. SAP, http://www.sap.com/
85. Sun: Solaris containers,
    http://www.sun.com/bigadmin/content/zones/index.jsp
86. Andersen, D., Franklin, J., Kaminsky, M., Phanishayee, A., Tan, L., Vasudevan, V.: Fawn: A fast array of wimpy nodes. In: Proceedings of the ACM Symposium on Operating Systems Principles (2009)

Author Index

Agrawal, Divyakant   57
Aime, Marco D.   81

Brunnert, Jan   257

Candan, K. Selçuk   155, 283

Dai, Jinquan   31, 209

Eckart, Benjamin   257
El Abbadi, Amr   57
Emekci, Fatih   57

Gao, Bo   1
Guo, Chang-Jie   1

He, Juzhen   185
Huang, Bo   31, 209
Huang, Jie   209
Huang, Shengsheng   209
Huang, Ying   1
Hung, Patrick   185

Jacobs, Dean   257
Jiang, Zhong-Bo   1

Kim, Jong Wook   155

Li, Wen-Syan   283
Lioy, Antonio   81

Metwally, Ahmed   57

Nagarkar, Parth   155
Nagendra, Mithila   155
Ng, Wilfred   185

Phan, Thomas   283
Pomi, Paolo C.   81

Risch, Tore   132

Sabesan, Manivasakan   132
Schaffner, Jan   257
Schwarz, Christian   257
Sion, Radu   112
Sun, Wei   1

Tatemura, Junichi   112

Vallini, Marco   81

Wang, Shiyuan   57
Wang, Xiaoling   185
Wang, Zhi-Hu   1

Xie, Tao   209

Yan, Jianfeng   229
Yu, Renwei   155

Zeier, Alexander   257
Zhang, Bo   229
Zhou, Aoying   185
Zhou, Minqi   283